RURAL DEVELOPMENT
UNDER DECENTRALISED GOVERNANCE

By the same Author—

Developmental Issued in Contemporary India.

About the Editor

M.R. Biju, Editor of South Asian Journal of Socio-Political Studies (SAJOSPS) has been actively engaged in his researches on the area of decentralized governance in the past 25 years. He has made significant contributions to the theory and practice of grass root governance in India. As a mark of its national recognition he has been conferred with the post-doctoral research award by the University Grants Commission, New Delhi in 2004.

As prolific writer, he has published 21 outstanding books and 98 research papers on various aspects of decentralization, development, democracy, human rights, development management, strategic management, women empowerment, etc. He is also heading two major research projects on Panchayati Raj funded by the Ministry of Panchayati Raj, Government of India and University Grants Commission, New Delhi. Dr.Biju is currently Head and Associate Professor of the Post-Graduate and Research Department of Political Science, Sree Narayana College, Kollam, Kerala.

RURAL DEVELOPMENT

Under Decentralised Governance

Edited by

M.R. Biju

Head & Associate Professor of Political Science
Sree Narayana College, Kollam,
University of Kerala

CONCEPT PUBLISHING COMPANY PVT. LTD.

NEW DELHI-110059

ISBN-13 : 978-81-8069-838-5

First Published 2012

Published and Printed by

Concept Publishing Company Pvt. Ltd.
A/15-16, Commercial Block, Mohan Garden
New Delhi-110059 (India)
T: 25351460, 25351794, *F*: 091-11-25357109
E: publishing@conceptpub.com, W: www.conceptpub.com
Editorial Office: H-13, Bali Nagar, New Delhi-110 015, India.

Cataloging in Publication Data--*Courtesy:* D.K. Agencies (P) Ltd. <docinfo@dkagencies.com>

Rural development : under decentralised governance / edited by M.R. Biju.
p. cm.
Contributed articles.
Includes bibliographical references and index.
ISBN 9788180698385

1. Rural development—India. 2. Decentralization in government—India. 3. Panchayat—India. 4. Women in development—India. 5. Self-help groups—India. I. Biju, M. R., 1965-

DDC 307.14120954 23

Acknowledgements

I would like to express my gratitude to those who have been kind enough to help me in the preparation of this volume. I wish to express a deep sense of gratitude to the esteemed contributors to this anthology of articles. The views and opinions expressed by the contributors are of immense value for researchers, policy-makers, planners for rejuvenating policies and strategies on Rural Development and Decentralized Governance in India. I am extremely thankful to Shri Ashok Kumar Mittal of Concept Publishing Company Pvt. Ltd., New Delhi who brought out the volume in an elegant form. I also wish to express my sincere thanks to Dr. C.Mohan Sreekumar, Principal, Sree Narayana College, Kollam for his support.

I am also grateful to my wife Jaya, daughter Aishwarya and son Anantha Padmanabha for kindly sparing me the time for completing the volume.

Dr. M.R. Biju

Head & Associate Professor

PG & Research Department of Political Science

Sree Narayana College Kollam, Kerala, India.

Acknowledgements

Contents

About the Contributors

Rakesh Hooja, Ph.D., is now in his 36th year of service in the IAS, having earlier taught Political Science at University of Rajasthan. An able administrator, he has worked in both Government of Rajasthan and Government of India. In addition he has authored or edited 30 books and written over 410 articles, reviews and research papers for books, journals, seminars/conferences and magazines on development, public policy, governance and administration, land-water management, district and decentralized planning, rural development and development administration, state and district administration, panchayati raj, participatory irrigation management, training and capacity building, federalism, disaster management, natural resource management in desert areas, etc. He is actively associated in the editing of some journals and magazines. He has been awarded State Government of Rajasthan cash awards and merit certificates for original writing in 1988 (for a book on District Planning) and in 2007 (for a book on Managing Water for Agriculture). I.I.P.A. Delhi awarded him T.N.Chaturvedi Prize in 2009 for his writing on public administration. His two immediate previous postings have been Additional Chief Secretary, Development and Development Commissioner and Additional Chief Secretary Training and Director, H.C.Mathur Rajasthan State Institute of Public Administration, Jaipur I.I.P.A — Indian Institute of Public Administration Chairman of the Board of Revenue for Rajasthan at Ajmer. Currently he is the Director of I.I.P.A, New Delhi.

S.M.Vijayanand, IAS is a distinguished Civil Servant of

India. He has contributed immensely on the theory and practice of Decentralised Governance in India with special focus on Kerala. Currently, he is working as the Additonal Chief Secretary and Principal Secretary, Local Administration Department, Government.of Kerala.

G.Palanithurai, Professor in Rajiv Gandhi Chair, Gandhigram Rural Institute is an academic activist working with people in rural areas. He is heading the Department of Political Science and Development Administration in Gandhigram. He is closely associated with the various global and national research, funding agencies. He has to his credit 29 books and 75 articles on the areas of Panchayathi Raj, Legislative Behaviour and Ethinicity. He has also received fellowships from Shastri Indo-Canadian Institute, World Academy of Art and Science. He is also a member of the expert committee of Government of Tamil Nadu to monitor training programme for local body leaders.

M.R. Biju (b.1965), currently working as Director of Asian Institute of Development Research (AIDR), Editor of South Asian Journal of Socio-Political Studies (SAJOSPS) and Head and Associate Professor in the Post-Graduate and Research Department of Political Science, Sree Narayana College, Kollam, Kerala. In 2004 he was conferred with Post- Doctoral Research Award by the University Grants Commission for his exemplary contribution to the field of decentralised governance. He is heading two major research projects on Panchayati Raj funded by the Ministry of Panchayati Raj, Government. of India and University Grants Commission, New Delhi. Dr. Biju is a prolific writer on socio-political and developmental issues. He has published twenty one outstanding books and Ninety-Eight research papers in the prestigious journals.

Archana G.Gulati is a 1989 batch Civil Services Officer belonging to the Indian P&T Accounts and Finance Service. She is currently posted as Joint Administrator (Finance) of the Universal Service Obligation Fund (USOF), Department of

Telecommunications (DOT), and Government of India. The USOF is an attached office of DOT and has the mandate of providing access to telecommunication services to people in rural and remote areas at reasonable and affordable prices. As Joint Administrator (Finance) USOF Mrs. Archana G.Gulati is actively involved in formulation, detailed designing and implementation of USO Schemes. She also supervises the disbursement of USO subsidy through 22 Controller of Communication Accounts (CCA) Offices spread across the country who assist the USOF HQ in implementation of USOF schemes. These offices disburse USO subsidy against claims preferred by service providers and carry out post-payment verification of claims. In her previous tenure she headed the CCA Office in Haryana.

Shankar Prinja is a public health specialist. He has worked as a Senior Research Scientist in the ICMR- Johns Hopkins research project for assessment of preventable burden of Haemophilus influenzae type 'b' pneumonia and meningitis in India. His area of interest is health systems research and is currently working as Senior Resident in the School of Public Health, PGIMER, Chandigarh (India).

Prof. Sunder Lal is an eminent public health specialist who has held several important positions. He had been the Head of Community Medicine department in PGIMS, Rohtak, for more than 20 years, Secretary General of Indian Association of Preventive and Social Medicine (IAPSM) and Chief Editor of Indian Journal of Community Medicine (IJCM) for 10 years. He has been on the national advisory panel of Integrated Child Development Services Scheme (ICDS). His publications include numerous operational studies on implementation of Reproductive and Child Health Programe (RCH) and ICDS programe.

Prof. Amarjeet Singh is a Professor in the Department of Community Medicine, School of Public Health, PGIMER, Chandigarh. He has been working in the department since more than 20 years and has pursued many research projects in the field of social medicine.

Ramesh Verma is working as Lecturer, in the Department of Community Medicine, Pt.B.D.Sharma, PGIMS, Rohtak.

Shankar Chatterjee is currently working as Senior Assistant Professor, National Institute of Rural Development, Hyderabad.

V.M.Rao, Professor and Head of Department, Centre for Research and Publications, joined VMNICM during 1992, and has been involved in research, training, and teaching. Dr. V. M. Rao has completed consultancy projects worth about Rs. 75 lakhs, the highest by any individual faculty at the Institute. He has published 15 books, over 90 articles in journals of repute, and contributed papers to national and international seminars. Prof. Rao is a recognized Ph.D. guide in the Department of Management Studies, University of Pune. His areas of interest include agribusiness management, rural cooperatives (dairy, credit, sugar, horticulture, forestry, etc.) gender integration, and animal husbandry economics.

V.Rama Krishna is a doctoral student at the Department of Political Science, Gulbarga University, Karnataka

Manmohan Singh. Gill is Professor in the Department of Sociology, Guru Nanak Dev University, Amritsar since 1986. He has served in the capacity of Reader, Academic Staff College and Programme Coordinator, NSS in the same university. He has also worked with industrial houses for sometime. With 24 years of teaching and research experience, Dr. Gill has specialized in the fields of Rural Sociology and Social Ecology. He has completed research projects of the Department of Social Welfare of Punjab Government on UNTOUCHABILITY and UGC project on Caste-Land Relations. He has published numerous papers in research journals, besides making presentations in various academic forums at national and international levels. He has authored books on Spatial Patterns: Socio-ecological Analysis (1991) and Punjab Society: Perspectives and Challenges (2003) and Environmental Conscience: Socio-legal and Judicial Paradigm (2009).

S.N.Dhar, is working as Professor of Commerce, University of North Bengal, Darjeeling, West Bengal. He has teaching for more than 23 years in PG level. Author of two books on Micro-Finance and one book on Cost Accounting, More than fifty published papers in national and international journals, presented equal number of papers in national and international conferences, delivered many lectures as resource person in different universities in India.

T. Krishna Kumar, currently working as a faculty member in Department. of Commerce and Business Management, Satavahana University, Karimnagar.

Anita Modi is currently working as Head of the Department of Economics, GSS Girl's Post-Graduate College, Chirawa (Rajasthan).

Jitendra Ahirrao currently working as Associate Professor in Department of Commerce and Post-Graduate Research Centre in Commerce and Management of Smt. Dankunwar Mahila College, Jalna (Mh.) affiliated to Dr. Babasaheb Ambedkar Marathwada University, Aurangabad since 1996. He possesses Post-Graduate degree in Commerce and obtained his Ph.D. degree in 'Co-operative Agricultural Finance'. Currently he is Ph.D. Research Guide of Dr. B.A. M. University, Aurangabad, Sant Gadgebaba Amravati University, Amravati and Yashwantrao Chavan Maharashtra Open University, Nashik and awarded four Ph.D. and one M. Phil. students under the supervision. He has authored thirty outstanding books in Commerce and Management. He has contributed Twenty-Five research articles published in National and International Journals.

Bhabesh Chandra Das is presently working as Assistant Professor in National Institute of Rural Development (NIRD), Hyderabad. He started his career as Training Specialist in Indo-Danish Project under Government of Orissa. He has also worked in various capacities in different Organizations like Indo-Swiss, DFID and Watershed Development Mission, Orissa.

He has published one book and more than 40 articles in National/International journals.

B.Vanitha, is currently working as Associate Professor in the Department of Economics, Bharathiar University has 22 years of teaching and research experience. She has completed 3 research projects funded by UGC & Malcolm and Elizabeth Adiseshiah Trust. She is currently working on a Major Research Project funded by UGC. She has published a book on Economic Analysis of Solid Waste Management, 15 articles in Journals and 10 articles in edited books. She has guided 2 Ph.Ds and 17 M.Phil. Scholars. She is Life Member and Executive Committee Member of Coimbatore Productive Council, Tamil Nadu Economics Association, All India Economics Association and Indian Society Labour Economics.

R.C. Mishra, currently working as Reader and Head of the Department, Economics, in KKS Govt. Women's College, Balasore, Orissa. He has 31 years of teaching experience at Under-Graduate level and 18 years at Post- Graduate level. His area of specialization is Agricultural Economics and Rural Economics. Dr. Mishra started his career as Lecturer in Economics in 1979 at F.M. Govt. College, Balasore. In 1995 he was promoted as Reader in Economics. He was awarded Ph.D. in 2001 from Utkal University, Bhubaneswar. Dr. Mishra has successfully guided 3 doctoral students and 4 M.Phil. scholars. He has published 5 books in Economics and more than 30 articles in state and national level journal. Dr. Mishra is a life member of Orissa Economic Association, Indian Economic Association, Member of Board of Studies, Subject Research Committee of F.M. University, Balasore.

K.C. Mishra, (b.1973), currently working as Lecturer in Economics in M.P.C. J. Govt. College, Baripada, Orissa. He had qualified NET conducted by UGC. His area of specialization is Rural Economics and Mathematical Economics. He is a prolific writer on Rural Development. He has published Twenty-Seven Research papers in various journals.

Niti Mehta is an Urban and Regional Planner and Ph.D. in Development Economics. She is Professor at the Sardar Patel Institute of Economic and Social Research (SPIESR), Ahmedabad. Her areas of interest are regional development, agriculture transformation and rural development, labour, employment and poverty issues, on which she has numerous published articles.

Anita Arya is a Ph.D. in Economics. She is Associate Professor at the Sardar Patel Institute of Economic and Social Research (SPIESR), Ahmedabad. Her areas of interest include macro economics, development economics and agricultural economics. She has worked extensively on issues related to agricultural marketing and institutional mechanisms.

B.K.Mohanty is currently working as an Associate Professor in the Faculty of Commerce, Banaras Hindu University. Dr. Mohanty had his early education in different Institutions in Orissa. He took his M.Com. Degree in 1979 from Berhampur University with First class third position. He was awarded Ph.D. in Commerce from Utkal University in the area of Finance and Banking in the year 1997. Currently he is engaged in a Major Research project entitled "Micro-financing and Rural Development in Orissa—A study on the Role of RRBs." funded by UGC.

Rajkumar Josmee Singh is a doctoral scholar at the Dairy Extension Division of National Dairy Research Institute, Karnal (Haryana)

G. Prasad Babu is a doctoral scholar at the Dairy Extension Division of National Dairy Research Institute, Karnal, (Haryana)

Vairagar Vishal Gulab is a doctoral scholar at the Dairy Extension Division of National Dairy Research Institute, Karnal, (Haryana)

Ram Kumar, is a Principal Scientist at the Dairy Extension Division of National Dairy Research Institute, Karnal, (Haryana)

K.V.Ramachandran is a Reader in the Department of Economics, University of Calicut.

Anupam Hazra, studied Master in Social Work (MSW) from Visva Bharati University. Currently Assistant Professor in Department of Social Work at Assam (Central) University Silchar. Associated with "*Consortium for Teaching, Research, Learning and Development*" *(U.S.A)* as Director and President of "East Central Service Region" of India. Earlier worked in development sector with different International and national-level NGOs. Areas of expertise: Rural development, Sanitation, Social development. Published over 30 articles in leading academic journals. Associated with different academic institutes and editorial board of different academic journals.

Introduction

Since an overwhelming majority of India's population lives in villages, a holistic development of its rural life is a requisite for the acceleration of the pace of overall economic development of the country. Rural development programmes are designed to facilitate a multi-faceted growth of the rural poor by extending the benefits development to them. It aims at the improvement of their living standards by providing them opportunities for the fullest utilization of their political capabilities through their active participation in the process of goal-oriented change. Rural development also tends to reduce migrational pressure on cities and towns. It also enables the use of human and national resources in the rural areas and to reduce area-wise differences. Evidence indicates that in India, public and governmental interest in rural development has been growing rapidly and a strong and various commitment towards it on the part of our polity-makers is clearly visible. The government has initiated a number of programmes to resolve the chromic problems facing village in India. In fact efforts to improve the rural economy were initiated soon after independence, particularly after the Constitution came into force. Notably, in the early phases, despite some efforts at involving the people though democratic decentralization community development and panchayati raj rural development programmes were virtually synonymies with agricultural development. This followed the prevailing worldwide thinking and India's excessive concern especially till the green revolution in the late 1960s with food sufficiency. In the seventies, however, it came to be realized that rural development is much broader in scope than merely agricultural development. Besides it was recognized that development in agriculture was not a panacea for all ills and that development should not be confined to a single area of change, however significance it may be. Therefore, if the strategy for rural development had to be made effective, a multi-pronged approach to rural problems was imperative. A package programme of rural development had to be devised, a multi-dimensional approach taken up and multi-institutional efforts had to be initiated.

As we have adapted policies of liberalization and globalization since 1991, we will have to look at the rural development from a holistic angle rather than from the angle of compartmentalization of between the urban and the rural. Moreover, during the recent past, the Indian economy has witnessed spectacular success in terms of achieving a higher growth rate. Especially since Independence and inception of plan periods, huge funds have been spent for the Rural Development in India. The Eleventh Five Plan (2007-2012) also lays priority on providing basic facilities including Education and Health to the masses of India, to enable them to avail the benefits of economic growth. However, the benefits of the same have not shared by the rural masses. The process of growth, therefore, has not been inclusive. Still it remains as an illusive goal. The visions and missions related to rural development strategies should be redefined by focusing on the new areas of advancement viz. rural technology, infrastructure, health-care, education, poverty eradication, employment generation for women and weaker section, micro financing, etc. All these efforts will certainly help to usher a new era in the developmental scenario of rural India.

In this context it has to be remembered that one of the key players of Rural Development Strategies in a developing polity like India is its adoption of decentralized governance as its key development approach. In the nation's march towards decentralized rural development, rural institutions have come to play a very vital role in the successful execution of the whole developmental strategies. The rapid growth of Rural Institutions in country like India during the past six decades, especially after the passing of the 73rd Constitutional Amendment Act, 1992 shows the ever increasing role being played by Rural Development Institutions to achieve the fundamental goals of decentralization.

Keeping all the above concerns, the present volume attempts to explore the ways and means for the development of rural India. The volume contains Twenty-three articles and research papers contributed by senior civil servants, renowned academics and activists with rich experience on the core areas of the study. In their submissions, the authors have tried to explore the existing problems faced by the rural development sector and present solid suggestions to revamp the system.

CONTENT OF THE VOLUME

In the inaugural paper **Rakesh Hooja** examines Rural Development with Development Administration in Indian context. According to Dr.Hooja, for a country like ours there continues to be a strong moral imperative to look after the development of rural people and rural areas. And for our country it is the rural human and physical resources and rural produce as well as rural demand for goods and services, which are the major engines for growth. Rural hinterlands form a unified system with urban centres and neither can grow or develop without the other. Thus, in common usage, in India, the term 'development administration' has got linked with rural development, so that administration for rural development tends to be referred to as development administration.

The author further observes that the statutory Panchayti Raj Institutions that came up in various states of the country after 1959 have now been constitutionalized following the 73rd Constitutional Amendment, many developmental activities still continue to be carried out by various State Government departments and these can only be coordinated on behalf of the Government by the District Collector. The general populace expects welfarism and rural development measures from the

State and Central Governments and not merely from the PRIs. Hence, State Governments (and even Central Government) would always be reluctant to give up their multifaceted role in rural development. Since, the rural development department coordinates the planning of PRI activities and the schemes of their own department, for meaningful comprehensive district planning the state planning department needs to undertake the coordination and planning involving the District Collectors, staff of various government departments including those at the district level, PRIs and district planning cells attached to the district collectorates. Similarly, the overall effort at rural development undertaken jointly by all departments and agencies of government has, in todays Indian scenario, to be overseen by the State planning department, and not by the rural development department which presently concentrates only on some aspects of rural development.

S.M.Vijayanand, the Chief Architect of Kerala's Decentralization Process has made an indepth study on the linkage between National Rural Employment Guarantee Act and PRIs. According to him the NREGA has created the legal framework to enable the political executive to structure effective decentralization. According to the author since NREGS is a programme which combines the economic development and social justice function in a context of local planning and implementation it is only in the fitness of things that PRIs play the central role as the Constitution itself assigns these two roles to PRIs. Further for realizing entitlements and broadening capabilities of the disadvantaged, democratization and participation are essential and sufficient pre-conditions and only PRIs can bring them about. S.M.Vijayanand further states that, if the potential for panchayati raj empowerment using NREGA as the entry point is not thought through and given operational features there is every danger of converting PRIs into mere agencies, just going through the motions without realizing their central place or even becoming potential cat's pass of the coterie of vested interests dominating the public works scene, snatching public resources for private gains. Thus, the legal empowerment of PRIs along would not automatically lead to their actual strengthening, unless a deliberate and purposive effort is taken to create capacity, develop process and build system to enable PRIs to play the intended role.

The author concludes his study by stating that people's plan in Kerala was the motive force which pushed decentralization, NREGA could be used for strengthening panchayati raj in the country. In that sense, NREGA could be called "Mother of all development schemes". According to him, to realize the potential it is necessary to move on a concerted capacity building exercise with focus on panchayat empowerment in the context of NREGA. Probably a policy shift is needed to make NREGA as much an instrument for panchayati raj empowerment as an instrument for poverty reduction.

G.Palanithurai, has presented a paper on the role of ICT in scientific data generation and management for scientific decision-making at the grass roots. According to him, data is fundamental for decision-making, policy making, resource allocation and for that matter anything which we want to do. Irrespective of the level of operation whether it is micro or macro data is essential and imperative. Further precision of data are more important. In all aspects of the society data have to be generated, validated and maintained scientifically from Gram Panchayat at the bottom to the Federal Government at New Delhi for all kinds of decisions, programmes and resource allocations. He further laments that there is no systematic generation of data done at grass-roots in an integrated manner. All data generation activities are *ad hoc*, occasional, need based and unscientific. People who are all involved in data generation for government departments at the grass-roots are not well trained in data generation as professionals. Hence, the data generated by the agencies mostly by the Departments of government at the grass-roots are not scientific and periodical and yet they are the only reliable data base for decision-making at different levels of government. Faulty decisions are made because of the unscientific data support provided to the decision-making process by the grass-roots agencies. Further the data generated by the researchers for specific purposes contradict the database generated by the government departments. It is to be noted that for all vital matters data are compiled from district data pool. The data generated and compiled at the district level are not considered to be the best and scientific. Down below the district level there is no disaggregated scientific database. As a result for any reliable decision-making, data generated at the district level should not be considered as scientific and dynamic. And yet there is no alternative. Hence, for all decision-making we rely on the data obtained from the District Administration. There is no such concept of data management of all aspects of economy, society and development for decision-making at grass roots. At the village level, and at the block level there is no break up of data on any aspect. The District is considered as a unit. Variations within district cannot be captured; variations within block cannot be explainied. Each department has its own way of keeping the data and each department has its own geographical area of coverage. Hence, one cannot get data relating to school going children in a Gram Panchayat area, anemia affected women in Gram Panchayat area and likewise all data in the geographical area of Block Panchayat. The author suggests that data have to be generated from the lowest unit of governance and administration to the highest level. Decisions are taken at Gram Panchayat level, at block level, at district level, regional level, state level and federal level. Data have to be maintained in such a way that they can be used at any level. If data are maintained in disaggregated manner, problems and issues could be identified and they can be solved easily. Periodical updating of the data is yet another needed activity. Before conclude the author underlines the significance of Information Conmmnication Technology (ICT) devices in data collection, generation and management. To him, if it is used scientifically a new and vibrant development culture at the grass roots can be assured. It will help to improve the whole decision making process, wastages can be curtailed and it will also help to reduce the corruption, to a considerable level. What is required at this moment is the political and administrative will from the concerned.

M.R.Biju has made a detailed study on the measures taken by the Government of India in the field of rural development in the context of globalization. According to him despite the serious commitment on the part of the government, the benefits of the programmes do not seem to reach the indented targets and they fail to serve fully the purpose for which they were launched. It has been observed that, more often than not, the rural development programmes are implemented without testing their local suitability. Theoretical perfection of a scheme is regarded as the criterion for the soundness of a programme, which should not be the case. Factors such as psychological receptivity, local conditions and constraints and lifestyle are often ignored while designing the rural development programmes. Most of the rural development programmes. Though indented for the poorest of the poor, have not full helped in alleviating their problems. There is a lacuna in the identification of the really poor, with the result that the rich farmers have benefited much more from these programmes. The programmes have, no doubt, generated a ray of hope for the underprivileged sections of society, by they have, as yet, not brought about a perceptible rise in the income of these sections. Further, some other programmes have succeeded only partially because of the low motivation level among the villages. The basic problem of being unable to arouse popular participation has plagued most of these programmes. Little wonder, most of the programmes did not affect the rural poor substantially. It was found that the village level workers, who ought to have worked as the rural animators, did not truly accomplish their role satisfactory. An impression exists that a VLW is of greater help to the rural elite than to the rural poor.

A look at the rural development programmes will also show that some of them have been launched by various political leaders with only an inadequate understanding of the complexity of the problems faced by the rural poor. It appears that, sometimes, they were simply forcing the programmes down the villagers' throats. Programmes with catchy slogans have also been launched in a haphazard manner just before elections and, hence, have been implemented in a half-hearted way.

He concludes his study by saying that the forces of globalization, liberalization and the revolution in information technology have shattered many a myth hitherto held sacrosanct about the government and more specifically concerning its primary institution of governance the public administration. No longer can governments afford to support, rigid, bureaucratic, reactive, rules driven administrative organizations. Rather, today's administrative system must be flexible, consultative, result-oriented and proactive-encouraging and supporting creativity and innovation from the bottom to the top in order to govern and provide services to the citizens at large. There has been a considerable rethinking the way the governments now conduct their business, and they are looking more and more towards innovative solution to respond to an increasing number of complex new environmental and global problems and pressure, which are further accentuated in a developing, multi-linguistic, and a multi-cultural country like ours having diversity of social and religious systems.

Archana G.Gulati's paper captioned 'Universal Service Policy in India – Theory and Practice' aims to delve into various aspects of the policy with the objective of highlighting both positive aspects and potential pitfalls. It looks at the theory and practice of prevailing methods of US Provision and also a possible way forward. According to Gulati USO funds become essential even in all developed nations with fully liberalized and mature telecom sectors in order to step in and bridge access gaps in areas where markets have failed. While it has done excellent work since its conception in 2003, the University

Service Obligation Fund (USOF) of India still has a long way to go before it can fulfil its mandate of fully connecting rural and remote India. When chalking out a plan for future schemes it is important for USOF to avoid any unintended negative impact through introduction of competitive distortions which could imbede the healthy growth and long term sustainability of rural telecom. It is also essential to keep a close eye on whether the desired socio-economic objectives of Universal connectivity are being achieved. This requires the undeniably tricky task of close co-ordination with other government departments so that connectivity is also supported by complementing content and the essential capacities of stakeholders to fully realize the potential of ICT to bridge the digital divide and thus ensure inclusive growth. Going forward targeted subsidies may be necessary to reach out to the specially disadvantaged sections in a cost effective manner. The eventual expansion of the definition of US to include the special services and unconnected urban population also merits consideration.

Shankar Prinjia *et.al*., have presented a paper on the role of PRIs in decentralized village health planning. The study was conducted in thirty subcentres of district Rohtak, The study participants included 30 *sarpanches* and 120 *panchayat* members/ *panches* (60 male and female *panches* each). Twenty-seven (90%) *sarpanches* and 101 (84.2%) *panches* selected belonged to subcentre village while the rest were from non-subcentre village which was under the service purview of the selected subcentre. The average population of the study subcentre was 5914. The study revealed that *sarpanches* were contacted more frequently than the *panchayat* members by the ANM. Twenty-eight (93.3%) *sarpanches* were contacted at least once during last six months as against 70 (58.3%) *panches* which was statistically significant (OR=10; OR 95% CI=2.1-63.7). Four (57.2%) female *sarpanches* were contacted by the ANM thrice or more in past six months while only 8 (34.8%) male *sarpanches* were contacted as frequently which was however statistically not significant (OR=2.5; OR 95%

CI=0.34-19.6). The contacts with all the *sarpanches* were utilized mainly to provide information regarding special campaigns like the Intensified Pulse Polio Campaigns (IPPC) or any other camp. Seven (23.3%) *sarpanches* were contacted for providing them health education in which 4 (13.3%) of them were also provided some educational material.

One (3.3%) *sarpanch* was provided with a copy of fixed work schedule by the ANM detailing her day-wise activities plan at the subcentre and home-visiting. None of the *panches* was provided with this information. Besides providing information on special campaigns, the four issues which were discussed most frequently with *sarpanches* included explaining the spectrum of services at subcentre (11; 36.7%), discussion on health information of women and children (8; 26.7%), health problems of women and children (7; 23.3%), and opinion seeking on health needs of women and children (8; 26.7%). Coverage of discussion of these four issues ranged from 4.3 to 30.4% for male *sarpanches* while it was 28.6 to 85.7% with female *sarpanches*. Barring the exception of discussion on spectrum of services, all other areas of discussion relating to heath information, health problems and needs ascertainment of problems of women and children were found significantly more with female *sarpanches*.

The study further reveals that almost all the *sarpanches* complained that the ANM did not stay in the subcentre which compromised the provision of intranatal and postnatal care to women and children. Majority of *sarpanches* opined that the management of subcentres should be handed over to the *panchayats*. This reflects that PRIs are ready and willing to shoulder the responsibility assigned to them. This situation should be carefully nurtured. Women members of village *panchayat* should take the lead in view of the camaraderie and congenial relation between them and the ANMs. However, awareness among the PRI members regarding their roles and responsibilities in health care delivery was minimal. Lack of capacity among PRIs to undertake development work and illiteracy are often cited as reasons by the health workers and medical officers for not involving them in the planning process. This issue needs urgent redressal, particularly in a sector such as health and family welfare, where some knowledge of basic structure of health care system, roles and responsibilities of service providers, functions of each tier of the health system are basic prerequisites before PRI can undertake Health and Family Welfare (HFW) related interventions. The form and content of capacity building processes also need to be tailored to the literacy levels and circumstances of PRI members. Where women PRI are to be trained, female trainers are much more acceptable. The study revealed that 26 (86.7%) *sarpanches* felt need for more financial resources at hand to undertake planning for developmental work. Transfer of funds to PRI is a critical must before they can be expected to play a meaningful role in HFW activities.

Shankar Chatterjee in his paper examines various rural development strategies for the employment generation. He has made a detailed critical enquiry on SGSY, NREGA, MGNREGS, IAY, etc. The author observes that employment generation programmes and housing programmes have benefited million of rural households. The people of rural areas *inte ralia* require employment and housing. To contain rural migration, employment and housing are *sine qua non*. Thus, if rural areas develop then only India will develop in true sense.

V.M.Rao has made a study on the empowerment of women through training in mushroom cultivation under support to training and employment programme. The study is the outcome of a project of ABGVS, Ahmednagar for organizing 500 women beneficiaries to take up mushroom cultivation in the project area in 2000. The overall objective of the paper is to understand procedures followed in organizing women and effective utilization of the grants received from the funding agencies. According to Rao, though women constitute half of India's population, due to historical social, religious, and economic factors their status has been low compared to their counterparts. Society has institutionalized a sharp demarcation of social roles according to sex, in which one-half of its members voluntarily accept a role subordinate to the other half. They still lack right to inherit property, own land, get education, obtain credit, earn income, work outside home, and control their fertility. They are widely under-represented in decision making at household and social levels and little control over money matters and assets even though they contribute substantially in asset formation, especially in rural India. Empowerment by means of modest income generation projects is clearly insufficient to ameliorate prospects for a high quality of life for women. Major problem in villages is that disadvantaged women are unaware of their rights and privileges. The author further feels that Arunoday has successfully completed Support to Training and Employment Programme (STEP) scheme and all 500 women beneficiaries were trained in mushroom cultivation and marketing. Implementing agency has completed the scheme as per guidelines, and successfully achieved targets. The project has resulted in providing both quantifiable and non-quantifiable impacts on beneficiaries. Adequate amount to start the activity should be made available in the scheme, at least to the target group members. Male orientation programmes also should form part of such schemes. This would enable men to extend support to the activity under consideration. Trainers may be selected from among the members by proper identification, and imparting training to such master trainers.

V. Rama Krishna in his paper 'women empowerment through panchayat' examines the history of women's political participation and their reservation in the rural self-governing institutions. The paper also highlights the recent decision of Government of India to raise reservation from one-third to 50%. Further, the researcher has made a comparative appraisal of women's reservation in the rural local bodies in various states. The author comments that, though women comprise about half of the Indian population they have been subjected to discriminatory social ethos resulting in denial of equality of status and opportunities in social, economic and political spheres. Ramakrishna's concerns is that, over the years the realization has drawn to us that women have no less concrete contribution in social and economic progress of the community and the country. Furthermore, in sharp contrast to their urban counterpart the hapless conditions of rural women are more glaring and galloping. Because of various socio-economic constraints, clear absence of acceptance of women's public role, more orthodox social milieu of agricultural society and utter confinement in subsistence struggle all have practically and comprehensively strangulated rural women political participation in almost every sense. The efforts towards integrating women in the development process through panchayats remained for decades elusive, a mere 'tokenism' and it could not bring any perceptible process. A change in political status may bring about a larger transformation is socio-economic processes. Extending the term of reserved seats for women up to two or three terms would allow women in panchayats the time and space to negotiate their own power relationships within them. If they are given 10 to 15 years of continued opportunity, it can perhaps nudge them in the right direction, and encourage and nurture their desire to be assertive and independent.

M.S.Gill in his paper on rural finance and commission agents, explores the role of moneylenders and agents to meet the aspirations of the farming community. The analysis provides that the institutional agencies are withdrawing from their social responsibility of catering. The demands of the rural society and making way for the moneylenders and other non-institutional agencies to lend in a big way in cash and kind. According to the author the system of their dependency has elements of exploitation because of the vulnerability of the farming community and lack of their borrowing power. Moreover, the populists policies of the respective governments are responsible for this unhealthy economic structure of the rural credit that has encouraged high level of institutional advance.

Strategic issues in financial sustainability of Self-Help Groups (SHGs) is the core area of discussion of the paper of **S.N.Dhar.** The study is based on primary data collected from SHGs having a vintage period of one year or more and graded at least level one under the Sampoorna Grameen Samridhi Yojana (SGSY) grading mechanism. While semi-structured checklists and data formats were used to collect specific information, examination of the records and documents of the groups formed the basis of computation of interest incomes and operating costs. In addition to these informal interviews were carried out with DRDC officials, GPRPs and group leaders and a structured questionnaire was administered to one member from each group chosen at random. According to S.N.Dhar the viability and attractiveness of SHGs. as micro-finance delivery mechanisms has been established India is a laudable phenomenon and the success is due to the reason that they are essentially low cost micro-banks operating for the members in distant rural areas. Efforts at increasing the number of groups and increasing outreach being the major success indicators, often draws ones attention from the fact that the groups need to be sustainable based on peer support and 'comfortable peer pressure'. Charging of abnormally high interest rates for inter-lending has become a practice which is less questioned on the premise that the groups are informal voluntary groups. Financial management of a group in order to attain sustainability cannot be centred round high interest rates, but needs to focus also on effective management of operating costs, repayment cycles and delinquency rates. Monitoring, training and capacity building efforts by the Government agencies and NGOs need to be geared up so that groups can be capacitated to generate surpluses. With adequate surpluses, the pressure to earn incomes from interests can be reduced and consequently the inter-lending rates can be scaled down. Voluntary reduction of rates may in many cases not be easy to bring about as there may be inherent fears of generating lower income for the group. Discussions regarding fixing of interest rates need to be frequently made. Here comes the role of clusters and federations where counselling can be done and the reductions can be then implemented through the Gram Panchayt Resource Persons (GPRPs). The SGSY guidelines and provisions of the Micro-finance Sector Development and Regulation Bill can be expanded to incorporate restrictive provisions on inter-lending rates. Prompt and adequate measures in this respect are a *sine qua non* for long term sustainability of the groups and the micro-finance movement.

T. Krishna Kumar highlights the problems of tribal agriculture development in the era of globalization. To him the role of agriculture in the development of any country needs no emphasis. It has more strategic role in the process of development of developing countries like India. Agriculture continues to be the main stay of the Indian economy even after six decades of independence. As it is playing a vital role in the progress of the nation, it is considered as the backbone of economy. But the importance of the agriculture sector in the country is gradually declining. The share of agriculture in GDP has declined from 59.2% in 1950-51 to 34.9% in 1990-91. It has now reached to 18.3% by 2007-08. Similarly, the percentage of population who depend on agriculture for their livelihood has also declined from 70 to 57%. In his conclusion the author states that globalization has broken the backbones of the agriculturists of Andhra Pradesh in the particular and the country in general by making the seeds and fertilizers scanty and dear. The author feels that the farmers are not able to get the required quantity of fertilizers and seeds of the good quality. Due to this the farmers are not in a position to get the quality output for getting the reasonable or good price for their yield. At the end of the study it has been concluded that the globalization is both boom and bane to the tribal agriculturists. And the agencies, government has to take an oath to develop the tribal agriculturist.

Empowerment of Rural Women through SHGs and Microcredit is the central theme of the paper by **Anita Modi.**

According to Anita, the condition, status and position of women are deplorable in all terms whether social, economic and political. Specially, rural women of India are victims of gender discrimination and their sad plight is a challenge for us. Rural women are the major workforce in the agricultural sector of our economy, but their work could not get the recognition in the society. They have no property, no education and no skill to get employment in the formal and organized sector.The sad plight of women is evident from the fact that women constitutes almost half of the population, performs nearly two-third of work hours, receives one-tenth of the world's income and owns less than one hundredth of the world property. The author warns that, gender discrimination involves the huge cost in the form of great poverty, slower economic growth, weaker governance and a lower living standard of the people. She further underlines that, to make SHG movement effective and successful for women empowerment, it is essential that the main motto of SHG "for the women, by the women and of the women" should be followed in every manner. There is an urgent need of massive support from the state, NGOs, civil society groups and local people to make SHGs more viable, successful and effective. Awareness camps, literacy campaigns and capacity building training programes should be organized periodically to bring a large of women under the umbrella of SHGs and thus empowering them.

Jitendra Ahirrao has presented a paper on Capacity building of rural poor through micro-finance. According to Rao, micro-finance has gained considerable importance in the last two decades as a tool of poverty reduction. It is also emerged as a powerful tool for rural development. Micro-finance is generally seen as small loans to poor people in general and rural poor in particular for self-employments that generate income allowing them to care for themselves. He further comments that, micro-financing through SHGs has transferred the real economic power in the hands of women and has considerably reduced their dependence on men. It is not only a financial system but also a tool for social change. Micro-finance provides the economic element to development. Rural people can earn income and build assets, families eat better, they can afford health care and children are more likely to attend school. Rao concludes his study by stating that micro-finance can be a powerful instrument initiating a cyclical process of growth and development. Micro-finance is expected to play a significant role in poverty alleviation and development. Micro-finance activity improved access of rural poor to financial services, both savings and credit. Micro-finance has gained considerable importance in the last two decades as a tool of poverty reduction. SHG has gradually received necessary support from the institutional structure. Central Government should be promoted SHGs in a very large way to extend credit to the poor rural people under SGSY. SGSY is being implemented by the DRDA with the active participation of Panchayati Raj Institutions (PRIs), the Banks and Non-Governmental Organizations (NGOs). In India, a variety of micro-finance schemes exist and various approaches have been practiced by both GOs and NGOs.

B.C.Das, discusses in depth the performance SGSY-SHGs in Bihar, one of the backward states in India, where concentration of rural poor is much higher than other states. From the state, two Regional Rural Banks (RRBs) having more than 25 branches were selected at the first phase. Again from each RRB, 25 branches were selected and from each branch, one SHG financed under SGSY for income generating activities prior to March 2007 were taken for the study. The reason for such selection of the SHG was that the groups those were financed at least two years before the data collection would have manifested some economic development. Therefore, 50 SHGs financed under SGSY by the 50 branches of two RRBs, viz. Bihar Khestriya Gramin Bank and Uttar Bihar Gramin Bank constituted the sample of this study. Primary and secondary data for the study were collected during December 2009 to February 2010.

For the purpose of measuring and ranking the performance of the group, a maturity index was developed with 20 key performance indicators. For each indicator, values (marks) were assigned as per the actual performance of the group. The maximum values allotted to each of the indicator aggregates to 100. The performance of SHG is assessed on the basis of total marks obtained on 20 indicators. According to B.C.Das, SHGs of the study sample were formed in a very routine manner without giving much emphasis in the process part. They were recommended to bank for revolving fund and credit for IGA without following right grading process. It was found that the most of the SHGs did not take up sufficient number of times of internal lending to acquire the minimum level of skill to manage their own fund before opting for higher amount of credit from bank. Many of the SHG members were found ignorant about the quantum of subsidy, interest rate and terms of loan repayment. The maturity level of the sampled SHGs was very poor and they performed very badly in all 20 performance indicators. These immature SHGs were not reckoned by the banks as serious micro-credit clients and the SHG-bank linkage process was not pursued seriously. To establish an effective linkage between SGSY-SHG and bank, the performance of the SHGs on the above discussed 20 indicators has to be improved through capacity building of different stakeholders involved in the process.

B.Vanitha in her paper made an enquiry on the rural credit access through micro-finance. To her, women empowerment is a process whereby women become able to organise themselves to increase their own self-reliance, to assert their independent right to make choices and to control resources which will assist in challenging and eliminating their own subordination. The goal of women empowerment is to address issues relating to women's subordination, inequality and inequity. Hence, women empowerment is a process where women are able to change from a state of powerlessness (I cannot) to a state of collective self-confidence (We can). This study has taken up to assess the level of empowerment interventions on the SHG members in Coimbatore District due to the implementation of SGSY. The author after a detailed enquiry concludes her study by stating that there are indications of positive interventions in the women empowerment process due to the implementation of SGSY in Coimbatore District. From the stage of mere passive beneficiaries of welfare benefit, women are tending towards the stage of taking appropriate action to close gender gaps and inequalities. It has been found that there have been improvements in the financial position, income control and skill levels besides access to savings and credit.

Experiences over the years have shown that, putting financial resources in the hands of poor women is not enough to bring about empowerment and improved welfare. Micro-finance programmes like SGSY when properly designed can make an important contribution to women empowerment by adopting a holistic approach that takes into account cultural, economic and political factors affecting empowerment. The schemes like SGSY can be ensured that women are more deeply and consistently empowered. Apart from the revolving fund and economic assistance extended to the SHGs, there should be more emphasis on other elements of empowerment such as leadership, self-management, and entrepreneurship in order to inch towards the overall empowerment of women.

G. Prasad Babu and **Rajkumar J.S.** have presented a paper on Self-Help Group (SHG) and its linkage with Micro Credit Rural Development. According to the authors SHG-Micro- finance has significant role to play in Indian economy for boosting micro entrepreneurial activities for creating productive assets coupled with employment generation. So, in order to cover all the poor households, particularly BPL households, there is need for providing full support by the Government, financial institutions, NGO's, SHG Promoting Institutions (SHGPI) to SHG's programmes. Political interference in the functioning of self-help groups should be avoided. The bottlenecks like indifference attitude of bank officers, exploitation by promoting NGO's, lack of marketing facilities for product/services. These bottlenecks should be rooted out on priority basis. Women groups should be given responsibility of running *Anganwadi*, fair price shops, so that they become permanent entities and also transparency and accountability can be maintained. The concept of financial inclusion should be followed by giving the equal opportunity to all the BPL families in the country so that balanced growth is maintained and also ensure social, economic empowerment of the downtrodden.

R.C. Mishra and **K.C. Mishra** have presented a paper on Bharat Nirman. In their paper, the authors points out that, the building and development of infrastructure in rural areas will ensure that every household will have a roof over head, a square meal, market access, higher productivity, road connectivity, electricity, communication facilities, better health facilities and better environment by 2009. As a result, it will not only help to develop agriculture, industry, trade and commerce in the rural areas but also help to banish poverty and unemployment from the rural areas. It is expected that through these programmes, provision of urban amenities in rural areas will check the exodus of rural people to the cities and minimize the rural-urban divide. Thereby it will bring about sustainable development. The authors concludes their study by stating that the Bharat Nirman programme along with eight flagship programmes if implemented with strong determination and true spirit will no doubt change the face of rural India. As a result it will not only alleviate poverty and unemployment in rural India but also provide urban amenities in rural areas leading to rural development in India. It is however concluded that just as Roosevelt's New Deal Policy could overcome the Great Depression of the Thirties, the Government of India's new deal for rural development will not only banish poverty and unemployment in the rural areas but also bring about sustainable development in the rural areas within a short span of time.

Niti Mehta and **Anita Arya** in their paper captioned Krishi Rath: An innovative approach towards rural development provides an overview of the "Krishi Mahotsava" or "Rath" being conducted annually by the Government of Gujarat since 2005. The "Rath" is held in the months of May-June just preceding the kharif season. The purpose of this note is to speculate upon the future course of action that the government could pursue and the manner in which this rather unique exercise can be institutionalized for addressing the needs of holistic, sustained and systemic agricultural and overall rural development. The Krishi Rath- a month long agricultural festival is a unique programme and first of its kind in the country. It is an intensive programme to facilitate agricultural planning and overall rural development with the objective that the state's per capita agricultural income doubles in a sustainable manner within five years of the programme's inception. The event aims at development of not only agriculture, including crop and livestock sectors, but touches the entire gamut of agricultural research and education, land resources, water management, cooperatives, marketing and processing, livestock, fisheries, etc.

According to the authors, agricultural research and extension play an important role in the growth of the agriculture sector. Efficiency and efficacy of the extension system are important determinants of technological change. The extension machinery faces tremendous challenges as of today. The farming community, if they are to reap the benefits of the globalized era, requires knowledge and scientific practices to modify their agricultural operations. In addition, sustainability of agriculture is being threatened; declining productivity, increased cost of cultivation, degradation of land and water resources are all playing havoc with the farm incomes and overall threatening the livelihood patterns of the rural population. In the process rural poverty and growing rural – urban disparities are becoming all the more glaring. They further states that, Gujarat Government's effort towards information dissemination for scientific agriculture by way of the month long Krishi Mahotsava is a commendable exercise in the direction of doubling rural incomes. The Rath followed a holistic approach to address the needs of the agricultural sector, but for it to develop as a successful and replicable model it needs to be institutionalized into a permanent and stable structure. The authors concludes their study by stating that Krishi Rath can be developed as a decentralized information bank besides being the technical arm to provide support for village level planning. In this image the Rath would have a continuous and sustained role to perform. It has the potential to act as a catalyst in transforming agriculture of the state, thereby ushering in rural prosperity.

B.K.Mohanty has presented a paper on Gene Revolution— A sustainable approach for food crisis. To him sixty years after independence India produces on an average, only 14 kg of rice and wheat per person per annum, just a little over one kilogram per person over a month. Over 60% of India's net shown area still remains at the mercy of the monsoon. About 60% of our farmers own only 0.4 hectares of land each. Another 20% of farmers hold an average of 1.4 hectares each. Therefore 80% of our farmers are small and marginal farmers. Nearly 87,000 farmers in India committed suicide between 2001 and 2005, within a span of four years. The per capita availability of foodgrains in India has declined from about 500 grams per day per person to less than 400 grams per day over the last two decades.

Since the mid-1960's, the traditional agricultural practices, according to the author are gradually being replaced by modern technology and farm practices in India and a veritable revolution took place in our country. The new technology was tried in 1960-61 as pilot project in seven Districts and was called Intensive Agricultural District Programme (IADP) and later High Yielding Verity Programme (HYVP) was added and was extended to cover the entire country. This strategy was popularly known as "Green Revolution". Now it is the time to launch a "Gene Revolution" instead of "Green Revolution" to feed the world and make Indian farmers rich. In his final observation, Mohanty underlines that Today's paramount need is to improve agricultural productivity across the Globe. Crop yields can be increased through the introduction of technologies such as drip irrigation or through education and training of farmers. If countries like India and China, which have large agricultural land, can boost their productivity to the levels attained by the developed world, it will no doubt mitigate food scarcity. From the first "Green Revolution" to the current "Gene Revolution", innovative new technologies have significantly improved our ability to feed our people. Farmers in India and around the world, who have pioneered the use of modern bio-technology have seen their innovation rewarded in terms of high production and lower environmental impacts. Further innovations like bio-fuels and drought tolerant crops will further contribute to sustainable production efficiencies.

Rajkumar Josmeesingh *et .al*. have presented a paper on extension approaches for promoting participatory watershed management for sustainable agriculture development. According to the authors extension agencies should take dynamic and vibrant approaches to make Participatory Watershed Management for ensuring sustainable and productive agriculture. This long term strategy of Participatory Watershed Management is directed towards increasing or maintaining the adaptive capacity of natural resources to produce material goods such as food, fibre, fuel wood, timber, non-timber forest products, meat, dairy products, fish, etc. including their value addition wherever required including the conservation of bio-diversity and services such as clean air and fresh water not only for the present but for future generations also.

K.V. Ramachandran, in his paper unfolds the issues and constraints faced by the housing sector in the state of Kerala. According to the author, in Kerala there is persistent gap between both the aggregate demand for and supply of housing stocks which causes a high level of housing inadequacy in the state. Due to the escalating rise in price of building materials and labour the housing has become totally inaccessible to many. Now, the price of building materials alone contribute to 60-70% of the overall cost of construction. Besides, the recent boosting up of the wage rate (i.e. in the year 2007–08, the maximum wage rate per day for the male worker in the construction field was Rs.250 while that of the female worker was Rs.180. But, by the beginning of the year 2009-2010, the wage rate among the both workers suddenly increased to Rs.450 and Rs.300 respectively) has also added much to the intensity of the housing problem. He further points out that the acute shortage of housing settlements is one of the basic problems confronted by the State at present. The soaring price of building materials is the main factor which causes this problem. It has a cascading effect on the overall costs of construction. If this trend is followed, the housing scenario in the coming years presents a grim picture. Housing has been a "neglected area" especially among the rural masses. It is still a "mirage to many". To the poor persons concerned, the "sky itself is their shelter". The non-availability of accessible land at reasonable price keeps the poor man away from building apartments. But, just converse to this, the need for more and more dwelling units arose on account of the formation of nuclear families caused by the rapid urbanization and development. It necessitates the construction of a large number of new houses in the State. After presenting the magnitude of the topic, the author proceeds to present the major reviews carried out on the research area and submits a series of solutions to remove the existing hurdles.

In the concluding chapter **Anupam Hazra** has made a detailed study on NREGA and sustainable development. According to Anupam, under the social protection umbrella, public works have probably had the largest outreach. But these have been criticized because they often fail to generate employment through the creation of productive assets and, without this, they cannot contribute to the generation of sustainable and productive employment. NREGA in India is an example of a public works programme with diverse social protection objectives that include providing a minimum income along side stimulating local development, and operating in a gender-sensitive manner. It can serve as a model and provide lessons for the development of similar social protection initiatives in developing countries. To conclude it can be said that NREGA is an unusual and instructive example of a social protection measure that is demand-driven and gender-sensitive, has nationwide coverage, and provides a minimum income along side stimulating local development.

To him without a doubt, NREGA has the potential to change the socio-economic landscape in rural India in the long term. But as with any other legislation, it is practically impossible to make it foolproof. Middlemen coming into illegal nexuses with corrupt govt. officials to swig away the NREGA funds are to be expected. The only way corruption can be stemmed is by proactive people's involvement in the implementation process. People should start questioning the officials for transparency in the process and get proper information about creation of muster rolls and disbursement of funds. And as such, it feels like RTI (Right to Information Act) should and will become the primary weapon for people.

The author further feels that, NREGA is already making a difference to the lives of the people. Yet there is a long way to go. There are some issues in terms of the benefits to be drawn from the assets created by the scheme. Also, the menial nature and the lack of encouragement for both skilled labour and further training is something that is of concern in the long run. Implementation issues like issuance of job-cards on time is also a concern. Facilities for workers would also have to be improved over time. From the labour market point of view, it would be important to create a safety net through NREGA for poor people without damaging the labour market and employment prospects.

Thus this volume has touched upon the major components needed for the development of rural India. Though the contributors have given insights and their approaches differently all of them have highlighted the areas of concerns linked with PRIs and Rural Development. It is believed that the volume will contribute positively to plan and execute policies, strategies, projects and programmes for the overall developments of these two areas of concerns which will ultimately decide the very destiny of rural India in the days to come.

M.R. Biju

1

Rural Development and Development Administration in India Need for a Comprehensive Approach

Rakesh Hooja

It is most likely that all possible types of developmental initiatives have been tried out in some part or the other of India over the last 60 plus years since the country gained independence. With governments of different ideological hues having remained in power at different points of time in different States of the Indian Union and at the Centre, and with different ideas about development, governance, planning, state welfarism, market-orientedness, administration, nation building, etc. having been accepted or fashionable at different time frames- as well as a willingness to try out and emulate or adopt what was being attempted in other parts of India, or in the countries of the West, or of the erstwhile Soviet bloc, or in other developing areas, all forms of administrative and governmental action and all types of developmental schemes, as well as types of organizational arrangements, have been tried out somewhere or the other in India. These have been commented upon by experts, scholars, researchers, practitioners, journalists as also the ordinary layman or common citizen. The various initiatives undertaken for achieving development have been as per the percieved needs, wants and aspirations of the Indian people because what is relevant in the Indian context may not prove to be so in other contexts in other countries, and even in India what is contextually relevant is undergoing changes with the passing of time.

Accordingly this paper aims at developing a perspective about development administration and rural development in Indian context and from an Indian viewpoint. (Thus even views of non-Indian scholars picked out for taking note of in this piece are those which in this authors opinion suit the Indian situation.)

Development aims at social and cultural change as well as economic growth. Thus, the term 'development' may be used to describe such changes as are positively valued or such quantitative and qualitative transformations as have been or are being desired.

When it comes to the concept of development administration, it originally evolved as a counterpoint to regulatory administration and, at least in India, alluded to differences in approach, attitude and way of doing things from what was being done as part of what was considered traditional regulatory administration under the British which gave way to development administration in independent India. Now, it has been realized that it is difficult, as well as inappropriate, to segregate the regulatory from the development in administration. However, administration of development, which is what development administration essentially is, does involve somewhat different types of organizations, administrative procedures and orientations and nuances to ensure that the administration helps in the achievement of our developmental goals. Thus, in addition to administration of development, development administration also refers to development of administration so that the administration develops the capacity to work in a better manner towards achievement of desired developmental goals.

The above view of this author is somewhere similar to that

of Weidner (1970) for whom development administration in government refers to the process of guiding an organization towards the achievement of progressive political, economic and social objectives that are authoritatively determined in one manner or another.

According to Swerdlow (1963) one way of defining development administration is as "the management of change". Swerdlow had set forth his view in the context of Paul Meadows opinion in Swerdlow (1963) that development administration can be regarded as the public management of economic and social change in terms of public policy.

As Inamdar (1992) points out development administration involves the whole gamut of developmental functions and tasks, structures, personnel, finances, organizational inter-relationships, control and supervision, communication, reporting, monitoring, and special relationship with the people.

For Riggs (1970) development administration refers not only to a government's efforts to carry out programmes designed to reshape its physical, human, and cultural environment, but also to the struggle so enlarge a governments capacity to engage in such programmes.

Inayatullah (1970) refers to development administration as the complex of organizational arrangements for the achievement of action through public authority in pursuance of socio-economic goals and nation building. It presupposes policies, plans and programmes with a distinct development bias as well as a bureaucracy which consciously and continually seeks to modernize itself to meet the demands of planned change.

Kuldeep Mathur (1985) has suggested that there are three important dimensions to development administration. The first relates to professionalization of administration for successful implementation of development programmes. The second relates to changing the behavioural orientation and mental make up of the bureaucracy (we may note that this is reflected in practice by civil servants identifying some amongst themselves as 'development minded' as opposed to the 'administration minded' who are more oriented to maintaining law and order and enforcing rules as well as following set systems and procedures). Thirdly, development administration involves people's participation.

In a slightly different vein, John Montgomery (1966) defines development administration as carrying out planned change in the economy (in agriculture or industry, or the capital infrastructure supporting either of these) and, to a lesser extent, in the social services of the State (especially education and public health).

Despite the fact that in today's world urbanization is ever increasing, a significant percentage of India's population is likely for quite sometime to come to continue to live in rural areas as it has done for centuries and also during the last sixty years since independence when development came to the fore-front. Thus for a country like ours there continues to be a strong moral imperative to look after the development of rural people and rural areas. And for our country it is the rural human and physical resources and rural produce as well as rural demand for goods and services, which are the major engines for growth. Rural hinterlands form a unified system with urban centres and neither can grow or develop without the other. Thus, in common usage, in India, the term 'development administration' has got linked with rural development, so that administration for rural development tends to be referred to as development administration.

Rural development is very broad in terms of scope and involves changes in attitudes, customs, beliefs, values; output both quantitatively and qualitatively; utilization of natural and human resources; employment patterns and magnitudes; technology and access to it; institutional and organizational frameworks; incomes and income patterns; spatial as well as social relationships; migratory trends; power structures; production structures and production relations; productivity and production; rural lifestyles and cultural patterns; living standards; policy initiatives related to land and water, livestock and forests; physical and as well as social infrastructure; inputs, supporting services (social, commercial, etc.); prices and markets; backward areas and deprived sections of society; areas enjoying comparative advantages; diversification of the economy; food security; livelihoods; resource generation; self-sufficiency and self-sustenance; equity; gender issues; changes in qualitative and quantitative achievements *vis-a-vis* welfare; productivity and infrastructure related indicators; social and environmental sustainability and corresponding implementation; government interventions; organization and administration; coordination and integration; people's involvement and participation; role of community based organizations; rural-urban balances and complementa-rities; and multi-level and decentralized planning. When people refer to rural development they often mean management of rural development.

Katar Singh (1986) has expressed it slightly differently when he defines rural development as a process of developing and utilizing natural and human resources, technologies, infrastructural facilities, institutions and organizations, and government policies and programmes to encourage and speed up economic growth in rural areas, to provide jobs, and to improve the quality of rural life towards self-sustenance.

Thus, programmes for rural development can be varied covering one, some, or all aspects of rural development. However, as Johnston and Clark (1982) have suggested rural development can be viewed as a three pronged strategy. The first, a production oriented prong, is a broad based and unimodal approach to agriculture development (in an aside we may point out that John Harris, 1982, emphasizes that rural development is at once broader and more specific than agriculture development) whose multiple benefits derive from opportunities to simultaneously expand the growth output and employment, both within and outside agriculture, and at the same time generate the incomes that enable the poor to improve their level of consumption. The second, consumption-assigned prong, involves programmes to strengthen social services- education, health, nutrition and family planning. And the third prong, which concerns organizational programmes is designed to enhance the institutional infrastructure and managerial skills needed for rural development.

Mehla and Mehla (reproduced in Hooja and Parnami, 2007) suggest that certain important policies are common to most rural development strategies and these policies relate to land, technology, agriculture, employment, education, research and extension, reforming rural institutions and agricultural pricing. In this context an agricultural strategy for rural development can comprise the following elements: (i) agriculture research, extension, rural education and training programmes for farmers, (ii) infrastructure building activity related to the growth of irrigation, transport, communications and health facilities, (iii) programmes to improve marketing facilities for the distribution of agricultural inputs and implements, and (iv) policies related to land tenure, agriculture output, prices and taxation of agricultural incomes.

A slightly different approach is indicated by Najmunessa Mahtab (1994), who states that (integrated) rural development has three objectives; economic development in its various dimensions, social development, and educational and cultural development (which last helps in the achievement of economic and social development).

Hoshiar Singh (1985) suggests that rural development activities fall into the following six categories: income generation, growth, target group development, area development, education and welfare.

As we have already indicated, in India when people refer to development administration, they often mean rural development administration, or the rural delivery system. Such a rural delivery system in India by and large consists of the following: the general administration of the province or state government represented by its line unit—the district—headed by the Collector; functional departments and corporations of the State Government and their field staff headed by respective District Level Officers; the general district administration popularly called revenue administration system directly under the Collector; local self-government bodies (the three tiers of Panchayati Raj, also referred to as Panchayati Raj Institutions or PRIs) comprising the elected non-officials and appointed officials with the latter being responsible both to the elected panchayat representatives and to their parent State Government departments as also (due to his continuing coordinational role) to the Collector; special project agencies or sub-agencies set up on an area or activity basis by State or Central Government departments or agencies; the institutional credit system of banks and cooperatives; Community-Based Organizations (CBOs), beneficiary or user groups and other local associations and groups; non-governmental agencies; universities and research or consultancy organizations; normal trading channels and private sector institutions involved in rural development; the mass media network; (in some cases) political party cadres, etc. Each, or a combination of them, has to interact with each other and with the local populace as also various segments of such populations (including district or local level associations of professionals, or traders, or industrialists or farmers, and other pressure groups and local level politicians and other elites or non-elites) who themselves may be operating within a web of interlocked factor markets and socio-politico-administrative relationships, as also with external change agents whether from the public, private or what is now being called third sector.

In addition regional officers of various State Government departments, often posted at divisional headquarters, are involved in rural development, and in many States the Divisional Commissioner is also assigned a coordinational role regarding developmental efforts for the districts within his charge.

The above-mentioned framework of development administration has undergone some changes especially in terms of nuances or emphasis and orientation over the years. It also differs slightly from area to area and state to state, and can be compared with rural bureaucracies in other developing countries. But the development administrative system as it evolved in the 1950, 1960 and 1970 has by and large remained unchanged in India.

In fact the rural development delivery system has by and large continued to grapple with similar issues over the last 30-40 years, though nuances have changed as programmes have given way to newer but similar programmes, technological developments have led to some changes in the abilities, styles and manners of functioning, and feedback about implementation have led to modifications in implementation and to some structural and administrative changes like the constitutionalization of Panchayati Raj or the creation of special project agencies and implementation mechanisms. This author notes that many of the issues, problems and suggestions regarding implementing rural development initiatives by government highlighted in his first book of essays on rural development (Rakesh Hooja, Administrative Interventions in Rural Development, 1987) almost 25 years ago continue to remain relevant today though some terminologies and details of programmes and schemes may have undergone change, technologies available have improved, a few new types of government schemes have emerged, and some issues may now be considered to be somewhat resolved, though attempts at improvement continue. Articles like "Speculation on the Agrarian Structure and Government Delivery System in 2000 AD" and "Machinery for Delivering Benefits to the Rural Poor" in Hooja (1987) contain many insights, issues and recommendations that continue to be relevant today, as do the contents of the chapter on the rural delivery system in Hooja (1986).

In 1972 the Planning Commission's Task Force on

Integrated Rural Development observed "we have belatedly decided to take what might be considered a rather restricted view of the expression 'rural development' choosing to equate it with agricultural development in the widest sense so as to embrace besides crop husbandry all the allied activities".

There is another comparatively limited definition of rural development exemplified by Robert Chambers (1983) when he said, "Rural development is a strategy to enable a specific group of people, poor rural women and men to gain for themselves and their children more of what they want and need. It involves helping the poorest amongst those who seek a livelihood in the rural areas to demand and control more of the benefits of rural development". People subscribing to this view equate rural development with poverty alleviation and the uplift of the poor, rather than taking a broader multifaceted view of rural development as the process of change in rural societies, or the overall development of rural areas aimed at transforming the rural scene and improving the quality of life of all rural people.

hus the World Bank Rural Development Sector Policy Paper of 1975 considered rural development to be a strategy designed to improve the economic and social life of a specific group of people – the rural poor - and thus considered poverty and inequality as the focus of rural development. It advocated extending the benefits of development to the poorest amongst those who seek a livelihood in the rural areas. According to the World Bank paper since rural development is intended to reduce poverty, it must be designed to increase production and raise productivity. Provisions of improved food supplies and nutrition, along with basic services such as health and education, not only contribute to the physical well being of the rural people but also raise their productivity and ability to contribute to the national economy. The objectives of rural development according to the World Bank paper are not restricted to any single department but spread over several government departments and agencies, and the resultant mix serves to raise agricultural output, create new employment, improve health and education, expand communication, provide housing, etc. Thus rural development was defined in terms of an improvement of the economic and social life of the rural poor.

In fact many countries in the world do not have separate rural development departments, but their agriculture department or Ministry also touches upon animal husbandry, irrigation, land improvement and soil conservation, and other aspects of rural development.

In India by the time of the Fifth Five Year Plan the following special programmes for backward areas and weaker sections of the rural society were being implemented:

1.	Resource/Problem based Area Programmes	Drought Prone Areas Programme, Command Area Development Programme, Hill Area Development, Intensive Agriculture District Programme
2.	Target Group Programmes	Small Farmers Development Programme, Tribal Development Agency Project
3.	Area Specific Incentive Subsidy Programmes	Concessional Finance, Investment and Transport Subsidy Schemes
4.	Comprehensive Area Development Programmes	Sub Plans for Hill and for Tribal Areas

Thus while the rural poor were a focus of rural development, programmes for the development of all rural people and all rural areas were also receiving significant attention.

India's Draft Sixth Five Year Plan (1978-83) had visualized the integration of the following programmes as part of Integrated Rural Development— (a) programmes of agricultural development, (b) programmes of animal husbandry, (c) programmes of inland water and brackish water fisheries, (d) programmes of marine fisheries, (e) programmes of social forestry to provide a base for fuel and fodder, etc.,

(f) programmes of farm forestry through small peasant householders, (g) village and cottage industries as a full or part time occupation, (h) services sector of the rural economy as self-employment sectors for farm families, and (i) labour programmes for skill formulation and labour mobility.

By 1992-93 the annual report of the Ministry of Rural Development of the Government of India was asserting that rural development has come to mean a direct attack on rural poverty through special employment programmes, land reforms, area development programmes, and measures to provide safe drinking water supply and rural housing and rural sanitation.

In fact until it got merged into the new Swaranjayanti Gram Swarozgar Yojana (SGSY) near the turn of the Century, what was called the Integrated Rural Development Programme (IRDP or IRD) was a major pillar of government's rural development administration efforts. However, the word 'integrated' was somewhat of a misnomer since IRD did not cover all aspects of rural development, but was a poverty alleviation programme targeted at the rural poor and aimed at providing them easy access to productive credit, provision at subsidized cost of assets which could be used to earn livelihoods, and encouragement of and training for the undertaking of self-employment activities. Only some poverty alleviation activities were integrated under IRD. This programme has made the term Below Poverty Line (or BPL) family, as selected by the Gram Sabha or '*majma-e-aam*' gathering of village elders, known throughout India in each of its languages or dialects. (It may be recalled that IRD had been preceded by the Small Farmers Development Agency and the Marginal Farmers and Agricultural Labourers Agency programmes).

This programme continues to be an important component of rural development in India. For long IRD was complemented by the National Rural Employment Programme (NREP), later renamed Jawahar Rozgar Yojana (JRY) and now replaced by one of Government of India's flagship programmes based upon the National Rural Employment Guarantee Act (NAREGA), which involves the taking up of rural works aimed at providing wage employment locally in each village. Originally such employment was intended for the rural poor, though NAREGA guarantees that if they so desire, then one member of each and every rural household would be provided with 100 days a year of wage employment upon works which are locally useful.

The Rural Development Ministry at the Government of India level, Rural Development Departments in State Governments and District Rural Development Agencies (DRDAs) in each district have concentrated on these programmes. Some other programmes, like Desert Development Programme, Drought Prone Areas Programme, Watershed Development Programme and now the Backward Areas Development Programme etc. have also been taken up as part of rural development by the Central Rural Development Ministry, State Rural Development Departments and DRDAs as well as District Level Offices of various State Government bodies and the PRIs. (State Government Rural Development Departments tend to concentrate on implementing Central Sector or Centrally Sponsored Schemes rather than formulating and implementing schemes of the State Government where State Government has to bear the entire costs). The Ministry of Rural Development of Government of India also manages other activities like supply of rural drinking water and the maintenance of land records. However, since at the State Government level such schemes are not the subject matter of the State Rural Development Department, many observers (including academicians) and even many government servants do not consider them to be part of rural development. This is a wrong approach. We have already noted above how the World Bank Rural Development Sector Policy Paper had stated that rural development has to be spread over several government departments and could not be restricted to any one department. Numerous observers (including the present author) writing about the IRD programme in the 1980s had noted how it had links with a number of schemes of various government departments. Even today when a State Government conducts a 'Prashashan Gaon Ki Or' ('Reaching Administration to Every Village') campaign then activities of a number of departments like Land Revenue, Rural Development, Agriculture, Horticulture, Cooperatives, Women and Child, Social Justice, Roads and Buildings, Power, Irrigation, Command Area Development, Rural Drinking Water (Public Health Engineering Department), School Education, Medical and Health, Food and Civil Supplies, Tribal Development, etc. are taken up simultaneously at each village camp because both the State Government and the people feel that all of them have a bearing on rural development.

Also the availability of correct and up to date land records are a prerequisite for rural development efforts since availability of land is a must for many public activities and purposes in the rural areas. Thus many actions of the land revenue administration also become a part of rural development initiatives.

Thus, for example, schemes like National Rural Health Management Programme, or Sarva Shiksha Abhiyan for primary education, or say a programme for ensuring literacy in the rural areas, though managed by other departments have to seen as part of rural development. Accordingly the 'Green Revolution' and the 'white revolution' or 'Operation Flood' involving daily farming and milk also have to be viewed as part of rural development. Similarly, many famine relief works undertaken in times of droughts also contribute to rural development.

Somewhat adapting the findings of a small group which this author had headed at the behest of the Governor of Rajasthan to formulate university courses for development studies and to examine possibilities of setting up development studies centres, it could be stated that rural development requires (and such focus and has often been provided in India)

(i) a *focus on area development* (desert area development, hill area development, coastal area development, irrigation command area development, backward area development, development of industrial areas including Special Economic Zones (SEZs), development of hinterlands and periphery areas of large habitations which act as growth centres where rural-urban linkages are extremely significant), (ii) a focus on certain *disadvantaged groups* (tribals, the poor, unorganized labour, migrants, other socially disadvantaged groups, small and marginal farmers, etc.), (iii) focus on *human resource development* (education, employability, population, health, livelihoods, nutrition and food security, responses to demographic changes, etc.), (iv) focus on *natural resource management and development* (land, water, livestock, energy, environment, etc.). Another focus one could suggest as relevant for rural development is on *the provision of basic minimum services, facilities and amenities and infrastructure* based upon distance and population threshholds for villages and hamlets in all rural areas (the then President of India, Mr. Kalam had given this approach, which has long been followed in India, the name PURA or provision of urban type amenities in rural areas); though the items considered to be part of basic minimum needs have changed over time as the country has undergone development, technological changes have occurred, and certain needs have been provided to all, while aspirations for other services and amenities have changed as per changing opportunities. The provision of basic services and minimum needs involves some overlap with the four broad areas of focus referred to earlier in this paragraph.

Even through irrigation Command Area Development (CAD) and tribal area development progammes are the subject matter respectively of the Water Resources and Tribal Ministries, they are essentially rural development programmes. In CAD it has been found that merely constructing canals and running water in the canals is not enough to ensure full utilization of the irrigation potential created. People who settle in the irrigation commands (also called colonization areas if it is a new area being provided irrigation water for the first time) require roads for agricultural inputs to be brought in and agriculture produce to be taken out, various types of agriculture support and back up services including in the spheres of livestock and rural cooperatives, schools for their children, medical facilities, drinking water facilities, marketing centres and small towns, etc. for them to be able to undertake irrigated agriculture properly and efficiently and to benefit accordingly. Thus CAD is essentially a water resource based rural development programme. Similarly, it has been felt that tribal groups can be provided livelihoods and other assistance best when the overall development (rural development) of the area where tribal groups live (which is often remote and backward) is undertaken along with special schemes for the tribals. Thus tribal area development programmes aim at rural development geared at the uplift of the deprived tribal population.

Interestingly in both CAD and tribal area development results have been found to be better when an integrated organization is created (may be under an Area Development Commissioner) with officers and staff from various related government departments being placed on deputation in the area development organization, integrated budgets being made available, and the entire rural development effort for the area being planned and implemented in an integrated manner. On the other hand where various departments are expected to contribute to area development under CAD or TAD through their own departmental hierarchies with some efforts at coordination of the various separate efforts, as is more often the case in various CAD or TAD projects, then the results are often less satisfactory. This would suggest that all rural development (including poverty alleviation and employment generation) should be undertaken through an integrated area development approach being adopted for each agro-climatical sub-region – may be a district, part of a district, or a couple of districts. But the world over the model of administration that prevails is one based on functionally segmented government departments rather than multi-functional and integrated area development organizations, because that has been found to be more convenient. Thus except for a few special area development projects which could be taken up in an integrated manner, the existing model of various government departments (including the state rural development department) contributing to rural development efforts in each district appears to be the most practical. In such a situation the coordinating role of the District Collector remains the most crucial.

A possible alternative could have been for the Zila Parishad to coordinate rural development in each district. However, despite the fact that the statutory PRIs that came up in various states of the country after 1959 have now been constitutionalized following the 73rd Constitutional Amendment, many developmental activities still continue to be carried out by various State Government departments and these can only be coordinated on behalf of the Government by the District Collector. The general populace expects welfarism and rural development measures from the State and Central Governments and not merely from the PRIs. Hence, State Governments (and even Central Governments) would always be reluctant to give up their multifaceted role in rural development. The PRIs tend to look up to the State Governments to provide them with funds, functionaries and functions so as to implement government programmes, rather than raising their own resources and implementing their own programmes. Naturally if State Governments are to provide funds and functionaries they would want to retain control over the activities and to lay down detailed guidelines as to how the PRIs are to implement various schemes, and also would like to get many programmes implemented through their own government department staff. Further in many states it is the Panchayat Samiti and not Zila Parishad that coordinates implementation of panchayat programmes and the Panchayat Samiti is too small and even less equipped to coordinate all development activities in a district or block. It may also be noted that panchayati raj is dealt with and coordinated/ supervised by one government department that is the Rural Development Department, which implements only a few schemes, while many departments are involved in rural development in actual practice. Also the list of activities suggested in the 11th Schedule of the Constitution which State Governments could consider transferring to the panchayat bodies is such that some aspects of each activity would perforce have to be continue to be performed directly by the State Government itself and only some can feasibly be transferred to PRIs. Thus rural development activities in a district would continue to remain a mix of many tasks performed by the district level hierarchies of state government departments or by special project agencies created by the State Government and other tasks performed by the PRIs usually as per State Government guidelines based upon State Government funding and State Government functionaries provided to the panchayat bodies to carry out the tasks.(Some activists and advocates of Panchayati Raj keep hoping that the PRIs could evolve and become full-fledged district governments, but this is likely to be resisted by State Governments, MLAs, and State-level politicians, bureaucrats and technocrats, etc. including District Level Officers, and thus appears unlikely. In any case these advocates of panchayati raj envisage PRIs as agencies for local self-government rather than as participatory and democratic instruments of development, and for that PRIs have to be willing to raise their own resources and the Constitution would need amendment since PRIs presently fall in the State list of the Seventh Schedule of the Constitution)

The District Collector who has traditionally has been the captain of the developmental team in the district and who heads about 70 odd district level coordinational and implementational committees (though the figure differs from State to State) would thus have to continue as the coordinator of all rural development efforts. The DRDAs have since their inception in late 1970s or early 1980s been headed by District Collectors and even though in some States the DRDAs have now been transferred to the Zila Parishads, in actual practice the Collector continues to play a significant role in their functioning even in such States.

In recent years the approach of bringing about convergence between various government programmes has gained acceptance within government. Such convergence is easier between different programmes of the same department. When different departments are involved then convergence has to be ensured in implementation at district and lower levels. Here again the Collector's role becomes significant.

Now under NAREGA (or Mahatma Gandhi NAREGA or MNREGA as it is now referred to) a large magnitude of Central and State Government funds are flowing to the Gram Panchayats for implementation. However, District Collectors have been assigned supervisory functions in the implementation of MNREGA and in the conduct of social audits of its implementation.

The Collectors also coordinate within their districts the Prashashan Gaon Ki Or campaigns and even special campaigns of various individual departments whenever they are conducted.

It may be added that the Sarpanch of the Gram Panchayat is the only elected representative in panchayati raj who himself performs executive tasks including maintaining of some records. In all other cases the PRIs have officers on deputation from State Government departments who are responsible for carrying out executive functions on behalf of the panchayat bodies.

A word about CBOs (like water users associations, watershed or forestry committees, etc., which come up due to the felt needs of the communities and possess much social capital. The panchayat bodies (who are the third tier of federalism) and their advocates who keep pressing for State Governments to grant them political and social space and autonomy, are not themselves willing to concede the same to CBOs. They want such bodies to be brought under the control of PRIs or to be banned. An alternate, more appropriate, view could be to treat such CBOs as useful and independent parts of the fourth tier of Indian federalism.

Now to turn to the issue of rural development planning or district planning. At least from the Second Five Year Plan period onwards numerous initiatives at district planning involving PRIs, District Level Officers and the District Collector have been undertaken from time to time. Sometimes the techno-economic and spatial planning aspects have predominated and at others the participatory aspects. The most recent such effort at district planning through panchayat bodies commenced in 2004-05. Some of the deficiencies noted by this author over the years in district level plans emanating from Panchayati Raj Institutions (PRIs) are (i) the plans have often been a mere collection of felt needs (wish lists or shopping lists) of the elected panchayat representatives and resultant demands for financial provisions without taking into account local resources and infrastructure, (ii) the plans have also often tended to be a mere collection, without much integration, of various departmental or sub-departmental proposals and plans which are often indicated or influenced by the State Government and its district functionaries, (iii) each lower administrative or panchayat unit and planning body has been reluctant to muster any resources at its own level, but has tended to depend upon funds and functionaries for undertaking implementation being provided from higher levels, thus limiting its own flexibility while planning, (iv) plan formulation and techno-economic appraisal skills have been lacking at district and sub-district levels, and (v) the plans prepared by panchayat bodies and District Planning Committees have primarily been plans of the activities that the PRIs would implement and have failed to include the various activities to be performed by the State Government departments, or which it is hoped would be performed by the private sector or by NGOs and by Community Based Organizations (CBOs).

Comprehensive District Planning in fact calls for district natural resource inventory and resource use planning, district manpower survey and employment planning, district livelihoods planning, district agriculture and livestock planning, district industrialization planning, district food security planning, district drought proofing and disaster management planning, assessment of all on-going government programmes in the district to identify spheres or areas requiring special attention in future, mapping of village-wise infrastructure, facilities and services already available and further requirements of the same so as to facilitate spatial or area planning, etc. Only then would district planning lead to the proper coordination and integration of the rural development efforts in the district which could then have a comprehensive and integrated impact.

Since the rural development department coordinates the planning of PRI activities and the schemes of their own department, for meaningful comprehensive district planning the state planning department needs to undertake the coordination and planning involving the District Collectors, staff of various government departments including those at the district level, PRIs and district planning cells attached to the district collectorates. Similarly, the overall effort at rural development undertaken jointly by all departments and agencies of government has, in todays Indian scenario, to be overseen by the State planning department, and not by the rural development department which presently concentrates only on some aspects of rural development.

Whether we consider development administration or rural development, the focus has to remain primarily on the people and secondarily on the development of the area since rural infrastructure, rural livelihoods, rural services, rural productivity and rural administration are all meant for the people.

References

Ahuja, A.K. and A.K.Ojha (ed.) (2009). *Welfare and Tribal Development Administration*, Aalekh, Jaipur.

Ambedkar, S.N. (1994). *Integrated Rural Development Programme : Implementation Process*, Rawat, Jaipur.

Arora, Ramesh K. (ed.) (1979). *Peoples Participation in Development Process*, HCMSIPA, Jaipur.

Arora, Ramesh K. and Sangeeta Sharma (eds) (1992). *Comparative and Development Administration*, Arihant, Jaipur.

Arora, Ramesh K. and Rakesh Hooja (1994). "The Mosaic of Rural Development: Cross National Concerns" in Ramesh K. Arora and Rakesh Hooja (eds.), *Administration of Rural Development: Indian and Comparative Perspectives*, Arihant, Jaipur

Bhattacharya, Mohit (1997). *Development Administration*, Jawahar, Delhi.

Chambers, Robert(1983). *Rural Development: Putting the Last First*, Longman, London.

Dutta, Prabhat (2004). "Development Administration: New Agenda" in Ramesh K.Arora (ed.), *Public Administration: Fresh Perspectives*, Aalekh, Jaipur.

Harris, John (1982). *Rural Development: Theories of Peasant Economy and Agrarian Change*, Hutchinson.

Hooja, Meenakshi, (2004). *Policies and Strategies for Tribal Development*, Rawat, Jaipur.

Hooja, Rakesh (1973). "Administrative Development: The Concept Re-explored" *Administrative Change,* Vol.I, No.1 1973

Hooja, Rakesh (1986). *District Planning : Concept Setting and State Level Applications*, Aalekh, Jaipur.

Hooja, Rakesh (1987). *Administrative Interventions in Rural Development*, Rawat, Jaipur.

Hooja, Rakesh (1990). *Planning, Interlocked Markets and Rural Development*, Rawat, Jaipur.

Hooja, Rakesh (1997). Rural Development Administration: A Bibliographical Review, *Administrative Change*, Vol. XXIV No. 2 January-June 1997.

Hooja, Rakesh (2001). *Greening the Desert*, Rawat, Jaipur.

Hooja, Rakesh (2006). *The Management of Water for Agriculture: Irrigation, Watersheds and Drainage*, Rawat, Jaipur.

Hooja, Rakesh (2007 a). *Local Government and Federalism in India*, Occasional Paper No. 11, HCMRIPA, Jaipur.

Hooja, Rakesh (2007 b). "Managing Water in Rural Areas : An Institutional and Multi Use Perspective" in Rakesh Hooja, Ramesh K.Arora and K.K.Parnami (eds.) *Water Management : Multiple Dimensions*, Rawat, Jaipur.

Hooja, Rakesh (2007 c). "The Evolving Role of the Collector and District Administration" in Suneel Dhariwal and M.C.Sharma (eds.) *District Level Administration and Role of District Collector*, Aalekh, Jaipur.

Hooja, Rakesh (2008). "The Contextual Character of Good Governance : A Viewpoint" in Ramesh K.Arora and R.M.Khandelwal (eds.) *Good Governance : Initiatives and Impact*, Paragon, New Delhi.

Hooja, Rakesh and Meenakshi Hooja (2007). *Democratic Decentralization and Planning: Essays on Panchayati Raj, District Planning and Development Administration*, Rawat, Jaipur.

Hooja, Rakesh and R.K.Choubisa (ed.) (2009). *Administration of Desert and Drought Prone Arid Areas*, Rawat, Jaipur.

Hooja, Rakesh and K.K.Parnami (ed.) (2007). *Development Administration and Rural Development*, Aalekh, Jaipur.

Hooja, Rakesh and Sunil Dutt (ed.) (2008). *District Administration: Re-inventing the Development Role*, Kanishka, New Delhi.

Hooja, Rakesh and Sunil Dutt (ed.) (2008). *Development Administration and Multi Level Planning*, Kanishka, New Delhi.

Hooja, Rakesh and Sunil Dutt (ed.) (2009). *Fifty Years of Panchayati Raj and Decentralized Development*, Kanishka, New Delhi.

Inamdar, N.R. (1992). *Development Administration in India*, Rawat, Jaipur.

Inayattulah (1970). Local Administration in a Developing Country – Pakistan in E.W.Widner (ed.) *Op.Cit*.

Johnston, B.F. and W.C.Clark (1982). *Redesigning Rural*

Development: A Strategic Perspective, The Johns Hopkins University Press.

Mahtab, Najmunessa (1994). "*Rural Development: Towards an Integrated Appoach*" in Arora and Hooja (eds.), *Op.Cit*.

Mathur, Kuldeep (1985). "Development Administration in India: Old Lessons and New Concerns", *Journal of Social and Economic Studies*, Vol. 2, No. 4.

Mathur, Kuldeep (ed.) (1996). *Development Policy and Administration*, Sage, New Delhi.

Mathur P.C. and Rakesh Hooja (1996). *Projects, Planning and Development Administration*, Rawat, Jaipur.

Mathew, George (ed.) (2000). *The Status of Panchayati Raj in the States and Union Territories of India*, Concept, New Delhi (revised and enlarged edition forthcoming in 2010).

Montgommery, John in J.Montgommery and William Siffin (eds.) (1966). *Approaches to Development: Policies, Administration and Change*, Mc-Graw Hill, New York.

Panandikar, V.A. Pai (ed.) (1974). *Development Administration in India*, MacMillan.

Ray, C.N. (1994). *Politics of Rural Development*, Rawat, Jaipur.

Riggs, F.W. (ed.) (1970). *Frontiers of Development Administration*, Duke University Press.

Sapru, R.K. (1994). *Development Administration*, Sterling, Delhi.

Sharma, Aruna and Rajgopal (1995). *Planning for Rural Development Administration*, Rawat, Jaipur.

Singh, Hoshiar (ed.) (1985). *Rural Development in India*, Printwell, Jaipur.

Singh, Hoshiar (1995). *Administration of Rural Development*, Sterling, Delhi.

Singh, Katar (1986). *Rural Development: Principles, Policies and Management*, Sage, Delhi.

Swerdlow Irving (ed.) (1963). *Development Administration: Concept and Problems*, Syrause University Press, New York.

Vyasulu, Vinod (2003). *Panchayats, Democracy and Development*, Rawat, Jaipur.

Verma, S.P. and S.K.Sharma (eds.) (1984) *Development Administration*, IIPA, New Delhi.

Weidner, E.W. (ed.) (1970). *Development Administration in Asia*, Duke University Press.

Wood, W. (1967). "Development Administration : An Objection" in *Indian Journal of Public Administration,* Vol. 13, No. 4, 1967.

2

NREGA and Panchayati Raj Institutions

Learnings from Kerala

S.M. Vijayanand

Introduction

Though the constitutionally-mandated Panchayati Raj system was ushered in more than 15 years ago, most of the mega schemes in the functional domain of Panchayats, since then, have largely ignored the Panchayats or given them only a perfunctory role. However, National Rural Employment Guarantee Act (NREGA) breaks new ground in this respect. Panchayats have been legally declared as the "principal authorities for planning and implementation" of the scheme made under the Act. Incidentally, NREG Act is the first developmental legislation which assigns a definite and important role to PRIs. Also it is significant to note that National Rural Employment Guarantee Scheme (NREGS) does not entail creation of parallel bodies for implementation; even the ubiquitous DRDA has not been given any functional role. The Act has created the legal framework to enable the political executive to structure effective decentralization. The Guidelines reaffirm this declaring the PRIs as the "key Stakeholders."

Theoretically, with this powerful legal entitlement backed up by substantial resources in a largely untied form, and, reckoning the potential synergy with other schemes like the Backward Region Grant Fund (BRGF), National Rural Health Mission (NRHM), Rashtriya Swasthya Bheema Yojana (RSBY), the launching pad for PRI empowerment and their transformation into "institutions of self-government" has been put in place. It is a debatable issue whether this potential has been fully realized and given concrete shape in practice. Since, NREGS is a programme which combines the economic development and social justice functions in a context of local planning and implementation it is only in the fitness of things that PRIs play the central role as the Constitution itself assigns these two roles to PRIs. Further, for realizing entitlements and broadening capabilities of the disadvantaged, democratization and participation are essential and sufficient pre-conditions and only PRI can bring them about.

If the potential for Panchayati Raj empowerment using NREGA as the entry point is not thought through and given operational features there is every danger of converting PRIs into mere agencies, just going through the motions without realizing their central place or even becoming potential cat's paws of the coterie of vested interests dominating the public works scene, snatching public resources for private gains. Thus, the legal empowerment of PRIs along would not automatically lead to their actual strengthening, unless a deliberate and purposive effort is taken to create capacity, develop processes and build systems to enable PRIs to play the intended role.

Legal Provisions

NREGA assigns PRIs the most critical role in its implementation. Some of the salient provisions illustrating this point are summed up below:

(1) Section 12(1) mandates the inclusion of representatives of the PRIs in the State Employment Guarantee

Council which is the paramount institution at the State level in implementing the Act, with wide ranging powers and functions.

(2) Section 13 declares the three tier PRIs as the "principal authorities" for planning and implementation and outlines the functions of intermediate and district level Panchayats in planning and supervision of implementation. The District Programme Coordinator, who, in most part of the country, is the District Collector, is given an obligation by this Section to assist the District Panchayat.

(3) Section 15 speaks of the Programme Officer at the intermediate Panchayat level (and not at the CD Block level). It further states that all or any of the functions of the Programme Officer can be discharged by the Gram Panchayat or any other local authority.

(4) Section 16 explains the role of the Gram Panchayat and mandates that at least 50% of the work in terms of cost has to be implemented through the Gram Panchayat. Further, it has given the responsibility of allocating employment opportunities among the applicants to the Gram Panchayat.

(5) Section 17 endows the Gram Sabha with the authority to conduct social audit and monitor execution of works.

(6) Schedule II explains the duties of the Gram Panchayat in registering the household, issue of job cards, assigning of work, maintenance of records, etc.

Thus the NREG Act assigns a wide ranging role to PRIs right from registering of workers up to monitoring and social audit. It vests powers of planning and implementation (at least 50%) with the PRIs and casts an obligation for transparency and accountability on them, especially on the Grama Panchayat. Probably the only deficiency with reference to PRIs is the non-mentioning of the District Planning Committees in the Act. Ideally the DPCs should have been assigned the task of coordinating the planning and preparation of the Perspective Plan, Labour Budget and the Annual Plan.

Panchayati Raj in Kerala

Kerala is the acknowledged pioneer and leader in strengthening Local Governments in the post-Constitutional Amendment phase. Following a "big bang" approach resulting in a series of reversals in the conventional sequence in decentralization – giving responsibilities and then building capacity, giving powers and then structuring administrative systems, giving funds and then putting up accountability mechanisms – Kerala launched its decentralization experiment, following a campaign mode which by itself not only set the agenda but generated expectations and forced the pace. Paradoxically, though the push was unorthodox, the principles and practices have been classical in their features. They include:

(1) Sharp mapping of functions and responsibilities among different tiers of Panchayats and a rational division of labour between the State and Local Governments – in this scheme of things, poverty reduction, human development, local economic development and provision of minimum needs including housing, sanitation, water, power, and connectivity are all predominantly Panchayat responsibilities.

(2) Devolution of funds matching expenditure responsibilities, in a largely untied manner, facilitating considerable local autonomy in prioritization and allocation of resources — the State gives about a quarter of its Plan Budget in this fashion, with every rupee allocated as per a formula ensuring transparency, fairness, equitability and predictability.

(3) Transferring staff to Local Governments to discharge the transferred functions and in putting in place a dual control system – even while the State Government is the staff-creating and cadre-controlling authority, Local Governments have full freedom in assigning work, supervising its execution, reviewing performance and even imposing minor punishments, if required.

(4) Setting up of independent umpiring institutions like Ombudsman and Appellate Tribunal to reduce executive control over local government functioning.

(5) Enhancing financial and social accountability through due process in budgeting, transparency in decision making, particularly in selection of beneficiaries and in expenditures and mandatory reporting of performance to constituents.

(6) Participatory planning to ensure incorporation of people's priorities.

(7) Creating space for formal people's participation in governance – in priority setting, in implementation and in monitoring.

Approach of Kerala

With more than a decade of experience in local level planning and development, the PRIs of Kerala were in a vantage position to take over full responsibility for implementation of a rights based pro-poor programme of large magnitude like NREGA. Therefore, Government consciously decided to internalize its operationalisation into the Panchayati Raj system to further empower it. The salient features of this approach are summed up below:

(1) NREGA was perceived as an opportunity for

strengthening and institutionalizing decentralization in all respects and therefore a decision was taken that the whole programme would be implemented through PRIs and, by and large, through Grama Panchayats which are closer to people.

(2) Right from the beginning an attempt was made at deconstruction and de-schooling vis-à-vis the employment generation schemes of the past so that NREGA does not get contaminated by vestiges of past practice. A clear distinction was drawn between the past schemes and NREGA and communicated to all stakeholders especially the elected leaders of Panchayats. The differences thus highlighted are summed up in the *Annexure*.

(3) Though it was widely realized that NREGA is not the main solution to the unemployment problem of the poor in Kerala where a large number of the poor seek not manual work but self-employment and wage employment in the formal informal sectors, at the same time, the State was able to foresee a niche for NREGA in reducing poverty of at least half a million poor agricultural labourer families who are expected to turn up for works under NREGA and get an additional annual cash income of Rs.12,500 per annum.

(4) Realising that the vast majority of the workers is going to be women it was decided to involve the Kudumbashree network of poor women in a big way— for awareness creation, for demand generation, for indentification of work; for organization of work and for concurrent social audit (Kudumbashree is a unique programme for poverty reduction and women's empowerment under which every BPL family in the State and a few APL families — families in rural areas are organized into — Neighbourhood Groups (NHGs) at the local level, networked with — Area Development

Societies (ADCs) at the Village Panchayat Ward level which are then federated into 999 Community Development Societies (CDSs), at the Village Panchayat level. This large community-based organization work in partnership with the PRIs.

(5) In a State which has very little public land, to enhance the quality of environment using NREGA, a policy decision has been taken to focus on natural resource management in forest areas, river basins and watershed areas in agricultural land.

(6) To prevent NREGA from being seen as an extraneous Centrally Sponsored Scheme the processes and procedures were designed in such a way that they could be woven seamlessly into the fabric of the administrative operating systems now existing in Panchayats.

(7) The potential of NREGA to strengthen good governance at the local level mainly through its consistent and coherent information and accountability systems and transparent and participatory processes was realized right in the beginning and acted on.

(8) A carefully focused and planned objective was to achieve zero corruption in the implementation of NREGA – whatever be the costs in terms of time and resources. Interestingly this approach was articulated in unambiguous terms by the political leadership sending powerful signals both to elected leaders and field level officials. It also gave freedom to senior officers to design systems, procedures and processes to attain this policy priority.

Features in implementation

The following features were purposefully designed to strengthen decentralization and Panchayati Raj.

(1) Capacity building was targeted at elected representatives and officials of the Panchayati Raj Institutions. Each member of every Panchayat was guided through the entire Act as well as key features of the guidelines. The "Operational Guidelines" issued by Government of India was circulated to all PRIs in its Malayalam translation.

(2) The roles and responsibilities of PRIs were clarified in minute detail. The Gram Panchayat was assigned the major responsibilities of awareness building and environment creation to spread the message of NREGA, mobilizing and registering the job seekers, issue of job cards, making special efforts to include outliers like tribals, preparation of shelf of projects and their approval, and technical clearance for execution, organizing execution, ensuring facilities to workers, making payments through Banks and maintaining records. In such a scenario the District Collectors as District Programme Coordinators and Block Development Officers as Block Programme Coordinators have become motivators, facilitators and monitors, assisting and enabling Panchayats and not directing or controlling them or using them as passive agents or mindless rubber stamps just to comply with the letter of the law.

(3) Taking cue from People's Planning highly participatory processes have been designed for the planning and implementation of NREGS as outlined below:

Identification of Works

(i) Meeting of Neighbourhood Groups (NHGs) of Women who are part of the Kudumbashree network and identification of suitable works.

(ii) Consolidation at the level of the Village

Panchayat Ward by the Area Development Society (ADS) which the network of NHGS at the Ward level.

(iii) Meeting of Workers' Gram Sabhas at the Ward level to give their preferences not only of works but also of time and locality.

(iv) Full Grama Sabhas to integrate these with their development demands so that NREGA priorities and People's Plan priorities merge properly.

(v) Working Group at the Village Panchayat level to put together the draft Action Plan – the Working Group is a unique contribution of People's Plan; it is a multi-disciplinary multi-stakeholder group headed by an elected member, convened by the official concerned with experts, activists, practitioners and officials. The objective of this variegated group is to provide multiple perspectives and come out with a well-rounded set of proposals for the Panchayat to decide.

(vi) Convene Workshops at the Village Panchayat to bring about linkage with People's Plan schemes.

(vii) Village Panchayat Committee meeting to finalize the Action Plan.

Implementation

- Organizing the workforce and co-ordinating the work through a "mate" identified by the ADS of Kudumbashree.
- Reading of the 'people's estimate' of the works to the labour gang and explaining the piece rates they are entitled to.

- Provision of facilities to the workers through the ADS.
- Maintaining of muster rolls by the "mate"
- Functioning of Vigilance and Monitoring Committees for each work for concurrent social audit – having seven members of which four are women and at least three belong to Scheduled Castes and Scheduled Tribes.

Transparency

- Project initiation meeting, just before the work starts, of workers, mate, technical staff, local people where all details of the work are explained in layman's idiom, photograph of meeting taken and minutes filed.
- Citizen's signboard displaying details of works.
- Photographs of work site at pre, mid and post–execution stages.
- Work diary by mate where every detail is recorded and on which workers, officials and public are free to write their comments.
- Completion report by Vigilance and Monitoring Committee before payment
- Project file containing all these and other records relating to payment are kept in the Village Panchayat office for public scrutiny, inspection, and audit.

(4) The PRIs especially the Village Panchayat have been strengthened to take up the additional work in the following ways.

(a) A Data Entry Operator and a Graduate Engineer (in case of non-availability a Diploma holder) have been posted in all Village Panchayats. The decision to increase the staff for Village Panchayat spending more than Rs. One crore per annum has been taken. Similarly, all Block Panchayats have got an additional Engineer and IT professional.

(b) The existing Overseers, Engineers and Agricultural Officers of Village Panchayats have been given powers of technical supervision, measurement, etc.

(c) Wherever there is shortage of manpower, Village Panchayats have been given the power to utilize the services of other engineers including non-government engineers on payment of a fixed fee.

(d) To ensure transparency and to bring in collective experience, the committee system for giving Technical Sanction another People's Plan innovation has been put in place at the Village Panchayat level. The committee consists of the Panchayat engineers, the NREGS contract engineer and one or more engineers from the public or private sector or from academic institutions. For larger works the existing committee at the Block-level issues the Technical Sanction.

(e) For overall coordination, popular committees under the elected President has been set up at the Village and Block and District Panchayat levels. A similar committee has been set up at the ward level also under the elected member.

(f) Soon the online MIS would start functioning

at the Village Panchayat level instead of the Block Panchayat level as of now. Computers have been installed in all but 30 Village Panchayats and action is under way to provide connectivity.

(5) A conscious effort has been made to integrate People's Plan with NREGS especially in the agricultural sector. As the first step watershed management activities are taken up under NREGS, giving priority to watersheds having paddy fields. This is followed up with Panchayats providing necessary inputs like seeds and fertilizers and subsidizing the cost of cultivation utilizing their People's Plan Funds. This is expected to improve local food security even while giving additional employment to the agricultural labourers.

(6) Even though NREG Act provides for implementation of works through departments, the reverse has been decided on in Kerala. Village Panchayats have been allowed by the Forest Department to carry out eco-restoration work within the NREGA framework in forest areas following the same processes and procedures with the only proviso that officers of the Forest Department would be involved in the Technical Sanction and supervision and measurement stages. This has created a scenario whereby Village Panchayats have emerged as the organizers and fund providers of Forest Development Projects.

(7) An elaborate social audit system has been prescribed. In order to ensure independence and credibility of the process even while the Village Panchayat supports in the organization, the social audit team is selected by the Gram Sabha and is headed by an expert from outside the Ward (which is the area co-terminous with the Gram Sabha in Kerala) and consists of another outsider and three local members; this team also co-

opts the services of a technical person not associated with the implementation of the NREGA to assist it. This team presents the report in the Gram Sabha and a panel oversees the process. This panel is interestingly chaired by the person who received the highest number of votes from among the defeated candidates in the last Panchayat election.

Assessment of Performance

Initial evidence from the field shows a lot of positive features in Panchayat empowerment even while throwing up challenges and concerns. The are summed up below:

Positive Features

Experience of the last two years has revealed that even in a State with proven track record in participatory planning and with strong Panchayati Raj Institutions (PRIs), NREGA could further consolidate Panchayat empowerment. The visible results include:

(1) The Gram Sabha had been a weak link in Kerala's Panchayati Raj. With NREGA there has been a perceptible strengthening especially in the functioning of sub-Gram Sabha fora like Workers Gram Sabha and Neighbourhood Groups of women. Also, two trained facilitators assist the Gram Sabhas in their deliberations relating to NREGS, enabling informed decision-making.

(2) The planning capacity of Panchayat especially the Village Panchayat has increased in response to the challenge of planning for NREGA as it has multiple dimensions of space and time linked to both human and financial resources. Whereas, the annual plan budget requires only matching of works and schemes

against available resources, the labour budget calls for identifying works location-wise with reference to specific time-periods to match the demand from a specified number of labourers and then to seek the funds required to pay the workers and meet the cost for the non-labour components.

(3) From simple planning now Panchayats are being guided by experts to move on to more complex areas of planning of works related to natural resource management where the inter-relationships and sequencing related to land, water and biomass present a formidable but interesting challenge.

(4) NREGA has improved the organizational and administrative capacity of Panchayats for, organizing works without a middleman and keeping the well-designed set of records and ensuring their consistency and currency are testing tasks.

(5) The elected member of the ward has gained in capacity as well as credibility. *De facto*, NREGA revolves around the elected member and its success is directly related to the commitment of the elected member. A new political culture depending on delivering development resulting in political acceptance and reward seems to have emerged in areas where NREGS is working well. It appears that good work has its own returns which could offset commissions, rents and illegal profits.

(6) Panchayats have been able to forge a closer relationship with the poor through a two-fold path – constant contact with the working poor in finding out their preferences and direct partnership with Neighbourhood Groups of poor women in organization of work, maintenance of records and general feedback. This has helped the Panchayats understand better the features of poverty at the local level and the poor to interact with Panchayats with confidence.

(7) Since natural resource management has been given policy priority in Kerala, NREGA has brought the Village Panchayat into direct engagement with the small and marginal farmers. It is widely believed that this positive relationship has drastically reduced the number of farmer suicides in Wayanad. Now with the accent on watershed management and food security this interface is expected to be more productive.

(8) Successful Village Panchayats have shown that they can bring about local economic development as well as provide social security through NREGA. By providing tangible benefits without patronage and corruption, the respectability of Grama Panchayats has grown.

(9) Incidentally r-governance has received a big boost. Though Kerala has been struggling for nearly 10 years to introduce e-governance in Panchayats, the well designed set of IT modules related to NREGA could be operationalized without much difficulty, so much so, the entire State is now on the verge of moving on to online mode with Village Panchayats taking the leadership.

(10) Several good governance features have become part of the Panchayat Raj system through NREGA. This includes proper maintenance of records, responsiveness to demand from the workers and Kudumbashree, increased transparency in all aspects related to execution of works, prompt grievance redressal and a totally corruption free environment.

(11) The very fact that more than 80% of the workers are women has imparted a positive gender dimension also. In a State where female work participation rate is low, a surprisingly large number of first-timers have turned up for work. Receiving wage only through individual bank accounts has not only boosted savings

but also given a new respectability to public works. And for the first time, equal wages is a reality. A gender-sensitive development process is emerging.

(12) Accountability both formal and informal has improved tremendously. For the first time a functional social audit system is in place. This complements a systematic inspection schedule from different levels.

(13) Manipulation by middlemen and corruption by power-brokers which proved to be the bane of the earlier employment generation work have more or less vanished so much so the optimists envisage a reverse influence of NREGS on the public works under People's Plan to fully free them from corruption – for now there is a robust working model for community execution.

(14) Panchayats have gained tremendously by getting flexible resources and, almost by definition funds have flowed to the backward pockets bringing in the element of equity in local level development. It is expected that once NREGS is in full steam, flow of funds to Village Panchayats would match the already high flow under People's Plan.

(15) Social capital has increased through networks of women NHGs, agricultural workers, farmers, activists and local leaders, paving the way for a cooperative model of public action.

Challenges and Concerns

The challenges and concerns in relation to implementation of NREGS by PRIs are:

(i) The work burden has increased tremendously particularly on the technical staff and those persons directly responsible for maintaining the registers and accounts, for the administrative system enshrined in NREG Act and guidelines does not brook any delay. It is clear that Panchayat requires additional support in manpower and this would translate into higher administrative costs.

(ii) The present system of execution of public works is totally inappropriate for direct execution of works through a mixed group of labourers of differing capacities. The standards and specifications and the schedule of rates of the Public Works Department are designed for works to be executed by contractors through specialized workers over whom they have total control. Therefore, at best they only serve as a baseline with reference to which open competitive bids are sought. And this system gives arbitrary powers to the engineer and it is opaque in all stages and is not amenable to social scrutiny. This points out to an urgent need for basic reform in the public works execution system to make it amenable to NREGA objectives by facilitating community contracting and public oversight.

(iii) Even in a literate and aware society like Kerala with a high degree of organization, it has been realized that a large number of eligible persons are not aware of even the basics of the scheme, let alone their entitlements. Therefore, there is need for continuous awareness creation, calling for launch of a specific programme for NREGA literacy. Otherwise, there is risk of the already excluded poor being continuously excluded.

(iv) Village Panchayats have tended to take up small works to satisfy local demand. But from the perspective of returns on investment and sustainable local development, there is need for more substantial works. Also to an extent, the restriction on taking up works of local and direct relevance for the poor like housing, maintenance of public assets, anganwadis and primary schools, local sanitation work and care services for the destitutes and the sick has narrowed the scope of local decision-making.

(v) Material procurement and hiring of skilled labour pose a major challenge in maintaining the corruption free environment. Appropriate systems for procurement are not yet in place.

(vi) Availability of public land is very low in Kerala. This has limited the scope in extremely vulnerable coastal areas and in areas of failed and closed plantations.

(vii) The integration with People's Plan is still not to the desired extent.

New Initiatives

In order to address the challenges and concerns and enhance the quality of NREGA implementation through PRIs certain new initiatives have been launched. They include:

(1) A time and motion study is underway. The intention is not to limit its application to NREGS works but move ahead in a phased manner within a limited time period to cover all public works implemented by PRIs.

(2) In order to make up the deficiency in availability of technical manpower, it has been decided to train "barefoot" engineers from among poor girls from the Kudumbashree network. While this would be of relief to Panchayats, it would open opportunities to the Kudumbashree members in the construction industry in the State.

(3) Government have decided to organize Labour Banks at the Village Panchayat level with multiple objectives. Since there is no middleman to organize works and,

whatever be the law, it is not easy to match demand with supply in all respects, it is felt that organization of workers utilizing the lessons of the SHG movement would make up this deficiency. Labour Banks could act as workers' collectives to articulate their performance in terms of time, locality and work and negotiate their rights properly. Further depending on their capacity, the skills of workwers could be increased through interventions from People's Plan so that they can graduate to higher forms of employment.

(4) To get over the problem of small works certain ambitious programmes are on the drawing board like rejuvenation of Bhrathapuzha and Kabini rivers. A joint meeting of Panchayat leaders, environmentalists and top professionals in river management was held recently. Once the idea gets fructified possibilities of joined-up action by Panchayats could be opened up.

(5) Forests constitute the only viable commons in State. Government have put in place a system by which Village Panchayats can use this potential using NREGS, leading to work opportunities, ecorestoration and additional gains from accessible usufructs.

(6) An important priority initiative is preparation of an Anti-Poverty Sub-Plan with NREGS as the nucleus. The components of this Sub-Plan would be:

☞ NREGA	for supplementary cash income
☞ NRHM ☞ Health Insurance	for health
☞ ICDS ☞ SSA	for education
☞ Special nutrition- through ICDS ☞ Mid-day Meals	for food security

- ☞ PDS
- ☞ Pensions } for social security
- ☞ Asraya of Kudumbashree } for social security
- ☞ People's Plan — for minimum needs like housing, sanitation,water supply, electricity
- ☞ Kudumbashree—for skill development and self-employment

Since all these are in the ambit of PRIs, community-led convergence to break the ratchet effect of different causes of poverty is eminently realizable.

Conclusion

The most important lesson from the Kerala experience is that, just as People's Plan was the motive force which pushed decentralization in the State, NREGA could be used for strengthening Panchayati Raj in the country. In that sense NREGA could be called "mother of all local development schemes". The possible ways in which the NREGA can contribute to Panchayat empowerment if properly planned, include the following.

- ✱ Providing much needed staff to PRIs
- ✱ Introduction of improved administrative systems
- ✱ Making available modern office equipment especially computers.
- ✱ Strengthening the planning and implementation capacity
- ✱ Improving governance functions
- ✱ Enhancing accountability
- ✱ Vesting Panchayats with status and credibility *vis-à-vis* the poor people and *vis-à-vis* other departments

by enabling them to play an important role in local level development.

To realize this potential it is necessary to move on to a concerted capacity building exercise with focus on Panchayat empowerment in the context of NREGA. Probably a policy shift is needed to make NREGA as much an instrument for Panchayati Raj empowerment as an instrument for poverty reduction. A great opportunity already exists in the BRGF districts. Once it can be proved that NREGA could strengthen PRIs then it could emerge as a nucleus around which other major programmes like SSA, NRHM, ICDS, Mid-Day Meals, PDS, SGSY, Health Insurance, RSBY etc. could converge into a viable anti-poverty initiative – to achieve inclusive growth through participatory development led by democratic institutions.

Annexure

National Rural Employment Guarantee Scheme and Ealier wage Employment Programmes— A Comparison

NREGS	*EARLIER PROGRAMMES*
	Concept
Legal guarantee of right to employment – a full blown entitlement – a new vision of rights-based development for the poor	No grand vision – concepts incidental to schemes – based on executive decisions and instructions
Non-exclusive and total coverage	Limited in scope and coverage
Demand-based	Supply-based
Self-targeting	Patronage-based
Focus on employment	Focus on assets
Focus on productive sector – for sustainable development	Focus on public works, predominantly roads
Natural resource management	Real estate development
Labour perspective – voice of the worker	Perspective of the bureaucrat / engineer / middleman-contractor
Gender sensitive	Male / machine – dominated
Off season employment	Peak season expenditure
Real participatory planning	Negotiated priorities – decision based on local power relations
Transparent	Opaque
Accountable	Manipulative
Vision-based perspective planning	Short term priority listing
Organic, central role for PRIs	Marginal agency role for PRIs

Planning	
Long preparatory phase	Hurried quick-fix plans
Elaborate communication and extension	Routine motions for form's sake
Real planning from below covering who, what, where, when and how.	Hotchpotch list of works
Elaborate budget – work to match demand	Financial budget – work to match resources
Can be integrated with varied development works	Limited to schematic works
Integrated plan	Isolated works
Statutory across-tier linkages in the Panchayat Raj system	Independent and repetitive plans
Multi-dimensional action plans covering time, space, manpower and resources	Two-dimensional action plan covering resources and works
Results-based and outcome-oriented	Expenditure oriented
Real People's Plan	Bureaucratic/technocratic plan
Organization	
Panchayat in central place — development from within	Middleman-contractor in central place — outsourcing development
Administrative Sanction and Technical Sanction before organization of work	AS and TS in response to middlemen contractor clout
All activities done inhouse • Getting together workers • Executing the work • Mustering • Material procuring • Measuring • Paying	Most of the activities carried out by the middlemen contractor except measurement and payment
Fortnightly measuring and payment	Often once or twice per work
People's estimates	Engineer's estimates
Minimum wages	Market wages
Equal wages – strong subsidizing the weak	Differential wages
Piece rate	Mostly bulk measurement
Local labour	Often outside labour
Payment through Bank	Direct cash payment
Payment by Government	Payment by middleman-contractor
Work without whip – new dynamics of mutual help and group discipline	Ruthless supervision by middleman-contractor
Actual material labour ratio	Notional and fictitious ratio
No abandoned works	Quite a number of abandoned works

Administration	
Outside DRDA	DRDA centered
Clear role for District Project Coordinator, Block Programme Officer etc.	Roles routinised over the years
Real records • Estimates • Muster rolls • Vouchers • Measurements	Often "created" records
Integrated and consistent database • Unique ID of workers • Unique ID of work • ID of muster rolls • Payment vouchers • Bank Accounts of individuals	No such database
Close monitoring • National level monitoring • State level monitoring • District level monitoring • Inspection schedule	Routine monitoring
Clear accountability systems • Proactive disclosures • Vigilance and Monitoring Committees • Social Audit • Penalties	Ritualized and routine
Special features	
Difficult to manipulate	Easy to manipulate
Criticality of Panchayat capacity	No such issue
Proactive role of Government of India	Routine role of Government of India
High visibility, watched with interest by supporters and opponents	No such interest
Clearly articulated political will	No such will

To illustrate the philosophical, conceptual and developmental differences between NREGS and its predecessors, the distinctions encapsulated below are significant.

NREGS	EARLIER PROGRAMMES
Qualitative Distinctions	
Rights-based	Patronage-based
Inclusive	Exclusive
Participatory	Co-optive
Redistributive	Rent-seeking
Liberating	Domesticating
Empowering	Exploiting
Transparent	Manipulated
Integrated	Automized
Engendered	Male dominated
Organic	Disjointed
Ecological	Mechanical
Outcome-based	Target-based
Developmental	Departmental
Democratic	Bureaucratic
Humanistic	Materialistic
Vision-based	Greed-based
REAL	MAKE BELIEVE

The points outlined above look quite obvious in the first reading. But if one reflects in detail and analyses in depth it will be clear how well-rounded a programme NREGS is and provide clues to unlocking the potential of this entitlement. The challenge is in building the capacity required to fully realise the potential.

Note : This paper has been reproduced from the website of Government of Kerala, Department of Rural Development, with the permission of the Author-Editor

3

Role of ICT in Scientific Data Generation and Management for Scientific Decision Making at the Grassroots

G. Palanithurai

I have been involving myself in doing research at micro level on many of the social development issues and on occasions, I have approached many of the government offices for data collection apart from collecting data from the field. What I found in all offices was that they maintain progress reports which do not reflect the real data. When I ask the question about the difference between the progress report and the field reality, the officials tend to confess that there won't be any match at all. Only a few offices maintain that the progress reports reflect the reality. They also confess that there may be difference but not too much. Further, in many of the reports I found terms such as (more or less, around and approximately) while indicating the trend. It is obvious that, we have lost scientific precision in maintaining data. As a result what we find is the mismatch between the decision, allocation of resources and the needs of the stakeholders. We spend huge money for which there is no need and by which we end up wasting money.

Further, the planning at micro level, that is for the Gram

Panchayat level we sought data from the panchayats as well as from many government departments. The Panchayats replied that they have not collected data. Government Departments informed us that they have the progress report of the activities carried out by their departments of the schemes given by the government where one can get data if they rely on them, but they cannot be disaggregated to the level of the Gram Panchayats. All Government Departments have lowest units of their administration. But they are not co-terminus with panchayat areas. Each department unit has its own geographical jurisdiction. Government departments are also collecting data on demand from above for proposal preparation to seek funding. Even these departments are not scientific systems of maintaining data. They generate data as and when they require. Data is fundamental for decision making, policy making, resource allocation and for that matter anything which we want to do. Irrespective of the level of operation whether it is micro or macro data is essential and imperative. Further precision of data are more important. In all aspects of the society data have to be generated, validated and maintained scientifically from Gram Panchayat at the bottom to the Federal Government at New Delhi for all kinds of decisions, programmes and resource allocations.

They also collect primary data from the field. But they are not validated. As and when they require data, they go to the field and collect the necessary data. The collected data are not reliable. They are with the government departments. Further, they are not updated periodically. At the lowest level there is no sense or sensitivity among the officials on the importance of data. There is yet another set of data available in census and on many of the occasions they do not reflect the reality at micro level. Even the census data are not updated. One has to wait for ten years. In the meanwhile one will find enormous reports of various kinds with the data support contradicting each other's observations. This kind of trivialities are due to the absence of sensitivity on data management at grass-roots.

Data is fundamental for decision making, policy making,

resource allocation and for that matter anything which we want to do. Irrespective of the level of operation whether it is micro or macro data is essential and imperative. Further, precision of data are more important. In all aspects of the society data have to be generated, validated and maintained scientifically from Gram Panchayat at the bottom to the Federal Government at New Delhi for all kinds of decisions, programmes and resource allocations. In India data generations at the field level is not sound, and they are not maintained scientifically. Moreover, there is no systematic generation of data done at grass roots in an integrated manner. All data generation activities are *ad hoc*, occasional, need based and unscientific. People who are all involved in data generation for government departments at the grassroots are not well trained in data generation as professionals. Hence, the data generated by the agencies mostly by the Departments of Government at the grassroots are not scientific and periodical and yet they are the only reliable database for decision-making at different levels of government. Faulty decisions are made because of the unscientific data support provided to the decision-making process by the grassroots agencies. Further, the data generated by the researchers for specific purposes contradict the database generated by the Government Departments. It is to be noted that for all vital matters data are compiled from district data pool. The data generated and compiled at the district level are not considered to be the best and scientific. Down below the district level there is no disaggregated scientific database. As a result for any reliable decision making, data generated at the district level should not be considered as scientific and dynamic. And yet there is no alternative. Hence for all decision making we rely on the data obtained from the District Administration. There is no such concept of data management of all aspects of economy, society and development for decision making at grass roots. At the village level, and at the block level there is no break up of data on any aspect. The District is considered as a unit. Variations within district cannot be captured;

variations within block cannot be explained. Each department has its own way of keeping the data and each department has its won geographical area of coverage. Hence, one cannot get data relating to school going children in a Gram Panchayat area, anemia affected women in Gram Panchayat area and likewise all data in the geographical area of Block Panchayat. As the departments function as per their own geographical area, desegregating the data is a difficult task. After the establishment of Local Bodies as units of governance after passing of the 73rd and 74th Amendments to the Constitution of India, the decision making takes place down below the district. With out proper data how will they make decisions?. It is a moot question.

Data collection is a science and it is an art also. How precisely data are collected and accordingly decisions can be made. Decision-makers fail to arrive at a exact decision and fail to solve the problem as they do not have exact data. Down below the district level in all offices, they are not maintaining data. They keep only progress report and beyond that they do not know the value of scientific data. To illustrate this I can quote an incident. When I was involved in preparing a report for an international agency, I requested the Health Department to supply me the data relating to anemia affected women, adolescent girls and school going children affected due to malnutrition, hamlet-wise or gram panchayat-wise. First they said that they have only progress report whereby what they have done and what they have achieved were provided in this regard. Secondly, there is no break up for hamlets or Gram Panchayat area. The lowest unit in the Health Department is functioning on population basis.

Sometimes a village nurse will look after two Gram Panchayat area. In some cases three or four villages depending on the strength of the population. In the same way I got reply from the school education department. If a researcher wants data for each village or hamlet on all aspects to compare the status and position of each village in terms of economy, wealth, income, livelihood, health education, skill, infrastructure, one cannot get such data with such a break up. At the district level as and when they need data they rely on the units of the Departments functioning at the lowest level. The lowest units supply the data available at that point of time and they are compiled and forwarded to the State level. Ration card is a very big issue today. Everywhere, bogus card brings lots of problem and as a consequence, we have to sell out huge quantity of materials for the public distribution system. It is a criminal wastage of the public money. It is because of the non-maintenance of database at panchayat levels. If there is a database at every Gram Panchayat, family-wise, all bogus ration cards will be eliminated very easily. If any one wants to know the status of unskilled labourers in the spread of different Panchayat areas in a block, status and position of the women and adolescent girls affected by anemia, status of children affected by malnutrition, agriculture productivity in villages etc. It is not for getting details alone. No one was trained in the Department at the lowest unit on how to generate data, and how to update the data scientifically and how they are to be maintained. These are the big questions. Since data are generated by different agencies a lot of confusion, conflict and corruption occur in development management activities. We are in the Eleventh Five Year Plan with regard to data generation and data management, despite the pronouncement of the importance of data from the First Five Year Plan by Mohalananobis. There are statistical institutes and officers and yet data are not precise, up to date and scientific. To overcome the problems, Rajiv Gandhi had started a new exercise by creating District National Informatics Centres through ICT. But they could not reach out to the lowest unit of governance and administration for data generation and data management. After the establishment of local bodies, the basic data about the villages are to be in position. It is not so, as it should be even after the computerization. If what should we do now? Long back, my friend from the management field argued with me that India has got all potential but unfortunately India does not have systems approach to make use of the potential available in India. He told me a formula and asked me to apply it. The formula is India + System = America in terms of wealth and income. India can do and achieve this. For this, we have to create a system.

Relevant data are not generated simultaneously. For example the labour department collects data from the rural areas, at a point of time and it has to collect during the Agricultural season and the non-Agricultural season. Data relating to migration have to be collected only during the off season. In our Departmental Administrative System we never sensitize the officials about the importance of scientific generation and management of data. As a result, they will go to the field as and when they require data. The same data are being recycled continuously till they get direction from their higher officials for upgradation. There is another issue i.e., data manipulation. If a state government wants to get more funds for poverty alleviation, the state government tends to manipulate data. This is the way, the Data Management System functions in India.

Statement of the Problem

At present there is no scientific data management system at Gram Panchayat level in India barring a few states. Hence, it is necessary to create a database in every gram panchayat by evolving a software and by using the computers provided by the Government to the Panchayats. How are we going to implement this scheme?

It is mandatory on the part of Gram Panchayat to develop a plan for each and every Gram Panchayat. In the same way, each and every block Panchayat should have a plan. Town Panchayat, municipalities, cantonments, corporations, and district Panchayats should have plans. Without having a scientific database how do they develop a plan perspective for the development of the region. Data generation at every level is imperative. This exercise has to be started atleast now.

Data have to be generated from the lowest unit of governance and administration to the highest level. Decisions are taken at Gram Panchayat level, at block level, at district level, regional level, state level and federal level. Data have to be maintained in such a way that they can be used at any level. If data are maintained in disaggregated manner, problems and issues could be identified and they can be solved easily. Periodical updating of the data is yet another needed activity. Data have to be owned and for which responsibilities have to be fixed. All government departments are doing the exercise but they are not integrated. Hence, the exercise has to be started from Gram Panchayat level. At every Gram Panchayat there is a computer. The computer can be used productively for the purpose of administration and providing services. For this, the clerk working in panchayat, or even Gram Panchayat President or a woman from the Self-Help Group can be trained in computer operation. Before data collection, a right mind set has to be created for the individuals who are going to carry out the activities relating to data generation. Computers have got potential and capacity and they are to be used fully by increasing the capacity of the individual who are operating the computer.

A software has to be developed to prepare a database which should be so comprehensive as to accommodate a variety of data from the villages. In the same way another set of software has to be developed for towns and cities. And they are to be linked and integrated at district level and state level. At a click of a computer mouse, data can be obtained from every village up to the level of the nation. At every level decisions can be taken precisely.

Data have to be generated for each and every hamlet and pooled at Gram Panchayat level. Town Panchayat has to generate data from each ward and they are to be pooled.

Municipalities and cantonments have to generate data for each and every administrative unit. In the same way Municipal Corporation has to maintain the database for each region of the municipal corporation area. From a Gram Panchayat ward to National Level Data flow can be ensured. Periodically the data have to be updated.

Basically all kinds of data have to be generated starting from the availability of natural resources, human resources, available human skills, and infrastructure and so on. A comprehensive data sheet has to be prepared. The data generated have to be validated. They are to be updated. There should be comprehensive software to accommodate all kinds of data.

The data confirmed and uploaded in the systems of all the institutions can be taken as validated data.

To attack many of the problems in the society, the basic data have to be brought to the level of the lowest unit of governance and administration. Since, the decision-making power has been given in the lowest unit through the 73rd and 74th Amendments to the Constitution of India, the data to each and every issue and aspect will enable them to take correct decisions. For example, the individual families which are ultra poor can be monitored at Panchayat level by keeping the family profiles in the Panchayat. Panchayats can intervene. In the same way the bio-diversity act insists that the Panchayats should have a register to keep all the details of the *flora* and *fauna* and all living animals. If the health department decides to free from anemia, malnutrition, it can achieve by tracking the families and individual women, adolescent girls and children. This data management will help in the planning for development and attacking all issues at the micro level.

What is the requirement?

It requires a computer at every gram Panchayat. In states like Tamil Nadu, all the Panchayats have good buildings, telephone connection and one computer each. Each Panchayat is managed by the Panchayat Council headed by the President assisted by a clerk. Along with the clerk, there is one more assistant (people welfare assistant) helping the clerk. Apart from the Panchayat, self help group women have independent buildings for their activities and in many of the places, they also have computers.

By developing a programme for compilation of data, every Gram Panchayat can generate data, compile, consolidate and validate the data. It is just like a ready reckoner. Data can be on population, infrastructure, skills, income, wealth and so on. Each and every family profile can be in the data sheet. What we need is a software. A data sheet has to be prepared and it can be explained to the members involved in data collection. Panchayat ward members can be trained for this work. Each and every ward member can do this work as he or she is familiar with the ward area. Further, Self-Help Group members from each ward area can be co-opted for this exercise and by which data can be generated systematically. Generated data can be entered into the system and for which one Self-Help Group member can be trained. Any institution whether it is a college, or a training institute, it can train them to operate a computer and by which data can be entered into the system. A printout from the system can provide basic data. Whatever, Panchayat wants, it can do with the data. Whoever, wants data from the Panchayats, they can get them from the system. They need not collect afresh from the field. Before serving the data; the collected data have to be validated. The collected data can be validated through Gram Sabha or through notification. Awareness has to be created among the public about the need of data. A new culture has to be created among every one that issues should be projected with accurate data and facts. Today's problems of bogus ration cards can be eliminated easily, ultra poor can be identified easily, and the benefits for the poor cannot be grabbed by the rich. Panchayat's financial details, expenditure details, scheme details can be obtained from the system. Hence, a scientific data management system will be in place. From the Gram Panchayat office to the President of India's office, data linkage can be given and further it can be tapped at any unit level.

Diagram Explaining the Data Generation

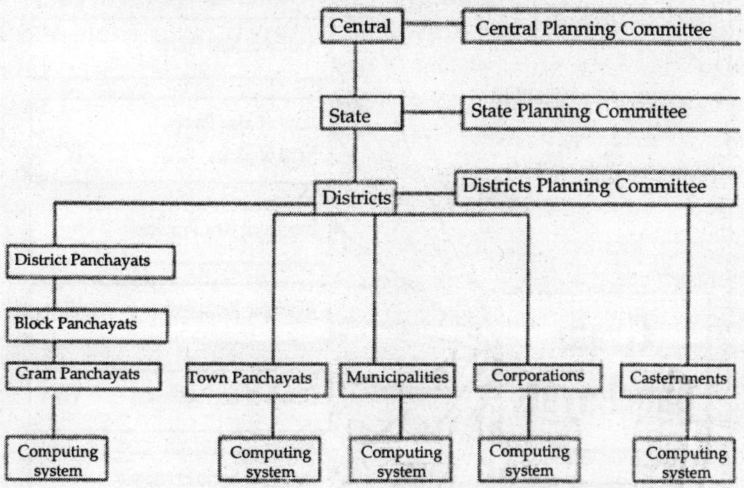

Conclusion

The present *ad hoc*, unscientific, unprofessionalistic way of decision making and implementation of programmes will be given a go by through placing a system of scientific data generation, data management, data validation at different levels of administration and governance starting from the lowest unit by using the ICT. ICT is an enabler, an instrument and a powerful tool to perform all the activities. By doing so, it can create a new culture of looking at things scientifically. Data available in every Gram Panchayat, Town Panchayats, municipalities, municipal corporations, Block Panchayats, and District Panchayats will improve decision-making and they will

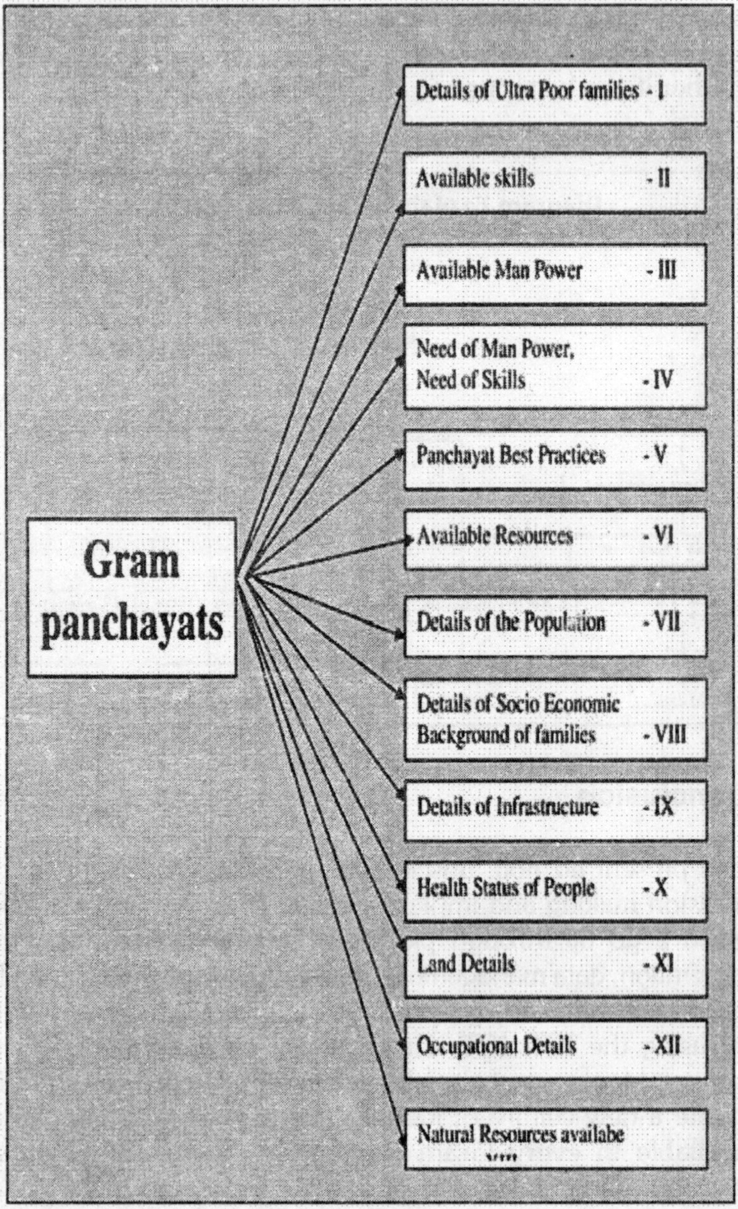
Gram panchayats
Details of Ultra Poor families - I
Available skills - II
Available Man Power - III
Need of Man Power, Need of Skills - IV
Panchayat Best Practices - V
Available Resources - VI
Details of the Population - VII
Details of Socio Economic Background of families - VIII
Details of Infrastructure - IX
Health Status of People - X
Land Details - XI
Occupational Details - XII
Natural Resources availabe

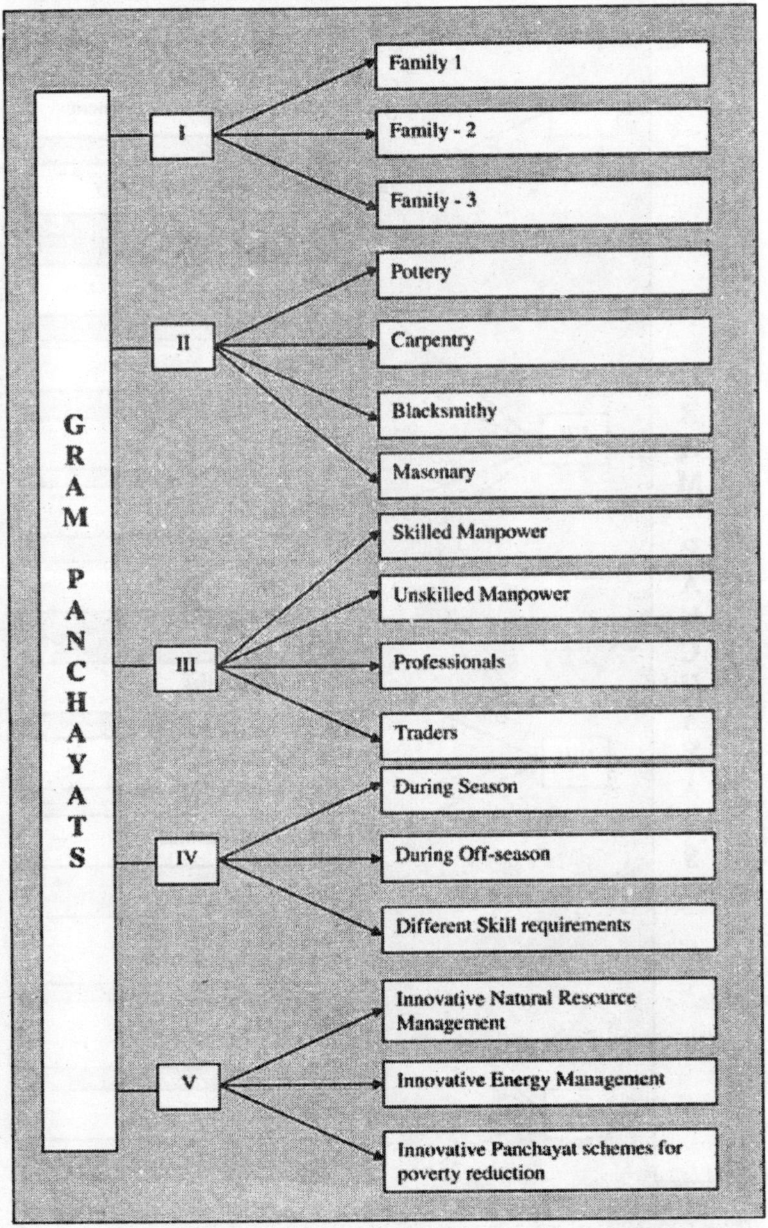
GRAM PANCHAYATS
I
Family 1
Family - 2
Family - 3
II
Pottery
Carpentry
Blacksmithy
Masonary
III
Skilled Manpower
Unskilled Manpower
Professionals
Traders
IV
During Season
During Off-season
Different Skill requirements
V
Innovative Natural Resource Management
Innovative Energy Management
Innovative Panchayat schemes for poverty reduction

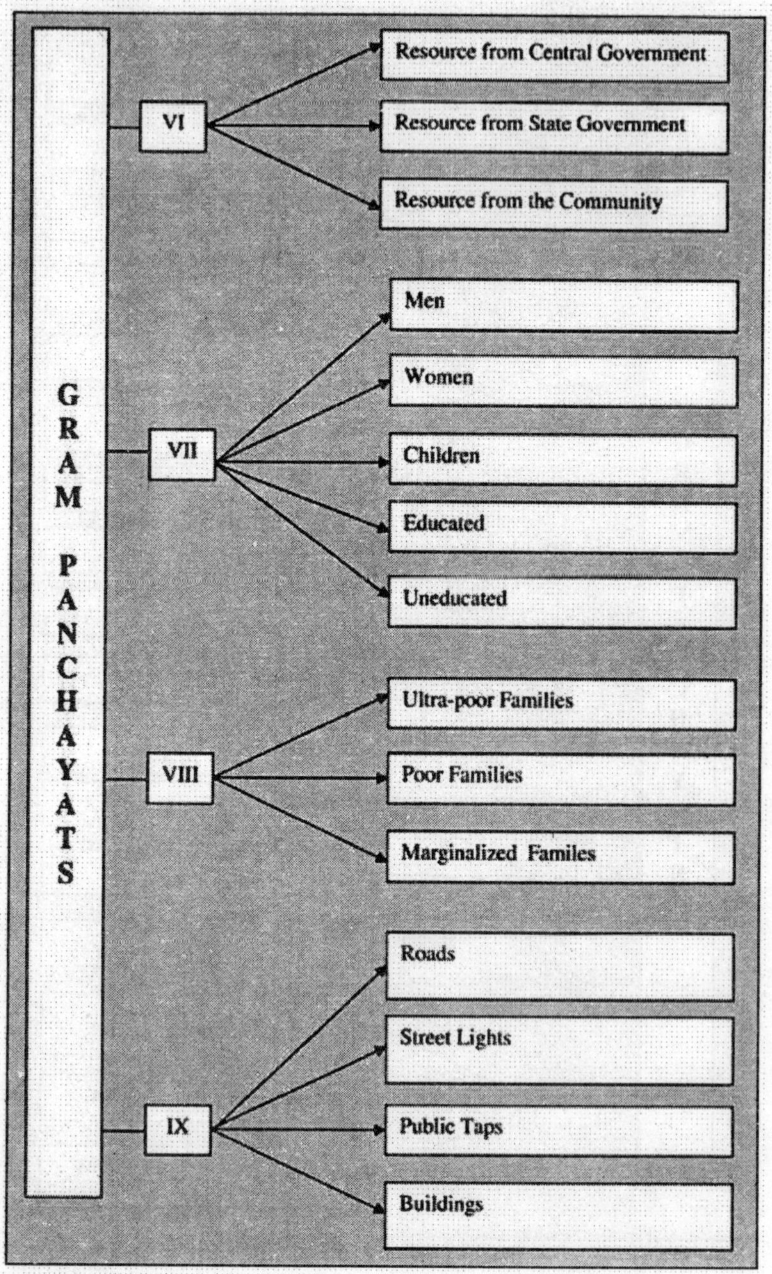
GRAM PANCHAYATS
VI
Resource from Central Government
Resource from State Government
Resource from the Community
VII
Men
Women
Children
Educated
Uneducated
VIII
Ultra-poor Families
Poor Families
Marginalized Familes
IX
Roads
Street Lights
Public Taps
Buildings

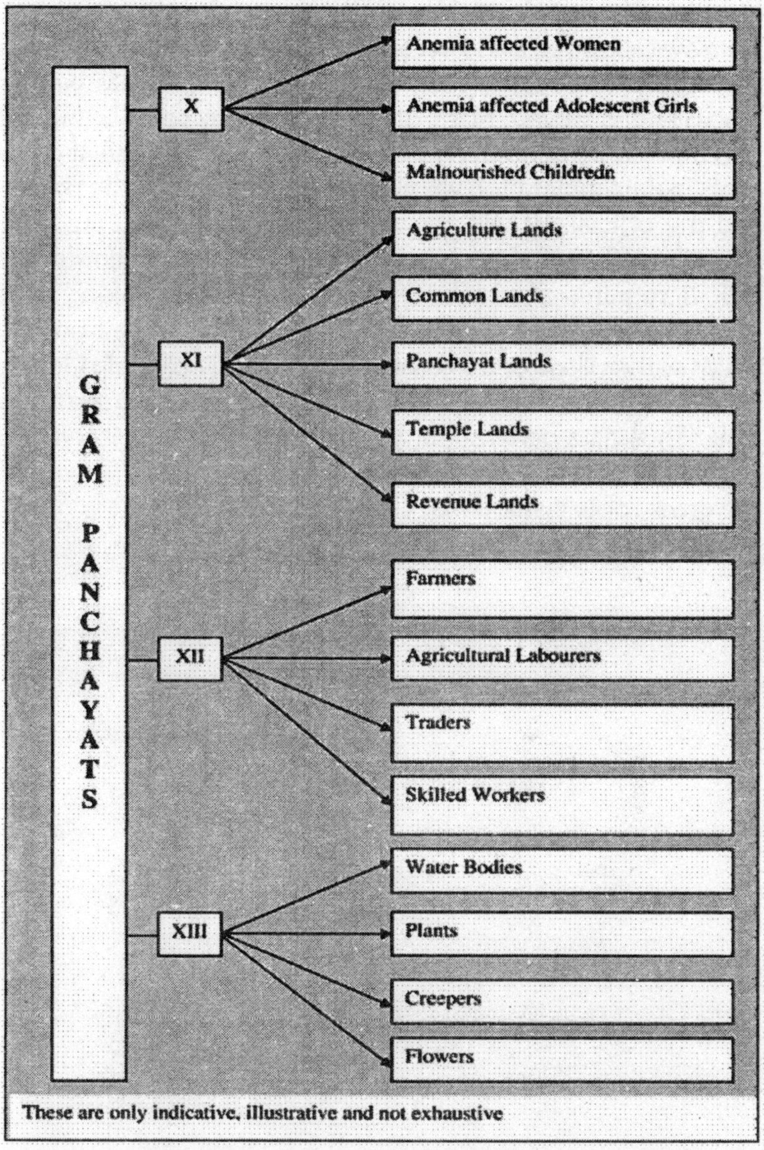

These are only indicative, illustrative and not exhaustive

help better policy planning and will enable better management of resources. Wastages can be curtailed. It will reduce corruption considerably. Every one is looking for a scientific database at grassroots for action. And for which data generation is essential. Data available in all the lower level units will help both grassroots institutions and higher level institutions for micro as well as macro level planning. Many of the micro issues could be tackled scientifically by generating data. This kind of exercise at grass roots in data generation will change the attitudes of the people and the officials. It will also reduce corruption and enhance scientific action. It requires only the political and administrative will. It requires a computer and a programme along with computer operators. The computer operator can be from the youth of the village or a woman from the local Self-Help Group. Once, they are trained and oriented, they will perform the task. Thus data generation, validation and data preservation or maintenance will become an indispensable routine work of the grass roots institutions.

4

Rural Development and Panchayati Raj in a Decentralized Polity

M.R. Biju

Since and overwhelming majority of India's population lives in villages, a holistic development of its rural life is a requisite for the acceleration of the pace of overall economic development of the country. Rural development programmes are designed to facilitate a multi-faceted growth of the rural poor by extending the benefits of development to them. Its aims at the improvement of their living standards by providing them opportunities for the fullest utilization of their political through their active participation in the process of goal-oriented change. Rural development also tends to reduce migrational pressure on cities and towns. It also enables the use of human and national resources in the rural areas and to reduce area-wise differences. Evidence indicates that in India, public and governmental interest in rural development has been growing rapidly and a strong and various commitment towards it on the part of our polity-makers is clearly visible. The government has initiated a number of programmes to resolve the chromic problems facing village in India. In fact efforts to improve the rural economy were initiated soon after independence, particularly after the Constitution came into force. Notably, in the early phases, despite some efforts at involving the people though democratic decentralization community development and panchayati raj rural development programmes were virtually synonymies with agricultural development. This followed the prevailing world- wide thinking and India's excessive concern especially till the green revolution in the late 1960s with food sufficiency. In the seventies, however, it came to be realized that rural development is much broader in scope than merely agricultural development. Besides it was recognized that development in agriculture was not a panacea for all ills and that development should not be confined to a single area of change, however significance it may be. Therefore, it the strategy for rural development had to be made effective, a multi-pronged approach to rural problems was imperative. A package programme of rural development had to be devised, a multi-dimensional approach taken up and multi-institutional efforts had to be initiated.

In the Era of Globalization

As we have adapted policies of liberalization and globalization since 1991, we will have to look at the rural development from a holistic angle rather than from the angle of compartmentalization. Against this backdrop, an attempt has been made here to examine the key aspects of Rural Development with Decentralized Governance.

Aspects of Rural Development

Broadly speaking there are four major aspects of rural development - Economic, Agricultural, Industrial Infrastructure, and Management.

Economic Aspects

The macro-economics policies of our country will have to be formulated with certain specific consideration that, at macro level the economic growth is reflected. This economic growth at village level will not only be in terms of statistics but it will have to be in terms of physical achievement including better standard of living, health facilitates, education and housing facilitates as also availability of electricity, drinking water, roads etc., - in which government's macro-economic policies will play important role from the point of view of distribution of resources. Integrated rural development will be one of the important dimensions of economic aspects. In our successive Five Year Plans, we have given considerable thrust on this aspect. Land in rural areas is the primary means of production to generate wealth. Although at the time of attaining our independence, the productivity of land was very low. But later we have been able to increase the productivity with the application of latest technology in agriculture and horticulture. Attention has now been drawn to top the rural market for industrial production to utilize the disposable income generated from agriculture and horticulture produces and also from the dairy industry. This will increase the trade and sincere in rural areas and villages. All these measures together will help in increasing the per capita income of rural people, which will give them a sort of social security. An important component of economic aspect is rural credit facilitates for different sectors such as agriculture, industry; individual trades and services as well as infrastructural facilities. These credit requirements are available from indigenous sector, scheduled banks with their lead bank branches, co-operative banks, regional rural banks and NABARD.

Agricultural Aspects

Agriculture is the backbone of Indian economy. When we became independent in 1947 the agricultural output was very low, the soil productivity was also very low and our agriculture was too much dependent on rains. After independence we build up high dams such as Bhakhra Nangal, Damodar Valley, etc. giant fertilizer plants such as IFFCO. KRIBHACO. GSFC, GNFC, etc. we could make green revolution and today we are self-sufficient on food front with mechanized framing and using improved verities of seeds and adoption of related technologies.

A glaring example is that of potato farming in the rural areas of a border town Deesa, situated in district Banaskantha in Gujarat state. This area is a traditionally potato growing area. The town Deesa has now become a 'Vegetable City'. The total annual turnover is Rs. 1000 crore out of which 65 per cent share is that of potato. This is completely a matter of good variety of seed quality, timely, credit facility and improved technology. Potato farrning has brought prosperity for Deesa.

Agriculture is one of the important means of production and much still remains to be done in this field, so that we can export our agricultural products such as wheat, rice, sugar, cotton, and horticultural product such as mango, apple, etc. in sufficient quantity with worlds class quality by establishing research centres and agro-industrial complexes with latest technologies for green house which can be established on large scale in different rural areas by forming co-operative societies of farmers, traders and agro-industrial services, for longer shelf life. With India taking a very strong stand and WTO, we will be in a very good position to export our agri-horti products to member countries of WTO in very large quantities and we will be earning a good amount of foreign exchange by establishing necessary mechanism for the same.

As this policy would get momentum it would generate income for rural people and would make our villages and rural areas prosper at a faster rate than what it is today.

Industrial Aspect

The foregoing agricultural aspect is limited by the total availability of land. However, in view of fast increase in development obviously is inevitable to generate either the part-time employment during lean season or fulltime employment when there is no work in the fields to supplement the income of farmers and agricultural labour.

Although considerable rural industrialization has taken place in the last two decades it is still necessary to develop on a vast scale, cottage, small and medium scale industries. Also where other resources like minerals, agro-products, etc. are available in a particular rural area, large scale industries such as cement manufacturing industrial unit, salt based industrial undertakings in coastal areas, etc. too will have to be established. Down to the line, trades and other services too will have to come up in consonance with other developments taking place in rural areas.

Another important point to consider in industrial development is that, it would require to local entrepreneurs as well as those from outside he can invest money on a big scale. They will have to be invited even from outside the country what is now known as foreign direct investment. The technologies of production of different products and consumer items are fast changing. It is therefore necessary to have unskilled, semi-skilled and highly skilled manpower in giving boost to rural industrialization. This leads us to develop human resources for various types of manufacturing industries as well as trades and service industries, hence, the requirement of training institutes in rural areas appropriate to the types of rural development. This is one of the important factors for rural industrialization.

Infrastructural Aspects

As we go for rural industrialization and other socio-economic and agro-developments they will demand infrastructural requirements. These requirements are, good motorable all weather roads. Extension of railway lines wherever possible, power, water, telecommunication facilities, housing facilities, education facilities, etc.

We have already embarked upon Quadrangular Highway project together with other roads linking big cities, towns and rural areas to move fast the traffic all categories which would reduce the time of transportation. Railways too are moving thousands of tones of goods across the country's different cities, towns, village and rural areas. Now whenever the economic development takes place in rural areas they too will have to be connected by railways.

Today power requirements is one of our biggest requirement. Power is at the centre stage of our living. We are utilizing all resources, such as, thermal, hydro, nuclear, solar and wind energy to generate electricity. We will have to increase our efforts to give more power to rural areas which we want to develop at a faster rate. The economics of power is a complex matter which covers generation, transmission and distribution. Considerable efforts have made to improve the management of power sector in our economy by creating Central and State Electricity Regulatory Authorities, to improve the working of State Electricity Boards, so that rural areas would get power of as much time as possible at reasonable tariff.

Management Aspect

When we take a comprehensive view of the foregoing different aspects of rural development it is imperative that it will require modern concept of management in all the aspects. If we go by the definition of management, it can be said that management of any organization, is to take work from others. For this matter certain clear objective will have to be formulated for development of rural areas. This will involve planning and the implementing machinery for the goals determined. The organization will require expert in the field of management.

organization will require expert in the field of management. Subsequent to establishing this organization the rural people for whom the development is indented, will have to be involved to create an awareness for the need of development by educating them about the opportunities being created for their welfare, through the process of development. Once the development process states it will require monitoring by the concerned managers about the physical achievements within the stipulated time and corrections will have to be made whenever necessary. It is equally necessary to update the knowledge of managers in rural development for which institute such as IRMA for imparting education in rural management, established at Anand city in Gujarat State be taken as model for the same.

RURAL DEVELOPMENT, DEMOCRATIC DECENTRALIZATION AND MAHATMA GANDHI

'Mahatma Gandhi underlined the significance of rural India by saying that India lives in villages. Since then successive governments have been trying to develop the rural areas has been one of the most abiding concerns. Gandhiji wrote in *Harijan* on 29th August, 1936: "I would say that if the villages perishes, India will perish too. It will be no more India. Her on vision in the world will be lost. The revival of the village life is possible only when it is no more exploited."

Gandhiji's views on Rural Development

Relationship between City and Villages

It was Gandhiji who first understood the importance, role and place of Indian villages in the whole country. His objective assessment of villages in overall Indian economic and political sphere was the key which helped him to bring them to the main stream and ultimately win the freedom. The rural character of the economy and the need for regeneration of rural life was stressed by Mahatma Gandhi. He wrote in *Harijan* (4, April, 1936).

"India is to be found not in few cities but in its 700,000 villages. But we town dwellers have believed that India is to be found in its towns and the villages were created to minister to our needs. We have hardly paused to inquire if those poor get sufficient to eat and cloth themselves with and whether they have a roof to shelter themselves from sun and rain". He was thus critical of the role of the urban set ups as they did not share proportionate resources with their counterparts living in villages. He considered urbanization as an evil insofar as (i) it is based on the exploitation of the countryside, and (ii) is totally divorced from the rural way of life rooted in nature.

He said (in 1946) "I regard the growth of the cities as an evil thing, unfortunate for mankind and the world, unfortunate for England and certainly unfortunate for India. The British have exploited India through its cities. The letter have exploited the villages. The blood of the villages is the cement with which the edifice of the cities is built". He has asked whether it was possible to retrace the steps and, if this was possible, whether this would not be incompatible with progress. Gandhi gave a remarkably balanced answer to this question in the form of the following proportions: (i) "I want the blood that is inflating the arteries of the cities to run once again in the blood-vessels of the villages"; (ii) "I do not want to depopulate the cities and send the city folk back to the villages. All I want is that they should re-adjust their lives so as to cease to sponge upon the poor village folk and make to the letter what reparation is possible, even this later hour, by helping to resuscitate their ruined economy"; (ii) "in my picture of the rural economy the cities would take their natural place and not appear as unnatural, congested spots or boils on the body-politic, as they are today."

The views of Gandhiji on urbanization and its relationship with that of the villages are still evading us as we find the ballooning of the cities as population due to migration is increasing day by day, pollution, famines, shortage of soft drinking water, etc., as ringing problems today. In addition as size is increasing their share in the proportion of the total funds at disposal is also increasing disproportionately.

Co-operative form of Enterprise

In the East man has relied on his group – family, clan, caste, guide or the village community. Gandhiji thought that if the Indian economy as well as the Indian policy, if it has to be restructured from the bottom outwards (rather than upwards in a pyramidal structure) it would be necessary to refashion the village communities as an 'ideal type' and readapt them to the modern methods of "cooperative" operations.

Gandhiji did not think that the village communities in future India would be a replica of the old village communities. In answer to Louid Fisher's suggestions of the nature of the new order in India after the British left, Gandhi said in 1942: " I admit that the future society of India is largely beyond my grasp." But he took care to explain (i) that power concentrated now in New Delhi or in Culcutta and Bombay, in the cities, would have to be distributed among the 7,00,000 villages of India; and (ii) that "voluntary cooperation will produce real freedom and a new order".

An Ideal Village

In 1919 Gandhi wrote for the Navjivan a series of article on the condition of Indian peasants and the means of ameliorating it. The English translation appeared in the *Young India*. Gandhi said: " Mr. Lionel Curstis' description of an Indian village as a collection of in sanitary dwellings constructed in a dunghill is not much exaggerated. There should be some system about the structure of a well ordered village, there should be some ordered about the village lanes, and the roads should be so scrupulously clean in this land of crores of barefooted pedestrians that no body need not hesitate in walking or even sleeping in the streets. The lanes should be mechanized and have gutters for letting out water. The temples and mosques should be kept so beautifully clean that the visitors should feel an air of tranquil holiness about them. The village should, as far as possible, be full of shade giving trees and fruit bearing trees in and around them. It should have a *dharmashala*, a school and a small dispensary. Washing and privy arrangement should be such as may not contaminate the air, water and roads of the village. There was time when the Indian village satisfied most of these conditions. Every village should be self-sufficient, so far as its needs for food and clothing are concerned and should be capable of defending itself against robbers or wild animals. An ideal village should approximate to the description I have given for. Only such village could be called self-governing, and if all Indian villages should come up to that ideal, India should be free from most of its worries... it is my firm belief that these small units are easily capable of being well ordered and organized.

Gandhiji thought of a casteless egalitarian rural society against the stark background of a caste ridden village community. This was a contradiction. He not only faced it, but also tried to resolve it by means of a progressive interpretation of the ancient differentiation of social functions, which, in the course of social decay, and in his view, degenerated into a hide-bound, caste-ridden social order.

"Village Republic", A Vision of Gandhiji

This picture of a new India which Gandhi presented in Harijan article must be delineated in his own words as follows.

1. "Indian independence must begin at the bottom. Thus every village will be a republic or panchayat having powers. It follows, therefore, that every village has to be self-sustained and capable of managing its own affairs, even to the extent of defending itself against the whole world. It will be trained and prepared to perish in the attempt to defend itself against any onslaught from without.
2. "Ultimately, it is individual who is the unit. But this does not exclude dependence on the willing help from neighbours or from the world. It will be free and voluntary play of mutual forces".
3. "Such a society is necessarily highly cultured in which every man or women knows what he or she wants, and what is more, knows that no one should want anything that the others cannot have with equal labour.
4. "In this structure composed of innumerable villages there will be ever-widening, never-ascending circles. Life will not be a pyramid with the apex sustained by the bottom. But it will be an oceanic circle whose centre will be the individual always ready to perish for village, the latter ready to perish for the circle of villages till at last the whole becomes one life composed in individuals, never aggressive in their arrogance, but ever humble, sharing the majesty of the oceanic circle of which they are integral units. Therefore, the outermost circumference will not wield power to crush the inner circle, but will give strength to all within and will derive its own strength from it".
5. "In it there is no room for machines that would displace human labour and that would concentrate power in a few hands. Labour has its unique place in a cultured human family. Every machine that helps every individual has a place."

Gandhi was aware that by presenting a picture of republican

village India he was exposing himself to ridicule in political atmosphere in which politicians of the urban classes were dreaming of power-politics and power-structure of the usual run of democracies, while reflecting on the content of independence in conventional terms."

Democratic Decentralization and Gandhiji

A democratic policy involves decentralization of power in such a way that the affairs of the local people are managed by means of their positive participation. It implies the extension of democracy at the grass roots level in view of the fact that the people's participation signifies the Constitution of a Democratic Government not merely at the top but also at the foundation level of the political system.

Mahatma Gandhi made reference to democratic decentralization for the first time in February 1916. While appreciating the working of the ancient Indian Panchayat System. He said, India is really a republican country as it is because it has survived every shock hitherto delivered. He was sure that the problem of village sanitation would have been solved long ago and India would have been enjoying self-government suited to its requirements had village panchayats been acting as a living force.

In his presidential address at the Belgaum Congress, Gandhiji referred to the panchayat system as the right medium for securing cheap justice as well as for avoiding reliance of the government on the settlement of mutual disputes. During his term of office as president of the Indian National Congress he extensively toured the country, that reinforced his conviction that India would be benefited a great deal if the villages were governed by the village panchayats. However, he felt that, the reorganization of the village administration could not be taken in isolation. He was sure that Indian village life had great vitality and character. It was because of this that it has persisted all these long years and had weathered many a storm. Gandhi's view of democratic decentralization developed over the years. He laid emphasis on PR or democratic decentralization till the last moment of his life. Simple living and high thinking is the ideal, the very foundation and essence of the Gandhian approach to decentralization.

Gandhiji opposed all types of concentration of power. Since to him, centralization is a menace and a danger to democracy. Concentration of power in his view distorts all democratic values. So he argues, possession of power makes men blind and deaf; they cannot see things which are under their very nose and cannot hear things which invade their cars. In other words centralization is a system inconsistent with non-violent structure of society.

Moreover, he was convinced that moral progress was possible only in a decentralized setup in a nutshell, he argues that without decentralization it is impossible to ensure individual liberty and mental and moral growth of man. Similarly, it is equally essential for the realization of the ideal democracy, for the rule of the people; which it stands for, is not possible without adequate opportunities to individuals to participate in the management of their owns affairs.

Gandhiji rather pleads for decentralization of economic and political power. For the success of political decentralization. In his view depends upon economic decentralization. This follows from his conviction that a highly centralized political set up is likely to bring dictatorship of one kind or another by a self-increased and power-hungry minority imposing itself on a deluded and subservient majority. While elaborating his ideas on decentralization, Gandhiji keeps in mind two different structures. First, the power state structure of the west. Basically he reject it on the ground that it leads to centralization of power, exploitation of the weak denial of individual freedom and moral degradation. It is democratic in its external framework but dictatorial in actual practice.

Second is the Panchayati Raj – building up from below. In other words, it can be called democratic decentralization. Basically Gandhiji is drawn towards this model. One important feature of this model is economic self-sufficiency at the grass roots level. To him this is the only way to eliminate exploitation of the weaker sections in society and to bring happiness to the millions. Further this decentralization implies the fundamental principle of self-sufficiency. But it is not absolute sufficiency. It is mostly confined to the basic needs such as food. Clothing and shelter. He reiterated that if a new democratic egalitarian social, political order free from exploitation had to be established on firm foundations. Decentralization in economics must go side by side with decentralization in politics. Even success of political decentralization depends upon decentralization. In other words without economic decentralization, political decentralization would be meaningless. The manifesto of the Congress Parliamentary Board, July 29, 1934 which was drafted by Gandhiji declared. In order to end the exploitation of the masses political freedom must include real economic freedom of the starving millions. Similarly his advocacy of *charkha* and village industries only demonstrate his living faith in decentralization of economic power.

Gandhiji was not against the modern science and technology. His attitude is entirely rational and scientific his main thrust is that science and technology instead of becoming masters should function as the servants of the people. Basically, he has no objection to machines as such. But he argues that, it is wrong to carry the process of mechanization of industry so far as to kill the cottage industries and concentrate them within a narrow field. Accordingly, he wants villages to be production centres and towns to be clearing houses for such product instead of being the reverse as it is today.

Therefore, Gandhiji's concept of democratic decentralization bears the stamp of his passionate belief in non-yiolence, truth and individual freedom. He calls it PR village *swaraj*. He wants to see each village as a little republic self-sufficient in its vital wants, organically linked with the higher bodies and enjoying the maximum freedom of deciding the affairs of the locality. According to Gandhi, real India lives in its villages. So villages held an important place in Gandhi's scheme of life and social organization. He was a strong and ardent supporter of moral atmosphere, rural life and rural development. For him Indian villages were the backbone of India or real India. He believed that if village perished, India would perish too. It will be no more India. Her own mission in the world will get lost.

Till 1936 Gandhi had not made up his mind or he was not clear about the character of the structure of Indian polity. At the Faizpur Congress Session in 1936 he expressed the opinion that India must have a polity suited to her genius. But he could not give its blueprint. This shows that he was clear about the spirit but not of the form of Indian polity. He only indicated that the western mechanism of democracy was not suitable for India. This meant that India must seek its own institutional framework to realize the values of democracy. He made some loud thinking in this connection. The institution of the village panchayat which had provided a democratic structure at the grass root level for centuries in India showed him direction. The institution of panchayat, for him, was the fundamental unit of democratic decentralization.

Further in 1942, during the course of an interview with Louis Fisher. He remarked that voluntary co-operation and cooperation induced by Nazi methods was the essence of the panchayat system. He again pleaded for the distribution of power among the villagers. He said "you see, the centre of power now is in New Delhi or in Culcutta and Bombay in the big cities. I would have it distributed among the seven hundred thousand villages of India. That will mean that there is not power. In other words, I want the seven hundred thousand dollars now invested in the Imperial Bank of England, withdrawn and distributed among the seven hundred thousand villages.

Then each village would have it dollar which cannot be lost.," Emphasizing this point he said the seven hundred thousand dollars invested in the Imperial Bank of India could be swept away by a bomb from a Japanese plane. Whereas if they were distributed among the seven hundred thousand shareholders nobody could deprive them of their assets. This will then be a voluntary co-operation will produce real freedom and a new order vastly superior to the new order in Soviet Russia.

The above-mentioned interview reveals Gandhi's deep faith in decentralized democracy based on village panchayat drawing their powers from the initiative and willing cooperation of the people and it must belong to the people. He fully subscribed to the principle that power resides in the people and it must belong to the people. It seeks expression through democratic decentralization or Panchayati Raj. Again the 1946 Gandhiji while rejecting western political institution of Parliamentary Democracy laid stress on the concept of decentralized democracy consisting of concentric village republics. He elaborated his plan for independent India at the time of transfer of power. He asserted that independence must begin at the bottom. Thus every village would be a republic or panchayat having full powers. It follows, that every village had to be self-sustained and capable of managing its affairs even to the extent of defending itself against the whole world. It would be trained and prepared to perish in the attempt to defend itself against any onslaught from without. Thus ultimately, it is the individual who is the unit. But Gandhi points out that this does not exclude dependence on and willing help from neighbours or from the world.

Under the Gandhian Constitution, the scheme of Government was briefly as follows :

1. First the primary political unit was to be the village panchayat, whose member would be elected by the audits of the village. The panchayat would control

chowkidars, *patwaris* and police and schools. It would also assess and collect land revenue, supervise cooperative farming irrigation and interest rate as well as Khadi and other village industries.

2. Secondly, above the village panchayat came a hierarchy of indirectly elected bodies. First came Taluka and District Panchayat, each comprised of the sarpanches of the next lower panchayats and having only advisory power over them. Members from the district and municipal panchayat would from the provincial panchayat, which would elect President to serve as head of the provincial government. Presidents of a provincial panchayat would comprise the all-India panchayat whose President would be the head of the State and of the Government, which would be ministerial in character. Among the responsibilities of provincial panchayat would be transport, irrigation, natural resources and co-operative bank.

The national panchayat would be responsible for such things as defence, currency, customs, the running of key industries of national importance and the coordination of provincial economic development plants.

Functions and Powers of Village Panchayat

One of the most important functions, according to him, under the jurisdiction of institution of democratic decentralization, was the settlement of disputes between individuals. Its object was to make justice available to the village without incurring much cost or inconvenience. So he said in his Presidential address at the Belgaum Congress, administration of justice should be cheapened and with that end in view, the final court of appeals should be not in London, but in Delhi. Parties to civil suits must be compelled in the majority cases to refer their dispute arbitration, the decisions of these panchayats is to be final expect in cases of corruption or obvious misapplication of law. Municipality of intermediate courts should be avoided.

However, its jurisdiction was based on the voluntary principle. Thus in his instruction to the village panchayat of Nainital, he laid down that the panchayat might try civil suits if the parties to the suit referred their disputes to the panchayats.

To him every panchayat will be expected to attend to education of boys and girls in its village, its sanitation, its medical needs, the upkeep and cleanliness of village wells or ponds and the uplift of and the daily wants of the so-called untouchable.

Gandhi pleads for decentralization of both economic and political power. He staunchly believes in political decentralization. Gandhi visualize a social and political order passed on decentralization of both economic and political power. He wants to create convenient regions not only to manage their political affairs but also their economic and political power. He wants to create convenient regions not only to manage their political affairs but their economic affairs too. Thus he wants to transform every region into a small republic or a panchayat. For, the real freedom, to Gandhi, is the management of one's own affairs by oneself. And it can function effectively only in small units.

Conclusively, Gandhi's approach to democratic decentralization is based on the principles of non-violence, truth, individual freedom, non-exploitation and morality suited to the genius of the Indian masse. Conversely, his approach incompatible with compulsion, force, strict control from above and centralization of power. It does not begin from the top but has to grow from below.

As regards the implementation of Gandhi's view not much seems to have been achieved. However, some efforts were made at both the official level. After his death some of his followers made efforts to give shape to his views. In this context, a reference may be made to such loadable attempts as the Bhoodan movement, reconstruction of Indian polity through communication approach, total revolution, etc.

However, they failed in their mission to realize or develop Gandhi's dreams of decentralized social, political order or Gram Swaraj or Panchayati Raj or rural democracy. He could neither fill up the gap nor develop his scheme of democratic decentralization, due to various shortcomings, as the structure of local Government was systematically destroyed out of political consideration. There was a lack of commitment of democratic decentralization, rather they created confusion in their approach by introducing in it certain extraneous factors; the principle of unanimity as advocate by them failed to produce any fruitful thing. *Jana Shakti* (people's power) was hardly generated and *Raj Niti* (power politics) dominate the *gramdan* villages. Lack of team work was notable and workers who finally showed their skin deep differences and even Jayaprakash Narayan and Vinoba Bhave, parted with each other in the long run.

To come to the efforts made at the official level; we find that while the institutional fabric of the country was radically reshaped, little was done to build it according to Gandian principles. The Indian Constitution bears witness to this fact. The people were quite hopeful that the new construction would definitely reflect the Gandian spirit, but surprisingly the draft constitution that appeared immediately after the independence did not make a mention of democratic decentralization or PR of Gandhi's conception.

Thus, the neglect of Gandian concept of decentralization in Indian Constitution was not an accident of history; rather it was the end result of a chain of events and thought which had been secretly working at the back of the minds of most of those who mattered at time of constituting-making.

While reviewing and evaluating in Gandian terms the

functional competence of PRI in different parts of the country, it has been found that except in a few states like West Bangal, Karnataka, and Andhra Pradesh, these institutions have been rarely given a change to perform their functions on a sizeable scale.

Regarding the financial position of PRIs, it can be said that the financial resources are not adequate and satisfactory and as a result these do not fit into the scheme of Gandhian approach to democratic decentralization as Gandhi wanted the local bodies to be self-reliant and self-sufficient so far as the basic or daily requirements of these bodies were concerned. Similarly, they must be provided with adequate and independent financial resources to discharge their duties properly.

Further PRIs do not possess absolute autonomy as these are created as well as controlled by Central/State Government.

Thus, the PRIs failed to become a part of the whole democratic system of the country. There has been a lack of organic linkage among these institutions and these were kept aloof from the democratic set up at the state as well as the national level.

The irregularity of elections to its various institutions constitute another distortion of the system. In fact, the State Government never realized the growing importance and urgency of holding the timely and regular elections to these institutions.

In the end, the history of democratic decentralization in India repeats its own pages that the subject remained a controversial one ever since the independence. All politicians exploited it as much as possible in the name of Gandhi, intellectuals gave it a different colour by interpreting according to their own mental make up; peoples showed their apathy and lacked interest, initiative and cooperation and participation in its operational process; the officials and representatives showed their indifference towards it and misused their power too. The Government both at the Centre and the State levels have also spread no efforts to make a capital out of it, without doing any tangible efforts either to strengthen it or to improve its image. It would therefore be futile to suggest any remedy. For, the ills or distortion or lapses themselves speak of the remedy.

Rural Development Programmes in India : An Overview

The Ministry of Rural Development is implementing a number of programmes aimed at sustainable development of rural areas with a focus on weaker and vulnerable section. In order to catalyze development in rural area, top priority has been accorded to Rural Development, not only in terms of allocation of funds and resources but also through introduction of new programmes and restructuring of the existing ones. Development should be participatory, tapping the local talent and resources in order to be sustainable. Stress is being given to make the Gram Sabha is pillar of Panchayati Raj Institutions as an effective unit of local self-government and an effective and vibrant forum for decentralized planning an implementation of rural development programmes.

To ensure sustainable development of rural areas, the allocation for rural development was increased substantially. As against a budgetary allocation of Rs. 12,265 crore during 2001-02 the allocation in the year 2002-03 were Rs. 13,670 crore, which was further enhanced to Rs. 14,070 crore for the year 2003-04 and to Rs. 15,998 crore for the current financial year, 2004-05.

Anti-Poverty programmes are a dominant feature of government initiatives in the rural areas. The programmes were reviewed and strengthen in successive year in order to sharpen their focus on reduction of rural poverty. The results achieved are worthnoting. In percentage terms, rural poverty has reduced from 56.44 per cent of the country's population in 1973-74 to 37.27 in 1993-94 and again to 27.09 per cent in 1999-00. However, the cause for concern is that the estimated number of rural poor is still about 19.30 crore which has led to further review and restructuring of the anti-poverty programmes. The Swarnajayanti Gram Swarojgar Yojana (SGSY) is the result of such latest review and restructuring of programmes. Launched on 1st April, 1999, the SGSY is different from the earlier programmes in terms of strategy envisaged for implementation has been conceived as a holistic Programme of Self-Employment, viz., organization of rural poor into Self-Help Groups and their capacity building, training, planning for activity clusters, infrastructure build up, technology and marketing support.

Gainful employment, food security and strengthening of infrastructure in rural areas is a must for national renewal for a resurgent India. On 25th September, 2001, the Sampoorna Grameen Rozgar Yojana (SGRY) was launched to attain these objectives. The scheme envisages an annual expenditure of Rs. 10,000 crore. Under the scheme, 50 lakhs tonnes of foodgrain amounting to Rs. 5,700 crore (at economic cost) are to be provided every year to State/UTs free of cost. About Rs. 5,000 crore is to be utilized to meet the cash component of wage and material costs. About 100 crore man-days of employment is likely to be generated every year, besides creation of durable assets in rural areas as per the felt needs of Gram Panchayats. In order to ensure people's participation, the programme would be implemented through PRIs.

Notwithstanding the efforts made over the years at the state and central levels through different programmes, about 40 per cent of habitations are still without road connectivity. Even where the connectivity has been provided, the roads constructed are not all-weather roads. There is close link between rural connectivity and growth, be it in the area of trade, employment, education to health care. Keeping this in view the government launched a major initiative – Pradhan Mantri Gram Sadak Yojana (PMGSY) on 25th December, 2000 with the objective of providing connectivity to all unconnected habitations with the population of more than 1,000 within three years and similar such villages with a population of 500 by the year 2007 through good all-weather roads.

Considerable success has been achieved in meeting the drinking water needs of the rural population. With an investment of more than Rs. 45,000 crore or rural drinking water supply by Central and State Governments since independence, 94.37 per cent partially covered. The programme has been revamped to usher reforms by institutionalizing community participation in rural water supply sector with a view to gradually replace the government oriented, centralized, supply-driven and non-people participating Rural Water Supply Programme (RWSP) by people oriented, decentralized, demand driven and community based Rural Water Supply Programme.

Since land is a critically important national resource among the natural resources, the efficient management of which is vital for economic growth and development of rural areas. Around 20 per cent (63.85 million hectare) of the country's geographical area is wastelands/degraded land. To meet the imperative need to put in place an integrated mechanism capable of responding effectively to the challenges of managing country's scarce land resources, a separate department of Land Resources came into being in April 1999 under the Ministry of Rural Development. All the land-based area development programmes are being implemented through the watershed development approach since April 1995, in accordance with the recommendations of the Hanumantha Rao Committee.

Empowerment has to be an essential ingredient in planning and implementation of the programmes. Accordingly, under the programmes of the Ministry, a predominant role for Panchayati Raj Institution (PRIs) in their implementation has been envisaged through a four-pronged strategy viz., (i) Enhancing the level of awareness about the Schemes; (ii) Promoting transparency in the implementation of programmes; (iii) Encouraging people's partnership; and (iv) Ensuring accountability/social audit.

Pradhan Mantri Gram Sadak Yojana

The Pradhan Mantri Gram Sadak Yojana (PMGSY), a 100 per cent centrally sponsored scheme was launched on 25th December, 2000. The prime objective of the PMGSY is to provide connectivity, by way of an all-weather roads to the unconnected habitations in the rural areas in such a way that habitations with a population of 1,000 persons and above are covered in three years (2000-03) and all unconnected habitations with a population of 500 persons and above by the end of the Tenth Plan, i.e., 2007. In respect of the Hill States (North-East, Sikkim, Himachal Pradesh, Jammu and Kashmir, Uttaranchal), Tribal and Desert Areas, the objective would be to connect habitations with a population of 250 persons and above.

As on 1st April, 2000, about 8.25 lakh habitations in the country, about 3.30 lakh habitations were not connected by all-weather roads. The PMGSY seeks to provide connectivity to about 1.70 lakh unconnected habitations besides upgradation of some existing rural roads to prescribed standards by the end of the Tenth Plan. According to estimates based on a survey, about 3.70 lakh kilometers of roads will be constructed under the programme. The total cost of the construction and upgradation of other rural roads is likely to be of the order of Rs. 1,30,000 roads estimated to cost Rs. 14,377 crore have been cleared up to the end of March 2004 and 20,651 road works have since been completed. The remaining works are in various stages of execution. A cumulative expenditure of Rs. 6,559 crore was incurred till March 2004.

Rural Water Supply Programme

Drinking water facility to rural habitations are provided under state-sector programme. The Central Government endeavours to supplement the efforts of the states by providing assistance under the Centrally-Sponsored Accelerated Rural Water Supply

Programme. Powers have been delegated to the states to plan, sanction and implement the rural water supply schemes.

The government envisages provision of safe drinking water to all rural habitations. The strategy to achieve the objective revolves around the following issues to accelerate the coverage of remaining "not covered and partially covered" habitations with safe drinking water systems; to tackle the problem of water quality in affected habitations and to institutionalize water quality monitoring and surveillance system and; to promote sustainability both of systems and sources, to ensure continuous supply of safe drinking water in "covered" habitations.

An investment of more than Rs. 45,000 crore has been made in the water supply sector so far. Status of coverage of rural habitations, as per information received from states till 28th May, 2004 is 5,936 not covered and 71,463 partially covered rural habitations. During 2003-04, as per information received up to rural development 28th May, 2004, 3,716 not covered and 30,540 partially covered habitations have been covered with drinking water facilities. Ninety-nine per cent of rural habitations have access to drinking water facility.

The government has revamped the Rural Water Supply Programme (RWSP), which, *inter alia*, envisages institutionalization of community-based rural water supply system by incorporating the following basic principles for ensuring peoples participations: (i) adoption of demand-driven, responsive and adaptable approach of villages to ensure their full participation in the arrangements; (ii) shifting the role of Government from direct service delivery to that of facilitator; and (iii) partial cost sharing either in cash or kind or both and 100 per cent responsibility of operations and maintenance by end-users. Sixty-seven districts all over the country have been identified for implementing the reform projects on a pilot basis. The reform initiative launched has now scaled to Swajaldhara to cover the entire country.

Central Rural Sanitation Programme

Rural sanitation is a state subject. The efforts of the state are supplemented by the Central Government through technical and financial assistance under the Central Rural Sanitation Programme (CRSP).

The programme was launched in 1986 with the objective of improving the quality of life of rural people and providing privacy and dignity to women. The concept of sanitation was expanded in 1993 to include personal hygiene, home sanitation, safe water, and disposal of garbage, human excreta and waste water. The components of the programme included construction of individual sanitary toilets for households below poverty line (BPL), conversion of dry latrines of water-pour flush toilets, construction of village sanitary complexes of women, setting up of sanitary marts and production centres, intensive campaign for creating awareness and health education, etc.

Keeping in view the experiences of the Central and State Governments, NGOs and other implementing agencies and the recommendations of the Second National Seminar on Rural Sanitation, the strategy for the Ninth Five Year Plan was revised by the programme was restructured from 1st April, 1999. The restructured programme moves away from the principle of state-wise allocation of funds, primarily based on poverty criteria, to a demand driven approach in a phased manner. Total Sanitation Campaign (TSC) was introduced and the allocation-based programme was phased put by 31st March, 2002. TSC is community-led and people centred. There was a shift from a high subsidy to a low subsidy regime. The TSC approach emphasis awareness-building component and meets the demand through alternate delivery mechanism. School sanitation has been introduced as a major component to encourage wider acceptance of sanitation among rural masse. The State/Uts are required to formulate project proposals under the TSC in order to claim Central Government assistance.

Under the TSC, so far 398 projects in 29 States/Uts have been sanctioned with the total project outlay of about

Rs. 3,744.24 crore. The Central, State and beneficiary panchayat contributions are about Rs. 2,213.81 crore, Rs 826 crore and Rs. 703 crore respectively. The components sanctioned in the 398 projects are: (a) construction of 323-lakh individual household latrines; (b) 3,53,041 lakh toilets for schools; (c) 25,236 community sanitary complexes; (d) 59,562 toilets for *Balwadis/Anganwadis,* and (e) 2,942 Rural Sanitary Marts /Production centres. Besides, funds have been earmarked for start-up activities, Information, Education and Communication (IEC) and administrative charges.

The total number of household toilets constructed up to 2003-04 are 80,87,130 (provisional).

Rural Housing

To meets the shortage of housing in rural areas, the Indira Awaas Yojana (IAY) was launched in May 1985 as a sub-scheme of Jawahar Rozgar Yojana (JRY). It is being implemented as an independent scheme since 1st January, 1996. The Indira Awaas Yojana aims at providing assistance to rural people below the poverty-line belonging to Scheduled Caste/Scheduled Tribes, freed bonded labourers and non-Scheduled Castes/ Scheduled Tribes categories in construction of dwelling units and upgradation of existing unserviceable kutcha houses by providing grants-in-aid. From 1995-96, the IAY benefits have been extended to widows or neset-of kin of defense personnel killed in action. Benefits have also been extended to exserviceman and retired members of the paramilitary forces as long as they fulfil the normal eligibility conditions of the IAY. Three per cent of funds are reserved for the disabled persons living below the poverty line in rural areas.

The District Panchayat/District Rural Development Agency (DRDA) on the basis of allocation made and targets fixed decide the number of houses to the constructed/upgraded panchayat-wise under IAY, during a particular financial year. Accordingly, the targets are intimated to the Gram Panchayat concerned. Thereafter, the Gram Sabha selects the beneficiaries from the list of eligible BPL households, restricting this number to the target allotted as per the Programme Guideline. Selection by the Gram Sabha is final. No approval by a higher body is required. Zila Parishads/DRDAs and Block Development Office are informed accordingly to provide assistance to selected beneficiaries.

Under the scheme, allotment is the house is done in the name of the female members of the households or in the joint names of husband and wife. A minimum of 60 per cent of funds is to be utilized for construction of houses for the SC/ST. Sanitary latrines and smokeless chulhas should also be provided to beneficiaries. Selection of construction technology, materials and design is left entirely to the choice of beneficiaries. The ceiling on assistance for construction of new houses has been increased from Rs. 20,000 to Rs. 27,500 per unit for the plain areas and from Rs. 22,000 to Rs. 27,500 per unit for the hilly/difficult areas from 1st April 2004. The upper limit in respect of conversion of *kutcha* houses into semi-*pucca* houses (upgradation) and subsidy under credit-cum-subsidy Scheme has increased from Rs. 10,000 to Rs. 12,500 per unit. Up to 20 per cent of the IAY funds are allocated for upgradations and assistance under credit-cum-subsidy scheme. A household having annual income of Rs. 32,000 is eligible to get loan up to Rs. 50,000 under credit-cum-subsidy scheme.

Under the Indira Awaas Yojana, since its inception and up to March 2004 about 114.78 houses have been constructed with an expenditure of about Rs 20,023 crore.

Swarnajayanti Gram Swarozgar Yojana

The Swarnajayanti Gram Swarozgar Yojana (SGSY) have been launched as an integrated programme for self-employmnet of the rural poor, on 1st April, 1999. The objective of the scheme is to bring assisted poor families above the poverty line by organizing them into Self-Help Groups (SHGs) through the process of social mobilization training, capacity building and provision of income generating assets through a mix of bank credit and Government subsidy. The scheme emphasizes on process approach and building the capacity of the rural poor. Therefore it provides for involvement of NGOs/CBOs/ individuals/banks as facilitators/Self-Help promoting Institutions in nurturing and developing SHGs. The scheme provides for the cost of social intermediation and skill development training based on the local requirement.

The focus of the programme is on establishing a large number of micro enterprises in rural areas based on the ability of the poor and potential of each area, both land-based and otherwise, for a sustainable income generation. Due emphasis is being laid on different components such as capacity building of the poor, skill development, training, credit training, technology transfer, marketing and infrastructure. The subsidy allowed under SGSY is 30 per cent of the total project cost, subject to a ceiling of Rs. 7,500 (for SCs/STs and disabled persons subsidy limit is 50 per cent of the project cost subject to ceiling of Rs. 10,000). For Self-Help Groups (SHGs), subsidy would be 50 per cent of the project cost subject to a ceiling of Rs. 1.25 lakh or per capita subsidy of Rs. 10,000, whichever is less. There is no monetary ceiling on subsidy for minor irrigation projects for SHGs as well as individual *Swarozgaris*.

The SGSY has special focus on the vulnerable groups among the rural poor. Accordingly, the SCs/STs would account for at least 50 per cent of the *swarozgaris*, women for 40 per cent and the disabled for three per cent. The SGSY seeks to promote multiple credit rather than a one-time credit injection.

The SHGs may consist of 10-20 members and in case of minor irrigation and in case of disabled persons and in case of people living in difficult area, i.e., hilly, desert and sparsely populated areas, this number may be minimum of five. The

Self-Help Groups should also be drawn from the BPL list approved by the Gram Sabha. The SHGs broadly go through three stages of evolution such as group formation, capital formation through the revolving fund are skill development and taking up of economic activity for income generation.

Selection could be made up to 10 key activities per block based on local resources, occupational skills of the people and availability of market so that the *Swarozgaris* can draw suitable incomes of their investments. The SGSY emphasis on cluster approach, i.e., each block should concentrate on four to five selected key activities and attend to all aspects of these activities, so that the *Swarozgaris* can drawn suitable incomes from their investments. The SGSY lays special emphasis on development of *Swarozgaris* through well designed training courses tailored to the activities selected and the requirement of each *Swarozgaris*.

The SGSY is being implemented through the District Rural Development Agencies (DRDAs), with the active involvement of Panchayati Raj Institutions (PRIs), Bank and the NGOs. It is financed on 75:25 cost-sharing basis between the centre and the state.

Sampoorna Grameen Rozgar Yojana

The Sampoorna Grameen Rozgar Yojana (SGRY) was launched on 25th September, 2001 by merging the non-going schemes of EAS and the JGSY with the objective of providing additional wage employment in the rural area as also food security, alongside the creation of durable-community assets in the rural areas. The programme is self-targeting in nature with special emphasis on women, Scheduled Castes, Scheduled Tribes and parents of children withdrawn from hazardous occupations. While preference will be given to BPL families for providing wage employment under SGRY, poor families above the poverty line can also be offered employment under the programme. The annual outlay is Rs. 10,000 crore which includes 50 lakhs tonnes on foodgrains. The cash component is shared between the centre and the state in the ratio of 75:25 foodgrains are provided free of cost to the States/UTs. The payment of foodgrains is made directly to FCI at economic cost by the centre. However, the cost of the transportation of foodgrains from the FCI godown to the work-site / PDS and its distribution are the responsibility of the state governments. Minimum wages are paid to the workers through a mix of minimum five kg of foodgrains and at least 25 per cent in cash.

The programme is implemented by all the three tiers of PRIs. Each level of panchayat is an independent unit for formulation of Action Plan and executing the scheme. The resources are distributed among District Panchayat, Intermediate Panchayats and the Gram Panchayats in the ratio of 20:30:50

The Gram Panchayat can take up any work with the approval of the Gram Sabha as per their felt need and within available funds. Fifty per cent of the funds earmarked to the Gram Panchayat are to be utilized for infrastructure development works in SC/ST localities. 22.5 per cent resources must be spent on individual beneficiary shemes meant for SCs/STs out of Zila Parishads and Panchayat Samiti's share of resources. Contractors are not permitted to be engaged for execution of any of the works and no middlemen/intermediate agencies can be employed for executing works under the scheme. Evaluated through impact studies conducted by reputed institutions and organizations sponsored by the Central/State Government.

Council for Advancement of People's Action and Rural Technology

In order to encourage, promote and assist voluntary action in rural development with focus on injecting new technology inputs for enhancement of rural prosperity, the government set up the Council for Advancement of People's Action and Rural Technology (CAPART) in 1986.

CAPART has nine Regional Committees/Centres at Jaipur,

Lucknow, Ahmedabad, Bhubaneswar, Patna, Chandigarh, Hyderabad, Guwahati and Dharwad. The Regional Committees are empowered to sanction project proposals to voluntary agencies up to an outlay of Rs. 20 lakh in their respective regions. Since inception and up to June 2003, CAPART has sanctioned 21,621 projects involving an amount of Rs. 701.63 crore and has released Rs. 545.5 crore.

Watershed Development Programmes

The Department of Land Resources is implementing three area based watershed programmes for development of wastelands/degraded land namely Drought Prone Areas Programmes (DPAP), Desert Development Programme (DDP), and Integrated Wasteland Development Programme (IWDP). DPAP was launched in 1973-74 to tackle the special problems faced by those areas that are constantly affected by drought conditions. Presently, 972 blocks of 182 districts in 16 states are covered under the programmes. DDP was launched in 1977-78 to mitigate the adverse effects of desertification. Presently, 235 blocks of 40 districts in seven states are covered under the programme. IWDP has been under implementation since 1989-90. The projects under the IWDP are generally sanctioned in areas that are not covered under DDP or DPAP.

Since 1st April, 1995, the three programmes are being implemented on the basis of a Common Guideline for Watershed Development. Details of projects sanctioned and fund released from 1995-96 to 2003-04 are as under.

Name of Scheme	*No. of projects Sanctioned*	*Area covered (in lakh ha.)*	*Total fund released by the Centre (Rs. in crore)*
DPAP	18803	94.01	1442.21
DDP	9876	49.38	1085.82
IWDP	662	50.79	977.49
Grand Total		**194.18**	**3505.52**

The cost norm for all the three schemes is Rs. 6,000 per ha. Under DPAP and DDP, it is shared between the Centre and States in the ratio of 75:25 in case of IWDP, the cost sharing between the Centre and State is in the ratio of 11:1.

Funds are released in seven instalments – six instalments at the rate of 15 per cent and the last instalment at the rate of 10 per cent. The first instalment is released along with the initial sanction-order and subsequent instalments on receipt of reports of utilization of 50 per cent of the available funds as well as the following documents: (a) Quarterly Progress Reports; (b) Utilization Certificates; (c) The Audited Statement of Accounts for the previous year; and (d) Evidence of satisfactory completion of institutional arrangements.

Implementation

Projects are implemented by District Rural Development Agencies/Zila Parishads (DRDAs/ZPs) through Project Implementing Agencies (PIAs); PIAs could be a line Department (of the state government), Panchayati Raj Institutions or a reputed NGOs; one PIA normally handles 10-12 watershed projects covering an area of about 5,000-6,000 hectares; The PIA is required to maintain a technical team of 4 experts called Watershed Development Team (WDT), and Individual projects (500 hectares) are planned and executed by the local people living in the watershed area called the Watershed Association (IWA) through an elected body called Watershed Committee (WC).

Hariyali

Department of Land Resources launched a new initiative called, *Hariyali* with the objective of empowering PRI's both financially and administratively in implementation of Watershed Development Programme namely, Integrated Watershed Development Programme (IWDP), Drought Prone Areas Programme (DPAP) and Desert Development Programme

(DDP) would be implemented through the PRIs. New projects under the ongoing area development programmes shall be implemented in accordance with the guidelines for *Hariyali* from 1st April, 2003. Projects sanctioned prior to this date shall continue to be implemented as per the Watershed Development Guidelines of 2001.

In the new arrangements, the Gram Panchayat shall implement the projects under the overall supervision and guidance of Project Implementation Agencies (PIAs). An intermediate panchayat may be the PIA for all the projects sanctioned to a particular Block/Taluka. In case, these Panchayats are not adequately empowered, then the Zilla Panchayat can either act as PIA itself or may appoint a suitable Line Department like Agriculture, Forestry/Social Forestry, Soil Conservation, etc., or an agency of the State Government/ University/Institute as PIA. Failing these options, the ZP/ DRDA may consider appointing a reputed Non-Governmental Organization (NGO) in the district with adequate experience and expertise in the implementation of watershed projects or related area development works as the PIA after thoroughly examining their credentials.

The Project Implementation Agency (PIA) will provide necessary technical guidance to the Gram Panchayat for preparation of development plans for the watershed through Participatory Rural Appraisal (PRA) exercise, undertake community organization and training for the village communities, supervise watershed development activities, inspect and authentic project accounts, encourage adoption of low-cost technologies and build up on indigenous technical knowledge, monitor and review the overall project implementation and set up institutional arrangements for post-project operations and maintenance and further development of the assets creating during the project period.

Land Reforms

Two Centrally Sponsored Schemes viz, (i) Computerization of

Land Records (CLR) was started in 1988-89 with 100 per cent financial assistance as a pilot project in eight districts, viz., Rengareddy (A.P.), Sonitpur (Assam), Singhbhum (Bihar) Gandhinagar (Gujarat), Morena (M.P.) Wardha (Maharashtra), Mayurbhanj (Orissa) and Dungarpur (Rajasthan) to remove the problems inherent the manual system of maintenance and updating of Land Records and to meet the requirements of various groups of users. It was decided that efforts should be made to Computerize Core data contained in land records, so as to assist development planning and to make records, peoples/planners and administrators.

During the Eighth Five Year Plan, the scheme was approved as a separate Centrally Sponsored Scheme on Computerization of Land Records. The total expenditure under the scheme during the Eighth Plan period was Rs. 59.42 crore.

During the Ninth Five Year Plan , the Ministry of Rural Development released a sum of Rs. 169.13 crore for covering 259 more districts under the scheme. At present, the scheme is being implemented in 582 districts of the country leaving those districts where there are no land records. A decision has been taken during 1997-98 for operationalization of the scheme at the tehsil/taluk level for facilitating delivery of computerized land records to users and public at large. Under this programme, funds are released to the State Governmental to purchase of hardware, software and other peripherals. 3,142 tehsil/taluks have been covered under the programme. Since inception of the scheme, the Ministry has released Rs. 300.51 crore till 31st March. 2004. The utilization of funds reported by the States/Uts is Rs. 203.01 crore, which is approximately 68 per cent of the total funds released.

Strengthening of Revenue Administration and Updating of Land Records

With a view to assist the State/Uts in the task of updating of land records, Centrally Sponsored Scheme for Strengthening of Revenue Administration and Updating of Land Records (SRA & ULR) was started in 1987. Initially the scheme was approved for the states of Bihar and Orissa in 1987-88 and extended to other States/Uts during 1989-90. The scheme is being implemented by the state governments through their Revenue/Land Records Departments. It is financed by the Centre and the State on 50:50 funds sharing basis. However, Union Territories are provided full Central Assistance.

Under the scheme, financial assistance is given for purchase of Modern Survey Equipments like Global Positioning System (GPS), EDM, Total Stations, Theodolites, Work Stations, Aerial Survey, Office equipments like photocopies, Laminating Machines and basic facilities to improve work efficiency of lower staff of the Revenue Departments, construction of Office-cum-residence of *Patwaries* construction/repair/renovation of Training Institutes and equipments for training, etc. Financial assistance of Rs. 265.97 crore has been provided to the State Governments/UTs up to 31st March, 2004 towards central share under the scheme. The utilization of the funds reported by the State/UTs is Rs. 170.31 crore which is approximately 64 per cent of the total funds released.

Monitoring and Evaluation

The government lays great emphasis on monitoring and evaluation of all rural development programmes being implemented in various States/UTs. The monitoring mechanism includes; *inter alia*, the Performance Review Committee, the Area Officer Scheme, Periodic Progress Reports, Audit and Utilization Certificates, Video Conferencing and Field Visits. The government conducts quick evaluation/concurrent evaluation of all major programmes. States/UTs have been advised to reconstitute vigilance and Monitoring Committee at state and districtlevels to monitor the implementation of programmes and introduce greater transparency in the same. These committees, *interalia*, include MPs/MLA, representatives of Panchayati Raj Institutions and NGOs.

In order to strengthen the monitoring mechanism, the government has prepared a panel of National Level Monitors by involving ex-serviceman and retired civil servants to monitor and furnish periodic reports on the implementation of programmes in selected districts.

A system of District Level Monitoring also has been put in place in selected districts of the country through independent locally based institutions for physical verification of assets created under various rural development programmes and ensuring transparency in programme implementation.

Social Structure and Rural Development in the Context of Globalization

Rural India now contains 72 per cent of the population, and some 70 per cent of the labour force is engaged in agriculture. Despite the land reforms of late 1940s and early 1980s, the distribution of land ownership in rural India has been grossly unequal. In the early 1970s, over 96 per cent of India's household owned less than 20 acres of land; 43 per cent owned less than 5 acres; and 24 per cent owned no land at all with the percentage of landless labour increasing. The disparities in land ownership are revealed in the fact that 10 per cent of the rural families hold 70 per cent of the cultivable land.

As has been indicated earlier, the social structure in India consists of powerful status groups based on religions, castes and language. Although a class system has also begun to emerge in India, it still remains tenuous. The slow process of industrialization and urbanization had led to a highly uneven pattern of class-growth. Status group continues to cut across class lines. As a result, the development of class identities and political mobilization based upon class appeals has been securely inhibited. India's urban based class structure is small compared to the rural society. The 15 million industrial workers in the organized sector of the economy make up only 10 per cent of the total workforce of 150 million. Of these, only 3 per cent, or 5 million, work in large modern factories. The industrial workforce moreover is not only small, but its portion of the total labour force has also remained remarkably stable over the past several decades.

In comparison to this the size of the urban population represents a consumer market larger than the entire European Union. These changes in the rural/urban population and the merging class structure have meant the evolution of new administrative policies, strategies and institutions. In the past forty years, there has been a proliferation of a number of administrative institutions, authorities and agencies both at the centre as well as states to cater to the strategies of integrated rural development, and the needs of growing urban metropolises, incredibly crowded, lacking in adequate housing, transportation, water and electricity sewage and sanitation facilities. The administrative strategies evolved have ranged from technological and scientific innovations in the field of agriculture production to the establishment of institutions of democratic decentralization and a host of specified agencies for regulating industrial development, large, medium and small scale and a host of institutions for providing a number of services for good urban life have come into operation. Because of a growing concern for environmental degradation a number of regulatory agencies have come into being to protect the environment from further degradation, although with little success. All these developments have further meant a keen political competitions among various segmented social groups and cultural communities based on language, religion, region and caste, creating additional pressures on the administrative systems. The existence of a number of multifarious agencies with conflicting and overlapping jurisdiction have not only highlighted the problems of unified direction, control and coordination, but have also raised afresh the basic issue of centralization and the relative autonomy of various units of administration.

In the Era of liberalization

The Government of India has adopted policies of globalization, liberalization and market economy in the wake of the serious economic crisis owing to a steady decline in exports, negative growth rates in industry and agriculture, and 0.3 per cent decline in the domestic production of crude oil. Among the long-term domestic factors contributing to high cost and low productivity were: (a) the inadequate returns and continuing losses from the massive investments in the public sector undertaking, and (b) economic populism resulting in increasing state subsidies, especially in fertilizers and writing off loans to farmers and hidden payments incurred through lower tariff rates of state undertakings in power and transport sectors.

India's adoption of a programme of globalization, market economy and competitiveness came after more than six months of negotiations with the World Bank starting in January 1991. The package of reforms measures announced by the newly installed Narasimha Rao Government in July 1991 consisted of two separate economic policies: (a) a macro-economic stabilization programme (IMF Inspired) essentially focus on reducing the twin deficits on the balance of payment and on the state budget, and (b) a comprehensive programme for structural change of the economy (World Bank Inspired) in the fields of trade, industry, foreign investments, public sector and the financial sector among others.

'Globalization', 'competitiveness' and liberalization' come to India as a booster, and through the back door of "economic reforms". The sanctity of economic reforms had been derived from it. It was argued that progress is taking place through globalization, and economic reforms are the only means to join in this process. Hence, economic reforms are the only alternative for human security and India's future. Globalization as a phenomenon involves two different entries (a) finance capital through multi-national corporations and (b) new technologies such as computers and telecommunications. It was argued that the growth and internationalization of finance capital is good and desirable for projects because it promotes growth of technology. Globalization provides a useful means to develop technology necessary for the production of goods and services that improve our well-being.

The post-1991 economic reforms were initially launched under compelling balance of payments crisis. At the same time it was felt that by adopted market-oriented and globally competitive restructuring policies somewhat similar to those of Southeast Asian countries, the Indian economy could grow much faster and become more self-reliant in managing its balance of payments and could at the same time speedily accelerate growth and reduce the level of poverty, thus contributing to human security including freedom from hunger, disease, ignorance, unemployment and homelessness.

The Pre-reform (1991) Scenario

The Structural Adjustment Policy (SAP) and economic reforms were introduced in the Indian polity at a time when the domestic inflation raged at an annual rate of 17 per cent. The growth rate of Gross Domestic Product (GDP) in 1991-92 stood at 0.6 per cent. The industrial sector also showed the same growth rate, while the index number of agricultural production had declined from 148.4 in 1990-91 to 145.5 in 1991-92 with foodgrains production declining from 176.4 million tonnes in the previous year to 168.4 million tonnes. In the view of the fast deteriorating economic situation the fight of capital had started from the country. This resulted in a severe Balance Of Payment (BOP) crisis, the foreign exchange reserve touching the bottom line of $ 1 billion – from 4.4 months of inputs to 1.1 months in 1990-91 to attain that growth and to reduce poverty on a sustainable basis, a series of measures have since been undertaken to bring back the macro-economic balance of the economic and to initiate the necessary structure adjustment programme for improving efficiency in resource use. In this perspective, the emphasis in policy objectives has shifted to higher 'growth', with the expectation that higher growth will automatically percolate as benefits to the poor.

Reform Package

The New Industrial Policy of 24th July, 1991 spelled out the process of liberalization. It stated that foreign investment and technology collaboration was welcomed to obtain higher technology to increase export and to expand the production base. The number of industries reserved for the public sector was reduced to only eight, and compulsory industrial licensing was restricted for only eighteen industries. The policy indicated the need for more dynamic relationship between domestic and foreign industry than before in terms of technology and investment. The direct approval of investment up to 51 per cent of foreign equity in high priority industries was made without any bottleneck. Liberalized Exchange Rate Management System was evolved to help in the free working in the foreign exchange market and secure convertibility of the rupee. Coupled with changes in industrial licensing, the financial and banking sectors were also revamped. The directional paper of the Planning Commission (1991) had clearly indicated that the public sector should make investments of an infrastructural nature in areas were private participation is not likely to come quickly, but it should withdraw from areas were no public purpose is served by its presence. The paper stated that in large part of public sector operations, where commodities or services are produced and distributed, unless it is necessarily for protecting the poorest in society, the main operating principle should be that of the market economy.

The Role of the State

In the context of the new economic policy in operation since mid-1991, a controversial question that has often been raised is about the role of the state. State is not only required to achieve a balance between the functions of security, equity, ecology, development and safety, but also to provide an equilibrium between stability and growth. It is wrong to assume that under liberalization, the state folds up. The rolling back of the state on the economic issues necessitates a re-defining of its new role and a re-examination of its structures and process it may no longer remains to be the owner of strategic industries, but it is still a regulator – a pro-consumer regulator that oversees and prevents the abuse of the market and to provide the legal, physical and human infrastructure. It has to concentrate on 'Development dynamics' that would benefit primarily the poor and the disadvantaged.

To Protect the Living Standard of Poor

In order to protect the living standards of the poor during the transition period and provide for human society, the complimentary social measure reflecting india's commitment to good governance were also conceived to ensure equitable distribution of both the gains and costs of economic reforms. Since over half of india's population continued to live below the poverty line. A number of direct attacks on poverty were launched during 1980's. Prominent among these were special programme for backward areas, such as subsidized food supplies though a Public Distribution System (PDS), concessional loan schemes for marginal farmers and agricultural labourers, employment-oriented programmes sponsoring different employment schemes like Jawahar Rozgar Yojana (JRY), Nehru Rozgar Yojana (NRY), that are geared mainly towards urban housing improvement. After the introduction of the policy of globalization, market economy and liberalization, and despite the fiscal austerity, the government committed itself to increased outlay for clearly targeted social sector expenditure and rural development during the overall plan period 1992-97. In particular, employment creation and human capital development in rural India through (both Poverty Alleviation Programme [PAP] and Social Services, such as primary health care, elementary education and rural water supply-cum sanitation) were to be expanded and broadened. However, constraints on budgetary resources forced the government to postpone the provision of extra-funds for those programmes, and on the contrary to curtail them along with all other public expenditures. However, in February 1992, a National Renewal Fund (NRF), meant to provide assistance to workers who would become redundant as a result of the adjustment programme was created. Together with the rural development and social sector programmes, NRF was intended to constitute a comprehensive and permanent Social Safety net, providing adequate shelter for those who would be temporarily affected by India's SAP.

Employment Generation for Poverty Alleviation

During the last one and a half decade, poverty alleviation and employment generation programmes which have been in operation of several years have been redesigned for generation of self-employment and wage employment of rural areas and restructured to improve their efficacy and impact on the poor. An outlay of Rs. 9650 crore has been provided in 1999-00 (BE) as against 9345 crore in 1998-99 (BE). The former Integrated Rural Development Programme (IRDP) and allied programmes such as training of rural youth for self-employment, Development of Women and Children in Rural Areas (DWCRA) and Million Wells Scheme (MWS) have been restructured into a single self-employment programme called the Swarnajayanti Gram Swarozgar Yojana (SSGY) from April 1999. Simultaneously, Jawahar Rozgar Yojana (JRY) has been restructured and streamlined with effect from April 1999 and has been renamed as Jawahar Gram Samridhi Yojana (JGSY). The other ongoing programmes include, National Social Assistance Programme (NSAP), Urban Employment and Anti-

Poverty Programme (UEPP). The Swarna Jayanti Sahakari Rozgar Yojana (SJSRY) has subsumed the earlier three urban poverty programmes viz. Nehru Rozgar Yojana (NRY), Urban Basic Service for the Poor (UBSP) and Prime Minister's Integrated Urban Poverty Alleviation Programme (PMIUPEP) and has become operative from December 1997.

Conclusion

The foregoing analysis provides a summary of the various measures taken by the government in the field of rural development. Despite the serious commitment on the part of the government, the benefits of the programmes do not seem to reach the indented targets and they fail to serve fully the purpose for which they were launched. It has been observed that, more often than not, the rural development programmes are implemented without testing their local suitability. Theoretical perfection of a scheme is regarded as the criterion for the soundness of a programme, which should not be the case. Factors such as psychological receptivity, local conditions and constraints and lifestyle are often ignored while designing the rural development programmes.

Most of the rural development programmes, though indented for the poorest of the poor, have not full helped in alleviating their problems. There is a lacuna in the identification of the really poor, with the result that the rich farmers have benefited much more from these programmes. The programmes have, no doubt, generated a ray of hope for the underprivileged sections of society, but they have, as yet, not brought about a perceptible rise in the income of these sections. Further, some other programmes have succeeded only partially because of the low motivation level among the villages. The basic problem of being unable to arouse popular participation has plagued most of these programmes. Little wonder, most of the programmes did not affect the rural poor substantially. It was found that the village level workers, who ought to have worked as the rural animators, did not truly accomplish their role satisfactory. An impression exists that a VLW is of greater help to the rural elite than to the rural poor. A look at the rural development programmes will also show that some of them have been launched by various political leaders with only an inadequate understanding of the complexity of the problems faced by the rural poor. It appears that, sometimes, they were simply forcing the programmes down the villagers' throats. Programmes with catchy slogans have also been launched in a haphazard manner just before elections and, hence, have been implemented in a half-hearted way.

A number of programmes, such as the TRYSEM, JRY, DWCRA, etc., are employment-oriented. Yet, they hold little or no interest for the rural youth who perhaps feel that there is little future for traditional cottage industry. These programmes offer only manual jobs, whereas the youth today want opportunities that are gainful and yet decent. Some programmes also suffer because of lack of adequate trainers. The involvement of the rural poor in the process of rural development is low, particularly in the planning and implementation of such programmes. On the other hand, top-level planners and administrators, generally, have not held a 'correct' perspective of the values of traditional Indian society and, very often, they offer solution which do not have much bearing on the holistic development process in rural areas. For instance, a beneficiary may be supplied with a buffalo, but due to the poor water resources in the village or absence of a veterinary doctor, the animal may die. Or else, the villager may be forced to sell it. Involvement of beneficiaries can help in making programmes more realistic.

There are several cases of default on the part of the beneficiaries also. There have been cases when the beneficiaries, financed by a bank for buying an oil engine, sold the engine off without the permission of the bank. The concerned banks do not have adequate staff to monitor and provide after-case service to the beneficiaries. Hence, the process of recovery by banks, including taking legal action against the defaulter, must be made far effective.

A number of voluntary agencies are also involved in rural development. They are mostly dependent for their funds on the government those procedures are often slow and time-consuming, or on foreign donor agencies, whose grants may not be available on a regular basis. There is also lack of communication between the government and these agencies. As a result, the government funds may lapse because the agencies sometimes have no knowledge of these funds and when to avail themselves of them.

Financial institutions, chiefly the banks and cooperatives have a very crucial role to play in the success of the rural development programmes. It has been found in many cases that the loan sanctioned by the bank was inadequate and not timely, resulting in the diversion of funds for some other non-productive purposes. It was also found that some cooperative societies were charging the farmer more than the authorized interest rate. The banks also do not actively participate in the identification of the beneficiaries. They do not carry out pre-sanction inspection of the village before financing an activity. For instance, it has been found that, sometimes, an electric motor pumpset was financed without consideration of availability of electric power.

Regarding the involvement of the rural poor, all experiments in rural development including most of the present-day rural development schemes, emanate at the top. It is necessary that emphasis is laid on planning from the bottom and the exclusive reliance placed on the pyramidal structure approach has to be given up. Because of this approach to planning, the programmes also tend to have very high administrative costs. New technology, such as high yielding seeds, tractors, oil engines, etc., has no doubt been introduced in the agricultural and irrigation sectors, but it has helped the already rich farmers rather than the small and marginal farmers and agricultural labourers who have very little land to begin with. Had the measures of agricultural growth been preceded by land reforms, this problem could have been tackled more rationally.

And, lastly, the organizational dimension needs a reappraisal. With a number of models of rural development administration experimented with and applied over the last for decades and more, it is time that the respective efficacy of each was intensely examined. Since, the last one and a half decade, our general understanding of government and governance has been changing at a very fast pace. The forces of globalization, liberalization and the revolution in information technology have shattered many a myth hitherto held sacrosanct about the government and more specifically concerning its primary institution of governance in the public administration. No longer can governments afford to support, rigid, bureaucratic, reactive, rules driven administrative organizations. Rather, today's administrative system must be flexible, consultative, result-oriented and proactive-encouraging and supporting creativity and innovation from the bottom to the top in order to govern and provide services to the citizens at large. There has been a considerable rethinking the way the governments now conduct their business, and they are looking more and more towards innovative solution to respond to an increasing number of complex new environmental and global problems and pressure, which are further accentuated in a developing, multi-linguistic, and a multi-cultural country like ours having diversity of social and religious systems.

References

Biju, M.R., Gandhiji and Panchayati Raj, *Indian Communicator*, 5th October, 1995.

Chambers, Robert, *Rural Development: Putting the Last First, Longmans*, London, 1983.

Desai, Vasant, *Fundamentals of Rural Development : A Systems Approach*, Himalaya, Bombay, 1991

Government of India, India : 2005, A Reference Annual, Publications Division, New Delhi, 2006.

Haragopal, G and Sudharshanan, G, Liberalization Policy : Implication for Higher Education, *IJPA*, July-Sept: 1996

Hasnet, A. Hye, *Integrated Approach to Rural Development, Sterling*, New Delhi, 1986

Hooja, Rakesh, *Administrative Intervension in Rural Development*, Rawat, Jaipur, 1987

Jain, R.B., *Public Administration in India*, Deep and Deep, New Delhi, 2002

Jaiswal, N.K. and Kolte, N.V., *Development of Drought Prone Area Programmes*, N.I.R.D, Hyderabad, 1981

L.K. Tyagi and Rajesh Kumar, Rural Development in the New *Millenium, Kurukshetra*, February, 2000.

M.R. Biju Gandhiji and Panchayati Raj II, *Indian Communi-cator*, 6th October, 1996.

Maheswari, S.R., *Rural Development in India*, Sage, New Delhi, 1985

Mishra, S.N, Decentralized Planning for Rural Development, *Kurukshetra*, February, 2000.

Narain, *Iqbal, Panchayati Raj Administration in India, Laxmi Narain*, Agra, 1973.

Ramesh, K. Arora and Rajini Goyal, Indian Public Administration, Viswa Prakasham, Lucknow, 1996.

Sharma, S.K. and Malhotra, S.L., *Integrated Rural Development, Abhinav*, New Delhi, 1977

Singh, Manmohan, *Rural Development Administration and Anti-Poverty Programme*, Deep and Deep, New Delhi 1988

Sunder Raj, D., Peoples Participation in Rural Development, *Kurukshetra*, February, 2000.

Upadhyay, Yogesh and S.K. Singh, Rural Development - Gandhian View, *Kurukshetra*, May, 1999.

Vaidya, B.V, Some Aspects of Rural Development, *Kurukshetra*, April, 2002.

Varma, S.K., Rural Development Through Co-operatives, *Kurukshetra*, May, 1999.

Vijay, C.M., *Rural Development Administration in India, Pratiksha*, Jaipur, 1989.

5

Universal Service Policy in India : Theory and Practice

Archana G.Gulati

SECTION I

Background

India has seen the fruits of liberalization and effective regulation of telecommunications by way of the stupendous growth of this sector. This is obvious from the fact that while only 5 million telephone connections existed as on March 1999, as on March 2009 the country could boast of 429.72 million telephone connections. The most exciting development has been the Indian mobile revolution. What was hitherto a rich man's luxury item has become the poor man's basic lifeline connecting him to relatives, friends and employment opportunities. Today the mobile phone serves the common man as a safety net and aide to livelihood. Healthy competition combined with an enterprising and innovative private sector has placed India in the enviable position of being the world's second largest mobile market. Our huge billion plus population ensures that even so, there is plenty of scope for further growth. Today the Indian telecommunications sector has about five to eight operators already functioning in each telecom circle and still more licensees are awaiting spectrum allocation to commence services. While industry observers point out the inevitability of future mergers, acquisitions and market consolidation, there is no doubt that competition and multiplicity of players is a firmly established reality in the Indian telecom sector and one that is here to stay. The Universal Service (US) support policy of the Government of India is amongst the several excellent regulatory and policy measures adopted in the sphere of telecommunications. This article aims to delve into various aspects of Universal Service policy in India with the objective of highlighting both positive aspects and potential pitfalls. It looks at the theory and practice of prevailing methods of US provision and also a possible way forward.

Liberalization and Competition are Vital but not Enough

In the early days of telecommunications it used to be assumed that given this sector's need for huge, lumpy investments in the underlying networks (which only the public sector or big private sector companies could afford), and the large volumes needed to achieve minimal economies of scale as a proportion of the total market size, these networks constituted natural monopolies[1]. This assumption has been debunked by technological changes and the regulatory experience of the now developed nations. It has been now conclusively established that competitive provision of telecommunications services is not only possible, but is in fact the best alternative in order to ubiquitously serve entire populations, irrespective of income and location. A multiplicity of players ensures that the necessary investment in the underlying capital intensive networks is generated. Further, competition results in a much higher level of cost-efficiency, technological progress and innovation compared to the monopoly situation. This realisation has led many countries across the world to initiate telecommunications reforms by way of privatisation, liberalisation and regulated competition. As expected, these reforms have stimulated investment, ensured the modernisation of national telecommunications networks and resulted in the progressive extension of their reach by way of high quality, affordable services to increasingly larger proportions of their populations. Several countries have witnessed considerable success, especially in mobile communications. The sharp rise in mobile subscribers throughout the developing world has increased access, at least to voice services, to unprecedented levels. However, despite these promising gains, many rural areas throughout the developing world continue to remain un-served by any communications network, fixed line or mobile. Access to high-speed internet services also remains out of reach for most citizens of developing countries, especially in rural areas. Similarly, India which has undergone a veritable telecom revolution since the mid-nineties with the introduction of privatization and liberalization, has achieved an impressive growth in overall teledensity to 36.98 per cent as on March 2009.[2] This is made up of 37.96 million fixed lines and 391.76 million mobiles, taking total of telephony subscribers in country to 429.72 million. However, in spite of telecom reforms, our urban-rural telecommunication access gap has remained vast. Thus the urban teledensity as on 31st March, 2009 was as high as 88 per cent while rural teledensity was lagging at 15 per cent.[3] Such gaps in telecom access between developed and underdeveloped areas are seen across the world and typically arise on two accounts:

(A) Market Efficiency Gap

This gap denotes the current level of service penetration and the level achievable in a liberalized market, under suitable regulatory environment. It can be closed with a well known set of policy and regulatory measures such as introduction of competition, privatization, development of a transparent, non-discriminatory regulatory environment, creation of independent regulatory authorities capable of promoting a level playing field and enforcing service commitments of both incumbents and new operators alike. No direct public investment is required to close the market efficiency gap.

(B) Actual Access Gap

This gap continues to exist between urban and rural areas even under efficient market conditions, since a proportion of the population (relatively large in developing countries), cannot afford the market prices at which these services are normally offered. However, it must be borne in mind that people everywhere are willing to spend part of their income on telecommunications services. Across a wide range of developing and industrial countries, the percentage of income that is spent on telecommunications services typically varies from 1 to 3 per cent of GDP, and the worldwide average is 2.2 per cent. This share is not much smaller in rural areas, even in poor countries. In India, in spite of the existence of a booming mobile telecom industry, the second largest in the world, one is still confronted with very low rural teledensity. It is therefore clear that the liberalisation and competition alone will not solve the problem of lack of rural access. In order to close the Access Gap in challenging, uneconomic areas or to reach isolated poor customers, governments need to employ additional measures.

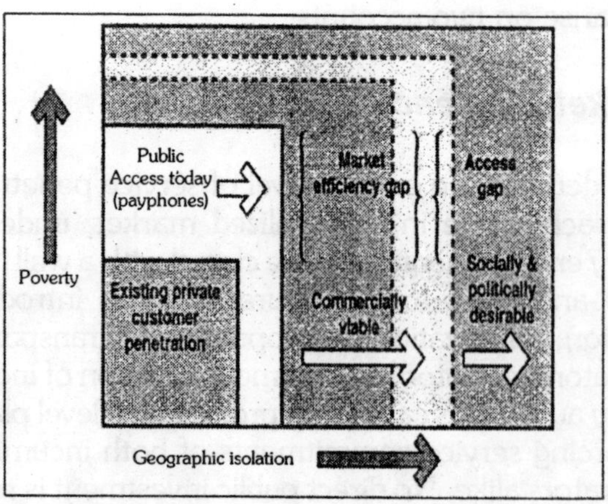

Fig. 5.1 : Pictorial Representation of Market Efficiency and Access Gaps[4]

The Concept of Universal Service

Apart from the higher capital cost of providing rural telephones, on account of distance/infrastructural constraints/difficult terrain, telecommunications services in rural/remote areas also generate lesser revenue due to lower population density and income levels. It is for this reason that normal market forces alone would not direct the private sector to serve backward and rural areas. Keeping in mind the inadequacy of market mechanism to serve rural and inaccessible areas on the one hand and the importance of providing the vital telecom connectivity on the other, most counties of the world have put in place policies to provide Universal Service. US may be defined as the long-term objective of making communications facilities available to every member of society on an individual or household basis. By some accounts, the term"Universal Service" was first used by Theodore Vail, the President of AT&T. In the 1910 Annual Report of the company, he described "Universal Service" by writing; "the telephone system should be universal, interdependent and intercommunicating, affording opportunity for any subscriber to any exchange to communicate with any other subscriber of any other exchange". In the more modern sense, US refers to having a phone and affordable phone service in every home. To be more legalistic, US means providing telecommunication service with access to a defined minimum service of specified quality to all users, everywhere, at an affordable price. The precise parameters for US are usually set by national law or regulation, or may be contained in the license of the dominant operator.The definition of US may include fax, phone booths, subscriber directories, emergency services or services for the handicapped as in developed countries. In Canada for e.g. definition of US includes individual line local service with touch tone dialling, provided by digital switch with capability to connect via low speed data transmission to the internet at local rates; enhanced calling features including access to emergency services, voice message relay services and privacy protection features; access to operator and directory assistance services, access to long distance network and a copy of current telephone directory.

Universal Service Obligation (USO)

USO is a term that refers to the burden, traditionally carried by an incumbent operator of providing services to all citizens of a country in a non-discriminatory manner, irrespective of the fact that some customers by virtue of their wealth, usage characteristics or location, might be easier and more profitable to serve than others. The USO might be defined as the cost of serving those customers whose monthly bills do not cover the cost of providing the service.

Methods of Financing Connectivity to Non-Remunerative Areas

US is generally funded world over by using the following methods:

(a) ***Mandatory Service Obligations.*** These are imposed by license conditions or other regulatory measures. This was tried in India with very little success. Under the National Telecom Policy, 1994, the government had made it mandatory for all private basic service operators to provide 10 per cent of all new lines in rural areas. A weightage of 15 per cent was given at the time of bid selection for service provision in rural areas. A penalty on a per day basis for each telephone not installed sought to prevent companies from delaying the meeting of rural targets. At the same time, the government encouraged new emerging technologies including local loop wireless, cellular telephony, and satellite-based communication systems that could help develop rural telecom in a cost-effective manner. Shockingly, against the targeted 10 per cent coverage in rural areas, as per the TRAI Report dated 3rd July, 2000, fixed service providers had provided only twelve village phones! They preferred to pay the penalty rather than engage in rural roll out and were able to get away from this onerous obligation very lightly[5]. Even operators who eventually fulfilled the statutory requirement of 10 per cent rural network did so by technically covering the area on the outskirts of the city, where villagers could seek a telephone by paying heavily for service charges. On the whole compliance was circumvented in various ways.

(b) ***Cross Subsidization*** between or within services provided by incumbent operators is another common method of financing US objectives. ILD and NLD services, for example, have traditionally been priced well above cost. Surplus revenues from these high priced services were intended to subsidise higher cost or lower margin services, particularly residential local access lines. This had been done by the incumbent service provider, BSNL, in India until the relatively recent rationalisation and lowering of ILD and NLD tariffs. World over cross subsidies between services are increasingly being viewed as impractical and anti-competitive. Further, with the opening up of markets to competition and falling international and long distance rates, this is no longer a viable source of funding universal access. Cross subsidies in any case are criticized as they promote inefficiency and depress demand for services. They also constitute a hidden form of taxation, which can be regressive. For example, poor migrant workers may have to pay high long distance rates. They have also not been found to be an effective tool to promote universality. They only subsidise all existing users, in areas with phones (urban) whether they can or cannot afford to pay full economic price and areas without telephones such as rural areas do not directly benefit from this form of subsidy. Developed countries are now tending to discard mechanisms of cross subsidies in tariffs and substitute them by the mechanism of Universal Service Funds that make for a more transparent allocation of subsidies and less distortion in markets, as well as facilitating clear identification of beneficiaries.

(c) ***Access Deficit Charges (ADC):*** paid by telecommunication operators to subsidise the access deficit of incumbents. An ADC is like a traditional cross subsidization regime, but modified to fit a competitive market. In an ADC regime, other operators pay subsidies (earlier on per minute of call basis in India) to finance the total cost of access deficit incurred by the incumbent (BSNL in India) in providing local services that are priced below cost. (Fixed line rental and call charges). ADCs have been criticized for being inefficient and potentially anti-competitive. In India ADCs were paid by mobile and unified access operators to fixed line operators and were progressively rationalized and reduced over a period of time. The result had been a substantial fall in NLD and ILD tariffs. Telecom Regulatory Authority of India (TRAI) has phased out ADC with effect from 1.4.08 except for a Rs 0.50 per call contribution from incoming ILD calls, which too stood terminated with effect from 1.10.08.

(d) ***Universal Service Funds*** collect revenues from a variety of sources. These could be government revenues, charges on interconnection services and levies on telecommunication services providers. In contrast to the other methods discussed above, Universal Service Funds are generally used to finance specific and targeted high cost areas and or low income subscribers. They can be used to efficiently provide a relatively small subsidy to motivate private operators to expand their services to otherwise uneconomic areas. They have the advantage of being an efficient and transparent mechanism of achieving universality in ICT access. They are generally administered independently from the incumbent operator and subsidies are normally used for specific schemes. They are based on the view that essentially all the participants in the market can and should take part in the collective effort to achieve universal access, since in theory they are all in a position to benefit as public networks expand. By the same token, no carrier should be expected to bear the risks and costs of US when its competitors are not similarly obligated. Distribution of universal service support may be via competitive bidding, allocation of funds to carriers who demonstrate ability to provide universal service or allocation of funds directly to end-users. These funds are committed to the notion that industry resources should be aimed as aggressively as possible at including previously ignored regions and populations within the scope of national ICT development. US Funds are not intended as a substitute for private market incentives and investments and should not interfere with competitive market forces. Nor are they inconsistent with other market-based measures to improve universal service/access, which may be implemented in parallel with other such measures.[6]

SECTION- II

USO in India

A reference to the Universal Service Obligation (USO) was first made in the National Telecom Policy, 1999 where it was mentioned that Universal Access Levy, as a percentage of the revenue earned by the operators under various licences would be imposed to raise resources for meeting the USO. The Universal Service Support Policy came into effect with effect from 1.4.2002. The universal service levy, which is at present, 5 per cent of adjusted gross revenue, is paid by all operators except value added service providers such as, voice mail. Statutory status to the Universal Service Obligation Fund (USOF) was given w.e.f. 1.4.2002 with the passing of the Indian Telegraph (Amendment) Act, 2003 on 9th January, 2004. Indian Telegraph (Amendment) Rules, 2004 governing the implementation of USOF were notified on 26th March, 2004. For the implementation of the US support policy the office of an Administrator USO fund has been instituted as an attatched Office of the Department of Telecommunications (DOT). Twenty-two Controller of Communication Accounts Offices of DOT performs state level monitoring of USOF activities and disbursement of Subsidy under USO. In the Indian Telegraph Act, USO is defined as the obligation to provide access to telegraph [telecommunications] services to people in the rural and remote areas at affordable and reasonable prices. Activities to be undertaken with the assistance from the USOF were identified and incorporated in the Indian Telegraph Rules. The Indian USOF India has one of the most comprehensive mandates compared to operational USO funds across the world.

The initial effort of the USOF Administration was directed towards tackling the need for public access to telephones by way of Village Public Telephones (VPTs) and Rural Community Phones (RCPs) and towards support for provision of household telephones (Rural Direct Exchange Lines or RDELs) in rural and remote areas. The USOF Administration develops benchmarks (or upper limit of subsidy) on the basis of studies carried out by it and telecom service providers were invited through open tenders to bid for providing these facilities. Through this process the lowest bidder was identified and agreements were entered into with the selected service provider(s) for carrying out the work. India is one of the few countries that have included broadband in its definition of Universal Service Obligation. This was done by an amendment in the Indian Telegraph Act and Rules in late 2006. This amendment allowed USOF to venture into a number of new areas beyond 'basic' telephony, such as, broadband, mobile services and general rural telecommunications infrastructure. Accordingly, the USOF immediately started working on number of new schemes through which it endeavours to bring the benefits of both voice and data connectivity to the rural population. These include :

A. ***The Shared Mobile Infrastructure Scheme.*** Under this scheme about 7,500 mobile infrastructure sites are being set up across about 2 lakh villages of the country. These sites are to be shared by three service providers to provide mobile services to rural population. There is a built in provision for accommodation of a fourth, broadband services operator, who is to be decided by USOF. On a similar basis another 10,000 towers are expected to be rolled out shortly by the USOF to cover another 1.5 lakh (approximately) villages.

B. ***The Rural Broadband Scheme:*** Under this scheme the USOF intends to leverage on existing infrastructure to provide access to broadband services to village schools, health centres, panchayats[7] and also individuals. The platforms for connectivity would include landline, satellite and the terrestrial wireless medium. An agreement has already been signed with BSNL for provision of broadband services to the villages falling in the coverage area of its approximately 28,000 rural wire line exchanges[8]. This scheme would create a capacity to serve about 18 lakh rural customers. In this scheme Customer Premises Equipment and Computer/Computing Devices are also being subsidised. In addition to these individual and institutional connections, the service provider has been assigned the task of rolling out at least one public access points or broadband kiosk from each of these exchanges. The idea is that these broadband kiosks will provide a range of e-services to the rural population, with access to locally relevant content. (This could include content developed by NGOs, business and government agencies). For this purpose the service provider will be free to adopt a franchise model assisted by a professional agency which would act as an aggregator of content. Underlying this model is the thinking that with the correct tie ups, the rural broadband kiosk, providing a mix of plain vanilla internet access and specialized flavour-full 'infotainment' could achieve good revenues in rural areas where individual connections may be relatively slow to take off. Similar agreements would be entered into with eligible private rural wire line service providers. Once the much awaited 3G and Broadband wireless spectrum auction takes place, USOF would be in a position to launch a similar scheme for wireless broadband. In the meanwhile at least the nation's existing rural wire line assets would be put to good use, providing public and private access to broadband facilities. Further, it is felt that the lessons learnt from the wire line based rural broadband kiosks would also help the USOF refine the scheme design, which would be beneficial for the planned roll out of rural broadband based on wireless technologies[9]. Provision of satellite based broadband services in areas where terrestrial means of broadband access are not possible is also under consideration. This is envisaged to be done by supporting BSNL to upgrade its infrastructure in the locations where they have already provided USOF supported public access (to voice) using Digital Satellite Phones. Again schools, health centres, *panchayats* and other government institutions in these areas would reap the benefits of broadband access and kiosks would be set up for the public, wherever viable.

C. ***Scheme for Optical Fibre Connectivity Augmentation*** : A critical component of effective connectivity is a high capacity backbone capable of high speed data transmission. Many rural mobile tower sites are forced to rely on microwave backhaul with its inherent limitations. Realizing that the lack of OFC backbone will hinder the growth of rural broadband, the USOF is soon to commence a scheme whereby the OFC networks between blocks and district headquarters will be provided /strengthened. The state of Assam has been taken up first and this project is expected to be followed by similar ones for other states and Union Territories in a phased manner. The infrastructure thus created would have the capacity to sustain future growth of broadband services and would be compulsorily shareable with other telecom service providers at discounted rates. It is hoped that this would create a favourable environment whereby the cheaply available high capacity backbone would spur the robust growth of a variety of affordable voice and broadband based services to residential, government and business users in rural areas. This in turn would offer a tremendous boost to the socio-economic development of these areas.

Thus it can be said that through a range complementary schemes for ICT connectivity USOF is aiming to create multiplatform access to rural voice and data services.

SECTION-III

TAKING STOCK OF ACHIEVEMENTS

Affordable Connectivity

The USO Fund has a number of ongoing schemes for the spread of rural telephony and broadband. Till date[10] around 5.58 lakh[11] VPTs, about 40,690 RCPs,[12] 63.82 lakh new RDELs[13] and about 109 lakh existing RDELs[14], have been supported from the Fund. There is also a scheme to replace old technology Multi Access Radio Relay (MARR) VPTs with reliable technology under which 1.83 lakh MARR VPTs have been replaced. Under the shared mobile infrastructure scheme where mobile towers are installed and shared by three mobile service providers with USOF support, a total of 5,666 towers have come up so far[15] and another 10,000 new towers are planned for Phase II of the scheme. The recently launched wire line broadband scheme has a target of subsidising about 9 lakh connections and 28,000 broadband kiosks while leading to capacity creation for 18 lakh rural broadband connections. In this scheme Customer Premises Equipment and Computer/ Computing Devices are also being subsidised.[16] Up to 31.3.09, there has been a total subsidy outflow of Rs. 7971.44 crore towards these USOF schemes.

Thus the issue of telecommunications connectivity is being tackled effectively by USOF. By mandating the sharing of USOF subsidized infrastructure and building in obligatory discounts on rental/leasing charges, such schemes make it possible for rural service providers to lower end-user charges in keeping with lower paying capacities of rural customers. Realizing the importance of innovation and new applications of existing technology in rural settings, USOF also supports pilot projects for rural and remote area technologies/applications. This includes pilots for new technologies such as micro BTS (Base Transceiver Station) or shared BTSs which would be particularly useful in the rural context.

Powering Connections

In India out of 5.93 lakh inhabited villages, fewer than 4.8 lakh villages have electricity. A village is considered electrified even if 10 per cent of the households have electricity[17]. Further the supply is more often than not restricted to a few hours a day. Recognizing that power is a major constraint in rural India, USOF has worked with the Ministry of New and Renewable Energy (MNRE) to initiate a project for solar powering of one lakh VPTs and for subsidizing installation of renewable energy installations in its shared mobile infrastructure sites on pilot basis. The possibility of including subsidised solar power installations as an option in future roll outs of USOF's shared mobile infrastructure schemes is under active consideration. Apart from saving on operating costs by way of diesel transportation and consumption, this option would also be environment friendly. The initial capital cost however seems to have deterred the large scale adoption of solar energy for BTSs, especially shared ones. Also, recognizing the power problem at the individual subscriber end, support for a pilot scheme for rural mobile charging stations is also under consideration. There is no doubt that more needs to be done to supply solar/renewable energy charging solutions to rural households. Without these, even the universal availability of phones or broadband connectivity in rural areas would not be very meaningful.

Creating and Connecting with Demand: Relevant Content

The growth of rural mobile telephony was initially driven by voice and now that sufficient volumes have been reached, a fair amount of content development is taking place even without subsidy support. However in case of broadband services, availability of relevant content has been recognized as a necessity for sufficient level of demand to be generated. The author has previously written about several efforts in this direction by government and private sector alike[18]. USOF schemes are also tackling this issue by encouraging tie ups between the service provider and content aggregators. Thus recognizing that relevant content in local languages is necessary to make rural broadband services meaningful, USOF has encouraged the adoption of a franchisee model in partnership with professional content aggregators for the subsidized broadband kiosks being rolled out by BSNL under USOF's wire line broadband scheme. Under its agreement with USOF, BSNL is to roll out about 28000 rural broadband kiosks within five years. These kiosks are meant for access to basic browsing and all types of commercial value added services (VAS) including entertainment, information, tele-education and tele-medicine. They are to be outfitted with facilities for video-chat and conferencing, printing and scanning and backup power supply.

USOF is also in talks with BSNL to undertake a possible pilot run of another content based scheme in Himachal Pradesh and Rajasthan. Under this scheme, coupled with subsidised broadband connections under its wire line broadband scheme, a secure device to be called the Rural Public Service Terminal would be offered to Self-Help Groups (SHGs). This device would enable them to sell banking, insurance and other financial services to rural customers for a fee with the help of a back end content aggregator and transaction facilitator. The device in question would also offer other VAS such as booking of railway, bus and airline tickets, mobile recharges and downloads and utility bill payments. The USOF scheme is aimed at women's SHGs as a gender empowerment initiative allowing these SHGs to supplement their means of livelihood through commissions earned on sale of online transactions. This device can also function as a mobile PCO. When combined with the National User ID initiative and increasing use of smart cards being planned by the Central Government, such ICT enabled secure access to online services would be a boon for both rural populations and the Government in its effort to reach out to and mainstream the former. The most significant service that this device can perhaps offer is financial inclusion. The Reserve Bank of India has in fact been vigorously propounding exactly such an interplay of ICT, local banks and SHGs to achieve much needed financial inclusion of rural populations. The idea behind RBI's stress on ICT enabled extension banking through its Lead Bank and Business Correspondent schemes is to allow the poor to open zero balance, no frill accounts with the help of mobile devices which provide biometric authentication and/or facilities to swipe smart cards. These devices access the government/bank servers at the back end through telecommunication infrastructure. This makes it possible to not only pay subsidies direct to beneficiaries but also to enable micro credit and insurance transactions.

Introspection—Learning from Past Schemes

USOF activities carried out since 2002 can serve to provide useful insights into implementation issues. These lessons serve as valuable guides to future policy and design of USO Schemes. For instance, public access schemes (VPTs and RCPs) have shown that organisation of subsidised activities along commercial lines is essential for ensuring provision of sustained services to end-users. In the absence of a commercial motive, the incentive to provide quality services is absent and this necessitates continuous monitoring to ensure service continuity and quality. Also, it is seen that awareness about USO schemes amongst target beneficiaries and effective grievance/feedback mechanisms are absolutely essential. Experience with USOF's individual access schemes suggests that subsidising and monitoring of a large number of individual connections is impractical and hence avoidable. Subsidising telecommunications coverage with minimum Quality of Service (QoS) criteria is a relatively better approach for USO support. Even if inevitable, individual connection based schemes should limit the per-connection subsidy outflow to a reasonable level needed to achieve business sustainability. In general past experience indicates that careful designing of schemes and absolute clarity about desired end results are important to ensure that objectives are achieved with minimum effort and time spent on monitoring. The idea should be to provide a smart subsidy[19] as incentive to service providers, thus seeding the area, after which USOF should be able to pull out. It is also seen that roll out periods should be appropriately shorter and earlier subsidy payout would be an additional inducement to operators. Sharing of created infrastructure should be mandated to the extent possible.

SECTION IV

FUTURE DIRECTION- CLARITY OF PURPOSE AND AVOIDING PITFALLS

It is clear from the relatively low rural teledensity and negligible rural broadband penetration that USOF has its work cut out. Rural telephony and broadband access are high on the agenda of the Indian Government. In the context of ICT as a tool for rural empowerment, the government has set a target of 40 per cent rural teledensity in the next five years and expanding broadband coverage to connect every panchayat to a broadband network in three years[20]. While chalking out a plan to move forward, it is necessary for USOF to think in big and bold terms about taking mobile services to smaller villages and ensuring universal access to broadband in all rural areas. However while planning careful thought should also be given to the impact of state supported schemes on the future development of the market. In the author's view every potential USOF scheme should be subject to a careful analysis to evaluate the impact on future demand and supply of services and hence long-term sustainability and growth of the relevant market in which the intervention is sought to be made. In this regard we could learn from the European Union(EU). In the EU, the concept of US is enshrined in law as a socio-economic equalizer and a tool in the hands of the State to promote equal access to e-communication services so as to ensure full participation in information society by all. It is recognised that the concept of US continues to be needed even in a competitive environment to take care of services, regions and sections of society which the market fails to serve adequately. Also apparent from the EU's regulatory framework *vis-a-vis* US are the underlying aims of balanced and vigorous development of the internal telecommunications market and protection of general and specific consumer interests across EU. The US Directive which incorporates these aims and is an integral part of EU's overall e-communications regulatory framework, is deliberately and specifically designed to promote US objectives without hindering competition or the healthy growth of the internal e-communications market. The US Directive thus religiously aims to avoid market distortions which would be discriminatory and harmful to effective competition in the e-communications sector and hence it's healthy development. Restrictions are therefore placed on the choice of activities to be supported ('minimum set'[21]), methods of implementation adopted (with respect to regulated tariffs, choice of service providers, transparency, non-discrimination and technological neutrality) and manner of funding (minimising competitive distortions and unfair burdens on any party). The scope of US is relatively modest and can be enlarged only under very specific conditions. The regulatory framework for US in the EU is thus quite stringent compared to other liberalised regimes of the developed world.[22] The concept of US as defined in EU complements rather than hampers competition and caters to those requirements which the market may fail to deliver[23].

It may be argued that as a developing country with about 27.5 per cent of population being below poverty line level[24] and with a rural teledensity of only 15 per cent, we cannot afford the luxury of pontificating about economic theory beyond a point. As communications are a vital means of mainstreaming the rural economy, we must address the vast digital divide urgently. Yet, it is important to bear in mind that whatever progress we have made thus far in telecommunications has been the result of sensible regulation and vigorous competition. These changes were often enforced while studiously ignoring criticism from conservative elements favouring the continuation of state monopolies and criticising policies that apparently favoured private sector firms[25]. To illustrate this argument let us take the case of rural landline telephony. In this area, the protective regulatory and policy interventions so far have led to a situation where the incumbent (BSNL) is practically the only provider of landline services in rural areas. BSNL offers the compulsory TRAI regulated below-cost tariff (in addition to others). In spite of concessional tariffs, the incumbent's rural wire lines have been declining steadily over the years[26]. As may be expected, below cost tariffs and high cost of wire line infrastructure have kept new players away from this market segment. Thus as on 31.3.09 only about 50,000 rural wire lines had been supplied by private players and this meagre coverage is limited to six states.[27]. The lack of competition has in turn held back the innovation and growth (that is so visible in the rural Indian mobile telephony segment), from similarly benefiting this segment. Rural wire lines were traditionally found in the houses of the upper crust in rural areas and in the absence of competition, not even their local clout was perhaps enough to ensure quality services. Wire lines in rural areas are difficult to maintain and frequent and prolonged faults have caused a steady switch over to wireless connectivity. The author has personally witnessed some improvement in customer services in the areas where USOF schemes brought in competition from subsidised fixed WLL phones. However, even this has not been able to arrest substitution of the incumbent's wire lines by wireless phones of competing service providers[28]. It is interesting to contemplate as to what may have happened if the wire line local loop had been unbundled and other service providers allowed to lease the rural wire line infrastructure from the incumbent. In the author's view this may have led to a healthier expansion of wire line telephony and DSL based broadband services in rural areas. What appears to be a policy decision against the incumbent's business interests may have actually helped it to realise much greater revenues from leasing lines to more aggressive and market savvy private players. It is anybody's guess whether this would have led to more investment towards expansion of the number of rural wire line exchanges by the incumbent and perhaps also eventually encouraged private sector investment in similar infrastructure. For example, in the U.K, since 2005 when the incumbent British Telecom was forced to unbundle the local loop, the broadband penetration has gone up from 37 to 68 per cent[29].

It is a widely acknowledged phenomenon that initially upon introduction of competition, new telecom players need to minimise risky and heavy investment by renting facilities from incumbents and after markets are sufficiently mature they tend to go in for investment towards creation of underlying infrastructure. Thus in telecommunications, service competition often tends to precede infrastructure competition and the best way to ensure sustainable growth, is for government intervention to recognise and assist this process. This is in fact being done in the case of the USOF's present approach to augmentation and creation of rural intra district OFC networks. The USOF Scheme for Assam, the first state[30] to be taken up for the project, envisages Capex subsidy towards creation of a high capacity intra district OFC network by the winning bidder which shall be compulsorily shared with other service providers at concessional rates (in relation to TRAI ceilings for various distance and capacity slabs). It is hoped that the availability of bandwidth at discounted rates will encourage the proliferation in the supply of affordable voice and data services in rural Assam as various telecommunication and application service providers step in to take advantage of the available infrastructure. In Scandinavian countries and Netherlands such open access models have been successful in bringing new competition and services to the people[31]. However, incumbent operators would if allowed tend to resist open access programmes which bring in their wake either service or infrastructural competition that threaten their monopoly position. In the American context, the open access angle seems to have kept big players such as AT&T, Times Warner Cable, etc. from applying for funding under the Government's recent economic stimulus related broadband initiatives[32]. The foregoing discussion would make it apparent that when considering subsidy support, the underlying theoretical analysis is very important and ignoring it would be at the peril of sustainable development of the rural telecommunications sector. It should certainly not be the aim of any USOF policy to fund schemes that lead to a system of service provision that is perpetually dependant on state support.

Another unfortunate trend in Indian developmental history which is now increasingly under critical re-evaluation is the stress on budgetary allocations rather than outcomes. In particular, there is a lot of impatience with Indian USOF for its disbursements not keeping up with accumulation of Universal service levies. At times, this translates into industry demands for methods and areas of funding that would lead to short-term gains for them but would not bring about sustainable growth of rural ICT. While criticism for not achieving universal coverage faster deserves consideration, just concentrating on budgetary allocations and disbursements, without commensurate outcomes on ground would not serve the nation. In the author's view, every USOF scheme must be meticulously designed to maximise outcomes in terms of universal service objectives and also ensure maximum socio-economic returns on Government and private sector investment. The reverse bidding approach generally followed by the Indian USOF to select Universal Service Providers (USPs) and to arrive at subsidy rates at which they will implement USOF schemes in rural areas, has been widely appreciated for its transparency and recently praised for its 'elegance' in The Economist[33]. Interestingly this praise has been recorded in the context of criticism of the American US programme for its bureaucratic working and its inability to achieve a better broadband penetration compared to other OECD countries. It is possible of course that tendering may at times not be feasible (e.g. where there are too few market players to lead to meaningful bidding and price discovery) or economical (e.g. in case of small project size and funding as in pilot studies). In such cases it may at times become necessary to offer a judiciously worked out subsidy rate to the USPs who meet eligibility criteria. Whatever be the manner of arriving at subsidy rates, US funding must be in any case be carefully planned to cost-effectively maximise positive impacts, to avoid competitive and market distortions and to ensure transparency.

Pressing Practical Matters

Once 3G and Broad Wireless Access (BWA) spectrum auctions are completed and wireless broadband becomes possible, USOF is expected to launch its wireless broadband subsidy scheme. While it is amply clear that initially the way forward for widespread rural broadband access is through the wireless medium, the experience of developed nations with successful wireless broadband roll outs suggests that eventually for high speed multi-media connectivity, investment in fibre networks is imperative. Thus clearly taking fibre to the larger villages has to be a priority area for USOF. Apart from the gap filling approach already being taken (as described above) encouraging the sharing of existing rural fibre networks through open access at discounted rates is also very important. TRAI in its recommendations on 'Growth of Telecom services in rural India-The Way Forward' dated October 3, 2005 had proposed that it be mandated that those who own optic fibre connectivity in rural/remote areas, must provide leased lines to others. These facility owners/service providers could be provided subsidy through the USO fund, possibly to the extent of covering 30 per cent discount on specified ceiling. Thus bandwidth users shall get a discount of 30 per cent on the ceiling specified by TRAI. It was further proposed that bandwidth owners should also get an incentive of 10 per cent on the ceiling tariffs specified by TRAI from USOF as an incentive for necessarily providing leased line. Thus the bandwidth owners would not only get the reimbursement of 30 per cent discount which is being offered to the other operators in rural areas but also a 10 per cent incentive on top of specified ceiling tariff. This is a good suggestion but perhaps requires some work from TRAI itself to rationalize its ceilings which have not been reviewed since 2005 and to come out with a more up to date ceilings and sharing formulae.

Ensuring the Desired Outcomes of Connectivity

It is interesting to observe that in the United States where Universal Service programmes have a much longer history, there is a vigorous ongoing debate on need for and methods of measurement of outcomes to justify and improve Universal Service funding. The basis of this argument can be understood from the following figure [34]:

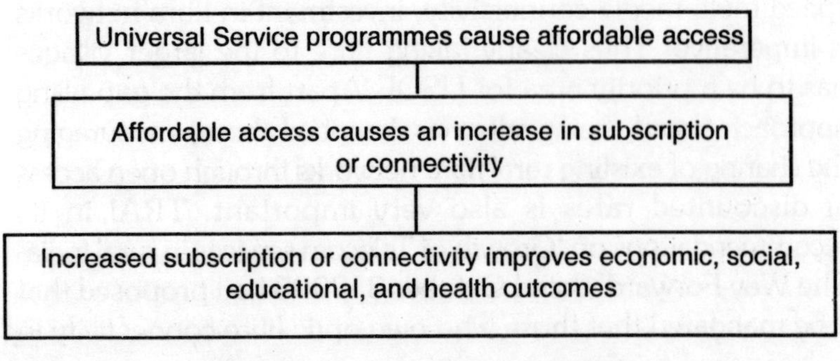

Fig. 2 : Desired Outcome of US Programmes

Thus it needs to be appreciated that connectivity is not an end in itself but that through universal connectivity it is hoped to bring economic, social, educational and health benefits to the rural population. In The U.S.A. Universal Service programmes such E-Rate[35] are specifically designed to achieve such objectives. It is unanimously accepted that apart from infrastructure creation which by itself will achieve very little, one has to address the real triggers of the multiplier effects of broadband connectivity. These are the useful applications that ride on the subsidised telephone/broadband infrastructure to bring about socio-economic development and political inclusion of the thus connected populations. The idea is to use ICT as the medium to reach the populations in rural and remote areas and enrich their lives through economic, social and welfare services that their physical/economic isolation normally deprive them of. Some may argue that for a developing country the focus should first be on universal connectivity and the rest may be tackled subsequently. In the author's opinion however, India must embark on a programme of not only rural connectivity but also its concurrent and urgent exploitation to quickly reach out and mainstream the populations of rural and remote areas. This requires multi-sectoral and cross-sectoral thinking and an unprecedented level of coordination of efforts from the Government and industry as opposed to the present tendency to plan in silos and to guard one's turf. The Department's of IT, Ministries of Human Resource Development, Rural Development, Women and Child Development, Panchayati Raj, Health and Family Welfare, etc. need to work together so that maximum utility is derived from the Government's spending on developmental schemes through mutual coordination and leveraging each others programmes. There would for example be little use of subsidised broadband for schools, heath centres and panchayats unless committed and trained computer literate teachers, health care providers and officials are able to access useful content and facilitate the use of the same by the rural population. In the author's interactions with teachers and private entities involved in education including software development for education, it was found that there is a heartening level of enthusiasm when it comes to tapping into ICT to progress rural education. However, the required capacity building and coordination amongst various government agencies is a very difficult task in India, more so in the more backward states. Even in U.S.A. studies have shown that the E-Rate programme is less effective in the poorer, more disadvantaged states. This is attributed to the lack of essential supporting capacities such as teacher training, technical support and relevant content required to make use of internet to improve education in such states[36]. It is not surprising therefore that the Government is opting for mission mode implementation of important national projects. These missions are increasingly headed by renowned experts rather than bureaucrats. This is perhaps a fall out of the acknowledged difficulty of coordinating efforts of the myriad of public and private agencies involved in such programmes.

Universal Service Obligation Fund (USOF) could also consider encouraging content development more directly. One way could be to use the Swiss Challenge route to identify good commercial broadband content applications. These would need to be rural specific and largely multi-media based in keeping with low literacy levels of rural India. Once USOF has a basic content package in place to serve as a minimal template (combination of information and entertainment, tie up with health education, micro finance institutions etc.), it could empanel content providers/aggregators that provide these services in regional languages. It could then make subsidy for content a part and parcel of service provision by way of both mobile and fixed telephony /broadband schemes. For example all USOF subsidised public access tele-centres would provide at least a minimal suite of services including e-education, e-medicine, einfotainment and financial services. Similarly, initial mobile/broadband connections given from subsidised infrastructure could have a subsidised content suite bundled compulsorily to add value for the rural subscribers. This would have the added advantage of spurring demand and increasing viability in otherwise sparsely populated, low income markets.

Affordability and the Target Beneficiary

One of the problems with respect to Universal Service or for that matter any subsidy programme that commonly troubles policy makers is the channelization of benefits to the genuinely needy. For example on the one hand we know that not every rural dweller in India is disadvantaged and in need of subsidised telephone connectivity. Yet on the other hand we must accept that a large number of rural folk may not be able to afford even the subsidised market prices of access. It is important for USOF to focus on the really needy segments of rural population who cannot afford services even when universal infrastructural coverage has been addressed and to provide a better package of services involving a greater amount of subsidization for them. In the U.S.A. there are two programmes specifically targeted at low income users. These are the 'Lifeline' programmes and the 'Link up' programme[37]. In India too it is being recognized that certain sections of the population will not be able to afford commercially determined tariff packages even when the underlying infrastructure is subsidised. This segment actually needs the livelihood enhancing connectivity and bundled content the most. In the Indian context however one must beware of the fact that most targeted subsidy programmes are fraught with problems of ensuring correct identification of beneficiaries and preventing misappropriation. The direct subsidy approach, though needed, presents onerous and daunting implementation issues. While initiatives such as the National Unique Identification Number scheme would eventually make such targeted subsidy models workable and leak proof, in the meanwhile the best one can do is to rely on low tariff, minimum usage plans as a proxy method for reaching the targeted population. This is done in the U.K. whereas Universal Service providers, BT and Kingston have to ensure that customers can afford telephone service. This is achieved through special tariff schemes aimed at customers on low incomes. BT's existing schemes, Light User Scheme (LUS) and In Contact — use a proxy of low usage in order to attract low income customers. It has been found that around 60 per cent of users are in fact from low-income households[38]. The Indian USOF's Wire line Broadband scheme adopts a somewhat similar approach by encouraging the provision of two low download but very affordable broadband packages named as USOF tariff plans. In the long run, USOF schemes could possibly incorporate a provision for prepaid coupons with a substantially subsidised, but low talk value service bundle with an inbuilt regionally relevant VAS content suite targeted at Below Poverty Line (BPL) families. A poor illiterate farmer could use this service suite to receive nominally priced market, agriculture and weather related daily voice updates and free e-Government (services, health, education micro-credit etc.) and other state sponsored applications including broadcasts about relevant government schemes. He would of course be able to increase talk time and access additional infotainment services, by paying more. However, this way, at least the basic service suite with its potential to transform the lives of hitherto unconnected masses starved of essential infrastructure would be made both available and affordable. Also very important is the fact that through this channel the Government can now reach the needy segments to solicit grass root level feedback on schemes. Imagine a scenario where apart from names and addresses the muster rolls in the NREGs scheme also contains each beneficiary's mobile numbers. Now monitoring would simply require a phone call to a randomly selected sample to establish the ground level working of the scheme. A comparable approach allowing prepaid access to broadband services from the local USOF subsidized broadband kiosks for target beneficiaries would truly empower the target population. Eventually Indian USOF would also need to think about incorporating added facilities such as compulsory access to location based emergency services and special services for the handicapped within the definition of Universal Service. The inclusion of connectivity programmes for the unconnected urban poor is also something which may be considered in time.

Conclusion

USO Funds become essential even in well developed nations with fully liberalized and mature telecom sectors in order to step in and bridge access gaps in areas where markets have failed. While it has done excellent work since its conception in 2003, the USOF of India still has a long way to go before it can fulfil its mandate of fully connecting rural and remote India. When chalking out a plan for future schemes it is important for USOF to avoid any unintended negative impact through introduction of competitive distortions which would impede the healthy growth and long term sustainability of rural telecommunications. It is also essential to keep a close eye on whether the desired socio-economic objectives of universal connectivity are being achieved. This requires the undeniably tricky task of close coordination with other Government departments so that connectivity is also supported by complementing content and the essential capacities of stakeholders to fully realize the potential of ICT to bridge the digital divide and thus ensure inclusive growth. Going forward, targeted subsidies may be necessary to reach out to the especially disadvantaged sections in a cost-effective manner. The eventual expansion of the definition of US to include special services and unconnected urban populations also merits consideration.

NOTES

1. Where only a single firm would be viable.
2. Source: *http://www.trai.gov.in/WriteReadData/trai/upload/Press Releases/671/pr21apr09no38*. Statistics as on 31.3.09.
3. CMIE Cell, DOT HQ.

4. Source:community.telecentr.*org/en-tc/wiki/two_gap_model.*
5. Jain R, " Review of the Indian Telecom Sector", chapter 8, India Infrastructure Report 2001.
6. Gulati Archana,G, Quest for Rural Telephony: Challenges and Choices, *Journal of Indian Institute of Public Administration*, July-Sept 2006 Issue.
7. Village level local Government office.
8. BSNL owns 99.5 per cent of the country's rural wire line network.
9. This will be possible after 3G/BWA spectrum auctions and allocations are completed.
10. As on 30.4.09 (source: Telecom Live, July 2009).
11. A lakh is 0.1 million.
12. VPTs and RCPs are public access telephones.
13. Installed after 1.4.05.
14. Installed before 1.4.05.
15. The target is 74440 towers which is likely to be achieved this year.
16. For more details visit www.dot.gov.in.
17. Venugopal K,'Running out of charge', *Business Line*, 11th February, 2009.
18. See Gualti Archana, G 'Broadband Services for Rural India-Connectivity and Content,', *Kurukshetra*, April 2009 and Planning for Rural Broadband Coverage-The ultimate bridge across the rural urban digital divide, Management in Government, July-September 2008.
19. The amount of money required by an operator to bring loss-making services to an acceptable rate of return over the long term.
20. President of India's speech to the joint session of the Parliament on June 4, 2009.
21 The minimum set of services of specified quality to which all end-user have access [independent of their geographic location], at an affordable price in the light of specific national conditions without distorting competitions' includes access at a fixed location for making and receiving local, national and international telephone calls and fax communications, and data communications at data rates that are sufficient to permit functional internet access; availability of at least one comprehensive directory and directory enquiry service

comprising all fixed and mobile subscribers who wish to be included; availability of public payphones; [with the possibility of making free emergency calls to the single European emergency call number 112] specific measures ensuring access and affordability of publicly available telephone services to users with disabilities or special needs, and those on low incomes.

22. For example, in USA under the 1996 Act, US is relatively rather loosely defined to include 'an evolving level of support-in short, as technological possibilities expand, so too, will the nation's US commitment.' It includes *inter alia* 'providing access to advanced services in all regions' and in particular to 'schools classrooms, libraries and health care providers.' The federal and state support mechanisms are required to be 'predictable, specific and sufficient' apart from ensuring 'competitive neutrality.' (*Source* : Benjamin, Lichtman, Shelanski and Weiser, Telecommunication Law and Policy, Second Edition, Carolina Academic Press, p-864.) In practice, the implementation of US in USA has resulted in a complicated set of programmes often criticised for leakages and raising concerns about their burgeoning financial implications.
23. Apart from activities falling under US, for promoting the spread of ICT to rural areas , national government's may support rural ICT projects through state aid (from general taxation rather than US funding) .The EU's state aid rules allow for public funding of such projects as long as the schemes are well-justified and proportionate to the remedy, there is a well-defined market failure necessitating state aid and they meet with other criteria for state aid including transparency, non-discrimination towards any product/service, technology or service provider and they do not cause market distortions.
24. Figures for 2004-05 as per Economic Survey of India, 2008-09.
25. For example, the introduction of Universal Access Service licenses in 2003 (allowing service providers to provide both fixed and mobile connectivity), had created a hue and cry on similar grounds. The Telecommunications Regulatory Authority of India (TRAI) and the courts had to find a balance between promoting service penetration and ensuring a level playing field among operators. This (then) controversial move has nevertheless undoubtedly been one of the factors involved in making the

Indian telecommunication success story possible.(Refer http://www.ictregulationtoolkit.org/en/PracticeNote.891.html).

26. In the year 2008-09 BSNL's rural wire lines declined by 100,0000 connections(*Source*: CMIE Cell DOT).
27. *Source*: CMIE Cell, DOT HQ.
28. The USOF's new wire line broadband scheme has however at least leveraged on this national asset to ensure that it is channelized into broadband for rural users. In the six months since its inception BSNL has added about 40,000 subsidised low tariff connections under the scheme. The scheme is also open to eligible private players.
29. Carol Wilson, 'Incumbents don't warm to stimulus funding' August 17, 2009 posted on Telephony online.
30. The state of Assam is a part of the relatively less developed and insurgency prone North Eastern belt.
31. Supra note 27. See also note 17
32. *Ibid.*
33. *The Economist*, August 15-21 2009.(This was with specific reference to the shared mobile infrastructure scheme.)
34. Public Interest Reply Comment on Comprehensive Review of Universal Service Fund Management and Oversight, Mecantus Centre, George Mason University, WC Docket No. 05-195
35. E-rate is a programme that allows rural schools and libraries to purchase telecommunications services and internet connections at a discount (20-90% depending on the degree of poverty and high cost of the population served) .Rural health care providers are also allowed certain discounted internet services. (*Source*: Telecommunication Law and Policy, 2nd Edition, Carolina Academic press)
36. Telecommunications Policy 28(2004) 227-232, www.sciencedirect.com.
37. The Lifeline and Link-Up Programmes are available to qualifying consumers in every state, territory, and commonwealth. Eligibility criteria vary by state. States that have their own Lifeline programme may have their own criteria. For states that rely solely on the federal Lifeline and Link-Up programme eligibility criteria, subscribers must either have an income that is at or below 135 per cent of the federal Poverty Guidelines, or participate in one of the following assistance programmes: Medicaid, Food Stamps, Supplemental Security Income

(SSI),Federal Public Housing Assistance (Section 8),Low-Income Home Energy Assistance Programme (LIHEAP),Temporary Assistance to Needy Families (TANF), orThe National School Lunch Programme's Free Lunch Programme. Residents of Native American Indian and Alaska Native tribal communities qualify for enhanced Lifeline and Link-Up support if they meet one of the criteria listed above, qualify under their state's Lifeline programme (if their state has its own Lifeline programme), or participate in one of the following assistance programmes: Bureau of Indian Affairs General Assistance, Tribally-Administered Temporary Assistance for Needy Families (TTANF), or Head Start (if income eligibility criteria are met).(*Source:* http://www.fcc.gov/cgb/consumerfacts/lllu.html)

38. http://www.ofcom.org.uk/consult/condocs/uso/uso_statement/

6

Panchayati Raj Institutions and Village Health Planning

Shankar Prinja, Sunder Lal, Amarjeet Singh
and *Ramesh Verma*

The National Family Welfare Programme in India underwent a paradigm shift in 1996 when it replaced method specific family planning targets with Target Free Approach, which was subsequently renamed more appropriately in 1997 as the Community Needs Assessment Approach (CNAA). Under this approach the Auxiliary Nurse Midwife (ANM) had to prepare annual action plans at subcentre level[1,2]. This involved estimation of their annual workload for each service delivery including contraception. Essentially, CNAA requires assessment of needs of community by the ANM for reproductive and child health services through consultation with eligible beneficiaries and community partners including members of Panchayati Raj Institutions (PRI)[3]. This approach indicates government's intention to decentralize the power by increasing the participation of the community partners including the *panchayats* in process of planning for health services starting from subcentre and village level. Apart from CNAA the Government of India has implemented National Maternity Benefit Scheme, Referral Transport Scheme (for referral of difficult delivery) and the recruitment of Accredited Social Health Activist (ASHA) through PRIs in various states [4].

Panchayats in India are an age old institution of elected representatives for governance at village level. In 1992, through the enactment of the 73rd Constitutional Amendment, Panchayati Raj Institutions (PRI) were strengthened as local government organizations with clear areas of jurisdiction, adequate power, authority and funds commensurate with responsibilities[5].

Panchayats have been assigned 29 rural development activities, including several, which are related to health and population stabilization. The XI schedule of the Constitution of India includes Family Welfare, Health and Sanitation, (including hospitals, primary health centres, and dispensaries,) and the XII schedule includes Public Health. Thus, the possible realm of influence of the Panchayats extends over a significant proportion of public health issues. The Gram Sabha (which includes the entire electorate of the village), has the potential to act as a community level accountability mechanism to ensure that the functions of the Village Panchayat in the area of public health and family welfare, actually respond to people's needs[6].

It is now over a decade since the constitutional amendments for PRIs were passed. Despite increasing policy articulation that decentralization is the cornerstone of planning, implementing and monitoring programmes for all social sectors including Health and Family Welfare, progress in involvement of PRIs in these activities has been uneven across various states. While fiscal devolution is a significant issue, lack of institutional modalities for PRI participation and variable capacity among PRIs are key lacunae[7].

Against this background it was decided to conduct an operational research with an objective to ascertain the nature and extent of consultation done by ANM with PRI members and to determine the factors affecting such consultation.

Material and Methods

Setting

There is a three tired system of Panchayati *Raj* Instistutions (PRIs) for decentralized and democratic governance in India. The electorate at the village level elect the *panches* (members of *panchayat*) and *sarpanch* (village headman/ chief of *panchayat*) of the *Gram Panchayat* which forms the first tier of Panchayati Raj Instistutions. There is a *Panchayat Samiti* at the block level which is constituted by the members elected by the electorate of the block. Each block has a BDPO (Block Development and Panchayat Officer) to serve as the representative of the district administration in rural area and serves as an extension and developmental executive at block level. At the district level is the Zila Parishad. The working of the Panchayat Samiti and Gram Panchayats is coordinated and administered by Zila Parishad. Various developmental works and projects at the rural level (Gram panchayat level) are run through Block offices.

The health care delivery system in India has evolved keeping in view the World Health Organization (WHO) goal of "Health for All by 2000" and the principles of Primary Health Care. The basic functional unit is a "subcentre" which is staffed by an Auxilliary Nurse Midwife (ANM) and a Multipurpose Health Worker male (MPHW) to provide reproductive and child health services and delivery of services under various national health programmes to a population of 5000 individuals. At a population of 20,000 to 30,000 is a Primary Health Centre (PHC) which provides preventive, curative and basic laboratory services by a doctor, besides a team of Multipurpose Health Supervisors (male and female), pharmacist and a laboratory technician to assist him. PHCs are equipped with facilities for selected surgical procedures (eg vasectomy, tubectomy, medical termination of pregnancy and minor surgical procedures). Community Health Centres (CHC) are located at block level over an approximate population of 80,000 to 1,20,000. It is proposed to provide specialist services of physician, gynecologist, surgeon and paediatrician at a CHC level.

Study Design and Sampling

This cross sectional study was done from June 2003 to September 2003 in Haryana. District Rohtak was purposively chosen. Under the system of Primary Health Care, Rohtak has 5 Community Health Centres (CHC), 30 Primary Health Centres, and 113 subcentres to provide comprehensive reproductive and child health services to the population at large. Functional subcentres, having both male and female (ANM) multipurpose health workers in position continuously since 1996-97 were considered for the study. Of these 41 functional subcentres, 30 subcentres were selected by stratified random sampling to include equal number of six subcentres from each of the five community development blocks of Rohtak.

A list of sarpanches/ village headmen/ chief of Panchayat (if more than one Gram Panchayat in the subcentre jurisdiction), and panchayat committee members/ panches was prepared for each subcentre individually. Using this sampling frame, one sarpanch and four panchayat members (two each, male and female) were selected by simple random sampling in each subcentre area. This constituted a total sample size of 150 PRI members (30 sarpanch and 120 panchayat committee members/panches) and 30 ANMs who were interviewed with the help of semi-structured, pre-tested interview schedule.

Informal discussions were held separately with 10 PHC Medical officers, 30 ANMs and 40 panchayat committee members to bring out the factors influencing the relationship and working of health department personnel and Panchayati Raj Institutions.

Informed consent was taken from all the participants. Data was analysed using the Epiinfo version 6.

Results

The present study was conducted in thirty subcentres of district Rohtak. The study participants included 30 sarpanches and 120 panchayat members/ *panches* (60 male and female panches each). Twenty-seven (90%) sarpanches and 101 (84.2%) panches selected belonged to subcentre village while the rest were from non-subcentre village which was under the service purview of the selected subcentre. The average population of the study subcentre was 5914.

The study revealed that sarpanches were contacted more frequently than the panchayat members by the ANM. Twenty eight (93.3%) sarpanches were contacted at least once during last six months as against 70 (58.3%) panches which was statistically significant (OR=10; OR 95 per cent CI=2.1-63.7) (Table 6.1). Four (57.2%) female sarpanches were contacted by the ANM thrice or more in past six months while only 8 (34.8%) male *sarpanches* were contacted as frequently which was however statistically not significant (OR=2.5; OR 95 per

Table 6.1: Frequency of Contacts Between ANM and PRIs in Last Six Months

Number of Contacts	*Sarpanch (n=30)*			*Panchayat Member (n=120)*			*Total PRI Members (n=150)*
	Male (n=23)	*Female (n=7)*	*Total (n=30)*	*Male (n=60)*	*Female (n=60)*	*Total (n=120)*	
0	2 (8.7)	0	2 (6.7)*	28 (46.7)	22 (36.7)	50 (41.7)*	52 (34.7)
1.	4 (17.4)	1 (14.2)	5 (16.7)	13 (21.7)	19 (31.7)	32 (26.7)	37 (24.7)
2.	9 (39.1)	2 (28.6)	11 (36.6)	8 (13.3)	12 (20)	20 (16.7)	31 (20.7)
3.	6 (26.1)	3 (42.9)	9 (30)	7 (11.7)	6 (10)	13 (10.8)	22 (14.6)
>=4.	2 (8.7)	1 (14.3)	3 (10)	4 (16.6)	1 (1.6)	5 (4.1)	8 (5.3)

* $p<0.05$

cent CI=0.34-19.6). The contacts with all the sarpanches were utilized mainly to provide information regarding special campaigns like the Intensified Pulse Polio Campaigns or any other camp. Seven (23.3%) sarpanches were contacted for providing them health education in which 4 (13.3%) of them were also provided some educational material.

One (3.3%) sarpanch was provided with a copy of fixed work schedule by the ANM detailing her day-wise activities plan at the subcentre and home-visiting. None of the *panches* was provided with this information (Table 6.2). Besides providing information on special campaigns, the four issues which were discussed most frequently with *sarpanches* included explaining the spectrum of services at subcentre (11; 36.7%),

Table 6.2: Exchange of Information Between ANM and PRIs

Information Exchanged By ANM	*Sarpanch**			*Panchayat Member**		
	Male (n=23)	*Female (n=7)*	*Total (n=30)*	*Male (n=60)*	*Female (n=60)*	*Total (n=120)*
Provided a copy of fixed work schedule	1 (4.3)	0	1 (3.3)	0	0	0
Explained availability of drugs and equipments	4 (17.4)	2 (28.6)	6 (20)	0	14 (23.3)	14 (11.7)
Explained spectrum of services at subcentre	7 (30.4)	4 (57.1)	11 (36.7)	6 (10)	16 (26.7)	22 (18.3)
Discussed Health information of women and children	2 (8.7)**	6 (85.7)**	8 (26.7)	4 (6.7)	20 (33.3)	24 (20)
Discused Health problems of women and children	2 (8.7)**	5 (71.4)**	7 (23.3)	3 (5)	20 (33.3)	23 (19.2)
Discussed health services utilization by women and children	1 (4.3)	4 (57.1)	5 (16.7)	3 (5)	16 (26.7)	19 (15.8)
Sought opinion on health needs and problems of women and children	3 (13)**	5 (71.4)**	8 (26.7)	7 (11.7)	27 (45)	34 (28.3)

*Figures in parenthesis indicates percentage.
** $p<0.05$ between male and female sarpanches.

discussion on health information of women and children (8; 26.7%), health problems of women and children (7; 23.3%), and opinion seeking on health needs of women and children (8; 26.7%). Coverage of discussion of these four issues ranged from 4.3 per cent to 30.4 per cent for male sarpanches while it was 28.6 per cent to 85.7 per cent with female sarpanches. Barring the exception of discussion on spectrum of services, all other areas of discussion relating to heath information, health problems and needs ascertainment of problems of women and children were found significantly more with female sarpanches ($p<0.005$).

During these meetings, help was sought by the ANM from the sarpanches for social mobilization in IPPI (26; 86.7%), arrangemements for health camp (9; 30%), accommodation/ land for building a subcentre (8; 26.7%) and construction/ repair of subcentre building (7; 23.3%). Support was provided by the sarpanches in the form of social mobilization during IPPI (26; 86.7%) and health camp (9; 30%). Construction/ repair of the subcentre was facilitated by all 7 (23.3%) sarpanches who were contacted for the same purpose. Repair of subcentres was undertaken by the panchayat was significantly more in villages headed by female sarpanches. Help was provided by the female sarpanches for identification and referral of RTI/STI cases (42.9%), identification of beneficiaries for family planning (28.6%) and social mobilization during routine immunization (28.6%). None of the male sarpanches interviewed provided help in these aspects (Table 6.3).

Only one (3.3%) sarpanch was aware of the scheme under RCH programme wherein the panchayats have been empowered to provide monetary help (Rs. 500/- per case) or vehicle for referral of difficult delivery to the nearest First Referral Unit (FRU). None of the sarpanches had identified any vehicle for such use in his area nor had provided monetary help to any beneficiary for the same during the past one year.

Informal discussions with PHC medical officers and ANMs revealed that low priority was accorded by the panchayat

Table 6.3 : Involvement of Panchayats In Health and Family Welfare Activities at Subcentre Level

Areas of Involvement	*Sarpanch (%)*		
	Male (n=23)	*Female (n=7)*	*Total (n=30)*
Social mobilization in IPPI*	19(82.6)	7(100)	26(86.7)
Construction/Repair of S/C**	3(13)	4(57.1)	7(23.3)
Accommodation/Land for S/C**	2(8.7)	2(28.6)	4(13.3)
Identification of Family Planning cases	0	2(28.6)	2(6.7)
Identification/Referral of RTI/STI cases	0	3(42.9)	3(10)
Social Mobilization during routine immunization	0	2(28.6)	2(6.7)
Well chlorination	1(4.3)	0	1(3.3)
Manage a DDC***	2(8.7)	1(14.3)	3(10)
Transport help for referral of complicated delivery	0	0	0

* Intensified Pulse Polio Immunization campaign.
** Subcentre.
*** Drug distribution centre for provision of presumptive treatment of malaria to fever cases.

members to issues related to health department. Illiteracy and ignorance of the PRI members regarding health related issues were cited as reasons for not consulting them by 24 (80%) ANMs and all the 10 medical officers (MO). It was observed that sarpanches had attended 7.5 per cent meetings organized by the MOs at PHC level while 28 (93.3%) sarpanches visited the BDPO office at least once a fortnight . Thirteen (43.3%) health workers told that they had contacted the sarpanch for some developmental work of subcentre. However, the panchayat did not do anything in response to such a request. Another 10 (33.3%) ANMs had not sought help of PRI for any developmental/repair work at the subcentre.

Awareness regarding 73rd Constitutional amendment and role and responsibilities of Panchayat in reproductive and child healthcare delivery was was found among 1 (3.3%) and 5 (4.2%) sarpanches and panches respectively. Issues related to healthcare delivery were taken up in only 3 (6.9%) meetings of panchayat in the last one year prior to survey. The perception of elected representatives about their functions and responsibilities in provision of healthcare varied across the tiers, with total indifference at the level of Gram Panchayat. Twenty-six (86.7%) sarpanches felt that the panchayat had much less funds at their disposal to carry out development work in the village. Twenty-nine (96.7%) sarpanches complained regarding non-maintainence of headquarter at subcentre by the ANM. Nineteen (63.3%) sarpanches felt that the administration of subcentres and the attendance of the health workers should be entrusted to the panchayats to improve their functioning and increase the involvement of local people.

Discussion

The National Population Policy, (NPP, 2000) includes decentralization and convergence of service delivery at village levels and recognizes the PRI as the agency responsible to ensure this[8,9]. The National Health Policy, 2002, also emphasizes implementation of public health programmes through local self-government institutions, especially relating to the national disease control programmes[10].

The Tenth Plan document (2002-2007) and more recently, in August 2003, the Central Council of Ministers of Health and Family Welfare, resolved "that the States would involve PRI in the implementation of HFW programmes by progressive transfer of funds, functions and functionaries, by training, equipping and empowering them suitably to manage and supervise the functioning of health care infrastructure and manpower and further to coordinate the activities of the works of different departments such as: Health and Family Welfare, Social Welfare, and Education which are functioning at the

Village and Block Levels" [11]. The effective implementation of the policy prescription and its continuous monitoring are issues which need to be addressed.

Devolution of powers to Panchayati Raj Institutions is an important evolutionary step in the democratic setup of India. The process of decentralization of powers to PRIs has been initiated in many states. In context of health care delivery system in rural India, Community Needs Assessment Approach (CNAA) provides a mechanism for decentralization of decision making pertaining to planning, implementation and evaluation of public health services through involvement of PRIs and the community.

Community health needs assessment entails regular monthly contacts between ANM and PRI members. However, our study revealed that such meetings continue to be rare. Though the ANM had contacted sarpanches, 50 (41.7%) panches were not contacted at all during the last six months prior to survey. This reflects the low importance accorded by the ANM to the panches. This may be because the main powers of decision-making are usually vested with the sarpanches. Attendance of the health workers at the meetings of the panchayat was also not very frequent. This implies that the feeling of oneness between the health workers and the PRI as a team is yet to generate.

Our study revealed that ANM's contact with female sarpanches were quantitatively and qualitatively superior than those with male sarpanches. Apparently, the ANM felt more comfortable in interacting with female sarpanches probably being of the same gender. This situation should be utilized further by declaring female sarpanch headed panchayat as model subcentre area for PRI-health worker team coordination. Specific RCH-II/ National Rural Health Mission (NRHM) linked projects may be initiated there – a kind of all women team which will further bolster women empowerment initiatives.

The contacts with sarpanches were used by the ANMs

primarily for disseminating information on special campaign like IPPI (91.3%) while only 27% and 28% of sarpanches and panches respectively were consulted on health needs and problems of women and children. Consultation on assessment of health needs and problems was thus inadequate. It seems that the sarpanches are contacted for special campaigns and not regularly for routine planning. Thus, ANMs contact with sarpanches is yet to become part of their routine work culture.

The panchayats are houses of wealth both capital and human. They have their own sources of income like the leasing of panchayat land, fisheries in local ponds, cutting and selling of trees and levying of taxes like *chulha* tax. Apart from this the panchayats get monetary grants from the offices of Block Development and Panchayat Officer on submission of proposal for undertaking any developmental work. This requires passage of a resolution in the panchayat with 50 per cent majority for undertaking any given developmental work. For this, there has to be endorsement from required number of elected representatives from socially backward classes. However, our study revealed that 10 (33.3%) health workers did not contact either sarpanch or panchayat members to raise funds for any developmental work for subcentre and 13 (43.3%) could not convince the sarpanch for the need to undertake requisite developmental work. Now that PRIs have been positioned as important stakeholders in primary health care at the peripheral level, the health workers will have to learn and develop skills of resource generation at local level. An active and regular dialogue should be established by ANMs and male health workers with sarpanches and other PRIs. Village panchayats with their resources should construct subcentres or hire building for establishing subcentres. The cost of construction should be borne by the government or else adequate administrative and financial powers including powers of resource mobilization should be given to panchayats.

In our study almost all the sarpanches complained that the ANM did not stay in the subcentre which compromised the provision of intranatal and postnatal care to women and children. Majority of sarpanches opined that the management of subcentres should be handed over to the panchayats. This reflects that PRIs are ready and willing to shoulder the responsibility assigned to them. This situation should be carefully nurtured. Women members of village panchayat should take the lead in view of the camaraderie and congenial relation between them and the ANMs.

However, awareness among the PRI members regarding their roles and responsibilities in health care delivery was minimal. Lack of capacity among PRIs to undertake development work and illiteracy are often cited as reasons by the health workers and medical officers for not involving them in the planning process. This issue needs urgent redressal, particularly in a sector such as health and family welfare, where some knowledge of basic structure of health care system, roles and responsibilities of service providers, functions of each tier of the health system are basic pre-requisites before PRI can undertake Health and Family Welfare (HFW) related interventions. The form and content of capacity building processes also need to be tailored to the literacy levels and circumstances of PRI members. Where women PRI are to be trained, female trainers are much more acceptable. Our study revealed that 26 (86.7%) sarpanches felt need for more financial resources at hand to undertake planning for developmental work. Transfer of funds to PRI is a critical must before they can be expected to play a meaningful role in HFW activities.

The ANM should increase her contacts with PRI members and utilize these in explaining her work schedule, services provided and the various health problems of women and children. Sharing of information will keep the panchayat members informed regarding the problems and activities of the subcentre, increase their involvement in planning process and build a sense of ownership amongst the panchayats regarding these institutions of health. The issue of ANMs staying at subcentre should also be suitable resolved.

NOTES

1. Mesham, A R, Heaver, A. R., Directions in development India's Family Welfare Programme: Moving to RCH approach. Washington DC. 1996.
2. Lal, S. A turning point in National Family Welfare Programme. Moving to Target Free Reproductive and Child Health Approach. *Indian J Community Medicine* 1997; 12 (2):43-6.
3. Ministry of Health and Family Welfare. Manual on Community Needs Assessment Approach (CNAA) in Family Welfare Programme. New Delhi, 1998.
4. http:// www. mohfw.nic.in/ nrhm. Retrieved on 16-09-06.
5. http:// panchayat . nic. in / 73rd Amendment Act. Retrieved on 10-09-06.
6. http:// panchayat . nic. in / eleventh schedule. Retrieved on 10-09-06.
7. Ministry of Health and Family Welfare. Manual on Decentralized Participatory Planning in Family Welfare Programme. New Delhi: Government of India: 6-7.
8. Ministry of Health and Family Welfare. National Population Policy 2000. Government of India; New Delhi: 12-14.
9. Lal, S. Implementation of strategies of National Population Policy 2000. *Indian Journal of Community Medicine* ;15(4):143-7.
10. Ministry of Health and Family Welfare. National Health Policy 2002. Government of India; New Delhi: 5-7.
11. Planning Commission of India. Tenth Five Year Plan (2002-2007). Government of India. New Delhi; 2002: 17- 19.

7

Rural Development Strategies in India Employment Generation and Housing Programmes

Dr. Shankar Chatterjee

Introduction

"India lives in her villages". This statement of Mahatma Gandhi still holds true. A little more than 70 per cent of India's population lives in rural areas and the issues are poverty, unemployment, quality housing, and infrastructure. In fact the Ministry of Rural Development, Government of India, has been implementing different type of programmes for bridging gap between rural and urban areas by addressing the above mentioned issues (MoRD, RD Prog., 2008). The programmes are mainly implemented from centre to different states through district level organization viz., District Rural Development Agency (DRDA)/ *Zila Parishad*. In fact in India, top to bottom institutions have been created for planning and implementation of rural development programmes. Rural development in India mainly focuses on removal of poverty, generation of employment, providing of housing facilities, and reduction of regional disparities. In this paper, some recent strategies followed in India for generation of rural employment and constructions of houses under Government of India sponsored programmes are discussed.

Swarnajayanti Gram Swarojgar Yojana (SGSY) : Self-employment Programme

The programme popularly known as SGSY is in operation since 1st April, 1999. It is a holistic programme covering all aspects of self-employment for rural Below Poverty Line (BPL) population. Some of the salient features of the Programme are (MoRD, Gram Vikas, 2009):

(i) *Objective* : To bring rural BPL families above the poverty line by ensuring appreciable increase in income on a sustainable basis through creation of income generating assets.

(ii) *Component of SGSY* : SGSY is a major on-going scheme to bring the assisted rural poor families (in India known as *Swarojgaries*) above the poverty line by providing them income generating assets through a mix of bank credit and government subsidy. The scheme involves organization of the poor into Self Help Groups (SHGs) and building their capacities through social mobilization, training and skill development, selection of key activities, planning of activity clusters, creation of infrastructure and other backward and forward linkages. The Programme is implemented through District Rural Development Agencies (DRDAs) with active involvement of Panchayati Raj Institutions (PRIs, local self-Government), banks, line Departments of the State Governments and Non-Government Organizations (NGOs).

SGSY is a credit-linked programme where credit is the key component and subsidy is the enabling element. Besides giving loan to the *Swarojgaries*, Banks' role is important for planning and implementation of the programme. The banks along with DRDAs/Block Officials are involved in selection of *Swarojgaries*, identification of key activities, preparation of the projects, infrastructure planning, capacity building, pre-credit activities and post-credit monitoring.

The programme covers two types of beneficiaries (*Swarojgaries*) – individual and group. For individual Swarojgaries of other category, subsidy is 30 per cent of the project cost, subject to a maximum of Rs. 7500. In case of SCs/STs and disabled persons, the subsidy is 50 per cent of the project cost, subject to a maximum of Rs. 10,000. Subsidy is one time only.

For group of *Swarojgaries* (SHGs), the subsidy is 50 per cent of the project cost, subject to per capita subsidy of Rs. 10,000 with maximum limit of Rs. 1.25 lakh, whichever is less. There is no monetary limit on subsidy for irrigation projects. However, subsidy is back-ended. Special safeguards have been provided to vulnerable sections by way of reserving 50 per cent benefits for SCs/STs, 40 per cent for women, 15 per cent for minorities and 3 per cent for disabled persons. (Please see note at the end for SC, ST and Minorities).

(iii) *Funding Pattern:* It is a centrally sponsored programme financed on 75: 25 cost sharing basis between the Government of India and the respective state government, except in the case of north-eastern states where it is 90: 10 basis. Pertinent to mention here that north-eastern states consist of 8 states are considered backward region of India.

Achievement under SGSY

Altogether 3.17 million Self-Help Groups have been formed since its inception in April, 1999 to November 2008. Statistics reveal that average size of each group is 10 members and from one rural family one member can join in the group. Thus roughly it can be said that 30 million families have been benefitted by forming self-help groups. By forming groups not only economically, women (in most cases women from self-help groups) are benefited but the same enabling them to have more bargaining power with the authorities. It was observed during field visits that women plan their credit needs, settle dowry related issues in the village, prevents child marriage, etc. Although there are millions of cases where BPL families have been benefited under SGSY, however, in this case one project related to irrigation is presented.

A case benefiting 49 farmers

This is a unique irrigation project located at Tambewadi village (Ahmednagar district, Maharashtra state) about 50 kilometers away from district headquarters and 5 kilometers away from main road. Out of 73 households in the village, 61 households live below the poverty line. Except 2 landless families, rest of them belongs to small (46 families) and marginal farmers (25). The major problem of the farmers was assured water up to March 2000. The village suffers from scanty rainfall, as the annual rainfall in the area is less than 450 mm although most of the villagers depend on agriculture. Under the circumstances, peasant community particularly small and marginal farmers were suffering immensely. Whatever, little crops were grown in rainy season was not sufficient to maintain a family. The winter crops were totally uncertain due to lack of water as a result most of the farmers were forced to work as wage labourer to harvest sugarcane in nearby villages, such type of work is very arduous. For harvesting of sugarcane, they have to stay in the area itself, leaving behind their families months together. Thus to get food throughout the year, they had to migrate although they are having agricultural land. The situation aggravated due to non-availability of water. With the launching of SGS in 1999 situation improved. Altogether, 49 farmers out of 61 came forward to take the benefit of SGSY for irrigation project; accordingly the project was sanctioned in February 2000 and within one-month Rs 2.00 million was disbursed - Rs 1.00 million as loan and Rs. 1.00 million as subsidy. Nine Self Help Groups (SHGs) consisting of 49 farmers (47 male and 2 female) of the village were assisted under SGSY. The cost of the irrigation project for 9 different SHGs varies from Rs. 0.15 million to Rs. 0.27 million per SHG depending upon the length of the irrigation pipe, as irrigation water was brought from nearby river through lift by using electric motor.

The agriculture land of each member varied from 0.7 hectare to 1.8 hectare. The SHGs were directly financed to start economic activities. Interaction with the villagers revealed that most of the farmers were getting one crop before the irrigation project in rainy season but after availability of water, crops were grown in winter also. That is, all the 49 farmers were growing crops in both the seasons. Apart from growing foodgrains, most of the farmers were growing sugarcane in some portion of their land, as sugarcane as a cash crop gives good return. Moreover, they all were well versed with sugar-cane growing. It was reported that for cultivating sugarcane first year some cost requires for plantation besides expenditure on labour and fertilizer. Second and third years onwards except fertilizer, no other major cost is required to be incurred. Moreover, the greatest advantage of cultivating sugarcane is that (as reported by the farmers), the chance of crop failure is very less. In the nearby areas sugar factories are located so marketing is also assured. Maharashtra State Electricity Board installed a transformer for smooth running of electricity. The farmers have been greatly benefited by the project. Earlier they used to migrate to other places now they employ workers on their land. Their income has gone up substantially. They have fully repaid bank loan. Striking feature is that earlier many of the farmers were going out of the village to work as agricultural labourers now the farmers themselves were employing labourers in their land, a shift in occupation from agricultural labourers to employers (Chatterjee, 2009).

Mahatma Gandhi National Rural Employment Guarantee Act (Mahatma Gandhi NREGA): Wage-employment for rural household

In view of the serious unemployment in the rural areas of India, Government of India has implemented a wage employment programme under by passing an Act in the Parliament on 7th September, 2005. It is known as the National Rural Employment Guarantee Act (NREGA) and as programme known as National Rural Employment Guarantee Scheme (MGNREGS). The objective is to "provide for the enhancement of livelihood security of the households in rural areas of the country by providing at least one hundred days of guaranteed wage employment in every financial year to every household whose adults volunteer to do unskilled manual work". Salient features of the scheme are (MORD, 2009):

- All adult members of a rural household willing to do unskilled manual work have the right to demand employment.
- Such households will apply for the Job Card to the Gram Panchayat (village level local self-government).
- The Gram Panchayat will verify the age and local domicile of the applicant.
- After verification, the Gram Panchayat will issue a Job Card to the household with photograph free of cost.

- The Job Card must remain in the custody of the household.
- Job Card holder can apply for work to the Gram Panchayat which will issue him/her a dated receipt of the work application.
- Employment will be provided by the Gram Panchayat within 15 days of work application, else unemployment allowance will be paid.
- A household may avail up to 100 days of guaranteed employment in a financial year, depending on its need.
- Payment of wages to be made every week, not later than a fortnight.
- At least one-third of the workers should be women
- NREGA workers are covered under life insurance

Achievement under MGNREGS

MGNREGS has tremendous impact among the rural communities. Rural persons both male and female are thronging for the works. As a result of implementation of MGNREGS employment opportunities and wage rates have gone up leading to significant dent in poverty in rural areas. Under the scheme 3508.70 million person days of employment created since inception February 2006 to October, 2008.

Minimum wages for agricultural labourers have increased after the implementation of NREGA in almost all the states of India. Another significant impact of MGNREGS is increase in purchasing power of the rural people as a sequel the same is causing "Multiplier Effect". It is heartening to mention that increase in income has resulted to access education and health care. Thus rural persons are not only benefited but due to creation of large number of water bodies water table has gone up in dry and arid regions. Many persons in India believe that through creation of water bodies as well as social forestry measures in future problem of "Global Warming" can be mitigated to a great extent. As we know this is a serious issue and in Denmark's Copenhagen lot of debate took place. Creation of water bodies /water conservation measures under MGNREGS may be a small step but we know "little drops of water and little grains of sand makes a mighty ocean and a pleasant land".

Another striking feature with regard to workers of MGNREGS is that more than 49.2 million savings accounts in the banks and Post offices have been opened (for the MGNREGS workers). Thus many of the persons who have earlier never visited banks/not transacted in the bank are well aware of the banking business.

With the launching of MGNREGS, not only employment opportunities are being generated but community assets are also being created. Thus through employment generation, economy is gaining by "Multiplier Effect" *vis-à-vis* community assets have been helping for the development of environment as most of the works are pertaining to water related activities. Altogether 1.31 million works were taken up under MGNREGS till January 2008. Of which water conservation and water harvesting works constituted 27.69 per cent, renovation of traditional water bodies 7.76 per cent, irrigation works including micro irrigation works 18.58 per cent, drought proofing 8.84, flood control and protection 2.35 per cent, rural connectivity 16.92 per cent and land development 14.42 per cent.

In this part two cases of workers who were benefited under MGNREGS are presented. Like this, millions of workers are benefited but these two cases will give us an idea about the level of benefit derived from working in MGNREGS.

Cases with MGNREGS workers

It is evident from the above discussion that millions of rural people/youths have been benefited under MGNREGS by getting employment in the rural areas. Only two cases of workers who have been benefited under MGNREGS are presented. The author visited more than a year back in an interior village namely Anwarpura village Sabarkantha district of Gujarat for the study.

Case-1

Hiraben, a widow belong to marginalized social category (58 years age) with her daughter is the card holders. Hiraben is a widow with 4 children (2 sons and 2 daughters) having a house only. They are having no agricultural land. Although one daughter was married but for 4 members family, (self, daughter and two sons) source of income is earning as daily labourers. Both Hiraben along with her daughter worked for 103 days for which the household could earn Rs. 6500 as time to time payment was made on the basis of piece-meal work. This was their additional income as besides their normal earning as daily labourers (mainly by the sons), they could earn some amount in their village itself. Pertinent to mention here that the sons being male persons can go other places, for the female from an interior area going to other places for work is not an easy task.

Case-2

Romilaben (40 years) and her husband belong to marginalized social category family are the job card holders. Although husband most of the times suffer from illness even then worked for few days as the family have no agricultural land except a small house. With one girl child pursuing higher study, the bread-winner of the family is virtually Romilaben. Although Romilaben and her husband worked under MGNREGS for 100 days but major chunk of work was done by Romilaben only. By working 100 days, the household could earn about an amount of Rs. 6500.

This amount was a great help for both the families as family members could spend this money for eating different type of fruits, vegetables and milk and milk products as with their usual income such items were not possible to consume. Even many workers in different parts of India while visited for the study informed that with additional income under MGNREGS, they could purchase durable goods like bicycle, television, etc.

Above two cases have been presented to throw some light about the benefit derived from MGNREGS. Even other workers like Monguben (Female, 55 years), Maniben (Female 50 years), Dibaben (Female, 58 years) whom author interacted expressed their happiness about the income derived from MGNREGS.

Few suggestions for better implementation of MGNREGS

Although MGNREGS is being implemented in many parts of the country with properly but in many other parts its implementation is a matter of discussion. Many issues are being cropped up which country has experienced while earlier wage employment programmes like National Rural Employment Programme (NREP), Rural Landless Employment Guarantee Programme (RLEGP), and Jawahar Rozgar Yojana (JRY), Sampoorna Grameen Rozgar Yojana (SGRY) were in implementation. The author also had come across many problems while doing evaluation studies on earlier wage employment programmes. Some of these were manipulation in muster roll, enhancing in man-days, discrimination in wage rate between male and female, etc.

Jean Dreze in his article on, "Employment guarantee or slave labour" published in *The Hindu* (20th September, 2009) has brought out some of the issues in payment, etc., and by quoting from the article "the delays in NREGA wage payments are not just operational hurdles – they reflect a deliberate attack on the scheme". As a faculty of National Institute of Rural Development (NIRD, Hyderabad) while visiting in many villages of the country, I have observed that villagers are not well acquainted with MGNREGS and demanding works is also a matter of concern, when most of the villagers are uneducated and socially backward unless and until, the labourers are well organized. Another issue is payment of wages through banks/ post offices. In interior parts of Chattisgarh, Jharkhand, Uttar Pradesh and difficult and hilly areas labourers face not only problem to collect wages but bank officials also face several problems. With limited bank staffs they have to open many accounts not only for MGNREGS workers but also for the members of self-help group of Swarnajayanti Gram Swarozgar Yojana (SGSY). For one self-help group of SGSY, three accounts have to be opened – one for self-help group's savings account, another is Cash Credit Loan (CCL) account and third one is loan account which is paid after second grading. Besides, the bank is having their regular savings account and accounts of many other government sponsored programmes, thus they are burdened with huge works. However, with respect to payment of wages it can be stated that in a country like India where 28.3 per cent rural population are Below Poverty Line (BPL) as per Uniform Recall Period (URP) of 2004-05 and as per N.C. Saxena, Head of Expert Committee set up by the Ministry of Rural Development, Government of India "50 per cent of Indians are Below Poverty Line if one takes into account the criterion of Calorie intake', (*The Hindu*, 20/09/09) waiting even for one day for getting wage is beyond expectation. In view of these, I would like to suggest following measures which may not be applicable in all the areas of the country but may be based on the geographical area and project site.

- 100 days employment may be taken up in the district/ block (mandal) at a stretch or in 2/3 phases, particularly in the lien season. Consequence of this is that at a time workers can come and work and chances of corruption will be less. Payment of unemployment allowance will not arise.

- Extensive campaign may be taken up to inform the villagers about the starting of the works and its completion.
- Starting time and ending time should not be changed in every year without any reason. Pertinent to mention here that in Andhra Pradesh Society for Elimination of Rural Poverty (SERP) has been working in many development and welfare programmes in the state. It is headed by one senior IAS officer. One of the SERP's programmes is minimum price support to the farmers, where farmers in the village can sell their agricultural commodities through village federation for which every year (60/40 days) days are notified.
- Payment of wages may be made in cash if post offices/ bank branches are not available nearby and payment should be made weekly.
- For better implementation of MGNREGS at the project site a supervisory team with one panchayat representative, one village elderly person, one person from a leading NGO and others may be constituted. Regarding my suggestion about others, I mean one priest if area (village) is dominated by Hindus or Moulavi in Muslim areas or Christian Priest in Christian areas, etc. Each member of supervisory team may be paid as per minimum wage rate. They should not perform works in all the time in a day but should attend sometimes.
- Wage rate for NREGA workers should be uniform in the country, may be Rs. 100 per person per day (minimum).

Indira Awaas Yojana (IAY): Housing Programme

The housing programme Indira Awaas Yojana (IAY) sponsored by the Government of India has been in implementation since 1985-86, to provide financial assistance for construction/up-gradation of dwelling units to the Below Poverty Line (BPL) rural households belonging to the Scheduled Castes, Scheduled Tribes and freed bonded labourers categories. From 1993-94, the Programme was extended to cover non-Scheduled Castes, non-Scheduled Tribes and rural BPL poor subject to the condition that the benefits to non-SC/ST would not be more than 40 per cent of the total IAY allocation. The benefits of IAY have also been extended to the families of ex-servicemen of the armed and paramilitary forces killed in action. Of the total expenditure, 3 per cent of the houses are reserved physically/mentally challenged persons. From 2006-07, funds and physical targets under IAY are also earmarked for BPL minorities in each state.

Under the Programme, financial resources are shared between the centre and the states on 75: 25 ratios. For north-east states, the funding pattern is in the ratio of 90: 10. The limit of assistance under the IAY is Rs. 35,000 per unit in the plain areas and Rs.38,500 in hilly/difficult areas from April 2008. For upgradation of shanty house, the financial assistance is Rs. 15,000 per unit. IAY units are allotted in the name of female member of the beneficiary household; alternatively, the same is allotted in the name of both husband and wife. In case there is no eligible female member in the family, the house is allotted in the name of an eligible male member.

Choice of design, technology and materials for construction of an IAY house is at the sole discretion of the beneficiaries. The construction of the houses is the sole responsibility of the beneficiary. Sanitary latrine and smokeless chullah (cooking stove) are required to be constructed along with each IAY house.

Achievement under IAY

This is a popular programme in India as many of the villagers are in need of good houses. In the absence of good house they had to stay worst than a shanty house. A few cases are presented here to justify the statement. However, about 19.02 million houses have been constructed under IAY since inception to December 2008. Thus, it is evident that millions of rural poor persons have been benefited from IAY. With a good house, one can lead quality of life as not only house is provided, along with house sanitary latrine and smokeless chullah (cooking stove).

Cases with IAY beneficiaries

Mrs. Firoja Begum hails from Domjur block of Howrah district, West Bengal state. The family is a poor one, belong to Muslim community and accordingly survey report put the family as Below Poverty Line (BPL). She is about 45 year's women. Due to lack of a quality house she had to face with severe problems to lead a descend life. The family came to know about housing scheme of Government of India for the BPL families. Accordingly they tried for a house under Indira Awaas Yojana (IAY) which is meant for housing for the poor families. An amount of Rs. 25,000 was sanctioned to her in 2007-08 for construction of a house. The family included some more money with this amount and constructed a good house. She happily informed that long standing desire has been fulfilled by constructing the house under IAY. According to her with the meagre income of family, they never imagined to construct such a good house, like the present one. A few more names from the area can be added here such as Mrs. Noorjahan Begum, Aklia Begum and others. Under IAY houses are allotted to a woman's name normally wife's name as head of the household or in joint name with the husband so women as owner of the house feel proud also. Like she many women informed to this author that their husband's attitude towards wife had been changed to a great extent as wife was the owner of the house.

The million families like Firoja Begum have been benefited under IAY throughout the country. As mentioned already 19 million houses have been constructed across the country under IAY which vividly reveals that millions of families could get quality houses for their stay.

Conclusion

The above discussion has vividly revealed that employment generation programmes and housing programmes have benefited million of rural households. The people of rural areas *inter alia* require employment and housing. To contain rural migration, employment and housing are *sine qua non*. Thus, if rural areas develop then only India will develop in true sense.

Reference

1. Chatterjee Shankar, "*Employment Programmes and Rural Development in India*" RBSA Publishers, Jaipur, India.
2. Ministry of Rural Development, Government of India (2008), "Four Years of Implementation of Rural Development Programmes (2004-08)", New Delhi, India.
3. Ministry of Rural Development, Government of India, (2009) "National Conference of Project Directors of District Rural Development Agencies", New Delhi, India.
4. Ministry of Rural Development, Government of India, (2009) "Gram Vikas: Programmes at a Glance (2009)", New Delhi, India.
5. Yunus Muhammad (2007) "Banker to the Poor" Penguin Books, India.

8

Women Empowerment Training and Employment Programme

A Study in Ahmednagar (Maharashtra)

V.M. Rao

Introduction

Women form half of Indian population. They have been managing and supporting survival system, particularly in poor households. Due to historical, social, religious and economic factors their status has been low compared to their counterparts[1]. Society has institutionalized a sharp demarcation of social roles according to sex, in which one-half of its members voluntarily accept a role subordinate to the other half. They still lack right to inherit property, own land, get education, obtain credit, earn income, work outside home, and control their fertility. They are widely under-represented in decision making at household and social levels and little control over money matters and assets even though they contribute substantially in asset formation, especially in rural India. Empowerment by means of modest income generation projects is clearly insufficient to ameliorate prospects for a high quality of life for women. Major problem in villages is that disadvantaged women are unaware of their rights and privileges.

Realizing this disparity, Government of India has made

number of interventions for social and economic emancipation of women. Mention may be made about constitution of Central Social Welfare Board, Ministry of Social Welfare, Intensive Child Development Scheme, Development of Women and Children in Rural Areas (DWCRA), Support to Training and Employment Programme (STEP), Indira Awaas Yojana (IAY), etc. Of all the programmes mentioned to above, STEP is unique. Under this scheme, implementing agencies are required to conduct a base line survey, and submit a detailed project proposal for funding by Ministry of Women and Child Development, Government of India. At the Ministry's level, these project reports are scrutinized by a project sanctioning committee and based on its recommendations; projects are sanctioned or returned for modifications.

What is STEP?

Support to Training and Employment Programme (STEP) aims at making a significant impact on women in traditional sectors (agricultural, small animal husbandry, dairying, fisheries, handlooms, handicrafts, khadi and village industries, social forestry, and wasteland development) by upgrading their skill and providing employment opportunities (Department of Women and Child Development, 1999). It advocates an integrated package of inputs aiming at integrated development of poor, assetless, and disadvantaged women in traditional sectors. Specific objectives of the scheme are : (a) providing training for skill upgradation, (b) mobilizing women in small viable groups, and making facilities available through training and access to credit, and (c) enabling groups of women to take up employment-cum-income generation programmes of their own, and (d) providing support services for further improving training and employment conditions of women.

The scheme was introduced during 1986-87 and being implemented by the Department of Women and Child Development, Ministry of Human Resources Development,

Government of India, New Delhi. So far, over 8 lakhs women were covered under 175 projects launched in various states. Apart from providing various economic benefits, there is a provision of 10-15 per cent of the total budget in the scheme for providing training and exposure visits to women. Of all the programmes of STEP, Women Dairy Project is popular. Number of state level dairy federations took up organizing Women Dairy Cooperative Societies (WDCSs) under STEP (Rao, 2004, and 2005). Non-Governmental Organizations too implemented various projects under this scheme.

The Project

Arunoday Bahhuddeshiya Gramin Vikas Sanstha, Ahmednagar submitted a proposal for organizing 500 women beneficiaries to take up mushroom cultivation in the project area in 2000. Various cost components included in the proposal were administration, establishment of cooperatives, training for skill upgradation, furniture, and equipments, infrastructure, raw material, marketing, support services, and contingencies. Proposal was submitted with an estimated budget of Rs. 39.90 lakhs over a period of 5 years[2]. Project sanction committee reviewed the proposal and sanctioned for 2 years with a budget of Rs. 12 lakhs of which Rs. 10.80 lakhs is the contribution of Government of India. Ministry of Women and Child Development released an amount or Rs. 6.56 lakhs in two instalments for implementation of the project for the first year.

Objectives

Overall objective of the paper is to understand procedures followed in organizing women and effective utilization of the grants received from the Ministry and its impact. The article has the following specific objectives:

1. To observe deviations in the purposes and amount received *vis-à-vis* project proposal,
2. To understand procedures followed and difficulties faced in organizing women from lower strata of society, and
3. To observe impact of the project on women beneficiaries.

Methodology

The study is based on both secondary data and primary data. Secondary data on grants received, disbursed, deviation, etc. are collected from the records of Arunoday Sanstha. 126 (25%) of the women members (beneficiaries) are interviewed to elicit their responses on socio-economic parameters, changes observed, and impact of the project. Data are collected through a special designed questionnaire using interview method and appropriate statistical tools are employed to analyze the data.

Background to Arunoday

Arunoday Bahuddeshiy Gramin Vikas Sanstha, Ahmednagar is a non-governmental organization registered in 1995 under Society Registration Act, 1860, Bombay Public Trust Act, 1950, and Foreign Contribution Regulation Act, 1976. It has been working for the upliftment of the poor and downtrodden people. It has been mainly concentrating on socio-economic problems and cultural development of people living in Shevgaon taluka of Ahmednagar district. The aim of organization is to develop social, educational, health and financial status of both rural and urban people located in Maharashtra. Sources of funds for the organization include member fees, member contribution, grants from Government of Maharashtra as also Government of India, tuition fees, admission fees and own funds.

Beneficiaries are selected from Scheduled Caste, Scheduled Tribe, other Backward Classes, families below poverty line, wage labourers, unpaid and underpaid daily workers, female headed households, migrant labourers, etc.

The Project

As indicated above, Arunoday organization has submitted a proposal to train 500 women beneficiaries from Shevgaon taluka of Ahmednagar. Main objective of the project was to provide training for skill upgradation and enabling groups of women to take up employment cum-income generation activities. The scheme included training on mushroom production, marketing, formation of viable women's groups, awareness building and support services, and formation of federation of women's groups.

The proposal was submitted in November 2000 and the same was scrutinized, recommended and forwarded by the Department of Women and Child Development, Government of Maharashtra in March 2001. Subsequently, Government of India informed the organization to revise the project for 2 years and sanctioned an amount of Rs. 12.00 lakhs (August 2005). Ministry released Rs. 3.56 lakhs on May 17, 2006 and Rs. 3 lakhs as second instalment.

Poor women drawn from above seven villages of Shevgaon taluka were trained in mushroom cultivation under STEP. The organization had a oyster mushroom production project in Najik Bahulgaon on its own farm and had experience in this sector for the last 5 years with good marketing network, know-how of cultivation, processing, packaging, etc. Agency has also arranged seminars, workshops for the women in this area training them the art of cultivation of oyster mushroom as a self-employment cottage industry. This experience came handy in the implementation of the project.

Funds utilization

Government sanctioned the project for Rs. 12 lakhs by contributing Rs. 10.80 lakhs and the remaining (Rs. 1.20 lakhs) has to come from the implementing agency (Table 8.1). Of the total grant, Government released Rs. 6.56 lakhs. However, implementing agency has completed the project by spending its owned money.

Table 8.1: Summary of funds sanctioned (Rs. lakhs) for the project

Sr. No.	*Particulars*	*GOI*	*Organization's share*	*Total*
1.	Amount sanctioned	10.80	1.20	12.00
2	Sanctioned amount for first year	6.56	0.73	7.29
3	Sanctioned amount for second year	4.24	0.47	4.71

Source: Records of Arunoday.

Implementing agency's share is 10 per cent at all levels. Allocation for the first year was Rs. 7.22 lakhs and Rs. 4.66 lakhs for the second year. It was implemented during July 1, 2006 to March 31, 2009. As against the sanctioned amount, agency spent Rs. 13.51 lakhs during the project period (Table 8.2). Table 8.3 provides particulars on percentage shares on item-wise expenditure. Training and technical skill accounted for 51 per cent followed by establishment of cooperatives (14.55%), and marketing (12.5%). Another important component is administration and project staff cost which accounted for 8.7 per cent. These four items together accounted for 87 per cent of the total cost.

Table 8. 2 : Item-wise and period-wise distribution of expenditure

S.N.	Item	July 1, 2006 to March 31, 2007	April 1, 2007 to March 31, 2008	April 1, 2008 to March 31, 2009	Amount	Total
1.	Administration					
	Salary	39150	52200	13050	104400	
	Contingencies	4520	6955	1597	13072	117472
2.	Establishment of cooperatives	44100	58800	14700	117600	
	Furniture and equipment	50029	–	–	50029	
	Society registration expenses	28000	–	–	21000	196629
3.	Skill upgradation					
	Staff salary	90000	120000	30000	240000	
	Training material	75150	90000	19524	184674	
	Travelling	45232	8500	2447	56179	
	Stipend	70000	100000	30000	200000	
	Water and power	4500	6000	1500	12000	692853
4.	Furniture and equipment					
	Central laboratory	1524	–	–	15241	
	Training hall	15451	–	–	15451	30692
5.	Infrastructure					
	Demonstration room	30154	–	–	30154	30154
6.	Raw material and equipment					
	For spawn production	15654	–	–	15654	
	Processing and packing	10620	–	–	10620	
	Mushroom drying machine	30254	–	–	30254	56528
7.	Marketing					
	Transportation	54841	62164	9625	126630	
	Salary of marketing personnel	15786	21048	5262	42096	168726
8.	Support services					
	Emergency need and credit	14548	20135	4925	39608	39608
9.	Contingencies	6712	9462	2298	18472	18472
	Total	**659942**	**555264**	**135928**	**1351134**	**1351134**

Source: Records of Arunoday.

Table 8. 3 : Item-wise expenditure of the grants received from Ministry

S.N.	Item	Amount (Rs. lakhs)	Percentage
1.	Administration and project staff cost	1.17	8.70
2.	Training and technical skill	6.93	51.28
3.	Infrastructure	0.30	2.23
4.	Raw material for training	0.30	2.27
5.	Raw material for production	0.57	4.18
6.	Marketing	1.69	12.48
7.	Establishment of cooperatives	1.97	14.55
8.	Support services	0.40	2.95
9.	Overriding cost	0.18	1.36
	Total	**13.51**	**100.00**

Source: Records of Arunoday

Training imparted

Coverage of beneficiaries during project implementation is presented in Table 8.4. In all, 500 women were covered in 8 batches. Project started on July 1, 2006 and completed on May 1, 2008. Each batch containing approximately 60 women were trained for 60 days in various issues of mushroom cultivation, processing, and marketing. Training on general health, sanitation, nutrition, etc. too were provided. These women were drawn from Najik Babhulgaon, Kurudgaon, Thakur Pimalgaon, Raytale, Rakshi, Gadewadi, and Takli villages. Fifty women were trained from Raytale while 75 each from the remaining six villages.

Table 8.4 : Coverage of beneficiaries during implementation

Sr. No.	*Batch*	*Beneficiaries covered*	*Training period*	*Total*
1.	Ist Batch	1 to 62 women	1st July 2006 to 31st Aug.2006	62
2.	IInd Batch	62 to 124 women	1st Oct 2006 to 30th Nov. 2006	63
3.	IIIrd Batch	125 to 187 women	1st Jan.2007 to 28th Feb.2007	62
4	IVth Batch	188 to 250 women	1st April 2007 to 31st May 2007	63
5	Vth Batch	251 to 312 women	1st July 2007 to 31st Aug. 2007	62
6	VIth Batch	313 to 375 women	1st Oct.2007 to 30th Nov.2007	63
7	VIIth Batch	376 to 437 women	1st Jan.2008 to 28th Feb.2008	62
8	VIIIth Batch	438 to 500 women	1st April 2008 to 31st May 2008	63

Source: Records of Arunoday.

Profile of beneficiaries

Vast majority (55%) of women are from farming community

(Table 8.5). Other important professions are agricultural labour (23%), shopkeepers (8%), artisans (7%), service (5%), and small scale business (2%). There are not many variations in distribution of occupations across villages.

Table 8.5 : Occupation-wise classification of beneficiaries

Sr. No.	*Village*	*Farming*	*Service*	*Shop-keeper*	*Labours*	*Artisan*	*Laghuud-yog*	*Total*
1.	Najik Babhulgaon	40	04	06	18	05	02	75
2.	Kurudgaon	40	04	06	18	05	02	75
3.	Thakur Pimpalgoan	40	04	06	18	05	02	75
4.	Raytale	35	01	04	07	02	01	50
5.	Rakshi	40	04	06	18	05	02	75
6.	Gadewadi	40	04	06	18	05	02	75
7.	Takli	40	04	06	18	05	02	75
	Total	**275**	**25**	**40**	**115**	**35**	**10**	**500**

Source : Records of Arunoday.

Socio-economic background

In all, 126 (Table 8.6) beneficiaries comprising 70 landless and 56 landed households spread over 7 villages are selected

Table 8. 6 : Village-wise distribution of sample respondents

S. No.	*Village*	*Landless*	*Landed*	*Total*
1.	Najik Babhulgaon	12	7	19
2.	Kurudgaon	13	6	19
3.	Thakur Pimpalgoan	8	11	19
4.	Raytale	4	8	12
5.	Rakshi	9	10	19
6.	Gadewadi	14	5	19
7.	Takli	10	9	19
	Total	**70**	**56**	**126**

Source : Field study.

for study. 19 beneficiaries each were selected from all villages except Raytale. Socio-economic background in terms of age, size of the household, literacy levels and landholding are provided in Table 8.7. Average age is 30 years with a household size of 5.7 persons. All the respondents are literates and as many as 72 studied between 1-5 classes. Average size of landholding is 2.8 acres.

Table 8.7 : Socio-economic status of sample respondents

S. No.	*Parameters*	*Landless (n= 70)*	*Landed (n= 56)*	*Total (n= 126)*
1.	Age (years)	30.4	29.5	30.0
2.	Size of the household	5.9	5.6	5.7
3.	Literacy			
	(a) Std. 1-5	42	30	72
	(b) Std. 6-12	28	16	44
4.	Landholding (acres)	0.0	2.8	1.0

Source : Field study.

These women spent as many as 855 minutes (14 hours 15 minutes) per day on household, agriculture, mushroom cultivation, off farm, etc. (Table 8.8). Women from landless categories spent longer hours (15 hours 20 minutes/day) than their landed counterparts (13 hours and 10 minutes/day). Landless women spent 38 per cent of their time on agricultural labour followed by household activities (30%). Mushroom cultivation consumed as much as 11 per cent of their daily time. On the other hand, women from landed category allocated 30 per cent of their total time on household activities followed by agriculture (21%). Mushroom cultivation consumed relatively higher percentage of time (16%) in this category of women.

Source-wise income of sample respondents is provided in Table 8.9. Average income/household is worked out 24585 of which 23 per cent is contributed through mushroom cultivation followed by agriculture (21%). Average income of landed households is Rs. 20520 of which 48 per cent is

Table 8.8 : Time allocation (hours/day) pattern of sample respondents

S.No.	*Activity*	*Landless (n= 70)*	*Landed (n= 56)*	*Total (n= 126)*
1	Household	280 (30.4)	240 (30.4)	260 (30.4)
2	Agriculture	350 ((38.1)	165 ((20.8)	257 (30.0)
3	Mushroom cultivation	100 (10.8)	125 (15.8)	113 (13.2)
4	Off-farm	90 (9.8)	130 (16.5)	110 (12.9)
5	Any other	100 (10.8)	130 (16.5)	115 (13.5)
	Total	**920** **(100)**	**790** **(100)**	**855** **(100)**

Source : Field study.

Table 8.9 : Source-wise income (Rs./annum) of sample respondents

S.No.	*Source*	*Landless (n=70)*	*Landed (n=56)*	*Total (n=126)*
1.	Agriculture	0 (0.0)	10200 (35.6)	5100 (20.7)
2.	Animal husbandry	2050 (10.0)	3100 (10.8)	2575 (10.5)
3.	Mushroom cultivation	5200 (25.3)	6300 (22.0)	5750 (23.4)
4.	Petty business	1500 (7.3)	3100 (10.8)	2300 (9.4)
5.	Wages	9900 (48.3)	3400 (11.9)	6650 (27.0)
6.	Others	1870 (9.1)	2550 (8.9)	2210 (9.0)
Total		**20520**	**28650**	**24585**

Source : Field study.

contributed by wages while mushroom cultivation contributed 25 per cent. On the other hand, income from agriculture constituted as much as 36 per cent in landed households followed by mushroom cultivation (22%). Petty business and others contributed around 10 per cent each to the household's income. Thus, most of the farmers are just around the poverty line and a small shock might push either ways. There is need for providing sustainable sources of income to the households under study.

STEP programme

Agencies instrumental in joining the programme are outlined in Table 8.10. These agencies included Arunoday, neighbours, husband and 'others'. Vast majority of respondents revealed that Arunoday as agency persuaded them to join the programme. The agency has been implementing various developmental schemes in the region and thus familiar with local people. Such association helped them in pursuing and identifying the target members. Neighbours and husbands contributed to about 15 per cent each in joining the programme. There are not many variations across landless and landed households.

Table 8.10 : Agency instrumental in joining STEP

S.No. Agency	*Landless (n= 70)*	*Landed (n= 56)*	*Total (n= 126)*
1. Arunoday	49 (70.0)	38 (67.8)	87 (69.0)
2. Neighbours	9 (12.9)	10 (17.9)	19 (15.1)
3. Husband	10 (14.2)	48 (17.9)	18 (14.3)
4. Others	2 (2.9)	0 (0.0)	2 (1.6)
Total	**70 (100.0)**	**56 (100.0)**	**126 (100.0)**

Source : Field study.

Awareness about STEP

Of the 70 landless households, 64 per cent are not aware of objectives of the STEP (Table 8.11). Relatively, higher percentage (46%) of households from landed category is aware of the objectives. On the whole, 40 per cent respondents are familiar with the objectives. When asked about the reasons for undergoing the training on mushroom cultivation, respondents provided as many as 7 factors (Table 8.12). They included no choice, could not get other job, saw good opportunities, for being impendent, availability of training, faith on Arunoday, and previous experience. Among all the reasons, faith on Arunoday came out to be major influencing factor in undergoing the training programme. Further, availability of training through Arunoday also motivated as many as 19 per cent of the respondents. More or less similar results are recorded among both landless and landed beneficiaries.

Table 8.11 : Awareness on objectives of STEP

S.No. Awareness	*Landless (n= 70)*	*Landed (n= 56)*	*Total (n= 126)*
1. Yes	25 (35.7)	26 (46.4)	51 (40.5)
2. No	45 (64.3)	30 (53.6)	75 (59.5)
Total	**70 (100.0)**	**56 (100.0)**	**126 (100.0)**

Source : Field study.

Feedback on training

As mentioned elsewhere in the paper, training programme on mushroom cultivation was conducted for a period of 2 months

Table 8.12 : Reasons for undergoing training on mushroom cultivation

S.No. Reasons	*Landless (n= 70)*	*Landed (n= 56)*	*Total (n= 126)*
1. No choice	3 (4.3)	0 (0.0)	3 (2.5)
2. Could not get job	4 (5.7)	2 (3.6)	6 (4.7)
3. Saw good opportunities	6 (8.6)	3 (5.4)	9 (7.1)
4. For being independent	11 (15.7)	7 (12.5)	18 (14.3)
5. Availability of training	15 (21.5)	9 (16.0)	24 (19.0)
6 Faith on Arunoday	30 (42.8)	33 (58.9)	63 (50.0)
7 Experience	1 (1.4)	2 (3.6)	3 (2.4)
Total	70 (100.0)	56 (100.0)	126 (100.0)

Source : Field study.

@ 2 hours/day at convenient time to beneficiaries. Cultivation practices, processing, marketing, etc. were covered in the training programme. Feedback (good/satisfactory/not satisfactory) on the training programme was recorded in Table 8.13. On the whole, majority of respondents from both the categories opined either good or satisfactory about the programme. Similar responses are noticed on reading material, guest faculty, refreshments, and venue. Thus, majority of respondents are satisfied with training programme conducted by Arunoday.

Grounding the scheme

Soon after completion of training programme Arunoday suggested respondents to start mushroom cultivation in their

Table 8.13: Feedback on contents of training programme and logistics

S.N.	Feedback	Good	Satisfactory	Not satisfactory	Total
A	**Landless category (n=70)**				
1	Production	28	15	27	70
2	Processing	33	18	19	70
3	Marketing	30	20	20	70
4	Reading material	30	17	23	70
5	Guest faculty	29	19	22	70
6	Refreshments	32	20	18	70
7	Venue	28	20	22	70
B	**Landed category (n=56)**				
1	Production	32	16	8	56
2	Processing	30	18	8	56
3	Marketing	28	20	8	56
4	Reading material	25	25	6	56
5	Guest faculty	24	20	12	56
6	Refreshments	25	18	13	56
7	Venue	24	20	12	56

Source : Field study.

respective houses. However, only 53 (42%) out of 126 respondents started cultivation (Table 8.14). Out of the 53 respondents who started cultivation, 38 (72%) reported to be either successful or break even (Table 8.15). Thus, success rate is relatively on the higher side and organizers need to be congratulated for the efforts put in.

As regards, sources of funds for starting the project, 54 per cent used owned funds, and 23 per cent borrowed funds from neighbours (Table 8.16). Money-lenders and bankers contributed 11 per cent each for grounding the project. These women started with an initial investment of Rs. 562 which increased to Rs. 1418 (Table 8.17). Similarly, initial sale was Rs. 1600 per annum which increased to Rs. 5750. Marginal difference across landless and landed households is noticed.

Table 8.14 : Grounding of the scheme by respondents

S.No.	*Training programme*	*Yes*	*No*	*Total*
1.	Landless	28 (40.0)	42 (60.0)	70 (100.0)
2.	Landed	25 (44.6)	31 (55.4)	56 (100.0)
3.	Total	53 (42.0)	73 (58.0)	126 (100.0)

Source: Field study.

Table 8.15 : Performance of the scheme

S.No.	*Particulars*	*Landless (n=28)*	*Landed (n=25)*	*Total (n=53)*
1.	Successful	12 (42.9)	12 (48.0)	24 (45.3)
2.	Breakeven	8 (28.5)	6 (24.0)	14 (26.4)
3.	Failure	8 (28.5)	7 (28.0)	15 (28.3)
	Total	**28** **(100.0)**	**25** **(100.0)**	**53** **(100.0)**

Source: Field study.

Table 8.16 : Sources of funds for grounding the project

S.No.	*Performance*	*Landless (n=28)*	*Landed (n=25)*	*Total (n=53)*
1.	Owned	14 (50.0)	15 (60.0)	29 (54.2)
2.	Neighbours	7 (25.)	5 (20.0)	12 (22.6)
3.	Money-lenders	3 (10.7)	3 (12.0)	6 (11.2)
4	Bank	4 (14.3)	2 (18.0)	6 (11.2)
	Total	**28** **(100.0)**	**25** **(100.0)**	**53** **(100.0)**

Source: Field study.

Table 8.17 : Improvement in the scheme over period

S.N. Content	*Landless (n=28)*	*Landed (n=25)*	*Total (n=53)*
1. Initial investment (rupees)	525	600	562
2. Present investment (rupees)	1236	1600	1418
3. Initial sale (rupees)	1500	1700	1600
4. Present sale (rupees)	5200	6300	5750

Source : Field study.

As can be seen from the above discussion out of 126,73 respondents have taken up mushroom cultivation. When probed about the reasons for not starting the scheme, respondents' revealed lack of raw material as the single major reason (Table 8.18). Other reasons mentioned are lack of resources, non-cooperation from Arunoday, inadequate training, etc. More or less similar reasons were noticed across landless and landed households. Those who reported success (successful and break even) of the scheme, mentioned training

Table 8.18 : Reasons for not grounding the scheme

S.No. Reason	*Landless (n=42)*	*Landed (n=31)*	*Total (n=73)*
1. Lack of resources	8 (19.0)	3 (9.7)	11 (15.0)
2. Inadequate training	5 (11.9)	3 (9.7)	8 (11.0)
3. Non-cooperation from Arunoday	6 (14.3)	4 (12.9)	10 (13.7)
4. Lack of raw material	18 (42.9)	15 (48.4)	33 (45.3)
5. Any other	5 (11.9)	6 (19.3)	11 (15.0)
Total	**42 (100.0)**	**31 (100.0)**	**73 (100.0)**

Source : Field study.

and support from Arunoday are instrumental in the success of the scheme (Table 8.19). Ready market for mushroom also contributed substantially for the success. Other reasons noticed are persistence and perseverance and support from family members. More or less similar observations are noticed across landless and landed households.

Table 8.19 : Reasons for success of the scheme

S.No.	*Reason*	*Landless (n=20)*	*Landed (n=18)*	*Total (n=38)*
1.	Training and support from Arunoday	8 (40.0)	7 (38.9)	15 (39.5)
2.	Support from family members	3 (15.0)	2 (11.1)	5 (13.1)
3.	Ready market	5 (25.0)	5 (7.8)	10 (26.3)
4.	Cooperation from fellow producers	1 (5.0)	2 (11.1)	3 (7.9)
5.	Persistence and perseverance	3 (15.0)	2 (11.1)	5 (13.2)
	Total	**20 (100.0)**	**18 (100.0)**	**38 (100.0)**

Source: Field study.

Similarly, reasons for failure of the scheme are also recorded from the 15 respondents (Table 8.20). These reasons included distance from market (27%) followed by lack of capital (13%), lack of raw material (13%), lack of transport (13%), etc. Implementing agency as also government departments may look into the constraints so as to make appropriate interventions for success of the scheme.

Respondents provided as many as 6 constraints in running the scheme (Table 8.21). Scheme was limited to only 'training' is the single major problem reported by as many as 60 per cent of the respondents. Thus, there is a need to prepare scheme for training as also initial landholding in starting the

Table 8. 20 : Reasons for failure of the scheme

S.No.	*Reason*	*Landless (n=8)*	*Landed (n=7)*	*Total (n=15)*
1	Lack of market	0 (0.0)	1 14.3)	1 (6.7)
2	Distance from market	2 (25.0)	2 (28.5)	4 (26.6)
3	Lack of support from Arunoday	0 (0.0)	1 (14.3)	1 (6.7)
4	Lack of capital	2 (25.0)	0 (0.0)	2 (13.3)
5	Non-cooperation from fellow producers	1 (12.5)	0 (0.0)	1 (6.7)
6	Production in small quantity	1 (12.5)	0 (0.0)	1 (6.7)
7	Lack of raw material	1 (12.5)	1 (14.3)	2 (13.3)
8	Excess supply over demand	0 (0.0)	1 (14.3)	1 (6.7)
9	Lack of transport	1 (12.5)	1 (14.3)	2 (13.3)
	Total	**8 (100.0)**	**7 (100.0)**	**15 (100.0)**

Source: Field study.

Table 8.21: Problems faced in running the scheme

S.No.	*Problems*	*Landless (n=28)*	*Landed (n=25)*	*Total (n=53)*
1	Inadequate support from Arunoday	4 (14.3)	1 (4.0)	5 (7.4)
2	Scheme was limited to only training	15 (53.4)	16 (64.0)	31 (58.5)
3	Lack of space	2 (7.1)	2 (8.0)	4 (7.5)
4	Inadequate capital	2 (7.1)	2 (8.0)	4 (7.5)
5	Indifferent attitude from men folk	3 (10.7)	2 (8.0)	5 (9.4)
6	Lack of technical know-how	2 (7.1)	2 (8.0)	4 (7.5)
	Total	**28 (100.0)**	**25 (100.0)**	**53 (100.0)**

Source: Field study.

project. Average budget for beneficiary may be increased to Rs. 15000-16000 as against the prevailing norm of Rs. 8000 beneficiary. This would go a long way in providing training as also arranging initial financial support, at least for the members of target group. Other problems mentioned are inadequate support from Arunoday, indifferent attitude from men folk, lack of space, etc.

Suggestions for improvement of scheme are provided in Table 8.22. About 37 per cent of respondents indicated to provide training along with capital to start the avocation. Women also requested for more demonstrations, to provide raw material, marketing support, etc. These suggestions are in tune with the difficulties encountered in running the scheme, and thus justified.

Table 8.22 : Suggestions for improvement of the scheme

S.No.	*Suggestion*	*Landless (n=70)*	*Landed (n=56)*	*Total (n=126)*
1	Training and capital	25 (35.7)	22 (39.3)	47 (37.3)
2	More demonstrations	7 (10.0)	9 (16.0)	16 (12.7)
3	Marketing support	18 (25.7)	10 (17.9)	28 (22.2)
4	Providing raw material	10 (14.3)	7 (12.5)	17 (13.5)
5	Supervision and guidance	6 (8.6)	5 (6.9)	11 (8.7)
6	Programmes for men also	4 (5.7)	3 (5.4)	7 (5.6)
	Total	**70 (100.0)**	**56 (100.0)**	**126 (100.0)**

Source : Field study.

Improved socio-economic conditions helped women to have bank account, account in post office, and life insurance which otherwise would not have been possible. Three-fourths of them have bank accounts, 10 per cent have accounts in post offices, and 14 per cent have life insurance. It is an achievement of the scheme.

Conclusion

Arunoday has successfully completed STEP scheme and all 500 women beneficiaries were trained in mushroom cultivation and marketing. Implementing agency has completed the scheme as per guidelines, and successfully achieved targets. The project has resulted in providing both quantifiable and non-quantifiable impacts on beneficiaries. Adequate amount to start the activity should be made available in the scheme, at least to the target group members. Male orientation programmes also should form part of such schemes. This would enable men to extend support to the activity under consideration. Trainers may be selected from among the members by proper identification, and imparting training to such master trainers.

NOTES

1. It is said that inequality in the labour market is rooted in inequality at home, which in turn is rooted in fundamental assumptions about women's biology, psyche and social roles. Employers pay women less because they believe them to be less skilled than men! Even in places where explicit efforts have been made, women continue to earn 50-80 per cent of men's wages. Because of low literacy, early marriages, confinement to home, social taboos, etc., women are unable to compete with their men counterparts.
2. Project sanctioning committee approved the proposal for Rs. 12 lakhs spread over 2 years and requested the agency to re-submit the proposal accordingly.

9

Women Empowerment through Panchayats

A Disquisition of Reservation

V. Rama Krishna

Jean Jacqus Rousseau (1712-1778) promoted political freedom and rights, though he belittled the advocacy of women's rights by his contemporaries (Sukhpal Kaur: 2009, p. 123). Mahatma Gandhi advised women to liberate themselves from their menfolks (Geralitine Forbes: 1996) "from the death grip of the existing government which is the greatest of all social evils with which society is cursed." Vats S. and Shakntala Mudgal (1999) said in the Indian context, there is a widespread misconception regarding the true status of women in ancient Indian society. It is mainly due to deplorable ignorance of the original Sanskrit texts, both Sruthi and Smriti, in which there are to be found the laws, customs and tradition which define the true status of women in early times. The neglect of education and the lowering of the marriage age, produced disastrous consequences upon the position of women. Their position in society further deteriorated with the prohibition of widow marriage, the spread of sati custom, the practice of purdah, increasing demand for dowry and the greater prevalence of polygamous marriages. Thus, in the eighteenth century the position of women was quite miserable (Suneera Kapoor: 2005).

Panchayat system in India has progressed a long way from its traditional to present day structure. In ancient period and before independence, there were traditional village level institutions based on traditional customs, which took important decisions in matters pertaining to village communities and to dispute among their members. But these institutions could hardly be described as democratic, depending as they did on the social legitimacy conferred on them by the existing power structure and social order. Women were denied the right to participate in the local bodies. Sukhpal Kaur (2009) despite the great progress made in the arena of women's rights in theory and policy formation, women are still facing violation of their social, political and economic rights in the family and community.

Panchayati Raj Institutions are the grass roots units of self-government. They are the instruments for participatory democracy and decentralization at the grass roots level. They carry back to the people the power that really belongs to them. They have an immense potential for democratic decentralization and devolving power to the people. They are the vehicles of socio-economic transformation. It is therefore, necessary that these bodies are effective and function meaningfully. This demands an active involvement of people, both women and men, in decision-making, implementation of development programmes, monitoring and evaluation of programmes and sharing of the benefits of development (Seema, Pradeep, 2009). There has to be a 'bottom up approach' rather than one where people are mere observers and total dependents. The people should operate and the government should co-operate.

The equality guaranteed by the Constitution of India, demands active political participation by women which is integral to the whole issue of the progress of women. Women constitute 50 per cent of the rural population (Panda, Snehalata, 1995). This gives them the legitimacy to play an important role at the grass roots level. Women's entry in village political system can ensure change in the political system of the village, the familial and social perceptions of the role of women and development of grass roots leadership among women. At the Gram Sabha and Panchayat levels a new leadership can emerge which is expected to administer better financial resources and provide constructive thinking in village administration and its development'. The champions of the Panchayati Raj desired that rural women should not only become the beneficiaries of development, but more importantly be contributors to it.

The 73rd Amendment has the following provisions relating to women (Art. 243 (D)):

1. Not less than one-third of the seats will be reserved for women (including SCs/STs). These may be allotted by rotation to different constituencies of a Panchayat.
2. There would be reservation for women in the seats that have been allotted to SCs and STs. Not less than one-third of the SC and ST seats may be reserved for women.
3. Not less than one-third of the total number of seats for the office of the chairpersons at each level would be reserved for women. This would be rotated among different Panchayat at each level.

The 73rd Amendment came in force in April, 1993 and accordingly, all the states amended their laws relating to local self-government. This led to a large number of women leaders coming to power at the grass roots levels.

Empowerment of Women in Democracy

Indian democracy is the biggest democracy in the world having large number of electorates. Though the Constitution of India has provided right to equality under Article 14, but in reality it is a myth. The Democracy in India is unworkable due to gender discrimination. This leads to women community being deprived of their rights, status, and position in public life. Democratic politics is not meaningful unless it provides equal opportunities to women at par with men in all walks of life. The equal participation of women in democratic process strengthens the quality of civic life.

It is necessary to provide adequate facilities or opportunities for women folk in social, economic and political fields. As women constitute half of the Indian population, they should get adequate representation in decision-making. This is possible only when they are empowered in real sense. Empowerment is followed by representation, which means power and responsibility (Malvika, 2007). This is based on two important principles like representing the interests of people and authority to act as per the aspirations of people. Until and unless women are politically empowered, the social and economic empowerment will be meaningless. It is through the authority or power one can tackle their problems effectively by legal and constitutional measures.

Even though the world is moving towards globalization, women are deprived of their rights and status. Discrimination of women from conception to cessation of life is well-known. According to United Nations report "Women constitute half of worlds income and own less than 1/100th of the world's property" (Malvika, 2007, p. 103). Women despite of their value in family, society and state are not treated at par with men. The inferior position of women has spread in all walks of life. Empowerment is one of the basic requirements to provide opportunities and facilities to improve the condition and status of women, and also it is an essential starting point and process for the realization of the values of women's liberation and freedom.

Women in Local Self-Government

The passage of 73rd and 74th Amendments is a milestone in

the Constitutional history of India, which brought remarkable changes in the local governing institutions by providing 1/3rd seats for women members as well as chairpersons (including SCs and STs) at all levels of Panchayati Raj Institutions. As a result of this there are one million women members along with women members or urban local bodies like Municipal Councils and Corporations (Women's Link, 1998). These Amendments to Constitution of India provide an opportunity for women to participate in the functioning of local governing institutions as the local political elites. This would certainly contribute to strengthen the democratic process and decentralization at all the local levels.

Empowerment framework is a process of development planners determine a project or programme of the welfare, access, containerization, participation or control levels and determine intervention to move women to higher levels of equality (Sreeramulu, 2007). Efforts to uplift women in our society are made by securing for them economic independence and by integrating them into political process. Against this background, the 73rd Constitutional Amendment passed in April 1993, by Parliament and all the State Governments ratified by April 1994, which give women 33 per cent of the seats at all levels of the Panchayat System, is a significant measure. It has been widely perceived as a crucial step for empowering women and raised hopes for their increased participation in local decision-making structures.

Women Political Participation in Different Local Bodies in India

In states where the social status of women has traditionally been better and levels of literacy, status in society, participation in the workforce and even, in local politics higher, women have been able to take advantage of the new measure. In Andhra Pradesh, Karnataka and Maharashtra, prior to the new legislation, women had contested elections, occupied reserved positions and contributed to the functioning of panchayats. In all women panchayats this was even, more clearly recognizable. Quite a few studies had pointed out the difference, that women members made to the nature of the decisions and the process by which they were formulated.

Karnataka was the one of the first state to provide reservations for women in Panchayati Raj Institutions. The Karnataka Zilla Panchayat, Taluk Panchayat Samiti, Mandal Panchayat and Nyaya Panchayat Act of 1983 provided for 25 per cent reservation for women along with reservation for SCs, STs and Other Backward Classes. The term of panchayat members began in 1987 and thousands of women were elected to local bodies. The 73rd Amendment in the Constitution was passed in 1992 that guaranteed one-third reservation for women and Karnataka was the first state to introduce these measures. The Karnataka Panchayat Act of 1993 provides for reservation of not less than 33.33 per cent seats for Backward Classes, 15 per cent for SCs and 3 per cent for STs. In all these categories and in the general unreserved group, not less than one-third seats are reserved for women. The State of Karnataka is ahead of all other States even in providing reservation for women in public employment. For this purpose Government Orders were issued on 30.10.1991 and 4.12.1992, which were enforced by an order of Karnataka Administrative Tribunal issued on 3.11.1995 (KAT: 1992).

The origin of the panchayats in Goa, can be traced back to the local self-governing institutions, which existed in the pre-liberation period, like the communidades, the ancient local self-governing unit were called as 'communidades', who owned the village land collectively. The Portuguese Government had full control over this body. In 1962, elections to the panchayats were held for the first time, followed by elections to the state assembly. In Goa, democracy and its roots right at its base. Thus, for the first time institutions were setup, which represented people in the villages. Goa has a single tier system of Panchayati Raj located at the Gram Panchayat level. The strength of the membership of the gram panchayats varies according to the population covered. Before the implementation of 73rd Amendment, one seat in each Gram Panchayat was statutorily reserved for women. All the village panchayats are grouped into taluka-wise blocks. In Goa there have been timely elections to the panchayats. The new Panchayat Raj Act, 1994, has been brought into force through an ordinance on 20th April of 1994, the January, 1997, elections to Panchayats in Goa, under the 73rd Amendment, saw a sizeable number of women assuming the mantle of grass roots leaders. The cumulative representation of women in Sarpanch and Deputy Sarpanch positions came to 40 per cent (Seema : 2000).

Uttar Pradesh is one of the states, where local institutions were established quite early, but their working has not been as satisfactory as in many other states, both in the colonial and post-colonial period. It was only with the passage of UP Panchayat Act, 1947 that an attempt was made to remedy the shortcomings and establish panchayats in all parts of the state. These bodies were envisaged as purely a people's institution, free from official control and based upon adult franchise, with seat reservation for SC/STs and minorities. In UP, Gram Sabhas and Gram Panchayats were established in 1949, throughout the state much earlier than in any other state. In 1960, based upon the Balwantrai Mehta Committee Report, which led to the UP Kshettra Samitis and Zilla Parishad Adhiniyam, there were changes introduced, which envisaged further democratic decentralization. The 73rd Amendment Act given panchayats a constitutional position i.e., they now form a third-tier below the state and elections must be held regularly. The finances available to these bodies and their responsibilities have increased. Reservations have been given to lower castes and women and it is hoped, an opportunity to play a role in local politics (Sudha Pai, 2000).

Reviews

Various research studies have been conducted to study the women's leadership at panchayat level in different states. The panchayat elections that took place in the State of Madhya Pradesh in 1994, brought forward a large number of women, many of whom belong to the Scheduled Castes and Scheduled Tribes. The study on role of women in Panchayati Raj in Madhya Pradesh by Rashmi Arun (1996), found that a majority of women Panchas are housewives and are either illiterate or educated merely up to the primary level. In large number of case the decision to participate in the election was not their own. If a seat was reserved for a woman, the men who were politically active convinced their wife, mother or sister-in-law to contest election, in order to keep the family's presence intact in local politics. And in fact, it is the men who are exercising the power by proxy today. The institution of '*Sarpanch-Pati*' or '*Adhyaksha-Pati*' might not have any legal sanction, but it is thriving in many panchayat in the states.

The Institute of Social Sciences, New Delhi, monitoring the performance of women Panchayat members in Orissa after the recent elections, revealed a mixed picture. Mathew, George (1995) while a woman Sarpanch from Jagatsinghpur district, who although educated, took time to assert herself, while, other woman Sarpanch from Rayagada district with no education whatsoever, took up her job confidently from the beginning. At the same time, both these districts had instances of women panchayat meetings, pointing to the need of proper training of the elected representatives, particularly women.

Ujwala Hiremath (1997) conducted a survey of 40 women members of ten village Gram Panchayats in Karnataka. Her studies show the same trend that is seen at the national level politics—members of influential families always seen to have an edge over the rest. However, it was interesting to note that all these women had a manifesto of development items for the village—shelter for the poor, electricity, toilets, roads, schools, water facility, doctors for primary health centres, sewing machines for young girls and many other things, including old-age and widow pensions, employment for youth, girls education, transport facilities, etc.

Pai, Sudha (1998) cautioned, after brief study of three villages from Meerut district in Uttar Pradesh, that female literacy, independent voting rights and change in the status in the family and society are required for women to play active role in the village politics. The Pradhanis played an almost insignificant role in the functioning of the gram and block panchayat level bodies. They have never attended any meeting or made any decision about allocation of funds to individuals or schemes. (Bhaskar, Manu, 1997) in her study of women Panchayat members in Kerala, found that only about 30 per cent of the members belonged to the forward caste/ communities, while the bulk of them were from the backward caste/communities.

Reservation for Women in Panchayats

The decision by the Union Cabinet to raise reservation for women from one-third to 50 per cent of seats at all three levels of panchayats is a welcome one. However, this decision was taken without addressing the problems caused by mandatory rotation of reserved seats, which women have been drawing attention to and the impasse over the Women's Reservation Bill remains. The latter in particular suggests that the 50 per cent reservation in panchayats is a sop to cover up the government's inability to ensure reservation for women in Parliament and State Legislatures. In August the Union Cabinet decided to reserve 50 per cent of the seats in panchayats at the village, district and intermediate levels for women. The posters of the women's movement have always proclaimed that "women hold up half the sky". However, their right to one-half of property or land or political space has not been recognised and until now the reservation initiatives have stopped at 30 per cent or one-third seats.

The current minimum reservation of one-third positions in panchayats for women was introduced by the 73rd Constitutional Amendment in 1992. This indicated an acceptance that the reservation should have been proportionate to women's share in the population as the bill included women from the Scheduled Castes (SCs) and Scheduled Tribes (STs) too. But the State was not ready for it. It has taken the state 17 years to decide to enhance the reservation for women to the proportion that it should have been legislated in 1992 itself (Nirmala Buch, 2009). The Committee on the Status of Women in India (CSWI), 1971, in view of the ineffectiveness of token representation of women in panchayats, recommended constituting separate women's statutory panchayats at the village level. But the idea could not be fructified as none of the states were in favour. The interesting turning point on the debate took place when the government of Andhra Pradesh in 1979 recommended 5 per cent reservation for women for the post of Sarpanches in each block for women where the percentage of women electors is comparatively higher (Mahi Pal, 2009).

The major breakthrough took place in 1988 after the emergence of the National Perspective Plan for Women (NPPW) which recommended. Reservation should be made of 30 per cent seats at Panchayat to Zilla Parishad level and local municipal bodies for women. Wherever possible, higher representation of dalits, tribals, women of weaker sections should be ensured. 30 per cent of executive heads of all bodies from Village Panchayat to district level and a certain percentage of chief executives of Panchayati Raj bodies at lower, middle and higher levels must be reserved for women. A more effective step would be to declare a certain percentage of constituencies in the lower tier of Panchayati Raj as exclusively women constituencies and all executive positions in certain number of territorial jurisdictions reserved for women candidates. (National Perspective Plan, 1988, 164-65). This was probably the basis for giving positive discrimination for women in panchayats by legislating the 73rd Amendment Act. Before this enactment, some positive changes took place for women participation in Panchayats as exemplified by the Karnataka Panchayat Act, 1983 reserving 25 per cent seats for women in both at Zila Parishad and Mandal Panchayat levels.

Similarly, Orissa, Maharathara and Kerala also introduced 30 per cent reservation for women in the membership of the panchayats. It may be deduced from above that reservation for women had been confined to membership and rotation was not an issue at all. Rotation Component rith this evolutionary trajectory of women reservation in panchayats let us come to the rotation aspect of reservation for women. The provision for reservation for women and its rotation is mandatory, but how it will be rotated or its periodicity is left to the State Legislatures. That is the reason that in some states the seats are rotated bi-yearly. In this context, it becomes relevant to refer to the resolutions of the Seven Round Tables of Ministers In-Charge of Panchayati Raj which charted out the course of action by both the centre and states to deepen cooperative federalism in the country and in the context of rotation the compendium of resolutions says: There are different practices being adopted in the different States and there are different practices under contemplation in several States. This being so, the option to reserve seats for more than one-term is open but it is for the State Legislature to decide the number of terms for which seats will remain reserved (GoI 2004: 12).

Rethinking Reservation in Panchayats

The belief that women in decision-making is an index of empowerment is reflected in the United Nations Gender Empowerment Measure (GEM), which tracks the percentages of women in Parliament, legislative assemblies, and in senior professional and technical positions. Tracking women's progress through numbers is not new and there is a growing demand that women be accorded a larger role in political decision-making. It is argued that women need to be "empowered" in this realm to facilitate their "real" empowerment. Nupur Tiwari (2009) The Women's Reservation Bill, which aims to reserve 33 per cent of seats in the National and State Legislatures for women, has not yet been passed by the Parliament but the impact of reserving a third of seats in Panchayati Raj Institutions (PRIs) for women has certainly been immense. The biggest success of Panchayati Raj in India is that it has politically and socially empowered women. Of the 26,00,000 panchayat representatives in the country, 9,75,000 are women, 8,50,000 of them from the Scheduled Castes and Tribes (SCs/STs).

Though under the Panchayati Raj System only 33 per cent of seats are reserved for women, Bihar took the bold step of pushing up the figure to 50 per cent in 2006. Elected Women Representatives (EWRs) now occupy 54 per cent of the seats in Bihar's panchayats. Bihar's example was followed by Sikkim, which increased its reservation for women to 40 per cent and held elections in January 2008. Chhattisgarh, Madhya Pradesh, Rajasthan and Uttarakhand have also passed laws increasing the reservation for women in panchayats to 50 per cent, a change that will come into effect when elections are next held. These measures have brought political and social exposure to women from among the dalits, the backward, the poor, and the illiterate.

This development has seen issues like education, water, roads and health gaining more importance on the agendas of Gram Panchayats. Union Minister of Panchayati Raj, Mani Shankar Aiyar says that "the rotation term of reserved posts for women should be extended up to two or three terms because generally the first term for women representatives has proved to be a period of learning and only in the second and third terms do women representatives start showing their real performance". The empowerment of EWRs will be difficult if the rotation system of reserved seats for women is not amended to give them 10 to 15 years of continued opportunity. However, such advocacy will definitely be opposed by forces in the country that are against reservation for women (Nupur Tiwari, 2009. p. 24). The Constitution (Seventy-third and Seventy-fourth Amendment) Act, 1992 sets out in detail, in Article 243D, the manner in which reservations are to be provided to women and others belonging to the SCs/STs.

(a) Reservations to elected seats are mandated by the Constitution in the following pattern:
  (i) One-third of the total number of seats to be filled by direct elections in every panchayats are to be reserved for women. This is inclusive of the reservation provided for women belonging to the SCs/STs (See Article 243D (3)).
  (ii) Within the reservation provided for persons belonging to the SCs/STs as detailed above, not less than one-third of the total number of seats that are reserved for different categories in each panchayat are to be reserved for women belonging to the SCs/STs (See Article 243D (2)).

(b) These seats may be allotted by rotation to different constituencies within a panchayat (See Article 243D (1) and (3)).

(c) The provision for reservation to the office of chairperson is nearly identical to the above provisions.

A recent survey, commissioned by the Ministry of Panchayati Raj and executed by AC Nielsen-ORG MARG under the guidance of an academic advisory committee, provides many new insights into the social and political empowerment of women in PRIs. This large survey covered Gram Panchayats in 23 states and had a total sample size of more than 20,000, including EWRs, Elected Male Representatives (EMRs), former EWRs, and official functionaries. Nearly three-fourths of the EWRs in the sample belonged to the SC/STs and other backward communities, and were evenly divided above and below the poverty line. Reservation has played a significant role – four-fifths of all the EWRs were elected from reserved seats. Its role was also evident in that it emerged as an important motivator, persuading 43 per cent of women representatives to contest their first election. Its absence dissuaded 39 per cent of former EWRs from seeking re-election. A majority of the EWRs had contested only one election (87%) and the proportion of first timers in politics was therefore high (86%). Around 14 per cent were re-elected more than once at the Gram Panchayat level (Nupur Tiwari, 2009, p. 24-25). Further analysis showed that a majority of former EWRs could not get re-elected because their seats had been de-reserved when the poll came around.

While no gender discrimination in panchayats was reported by 60 per cent of the EWRs, acceptability and the ability to raise issues freely in panchayat meetings was mentioned by 94 per cent. A supportive professional environment evidently motivates EWRs to perform better, as 60 per cent to 64 per cent reported an increase in their interaction with line departments and parallel bodies. Even the participation of other women citizens in various activities such as attending gram sabha meetings had reportedly increased (68-78%). However, issues related to planning rural development works and identifying families below the poverty line were discussed mainly by the male pradhans and ward members. In the case of EWRs, prior association with any form of politics was low, and for most, the act of contesting the first election signalled their entry into active politics. Whatever prior association they had was of a limited nature. A significant proportion of EWRs said that they were earlier associated with groups or committees and that this association had helped them.

The successful EWR now acts as a role model to others. The increased proportion of EWRs has ensured that the principles of justice between the sexes prevail and this has certainly led to the fulfilment of certain interests of women, which may otherwise have been neglected. It is for sure that without the system of reservation women would have had no role to play in grass roots politics in India. Statistics show that 95 per cent of EWRs claim they would never have acquired positions in panchayats if there were no reserved seats for them (Centre for Women's Development Studies, 1999). Reservation has at least succeeded in bringing women in rural India into the political forum and EWRs can now imagine contesting against men in the future.

It is possible for the states to reserve 50 per cent of the seats in panchayats for women through an amendment to their panchayat laws without a central initiative for a constitutional amendment. The 73rd Amendment says the reservation for women should be "not less than one-third" and not one-third of the seats. So legislation in the states could have included more than one-third reservation for women at any time. However, no state saw fit to do so. Most of them just reiterated "not less than one-third" without stipulating any specific percentage. Now that all political parties are in search of new allies, reservations for women in panchayats have been enhanced in the states. Bihar took the lead in 2006 under Chief Minister, Nitish Kumar when he was exploring new social coalitions that included sections like the most backwards and women. This state, which was dragging its feet on panchayat elections, finally held them after including 50 per cent reservation for women. Thereafter, other states like Madhya Pradesh (MP), Chhattisgarh and Rajasthan have amended their panchayat laws to provide 50 per cent reservation for women.

Conclusion

Though women comprise about half of the Indian population they have been subjected to discriminatory social ethos resulting in denial of equality of status and opportunities in social, economic and political spheres. Over the years the realization has drawn to us that women have no less concrete contribution in social and economic progress of the community and the country. Furthermore, in sharp contrast to their urban counterpart the hapless conditions of rural women are more glaring and galloping. Because of various socio-economic constraints, clear absence of acceptance of women's public role, more orthodox social milieu of agricultural society and utter confinement in subsistence struggle all have practically and comprehensively strangulated rural women political participation in almost every sense. The efforts towards integrating women in the development process through panchayats remained for decades elusive, a mere 'tokenism' and it could not bring any perceptible process. A change in political status may bring about a larger transformation is socio-economic processes. Extending the term of reserved seats for women up to two or three terms would allow women in panchayats the time and space to negotiate their own power relationships within them. If they are given 10 to 15 years of continued opportunity, it can perhaps nudge them in the right direction, and encourage and nurture their desire to be assertive and independent.

Women in general could not gain much, if at all, from the political and development process at the grass roots. If this was the overall pattern since the inception of Panchayati Raj experiment, form the fag end of 1980's women's involvement in wider scale sought to be secured in some states like Karnataka and Kerala. From 1993 onwards women have got the meaningful and even chance to occupy one-third seats and post in all panchayat institutions everywhere. Enhancing women's reservation in panchayats is good but it is not enough. Seventeen years after the Constitution was amended to reserve one-third of the seats in panchayats for women, the Union Cabinet has approved increasing this reservation to 50 per cent. Thus the women's engagement and participation has begun virtually from a scratch and women's role herein has to be viewed and grasped from this perspective. Role of Panchayats woman members (as well as male) should be posited on the overall functional context of panchayats. If one has to get into rural development or women's development role of woman members one should reflect on what is feasible and what is the role performance.

References

Bhaskar, Manu, (1997), 'Women Panchayat Members in Kerala', *Economic and Political Weekly*, April 26, p. ws. 15.

Centre for Women's Development Studies (1999): "From Oppression to Assertion: A Study of Panchayats and Women in MP, Rajasthan, and UP" (New Delhi: CWDS).

Government of India (1988): National Perspective Plan for Women 1988-2000 AD, Report of the Core Group set up by the Department of Women and Child Development (New Delhi: Ministry of Human Resource Development).

——,(2004): A Compendium of Resolutions of the Seven Round Tables of Ministers In-Charge of Panchayati Raj (New Delhi: Ministry of Panchayati Raj), July-December.

Geralitine Forbes (1996), *The New Cambridge History of India, Women in Modern India*, Cambridge University Press, 101.

Karnataka Administrative Tribunal, (1992) "Writ Petition Nos. 3823 and 3824 of 1992.

Mathew, George, (1995). "Will Reservation Ensure Participation," Vol. 42, Nos. 5-6, 'Social Welfare', August-September, p. 24.

Mahi. Pal (2009). "Why Rethink Rotation of Reservation in Panchayats?" *Economic and Political Weekly*, VOL 44. No. 23, June 06 - June 12, pp. 70-71.

Malvika, M. Deshpande (2007). "Democratic Politics Through Empowerment of Women," *Karnataka Journal of Politics*, Vols. VIII & IX, October, p. 102.

——, (2007). "Democratic Politics Through Empowerment of Women," *Karnataka Journal of Politics*, Vols. VIII & IX, October, p.103.

Nirmala Buch (2009) "Reservation for Women in Panchayats: A Sop in Disguise?" *Economic and Political Weekly*, Vols. 44, No. 40, October 03 - October 09, p.8.

Nupur Tiwari (2009). "Rethinking the Rotation Term of Reservation in Panchayats," *Economic and Political Weekly*, Vol. 44, No. 05, January 31 - February 06, pp. 23- 25.

——, (2009). "Rethinking the Rotation Term of Reservation in Panchayats," *Economic and Political Weekly*, Vol. 44, No. 05, January 31 - February 06, pp. 24-25.

Pai, Sudha (1998). 'Pradhanis in New Panchayats', Field Notes from Meerut District, *Economic and Political Weekly*, May 2.

Panda, Snehalata (1995), "Women in Rural Local Government," *Kurukshetra*, April, Vol. XLIII, No. 7, p. 103.

Rashmi, Arun,(1996). "Role of Women in Panchayati Raj"; Vol. XLI, *The Administrator*, April-June, p. 115.

Seema, Pradeep B. (2009), "Panchayats and Women Self Help Groups: Understanding the Symbiosis," *The Indian Journal of Political Science*, Vol. LXX, No. 2, April-June, p. 451.

Seema P. Salgoankar (2000). "Women in Panchayati Raj Institutions: A case study in Goa," (Ed) Kiran Saksena, *Women and Politics*, Gyan Publisiing House, New Delhi, pp.146-147.

Sreeramulu, G. (2007), "Women Empowerment Through Self Help Groups: A Study in Karnataka," *Karnataka Journal of Politics*, Vols. VIII & IX, October, p.116.

Sudha Pai (2000). Pradhanis in the New Panchayats: A study from Meerut Distirct," (Ed) Kiran Saksena *Women and Politics*, Gyan Publishing House, New Delhi, pp. 127-128.

Sukhpal, Kaur, (2009) "Women's Rights: A Historical Perspective", *The Indian Journal of Political Science*, Vol. LXX, No. 1, January-March, p. 123.

——, (2009) "Women's Rights: A Historical Perspective", *The Indian Journal of Political Science*, Vol. LXX, No. 1, January-March, p. 128.

Suneera Kapoor (2005). "Status of Women in India Society: Empowering Women through Legislation", in Bhardwaj (ed.), *Gender Discrimination: The Politics of Women Development*, Anamika Publishers and Distributors Pvt. Ltd. New Delhi, p. 144.

Ujwala Hiremath, (1997). "Women in Grass root Politics," Vol. 44, No. 2, '*Social Welfare*,' May, p. 13.

Vats, S. and Shakntala Mudgal (1999) (ed), *Women and Society in Ancient India*, Om Publications, Faridabad, p. 1.

10

Rural Finance and Commission Agents
Social Reality

Manmohan Singh Gill

Adoption of farm technology is capital intensive and its application requires sufficient supply of credit to meet input demands. The development of infrastructure in the form of cooperatives societies especially credit cooperatives and Gramin banks have supported the needs of the farming community. The financial and technical support provided by the cooperatives to the farmers have helped tremendously in achieving higher production of various crops and saved the farmers from the exploitative structure of the moneylenders (Singh, 1998). The credit cooperatives besides helping the farmers in achieving higher production were expected to save the farming community from the exploitative structure of money-lenders and bring lenders and borrowers close to each other (Singh, 2003). Darling (1984) holds that Cooperative Village Bank will not lend unless credit and object are good and it insists upon punctual repayment to make farmers free of any kind of indebtedness. At the same time, this will taught farmers to be on sound finance for future borrowing. The cash requirement for cultivation with new agrarian technologies is eleven times higher than the traditional methods (Prasad, 1991) and it is much higher at the present level of technological adoption and use of other inputs. In addition, so as to diversify the cereal oriented production pattern towards allied activities, lot of financial assistance is needed to the farmers because their own sources are not sufficient to meet the expenses of diversified production programme (Brar, 2001). With such an increase in the demand for capital, a question arises: Can a farmer have access to the financial resources that are prerequisite for the present farming needs? Studies (Kaushal, 1971; Gulati, 1996; Lekshmi *et al.*, 1998; Chahal, 2005) reveal that there exist a big gap between what a farmer owns and what he requires in terms of finance. The cost of different inputs has increased enormously as compared to the increase in the farm output prices and it is going to be more on the higher side with the type of policies being initiated whereby the subsidies on fertilizers are to be withdrawn overcoming years. Nevertheless, cooperative credit societies and other formal institutions of finance have been made functional to meet the rising demand of farming community but the credit advanced by these institutional agencies is inadequate to match the demand and so the farmers are made to depend upon non-institutional sources of credit (Patel, 1963; Thingalaya, 1978; Bell, 1990; Gill, 2001).

This paper addresses to one of the important non-institutional source of rural finance. With the help of secondary sources of information, this paper analyzes the importance and the shortcoming of such source of farm credit. Also it highlights the circumstantial forces that keep this non-institutional source in vogue despite its adverse effect on the socio-economic life of the rural farming community particularly in the light of rising rate of suicides among the community. In addition, the study particularly draws its conclusion on the basis of studies undertaken in Punjab.

Among the non-institutional agencies, commission agents/ *arhtiyas* have emerged as an important financier of the rural society. A great proportion of the funds and inputs requirements of the farming community for diverse agricultural needs come from the *arhtiyas* who have been able to appreciate the multifarious demands of farmers and lend them in all seasons and for all purposes. Studies by Khan and Tripathi (1972), Desai (1990), Jodka (1995), Gill (2003) have concurred similar inferences. In Andhra Pradesh, as against 20 crores advance by banks and credit societies, Rs. 90 crores of credit is being advanced by the *arhtiyas* in the form of inputs (Parthasarthy, 1993). Another report on the situation in Punjab states that 61.3 per cent of the farmers' needs are met by 63.85 per cent of the credit advanced by *arhtiyas*. Further, small and marginal farmers due to their inability to finance high cost inputs are forced to cultivate low value crops and if their credit needs are fulfilled only then they will shift to high value crops. On the other hand, large farmers have large resources and manage to avail credit from the institutional sources to their advantage to reap the scale of agricultural development. In the process, the small and marginal farmers are at the disadvantageous position in terms of operation and management of credit needs. Thus, there is difference with regard to credit availability among various classes of cultivators. Likewise, Mehta and Prasad (1988) have reported that cultivators in the more advanced states like Punjab, Gujarat, Tamil Nadu and others have more access to credit from institutional agencies and there is uneven flow of credit among the farming communities of different states. Epstein (1978) finds that cooperatives particularly credit societies are serving the wealthy farmers due to which they are able to make use of advanced agricultural technology to raise production and productivity of the farm. Under such situations, the poor farmers have to depend upon the non-institutional sources of credit. The data in the Table 10.1 reveals that out of the 83.9 per cent households with landholding up to 2 hectares, 79.9 per cent are under debt and 49.7 per cent have taken loan from the non-institutional agencies. Secondly, the households possessing more than10 hectares of landholding have their outstanding loan more from the institutional agencies as compared to that of the non-institutional agencies. This amply justifies that the outstanding loan of the large farm households is from the institutional credit agencies rather than the non-institutional ones.

Table 10.1 : Total and Indebted Farm Households and their Source of Debt by Landholding Size, 2003

Size of land possessed (hectare)	*Total Households %*	*Total Indebted Household %*	*Loan from Institutional agencies %*	*Loan from Non-institutional agencies %*
< 0.01	1.4	1.3	22.6	77.4
0.01 – 0.40	32.8	30.0	43.3	56.7
0.41 – 1.00	31.7	29.8	52.8	47.2
1.01 – 2.00	18.0	18.9	57.6	42.3
Up to 2.00	79.9	79.9	51.3	49.7
2.01 – 4.00	10.5	12.5	65.1	35.0
4.01 – 10.00	4.8	6.4	68.8	31.1
10.00+	0.9	1.2	67.6	32.4
All sizes	100.0	100.0	57.7	42.4

Source : EPW Research Foundation, 2008.

An analysis of non-institutional sources of credit requires having an overview of the situation with regard to agriculture credit advanced by institutional agencies like cooperative credit societies, banks and the like. Going through the data regarding loan advanced and recovered of the agricultural cooperative societies of Punjab, it is found that the loan advanced and loan recovered varies considerably. In 1970-71, the outstanding amount of loan advanced was 90.76 per cent and it increased to 139.07 per cent in 1990-91 (Table 10.2). With reforms setting in 1990's, banks profitability increased but their availability for rural credit and for backward regions has been adversely affected (Shah, Rao and Shankar, 2007). In other words, the rural sector was left at the mercy of moneylenders and the banks priority shifted from agriculture sector to industrial one. It may be because of the lack of collateral as security with the vast majority of small and marginal farmers. This indicates at the same time that farming community is under heavy debt as they either have not paid the outstanding advance or have not been able to get remunerative returns on the farm. This is amply evident from 2001-02 onwards trends of loan advanced. Equally, there has been a trend of decreasing outstanding loans; the outstanding amount has not increased more than 70 per cent.

Table 10.2 : Progress of Primary Agricultural Credit Societies in Punjab

Year	*Number*	*Loan Advanced*	*Loan Outstanding*	*Societies showing loss*
1970-71	10,932	5,726.59	5,197.32 (90.76)	2001 (18.30)
1980-81	4,266	19,920.65	14,625.88 (73.42)	1022 (23.96)
1990-91	4,633	34,630.66	48,161.63 (139.07)	962 (20.76)
2000-01	4,084	2,13,899.47	1,53,029.93 (71.54)	808 (19.78)
2003-04	3,996	3,32,817.83	2,31,948.64 (69.69)	1203 (30.11)
2004-05	3,985	3,78,947.69	2,66,475.56 (70.32)	1272 (31.92)
2005-06	3978	4,55,191.12	3,03,515.18 (66.68)	1171 (29.44)
2006-07	3981	5,106,17.43	3,612,48.39 (70.75)	1183 (29.72)

Source : Statistical Abstract of Punjab, Various Issues.

Moreover, the data provides that the number of societies going under loss has increased from 18.30 per cent in 1970-71 to 31.92 per cent in 2004-05 and it is 29.72 per cent in 2006-07. It amounts to the level of non-payment of debts by the farming community in Punjab; considered as the food basket of India. The amount of loss increased from Rs. 36.44

lakh in 1970-71 to Rs. 2334.50 lakh in 2004-05. This amply depicts the plight of farming community. Since data pertaining to class structure of agrarian society is not available, it cannot be generalized that the outstanding amount is with the rich and influential farmers or the small and marginal farmers. The analysis of EPW Research Foundation finds that with increase in size of holding, non-institutional loan decreases and that of institutional loan increases (2008). According to another estimate (Shergill, 1998 cited from Punjab Development Report, 2004), per acre indebtedness of the small and marginal farmers is the highest (Rs. 10,105) followed by that of the farmers with landholding between 5 to 10 acres (Rs. 7941) and those between 10 to 15 acres (Rs. 4230). Keeping the size of landholding into consideration, it is very clear that the upper strata of landholders have greater outstanding amount as compared to that of the lower strata. Even the study (Epstein, 1978) points out these credit societies are serving the wealthy farmers as against the poor one and the outstanding amount is largely with the rich class of the farming community. Bardhan (1984), Gill (2001), Kaur (2003) find that landless and small farmers remain dependent on informal sources for most of their credit requirements, thus supporting the above inference that the outstanding loan is invariably of the farmers above the category of small ones. Not only this, there is growing interference of governmental officials and these cooperatives have not been able to fulfil the aspirations in terms of new technology and cash requirements (Singh, 2003). Under such circumstances, the small and marginal farmers stand at the disadvantageous position if Government waive off the debt as the debt waiver specifically for the institutional outstanding credit. In other term, the debt waiver is in the interest of the already 'have' class. It is also the political compulsion of the so-called farmer's oriented parties to justify the waiver of farm credit so as to bail out themselves of the covert economic rhetoric of dwindling position of the farm sector in the light of globalization. It is the expectation of the borrowers that the loan will be waived off, has eroded the repayment behaviour of the farmers (Chaudhary and Makhija, 1999). Secondly, looking at the distribution of landholding, the small and marginal farmers account for 78.2 per cent of the agricultural holdings in the country (Punjab Development Report, 2004). The share of marginal and small holding increased to 77.65 per cent between 1970-71 and 1990-91.Consequentially, the small and marginal farmers will lag behind in the process of debt waiver and their dependency on the non-institutional sources of credit further deteriorate their position in the agrarian society. Equally, the rural elite dominates the cooperative structure as they used to during the colonial rule and hence, keep control of the credit advanced in their favour as against those without political or economic power.

Moreover, another institutional source of farm credit that is commercial banks advanced agricultural credit and it increased from Rs. 165.27 crores in 1984-85 to 245.59 crores in 1986-87 and after that there was drastic fall in the credit advanced by the commercial banks (Sekhon and Kaur, 2003) due to low returns and high transaction costs and overdue. At the same time, the cost of production increased, degradation of soil and water resources continued and farmers carried out their wheat-paddy rotation that resulted in increase demand of the credit. Since, the commercial bank continue to withdraw from agricultural advance and cooperatives standing advance continued to soar and many cooperatives come under losses, the non-institutional sources became important source of finance to fill the gap. Mukherjee and Bandyopadhyay (1993) narrate that with the cooperative structure going in disarray and the institutional finance from the commercial banks is in a state of destitute, the poor farmers have no option except to non-institutional credit sources and for this reason, moneylenders continue to hold ubiquitous position in the rural India. Even the Regional Rural Banks with their domain being confined to weaker sections of the rural areas (Misra, 2006) are finding it difficult to curb loan default and so treading a safe path by cutting advances to the rural poor. Such trends amplify the need and existence of non-institutional sources of credit. The observation (Kaur *et al*, 2001) that formal agricultural credit agencies shall have to review their lending policies in order to cater to the credit needs of the farmers to reduce the presence of informal agencies in the agricultural credit markets, justifies the hold of non-institutional agencies over the credit market in the agriculture sector.

The inadequate supply of institutional credit has increased the dependency of farming community in particular the small and marginal farmers on the non-institutional sources of credit. Also, their inability to provide sufficient collateral as security debars them to avail the institutional credit. Shah, Rao and Shankar (2007) have in their observation regarding rural credit point out that the reforms have made the return of moneylenders especially to meet the needs of the peasantry. Reddy (2006) states that it is distressing that government is considering to bring in moneylenders to solve the problem of rural credit. The fact is that the main source of credit for the pure tenants and mixed tenants are the traders (Kaur, 2003). Singh (2003) finds that majority of the farmers take loan from the cooperative societies and the private moneylenders. Nearly 21 per cent of the farmers have taken loan from the private moneylenders in their study of 150 respondents of four blocks of Muktsar district. Another study of a Ludhiana village reveals that majority of the respondents have taken advance from the commission agents for inputs like insecticides, pesticides, fertilizers, seeds and even to run the diesel pump for irrigation (Gill and Kaur, 2003). Parthasarthy (1997) finds that 90 crores of credit is advanced by the *arhtiyas* in the form of inputs as against 20 crores advance by banks and credit societies in Andhra Pradesh. Sengupta (2008) in his analysis of Vidharba region finds that moneylenders have considerable hold on the farmer's entire life cycle. The farmer borrows for diversification without realizing its prospects and borrows money for tapping groundwater sources and application of fertilizers. The downward global trends of cash crops many a times leave farmer indebted to moneylenders and other institutional credit sources. According to Chahal (2005), it is not easy for the farmers to get requisite amount of credit from cooperative banks and credit societies. They still have to depend on the moneylenders and commission agents to get loan for their investments. He further holds that the bulk of the loans have been arranged from the commission agents and moneylenders, which is estimated to be about Rs.5500 crores. Even the study by the Punjab Cooperative Department reveals that commission agents provided 61.31 per cent of the credit during the two major farm operations in 1997 (cited from Kaur *et al*, 2000). According to Singh (2008), 43 per cent of the farmers' needs are met by the commission agents/ *arhtiyas* who have their share of 43 thousands crores of business in Punjab only (cited from Dhanik Bhaskar, 2008). If this is the situation in Punjab, the Indian scenario cannot be at variance from that of Punjab. In other words, commission agents and moneylenders are the powerful groups that support Indian agriculture in its road to agrarian development and plight of the farming community.

The credit advanced by the commission agents or *arhtiyas* is mostly for the purchase of farm inputs like fertilizers, insecticides, etc. besides their non-productive purposes. Reddy (2007) finds that over the last 20 years there is decline in the borrowing for consumption purpose and increase in that of for production purpose. The moneylender lends in kind to the tune of 77.71 per cent for seed and fertilizers. On the other hand, Jeromi (2007) finds that 66 per cent of the loan is utilized for non-productive uses. In Punjab, majority of the farmers take loan from the *arhtiyas* for meeting their non-productive purposes, such as socio-religious ceremonies, housing and the like (Gill and Kaur, 2003; Kaur, 2003; Singh and Kaur, 2003). Secondly, the rate of interest charged for the advance extended by the *arhtiyas* or moneylenders is quite exorbitant ranging from 24 to 36 per cent. Ahlawat (2002) has reported 30 per cent rate of interest rates charged for the loan advanced by the traders whereas Gill and Kaur (2003) and Reddy (2007) have reported 14 to 21 per cent as rate of interest on the credit advanced by the commission agents. Irrespective of the high rate on interest, the easy availability of loan is another factor conducive to their hold over the credit market in the agriculture sector. The cumbersome procedure and file work makes it difficult for the farming community to procure loan. Getting advance from the banks requires sureties as well as collateral as security, which is often difficult for the small and marginal farmers. Many a times, farmers take loan from the *arhtiyas* to repay their loan instalment of the banks to keep their account in continuity. Gill and Kaur (2003) have come out with this observation in their study besides pointing out the ease of securing loan from these non-institutional sources.

Further, *arhtiyas* extend loan depending upon the credit-worthiness of the loaners and their social relations with the commission agents. Also, the *arhtiyas* make sure that the sale deeds are processed through them which act as collateral for the advance made to the borrower. This rider demeans the bargaining position of the farmer in the market: also provide sufficient ground for his exploitation. Darling (1925) has long time back observed that traders and moneylenders used to purchase the produce of the borrowers at much cheaper rates besides referring to the fact that moneylender cares nothing but tempt his client to borrow more. The analysis thus, points out that non-institutional sources are concerned with the continuity of indebtedness of the farming community.

No doubt, the situation has changed with the emergence of markets and procurements made by government agencies and the debtor is not under compulsion to sell his produce at the prearranged price. But the *arhtiyas* still rule the roast especially in the case of farmers where they have lent the credit for one or the other purpose. According to Ghuman (2008), 52 per cent of the debt is from non-institutional agencies. In this way, the borrowing farmers are under compulsion to maintain continuity of the economic ties through the services of their lenders. Not only this, they participate in their social ceremonies to strengthen the economic relationship. Gill and Kaur (2003) have found that *arhtiyas* lend helping hand in all odd situation and their mutual trust and keeping parity of the accounts consolidate their economic relations. Such bondage gets further strengthened with their participation in socio-religious ceremonies and offering gifts on such occasions. The vulnerability and weak bargaining position of the borrower define his subordination to the lender and for this, the scale remains in favour of the lender not borrower. This relationship is of exploitative type in which the lender position gets strengthened with poverty of the borrower and his vulnerability for credit needs for non-productive purposes. The issue emerges how long farming community will continue to hold their weak position in the credit market? Secondly, is there a way for providing credit support to meet other exigencies so bring him out of the control of non-institutional sources of credit?

With its entire shortcoming, the *arhtiyas*, moneylenders and other informal institutions of rural credit play positive role of providing credit under distress situations where institutional agencies fail to address the demand and needs of the farming community. They also play a negative role as exploiters and are largely responsible for rural indebtedness. They are charging exorbitant rate of interest and defining the buying and selling domains of the farming community.

Conclusion

The above analysis based on secondary sources of information depicts the exploitative and volatile situation of the rural society. The institutions meant to serve the needs and demands of the rural community have not been able to appreciate the non-productive needs of the farming community. Secondly, the greater outstanding advances have made the institutional agencies to think twice before lending in the rural sector for agricultural development. The cumbersome procedures and collateral as security for loan are the major hurdles in realization of the needs and aspirations of the farming community. This inference is corroborated by a study undertaken by the EPW Research Foundation in 2008. With the result, these institutions are giving way to informal credit agencies to operate on a large scale. Moneylenders or commission agents are of course lending at a high rate of interest but are able to cut their costs of lending because they are better informed about the borrower and the borrower keep their economic relations with the bonding of social ones. For this reason, they are ought to survive in the rural setting and continue to fill the credit gap created with the resultant no advance for the consumption and distress need of the farming community. The government may exonerate the farming community by writing off their outstanding in the institutional credit agencies but what about the outstanding credit farmers have with the non-institutional agencies. Small and marginal farmers have more than 75 per cent of their outstanding loan from the non-institutional sources. Secondly, the process of waiving off the loan will encourage the farming community to get advances from the institutional agencies on a large scale and then wait till the government again waive off the loans. Meanwhile, they will take the support of the non-institutional agencies to meet their credit needs and consolidate the position of the moneylenders or commission agents. How long will the government continue to waive off loans rather the public continue to pay for none of their fault? Did ever the planners or farmers oriented political parties realize the consequences of such a waiver? Why not to help those who regularly pay instalments of their outstanding farm credit? All these questions have to be answered if farming community has to bring back to the path of development and set the economic structure of the society but the political compulsion of regional parties who venture on rural vote bank never want to reverse the process of lending or putting a curb on those who are defaulters for long time. Interestingly, if a study is carried to ascertain the defaulters of the institutional credit, one may come out with facts that credit defaulters (particularly that of institutional credit agencies) are mostly the rich and influential and they are the actual beneficiaries of any debt waiver. Of course, in the whole scenario despite the exploitative nature of the informal credit agencies, these are a social and economic reality.

References

Ahlawat, S. R., "Political Economy and Peasant Suicide", *Guru Nanak Journal of Sociology*, Vol. 23, No. 1, 2002.

Bardhan, P. K., *Land, Labour and Rural Poverty: Essays in Development Economics*, Oxford University Press, Delhi, 1984.

Bell, C. "Interaction between Institutional and Informal Credit Agencies in Rural India", *The World Bank Economic Review*, Vol. 4, No. 3, 1990.

Brar, S. S. "Capital Requirements for Diversified Production Programme in Punjab", *Indian Economic Panorama*, Vol. 11, no. 2, 2001.

Chaudhary, R. L. and Makhija, "Repayment Performance of Crop Loan", *Indian Economic Panorama*, Vol. 9, No. 3, 1999.

Chahal, T. S. *Forced Fall: A Case of Punjab Farmers*, Institute of Development Planning, Amritsar, 2005.

Darling, Malcolm, *The Punjab Peasantry in Prosperity and Debt*, South Asia Book, Columbia, 1925.

Desai, S.M. *Agriculture and Rural Banking in India*, Himalaya Publishing House, Bombay, 1990.

Epstein, T., *South India: Yesterday, Today and Tomorrow*, Macmillan, London, 1978.

EPW Research Foundation, "The Loan Waiver Scheme", *Economic and Political Weekly*, Vol. XLIII, No. 11, 2008.

Gill, Anita, *Rural Credit Markets*, Deep and Deep Publications, New Delhi, 2001.

Gill, M S. *Punjab Society: Perspectives and Challenges*, Concept Publishing Company Pvt. Ltd., New Delhi, 2003.

Gill, M. S. and R. Kaur "Commission Agents in Rural Setting" in Gill (ed.) *Punjab Society: Perspectives and Challenges*, Concept Publishing Company Pvt. Ltd., New Delhi, 2003.

Ghuman, R. S., "Socio-Economic Crisis of Rural Punjab", *Economic and Political Weekly*, Vol. XLIII, No. 7, 2008.

Gulati, A. "New Economic Policy and Agriculture", *Indian Journal of Economics*, Jan-June, 1996.

Human Development Report, Government of Punjab, 2004.

Jeromi, P. D., "Farmers' Indebtedness and Suicides", *Economic and Political Weekly*, Vol. XLII, No. 31, 2007.

Jodka, S. S. "Changing Structure of Informal Credit in Rural Haryana", *Economic and Political Weekly*, Vol. XXX, 1995.

Kaur, Gian, "Tenancy and Demand for Agricultural Credit" in Gill (ed.) *Punjab Society: Perspectives and Challenges*, Concept Publishing Company Pvt. Ltd., New Delhi, 2003.

Kaur, P. *et al*, "Role of Cooperative Credit Institutions in Agricultural Development of Punjab", *Indian Economic Panorama*, vol. 11, no. 2, 2001.

Kaur, Milkho *et al*, "Institutional Agricultural Credit in Punjab: An Overview", *Indian Economic Panorama*, vol. 10, no. 2, 2000.

Kausal, G., *Economic History of India*, Kalyani Publication, Ludhiana, 1971.

Khan, W. and R. N. Tripathi, *Intensive Agriculture and Modern Inputs*, National Institute of Community Development, New Delhi, 1972.

Lekshmi, R. *et al*, "Characteristics of Defaulters in Agricultural Credit Use", *Indian Journal of Agricultural Economics*, Vol. 53, No. 4, 1998.

Mehta and Prasad, *Agrarian Relations and Rural Exploitation*, Ashish Publishing House, New Delhi, 1998.

Misra, B. S., "The Performance of Regional Rural Banks In India", cited from *Economic and Political Weekly*, Vol. XLII, No. 15, 2007.

Mukherjee, N. and D. Bandyopadhyay, "New Horizon for West Bengal Panchayats", *Indian Journal of Agricultural Economics*, Vol.48, No.4, September-October 1993.

Parthasarthy, V. P. "Supply of Short Term Credit and Estimation of Credit Gaps", *Indian Cooperative Review*, 1997.

Patel, M. L., "Direction of Cooperative Review", *Indian Cooperative Review*, 1963.

Prasad, K. N. *India's Rural Problems*, Concept Publishing Company Pvt Ltd., New Delhi, 1991.

Reddy, S.T.S., "Diary of a Moneylender", *Economic and Political Weekly*, Vol. XLII, No. 29, 2007.

Reddy, Y. U. *Rural Banking: Review and Prospects*, Centre for Economic and Social Studies, Hyderabad, 2006.

Sekhon, M. K. and Parminder Kaur, "Role of Institutional Finance and Government Investments in Capital Formation of Punjab Agriculture", in Gill (ed) *Punjab Society: Perspectives and Challenges*, Concept Publishing Company Pvt. Ltd., New Delhi, 2003.

Sengupta, J. "Why Farmers Commit Suicides", *The Tribune*, Feb. 16, 2008.

Shah, M. *et al*, "Rural Credit in 20th Century India", *Economic and Political Weekly*, Vol. XLII, No. 15, 2007.

Singh, Sukhdev, "The Lot of Small, Marginal Farmers Remains Same", *The Tribune,* May 8, 1998.

Singh, S. and Mandeep Kaur, "Socio- Economic Adversities of Farmers" in Gill (ed.) *Punjab Society: Perspectives and Challenges,* Concept Publishing Company Pvt Ltd., New Delhi, 2003.

Statistical Abstract of Punjab, Economic and Statistical Organization, Government of Punjab, Chandigarh 2005.

———,"Siyasat ke Pale me kisano ka Bhagya", *Dainik Bhaskar*, July 9, 2008.

Thingalaya, N. K. "Report of Rural Credit Structure and Flaws", *Indian Journal of Agricultural Economics*, Vol. 33, 1978.

11

Strategic Issues in Financial Sustainability of Self-Help Groups in India : An Empirical Study

Samirendra Nath Dhar

Micro-finance as a Movement for Financial Inclusion

The majority of accepted and effectual approaches to developmental planning across the globe including India have been raising the income and asset levels of the underprivileged and poverty stricken mass through the provision of self-employment. Over 500 million of the world's poor subsist on $2-3 per day but are economically active and earn their livelihoods by being self-employed or by working in micro enterprises (very small businesses which may employ up to 5 people). However, these poor households are severely constrained because they do not have access to financial resources, loans or a safe place to hold savings. Over 80 per cent of all households in developing countries do not have access to institutional banking services. It has been estimated that 93 per cent of India's workforce i.e., about more than 370 million people are in the informal sector and more than one-third of the workers are women. " The challenge before us is how to evolve a holistic and effective strategy to transform the informal sector into the main driver of income-enhancing and life-fulfilling opportunities for employment, self-employment and entrepreneurship"(Vajpayee, 2003). However, when there are no financial institutions to cater to their financial requirements for self-employment, poor entrepreneurs in search of just eking out a livelihood rely by and large on informal sources such as family, friends, suppliers or moneylenders who frequently play the role of extortionist and drain them even of their paltry livelihood means by charging inordinately high rates of interest and demanding exorbitant collaterals. "Moneylenders and pawnshops are more costly in direct terms. Sometimes charging very high annual interest rates of 60 to 200 per cent, especially when the amounts are small (< Rs. 5000) and are urgently required" (Sinha, 2005). Here stems the need for financial inclusion so that delivery of banking and financial services can be made at an affordable cost to the vast sections of disadvantaged and low income groups, especially poor women in a country. Therefore, "increasing women's access to micro-finance is assumed to initiate a series of 'virtuous spirals' of economic empowerment, increased well-being for women and their families and wider social and political empowerment" (Mayox, 1999). The last decade has witnessed numerous micro-finance programmes being taken up throughout the world aiming at financial inclusion of the impoverished by providing thrift, credit and financial services and products of very small amount to them in rural, semi-urban or urban areas for enabling them to raise their income levels and improve living standards. Though the pioneering efforts at providing micro-credit was made by Prof Yunus in the seventies, the worldwide impetus really took off after the 1997—World Micro-credit Summit, held in Washington DC-target which targeted at eradicating poverty of 100 million poorest families within 2005. Declaration of 2005 as the international year of micro-finance and awarding Prof. Yunus and Grameen Bank with the Nobel Peace Prize in

2006 are recent phenomenon which highlights the significance and recognition of this movement.

SHGs as effective change agents for better livelihood

The new micro-finance movement has made a paradigm shift in the quality of finance delivered to the rural and urban poor. Most of the micro-finance programmes operates on the principle 'Borrower know the best' and shifts its focus from individual to group approach as Self-Help Group (SHG) in an effective manner. Harper (1998) described that group system of micro-financial services evolved in particular in Bangladesh (the Grameen Groups) and in Latin America (Solidarity groups and village banking), as well as in India (Self-Help Group). Sen (2003) observed that " the first and foremost element of self-help is the involvement of the poor in their own development preferably as a group. Isolated and dispersed, they have no power or influence over the aspects that affect their lives. Organised, they have the power to ensure that their interests are protected and their opportunities are enhanced." The collective coming together of individuals as groups commonly called Self-Help Groups is the building block of micro-finance in India. The Self-Help Group (SHG) is a viable alternative to achieve the objective of rural development and to get community participation in all rural development programmes. Self-Help Groups (SHGs) are voluntary associations of people formed to attain certain collective goals, both economic and social goals. SHGs are normally formed with the people coming from rural or semi-urban areas. Each group consists of 10 to 20 members who are generally landless agricultural labourers, rural artisans and women folk micro entrepreneurs. A SHG is a homogeneous affinity group of rural poor voluntarily formed to save small amounts out of their emergent credit needs and revolving their resources among the members both for consumption and small production at such rate of interest.

Credit follows thrift. Periods of loans and other terms are decided by the group. Such groups may be informally registered and should not have a membership of more than 20 if they were to be unregistered. Self–Help Groups (SHGs) are mostly informal groups whose members pool savings and re-lend within the group on rotation or needs basis. The dynamic elements of the groups makes them grow on the resources and management skills of its members and their escalating confidence to get occupied in the issues and programmes that entail their association in the public and private arenas. The Self-Help Groups endow the benefits of collective learning, participatory culture, firm base and platform for discussion and cooperation, economies of scale, and cost effective alternatives for different financial services needed by the micro-finance beneficiaries. "Beyond the cost-effective provision of sorely needed financial services, self-managed savings and internal lending groups around the world have also become catalysts of economic and social development" LACRO (2008). Bringing out the character of SHGs as micro-banks researchers have described them as thrift and credit groups formed and managed by members who practice regular savings, democratically decide the credit needs and disburse credit through periodic meetings, ensure prompt repayment through peer pressure and support, acquire formal credit and administer its proper use and repayment of loans .(Rao, 2002, Khandker, Khalily and Zahedkhan, 1995, Karmakar, 1999, Dasgupta, 2001).

Due to the large segment of the population living in poverty, India is tactically important in the global context to alleviate poverty and to achieve the Millennium Development Goal of halving the world's poverty by 2015. The swiftness with which the movement took off in India in the early nineties and the short span in which the micro-finance system gained maturity in India is unparalleled. No country in the world having a matured micro-finance system works with a single model. In India while the Self-Help Group model predominates, there are variations in forms and linkage systems depending on whether the programme is a Government one or is being monitored by NABARD or other MFIs. Many MFIs have been able to successfully replicate the Grameen model and also provide micro-financial services to joint liability groups, individuals and CDFIs. In the year 1992, NABARD issued operational guidelines to the commercial banks for a pilot project for linking 255 Self-Help Groups to the Banks. The SHG-Bank linkage model was innovative and endeavoured to link the formal banking system to the informal groups in a cost effectual manner. The SHG-Bank linkage programme has registered tremendous growth under the NABARD initiatives and the launching of the Swarnajayanti Gram Swarojgar Yojana. According to NABARD reports, at the end of March 2008 total 34,77,965 SHGs have been linked and financed by banks. The rapid rate at which the model has scaled-up, particularly since the late 1990s, is truly remarkable. The micro-finance movement in the form of SGSY has been initiated in India on 1st April 1999. As an initial breakthrough, total 292426 groups were formed under SGSY in 1999-2000. Registering a ten-fold growth in eight years only, the total count of SHGs under SGSY at the end of March 2009 stands at 32,225,963. The loans outstanding are to the tune of 1934 billion rupees. The cumulative figure under these two programmes has crossed the 5 million mark already, surpassing the target of linking 1 million groups by 2008.

Financial Sustainability of SHGs— The Governing Factors

While the micro-finance beneficiary base in India has witnessed an unparalleled growth and is a reason for applaud, yet concerns regarding the functions, maturity and sustainability of Self-Help Groups are being expressed as cases of groups being defunct or dissolved or attrition of members are being frequently reported. Tankha (2002) drew attention to the fact that "The quality of SHGs being promoted, especially as the SHG bank linkage programme has become increasingly target-driven. The experience of Andhra Pradesh where a massive state promotion drive has resulted in thousands of defunct SHGs, which are now being rehabilitated, provides a warning signal for SHG promotion in future." (Tankha, 2002), SHGs are informal voluntary groups supposed to generate their cohesive characteristics from the homogenous composition of members. However, the basic motive for which groups are formed, i.e., economic and social benefits, if hampered can lead to dilution of cohesiveness and subsequently dissolution of groups. Rutherford (2000), points that informal money management groups are short-lived and changing in their membership for good reasons — to maximise returns and safety. The desire of donors and MFIs to work with stable groups necessitates much investment in management style and leadership towards the development of sustainable structures based upon SHGs." The question of sustainability of the groups is therefore immensely important when viewed in the context of the desire of the micro-finance providers to work with stable groups. "Within micro-finance, sustainability can be viewed at several levels - institutional, group and individual — and can relate to organisational, managerial and financial aspects." (Tankha, 2002) A considerable amount of research has been made regarding the sustainability, specifically financial sustainability of Micro-finance Institutions , but the sustainability of the Self-help groups which form the grass root structures have hitherto been neglected. "However, it is the financial sustainability of micro-finance institutions that has become the critical point of focus of mainstream analysis at the expense of the sustainability of the client/borrower." Therefore, "The sustainability question in respect of SHGs needs to be reviewed given the character, context and objectives of their promotion." (Tankha, 2002)

The attractiveness of SHGs stems from the fact that they are essentially low cost micro-banks operating for the members in distant rural areas. Therefore, the financial sustainability of these groups is achieved when their credit programme is able to cover its operating cost and from the fee and interest income it receives. The process through which SHGs are formed and function in India is essentially savings led. The members are required to pool their savings in a common fund and deposit them into a bank at least for a period of six months before they can be eligible for credit linkages with banks. While the group corpus, which is initially formed with the savings of the members is initially small it increases in size when the groups are credit linked and receive the subsidy and initial credit doses. The financial sustainability of the group depends on the effective financial management of the group corpus as this money is used for inter-lending between group members for their economic as well as consumption purposes. The financial management procedures thus are centred on monitoring the savings of the members, establishing the bank savings- credit linkages and ensuring timely repayment of the loans and the interest on loans granted to the members. In cases of groups which have not taken up economic activities as groups, the financial sustainability of the groups rest on whether the interest income from the inter-loans have been able to cover the operating costs of the groups. Interest incomes depend on the interest rates and the recovery of the loans and the interest on loans. What matters to poorer borrowers is not only the access to money, but also the cost of it. Interest rates should reflect market rates and real costs; especially when the beneficiaries are in the informal sector and prone to be in the nets of moneylenders with their apparently outrageous rates. However, interest rates charged on inter-lending in India has been found to be quite high, in the ranges of 24 to 60 per cent in many cases (CARE, CRS, USAID, 2006, and Karduck and Seibel, 2004) and has raised questions as to whether such high interest rates are necessary for financial sustainability or are they too exorbitant. Is it possible that the delinquencies and dissolutions of groups are as a result of high interest rates on inter-lending? Can the groups be made financially and physically sustainable as well by reducing the interest rates? This study attempts to delve into the issues and find whether a group can be made financially sustainable through monitoring of inter-loan interest rates, recovery of loans and interest amounts so as to cover the operating costs.

Objective, Scope and Methodology of the Study

Drawing from the discussions made in the previous section, it is evident that financial sustainability of a Self-Help Group is dependent on a number of factors such as the rate and frequency of savings, amount, and frequency and pricing of inter-loans, the quality of portfolio on the basis of timely recovery of loans and interests and the operating costs of the groups. The objectives of the study are therefore:

(i) To analyse the thrift and credit mechanisms operating in SHGs under the SGSY.

(ii) To find out the annual operating costs of the SHGs and the components of such operating costs.

(iii) To examine the inter-lending rates, patterns and frequencies of inter-loans, delinquency rates and interest incomes of the SHGs..

(iv) To examine whether the groups are self-sustainable on the basis of coverage of operating costs by interests earned and examine whether inter-lending rates can be reduced.

The study is based on primary data collected from SHGs having a vintage period of one year or more and graded at least level one under the SGSY grading mechanism. While semi-structured checklists and data formats were used to collect specific information, examination of the records and documents of the groups formed the basis of computation of interest incomes and operating costs. In addition to these informal interviews were carried out with DRDC officials, GPRPs and group leaders and a structured questionnaire was administered to one member from each group chosen at random.

The sample consists of 225 Self-Help Groups which were chosen at random from 18 blocks in Jalpaiguri district and Siliguri sub-division in the state of West Bengal . Initially, the list of SHGs having at least grade one as on December 2007 was obtained for each block from the DRDC. For each block a random sample of 30 SHGs was made from the list, taking the total to 540 groups. These groups were contacted to find out whether the maintenance of their books were quite satisfactory and the required information could be obtained. Each SHG has to maintain at least three vital books, a register in which proceedings of the meetings are recorded, a saving-cum-loan register, which keeps almost the entire financial account and cashbook which records the entire bank transactions. In many cases it was found that the DRDC supplied these books free of cost to the SHGs. Out of the 540 groups only 276 groups were found to maintain these books properly to our level of satisfaction. Some groups out of these could not provide information on interest rates or some transaction costs; others were not eager to respond to our queries and were thus eliminated from our sample. The final sample was finally fixed at 225 groups. The following Table 11.1 shows the groups according to their maturity.

Table - 11.1 : Vintage-wise distribution of groups

Vintage of groups	*No. of groups*
12months ——24 months	42
25 months —36 months	65
37 months——48 months	72
49months—— 60 months	40
More than 60 months	6
Total	**225**

The transaction and operating costs, interest incomes, group corpus, inter-loan amounts, and self-sustainability indices was calculated on the basis of the records of these sample groups, loan ledgers of banks and data generated from the checklists and data formats. The findings of the survey are reported below.

Findings of the Study

The findings of the study are reported in different sections, starting with reporting on the thrift and credit mechanisms operating in the groups.

Financial Operations in SHGs-Thrift and Credit Flows

All the sample groups under the study were started on the principle of 'savings first': members contributed weekly or monthly instalments ranging from Rs.20 to Rs.100 regularly for the first six months. The amount and frequency of the meetings were decided in the group meetings independently or sometimes on the advice of the officials of NGOs or the Banks. The initial group corpus developed solely out of these savings. A portion of this group corpus was lent out as loans to the members and a portion was deposited in the designated banks. After six months of the formation of the groups, they were examined and graded by officials of the DRDC on the basis of certain parameters like regularity of meetings, attendance of members, maintenance of books, loans provided to members, repayment pattern of loans etc. Groups qualifying in these grading tests were designate as first grade groups or grade one group and were given credit linkage from the bank in the form of revolving fund through cash credit under the SGSY guidelines. Those groups who could not pass the grading test were designated as weak groups and had to wait for months to qualify. Thus the group corpus was enhanced after the groups got credit linkage from the banks and was used again for inter-lending between the members for their individual economic activities or other purposes or for starting group based economic activities. Many of these groups were provided with a booster dose of revolving fund amounting to Rs. 10,000 after it was verified that they could use the revolving fund, savings on regular basis and has completed a cycle of drawal of total amount of cash credit sanctioned followed by a regular repayment of loan. The first graded groups were again tested for second gradation on the basis of certain parameters and on qualification was provided bank loan and an equal dose of subsidy from DRDC canalised through the banks. This enlarged their group corpus substantially. However, it was noticed many groups could not qualify as grade two groups within one year and had to wait for two to three years to satisfy all the parameters for second grading. Further, there were substantial time lags for groups in grade two to receive the subsidy and loan after gradation. On the whole, the savings and credit linkages of the groups with the banks helped in building up the group corpus or the capital of the group. A portion of this capital was used for inter-loaning purposes. The corpus was calculated as follows:

> *Group Corpus= Cash at group box + Savings Balance in bank + Interest on savings+ Inter-loans outstanding*

(Interest received on loans are automatically included in the group corpus as they are deposited in banks and/or held in cash)

The total fund under command of the groups were larger as many received bank loans which was four times their group corpus and nearly all of them received the revolving fund and the booster dose of the revolving fund. The total fund was calculated as follows:

Total fund of Group = Group Corpus + Revolving Fund + Booster dose of revolving fund+ Bank loan sanctioned.

The financial management of the groups revolved round segregating the group corpus into inter-loans and investment, timely depositing the savings component into the banks, monitoring and recording the loans advanced, calculating the interests and ensuring prompt payment of the principal and interest components of the loans and managing the transaction and operating costs. The following sub-sections will dissect some of these activities in details.

Operating Costs of SHGs—Compositional Analysis

SHGs as micro-banks do have some costs for their regular operations, some of the costs related to their management and operational activities and some other costs due to their social activities. Included in the cost of operations and management (which are usually referred to as transaction costs) are costs of making bank linkages, servicing a loan granted from a bank, cost of holding meetings, and maintenance of documents expenses for visit of officials, transportation costs, remuneration to external book writer etc. The cost of servicing a loan from a bank includes cost of stamp paper, cost of photos and interest paid on bank loan. In addition to these were certain costs which the groups expended for social activities, like provision of health and hygiene facilities, adult education, maternity services, anti-dowry campaigns, helping in marriage and other ceremonies in villages, providing potable water and sanitation, etc. These costs are essential for giving social benefits to beneficiaries, especially women as members of the SHGs. The other operating costs include membership fees for being members of clusters, which is Rs. 150 per month.

However, this cost was not included in the operational costs as being members of clusters were not compulsory and a very small percentage of the sample groups were cluster members. Therefore, the Operational Costs were taken as a sum of the Transaction Costs and the Cost of Social Activities.

The analysis of the cash books and checklists and data formats revealed the following composition of operating costs.

Table 11.2 : Mean Composition of Annual Operating Costs of SHGs

Items of expenditure	*% of total operating expense*
Expenses for conducting meetings	06
Cost of stationery and document, books	11
Documentation expenses for loans	07
Travel expenses to bank, panchayats, DRDC, etc.	15
Remuneration to external documenter/ book writer	03
Expenses during visits by officials	06
Interest on loans from banks	34
Miscellaneous expenses	02
Total Transaction Costs	84
Expenses for social activities	16
Total Operating Costs	100

Source : Field survey.

The Table : 11.2 given above is indicative of the fact that the number of heads of expenses is not many and does not need sophisticated accounting procedures or documents. Most of these expenses are recorded in the cash book of the SHGs, with no head of expenditure written in particular. In quite a number of cases there was no documentation of travelling expenses, meeting expenses, expenses relating to visits of officials and the information had to be extracted by asking the group leaders. The interest costs were available mostly from the loan ledgers of the banks to which they were credit linked. The major items of expenses as witnessed were the interest paid for bank loans, travelling expenses and expenses for social activities. The expenditure on remuneration to external book writers is low because of the fact that very few groups assigned book-keeping jobs to outsiders and book-keeping job was done by the group leader and/ or the treasurer.

The operating costs were found to be varied and ranged from about Rs. 1300 to a little more than Rs. 6000 per annum. These costs were calculated on the basis of the record books and the loan ledgers for the financial year 2007-08.

Table 11. 3 : Distribution of Annual Operating Costs of the SHGs

Transaction cost	*No.of groups*	*% of groups*
Below Rs.1500	22	9.8
Rs. 1500——Rs. 2500	42	18.7
Rs. 2500——Rs. 3500	58	25.8
Rs. 3500 —— Rs. 4500	52	23.2
Rs. 4500—— Rs.5500	45	20.0
More than Rs.5500	6	2.5

Source : Compiled from field data

The distribution shown above gives a clear indication regarding the quantum of operating costs. More than 75 per cent of the sample SHGs have operating costs lower than Rs. 4500 per annum, i.e. about Rs. 400 per month. This is an indication that the operating costs are not an inhibiting factor for operation of the groups.

It is not unnatural that as an organisation grows in size, the complexities of its operations increase and consequently drives the operating costs. This may be true for the SHGs as well, because as they mature, their number of members may increase, frequency of inter-loaning may increase. Travelling costs may increase due increase in the frequency of visits to banks and DRDCs, social activities and their costs may increase. Preliminary discussions with the SHG members disclosed that older groups had to spend more on operating costs. An attempt was made to statistically test the phenomenon by making a contingency table and formulating the following hypotheses:

H_o: The Operational costs of SHGs do not have any association with the vintage of the groups.

H_1 : The Operational costs of SHGs tend to increase with the vintage of the Groups.

Table 11.4 : Association between Operational Costs and Vintage of SHGs

Vintage of the group O. C. per year	*12 months – 24 months*	*25 months – 36 months*	*37 months – 48 months*	*49 months – 60 months*	*More than 60 months*
Below .1500	10	8	4	—	—
Rs. 1500-2500	18	13	6	5	
Rs. 2500-3500	8	27	13	8	2
Rs. 3500 -4500	6	12	22	12	—
Rs. 4500- 5500	—	5	25	12	3
More than Rs. 5500	—	—	2	3	1

Note : (For calculating the $\chi 2$ value, rows 4, 5 and 6 were coalesced and columns 5 and 6 were coalesced so that the expected cell frequencies were not lower than 5.)

$$\chi 2 = 68.295$$

The calculated value of Chi-square being larger than the table value rejects the null hypothesis and it is thus accepted that there is a positive association between the vintage of the groups and operating costs which is significant at 1% level. The phenomenon can also be observed from the pattern of the contingency table.

The operating costs were also tested on a multivariate basis using multiple regression analysis, where operating costs were taken as a function of Vintage of Groups (VN), No. of meetings held per year (MT), No. of members (N), No. of visits by Officials, (OV), Size of loan sanctioned by bank (L), Cluster membership (CL) and graded status (GR).

Therefore O.C. = f(VN, MT, N, L, OV, CL, GR)

For variables CL, dummy variables were used in the following manner-1 if member of cluster, 0 if not a cluster member, For variable GR, dummy variables 1 was used for grade I group and 0 for grade II group.

The regression result is as follows.

Table11.5 : Results of Regression Analysis taking Operating Cost as the Dependent Variable

R^2 = 0.869, F =22.04[a], D.W=1.015,

Explanatory variables	*Beta coefficients*	*t values*
MT	0.122	1.174
N	.002	0.015
OV	.020	0.191
CL	0.264	1.831[c]
L	0 .687	3.734[a]
GR	-0.049	-0.404
VN	0.669	3.613[a]

(a denotes significance at 1% level, and c at 10% level)

The results of the regression analysis show that the explanatory variables have been able to explain about 87 per cent variation in the operating costs. It is interesting to note that the variables vintage of the groups and being members influence the operating costs, as the beta coefficients are significant at 1 per cent level. As found in the analysis of association between the operating costs and the vintage of the groups in the bi-variate context earlier, the fact is also established in the multivariate context. The operating costs for groups which are members of clusters have also statistically found and is due to the fact that the monthly fees add to the operating costs.

Inter-loaning Operations—Pattern of distribution, repayments and interest rates

As discussed above inter-lending to members of the group is

a regular feature of the SHGs. The amount of inter-loans and the interest on inter-loans and the repayment schedules are discussed in the meetings and agreed upon by the members, but the regularity with which it is done is sometimes subject to question. However, previous studies have found that "fixing on internal loan plans do not find much place in group meetings" (Dhar, 2005).The first feature that will be examined is the amount of inter-loan that is disbursed out as a percentage of the total fund of the groups. This is given in the following Table. 11.6

Table 11.6 : Amount of inter-loan as a percentage of total funds

% of total funds	*No. of groups*
40%—60%	78
60%——80%	120
80%—100%	27

Source : Compiled from field data.

Table 11.6 shows that all groups have lent out quite a substantial portion of their total funds as inter-loans. No groups in the sample was found to have loans below 40 per cent of the total funds.

The second aspect that needs to be discussed is the frequency with which the inter-lending takes place in the groups. The findings are given in Table 11.7.

Table 11. 7 : Distribution of groups on the basis of frequency of inter-loan

Frequency of inter-loan	*No. of groups*	*% of Groups*
No specific time schedule	77	34.2
Once in a month	109	48.4
Once during 2—3 months	35	15.6
Once during 4—6 months	4	1.8

Source : Compiled from field data.

The pattern of the frequency of inter-loans as shown in the Table 11.7 indicates that about half of the groups are regular monthly lenders and about 18 per cent lent at lower frequencies. However, for 34 per cent of the groups no specific pattern was found. In the case of these groups, the inter-loans were given as and when needed to the members. Though this is a facility which is beneficial to the members, it creates problems in maintaining the financial discipline of the group. As disclosed by group leaders, irregular loan cycles lead to increase in delinquency tendencies as the members become less aware that their repayment is necessary to fund other inter-loan requirements which can come up.

The next interesting aspect, and probably the most disputed aspect is the rates of interest charged on the inter-loans made by the group. The following Table 11.8 gives the interest on the inter-loans.

Table 11.8 : Interest rates on Inter-loans charged by the Self-Help Groups

Rate of interest per month	*No. of groups*	*% of Groups*
2%	106	47.1
3%	72	32.0
4%	32	14.2
5%	15	6.7

Source : Field Survey.

The interest rates as shown above translate into 24 per cent to 60 per cent per annum. Though in about 80 per cent of the cases the interest rates are limited within 36 per cent per annum, yet for the others rates of 48 per cent and 60 per cent are others. Even rates of 24 per cent and 36 per cent are much higher than the rates at which the groups borrow from banks. Practitioners argue that since the groups are voluntary in nature, the determination of their internal activities be best left to them. Some argue that the interest incomes should be high enough to cover the operational costs of the groups so that they can be self-dependent. Contradictory opinions point out that these rates are exorbitantly high and are equivalent to interest rates charged by moneylenders. Further, it debilitates the repayment capacity of the borrowers and induces delinquencies.

It would therefore be prudent to examine the repayment patterns, the rates of recovery and the relationships between the interest rates and recovery rates of the inter-loans taken by the members. The following Table 11.9 gives an insight into the repayment schedules followed by the sample groups.

Table 11.9 : Repayment Schedule of inter-loans in Self-Help Groups

Pattern of repayment of inter-loan	*No of groups*
(i) Regular monthly instalment depending on term loan	Nil
(ii) Regular monthly instalment which determines term loan	10
(iii) Irregular payment on agreed terms	201
(iv) Bullet repayment at the end of the term of the loan	14
(v) Irregular payment on (i) & (ii)	Nil

Source: Field study.

The data in the above Table 11.9 reveals that in nearly all the cases the repayment is irregular. In a handful of cases a regular monthly instalment were found to be made and also in a handful of other cases the lump sum payment of interest and principal are made at the end of the terms which usually range from 3 months to 12 months. The problem lies with the irregular payments. As disclosed by the treasurers and group leaders of the SHGs, the irregular payments are due to the fact that though, terms are fixed for loan repayments, members usually fail to repay on time and request for extension of time frequently. Often request for extension of terms are made by influential members of local bodies and cannot be ignored easily. However, there are also genuine cases where the borrower has temporarily difficulties and disabilities to repay and there is no alternative but to give them more time for repayment. However, delays in repayment also lead to permanent delinquencies and the loan is never recovered.

It would therefore be worthwhile to examine the rates of repayment in the sample groups. The findings are given in Table 11.10. The recovery rates were calculated on the basis of the number of inter-loans repaid on time as a percentage of number of inter-loans given during the years 2006 and 2007.

Table 11.10 : Distribution of SHGs on the basis of rate of recovery of inter-loan

Recovery rate of inter-loan within specified time	*No. of Groups*
Up to 20%	12
20%—40%	48
40%—60%	59
60%—80%	72
80%—100%	33

Source : Field Survey.

The distribution given above does not present a very pleasant picture of the recovery of the inter-loans given to the members. More than half of the sample groups have recovered less than 60 per cent of the number of inter-loans given. 32 per cent of the groups have repayment rates averaging 60 per cent to 80 per cent, which is not satisfactory when compared to the repayment rates to banks, or even when weighed under the theoretical underpinning that peer-pressure and peer-support result in higher repayment rates.

The question therefore arises, are repayments not up to the mark due to high interest rates on inter-loans. This relationship is examined in the following contingency Table 11.11. The association between recovery rates and interest rates are tested using Chi-square test. For this purpose the following hypotheses have been formulated.

H_0: There is no association between recovery rates and interest rates on inter-loans.

H_1: Recovery rates are dampened as interest on inter-loans escalate.

Table 11.11 : Relationship between Recovery-rates and Interest-rates

Recovery rate *Rate of interest*	*Up to 20%*	*20% - 40%*	*40%- 60%*	*60%- 80%*	*80% - 100%*
2%	2	10	27	48	19
3%	2	25	20	16	9
4%	3	9	8	7	5
5%	5	4	4	2	-

Note : (For purpose of calculating $\chi 2$, rows 4 and 5 were coalesced and columns 2 and 3 were coalesced so that the expected cell frequencies were more than 5)

$\chi 2$ = 30.129 (significant at 1%)

It is quite clear from the Table 11.11 that when the interest rate is 2 per cent per annum, more number of groups have recoveries ranging from 60 to 100 per cent , than when the interest rates are higher. In addition when interest rate is 3 per cent, the number of groups having 20 to 60 per cent recovery is higher than those having 60 to 100 per cent recovery. Again the Chi- Square value being more than the table value leads to rejection of the null hypothesis. It therefore, stands that higher inter lending rates leads to lower recoveries of the interloans.

Income from Inter-loaning Interests—an analysis

This section deals with the interest income from inter-loans earned by the groups. The annual interest income from inter-lending was calculated as follows:

Total Amount of interest earned by a group during the vintage period

Total Amount of Loan outstanding as per loan ledger of the group —
Less: Amount of loan outstanding as per Cash Credit Account balance —

Loan from savings account of the group	——
Add: Amount of savings account balance	——
Less: Total amount deposited by all members of the group as thrift	——
Total amount of interest earned	——
Less: - Interest on savings from bank deposits	——
Total Interest earned from inter-lending	——

Annual interest income = Total Interest Income / Vintage of Group

The annual interest income of the sample SHGs are given below.

Table 11.12 : Distribution of SHG on the basis of amount of interest earned

Amount of interest earned per annum	*No of groups*	*% of groups*
Upto Rs.10000/	17	7.6
Rs.10000 — Rs15000/	65	28.8
Rs.15000 — Rs.20000/	84	37.4
Rs. 20000 — Rs.25000/	52	23.1
Rs. 25000 — Rs. 30000/	7	3.1

Source : Field Survey.

It can be seen that a large percentage (about 90%) of groups have been earning interests ranging from Rs. 10,000 per year to Rs.25,000 per year. Only about 3 per cent of the sample groups have been earning even more than that. The reasons for good interest earnings may be attributed to the fact that interest rates are quite high, the repayment periods short and the recycling of the loans are therefore more frequent. It may therefore be worthwhile to examine the variables which may influence the interest income of the groups in a multivariate context. To do this the following function was taken:

Int = f (IR, RR, VN, N,), where Int = Annual Interest income from inter-lending, IR= Interest rate on inter loans, RR= recovery rate, V=vintage of groups and N= number of members .The results of the regression are given below.

Table 11.13 : Results of Regression Analysis taking Annual Interest Earned as Dependent Variable

$R^2 = 0.812$, $F = 31.16^a$, D.W=1.604

Explanatory variables	*Beta coefficients*	*t values*
IR	0..114	1.112
RR	0.402	3.263[b]
VN	0.650	5.627[a]
N	0 .104	1.254

(a *denotes significance at 1% level, and* b *at 5% level)*

The regression results significantly prove that the variation in the annual interest earnings is explained to the extent of 81 per cent by the explanatory variables. It is interesting to see that the recovery rate plays an important role in explaining the interest earned, in the multivariate context. The coefficient being significant at 5 per cent level also corroborates the positive relationship established between recovery rates and interest earnings in the bi-variate context earlier.

Financial Self-Sufficiency—An Assessment

The next pertinent issue that has to be addressed is whether the interest income has been able to cover operating costs. If so the groups can be taken as sustainable at least from the view point of financial stability. In an effort to measure sustainability in a loan fund, researchers and practitioners have come up with a more comprehensive measure than just repayment rate. They use a complex sounding but actually very simple "Sustainability Index" to calculate their performance in this regard. The Sustainability Index is in fact nothing more than the percentage of total costs covered by income. Nair (2005) used Financial Self-Sufficiency Index developed by CGAP (Consultative Group for Assisting the Poorest) while measuring the financial performance of SHG federations.

According to their approach Financial Self-Sufficiency (FSS) is equal to Operational Income/(Operational Expenses +Financial Expenses + Adjustments for subsidies and inflation). Since, this study deals with SGSY groups where subsidy is given with bank loan to enhance total group funds and not to cover expenses, therefore, such subsidy has not been taken into consideration. Further, since the incomes and expenses were taken for the financial year 2007, no adjustment was made for inflation. The S.I. was thus calculated as follows:

$$\text{Financial Self-Sustainability Index} = \frac{\textit{Total income earned from credit programme during period} \times 100}{\textit{Total programme costs during the period}}$$

The sustainability index should be more than 100 to indicate that a group is financially sustainable. The more the index, the better it is for the group. The Table 11.14 shows the sustainability indices for the sample SHGs.

Table 11.14 : Distribution of Financial Self-Sustainability Indices of SHGs

Value of S.I.(%)	*No. of SHGs*	*% of total sample*
Below 100	nil	—
100–200	13	5.8
200–300	51	22.7
300– 400	69	30.6
400–500	54	24.0
500–600	23	10.2
600–700	08	3.6
700–800	07	3.1

Source : Compiled from Field Survey data.

Though the table is self-explanatory certain points need to be highlighted. None of the sample SHGs has the Sustainability below 100. This means that all the groups earn enough interest income to cover their operating expenses. More than half the groups have sustainability ratios ranging from 300 to 500, i.e. They are able to cover their operating expenses very comfortably. The mean Sustainability Index for the sample is 514 with a standard deviation of 317.75 . In order to test whether the sample mean indicates that the population also has a sustainability index greater than 100 the following hypotheses were framed.

Ho: Mean sustainability index for SHGs would be less than or equal to 100.

H_1: Mean sustainability Index for SHGs would be grater than 100.

The calculated Z score works out to be 19.528 and results in rejection of the null hypothesis. This is an indication that the income earned through inter lending would be covering the operating costs of the groups on the whole.

Conclusion

The fact that the viability and attractiveness of SHGs as micro-finance delivery mechanisms has been established in India is a laudable phenomenon and the success is due to the reason that they are essentially low cost micro-banks operating for the members in distant rural areas. Efforts at increasing the number of groups and increasing outreach being the major success indicators, often draws ones attention from the fact that the groups need to be sustainable based on peer support and 'comfortable peer pressure'. Charging of abnormally high interest rates for inter-lending has become a practice which is less questioned on the premise that the groups are informal voluntary groups. Financial management of a group in order to attain sustainability cannot be centred round high interest rates, but needs to focus also on effective management of operating costs, repayment cycles and delinquency rates. This study has empirically demonstrated that transaction costs are not high, though they tend to increase with the vintage of the groups and being involved as members of clusters. Further, involvement in social activities adds to the cost burden of the groups. Though controlling extra costs for older and larger groups are not easy as the scale of activities increase, costs can substantially be reduced if monthly membership fees for clusters can be reduced and the cost of social activities are either fully financed or subsidised by the Government. The study has demonstrated that there are problems in the repayment rates as well and delinquencies tend to increase with the increase in interest rates on inter-loans. This is of course natural as high interest rates put repayment pressures alike those put by moneylenders and consequently beneficiaries develop tendencies for skipping repayment instalments. This has been realised by many of the older groups who have reduced their interest rates. Further, the term of a loan should not be any longer than is actually necessary, and interest and repayment holidays should not be generalised. Repayment periods should weekly and some-times even daily wherever possible. Monitoring of repayment periods should increase the groups earning flow.

The average sustainability index found in this study is above five hundred, which means the groups can cover up to five times their operating costs through the interest incomes. It therefore, stems that even if moderate interest rates of 1.5 to 2 per cent per month are charged, the groups can sustain as well. The fundamental philosophy with which groups are formed is they are group micro entrepreneurs and will generate income from group economic activities. Though many groups have done that, there are thousands of groups who still resort to individual activities financed from inter-loans and contribute no surplus to cover the group operating costs. Monitoring, training and capacity building efforts by the Government agencies and NGOs need to be geared up so that groups can be capacitated to generate surpluses. With adequate surpluses, the pressure to earn incomes from interests can be reduced and consequently the inter-lending rates can be scaled down. Voluntary reduction of rates may in many cases not be easy to bring about as there may be inherent fears of generating lower income for the group. Discussions regarding fixing of interest rates need to be frequently made. Here comes the role of clusters and federations where counselling can be done and the reductions can be then implemented through the GPRPs (Gram Panchayat Resource Persons). The SGSY guidelines and provisions of the Micro-finance Sector Development and Regulation Bill can be expanded to incorporate restrictive provisions on inter-lending rates. Prompt and adequate measures in this respect are a *sinequo-non* for long-term sustainability of the groups and the micro-finance movement.

References

CARE, CRS, USAID (2006): "*Self Help Groups- A Study of Lights and Shades*"- A joint initiative of CARE,CRS, USAID and GTZ.

Dasgupta, R.(2001): "Rural Banking and Credit- Tale of many Committees", *Economic and Political* Weekly, March 3, 733-737.

Dhar, S.N.(2005): "*Micro-finance for Women-Necessities, Systems and Perceptions*" Northern Book Centre, New Delhi

Harper, M. (1998): Why Commercial Banks are not entering the micro-finance markets?", Paper produced as consultant to SDC. http:// www. alternativefinance. org.uk/cgi-bin/summer.pl.

Karduck, S and H.D.Seibel (2004)" *Transaction Costs of Self-Help Groups- A Study of NABARD's SHG Banking Programme in India*" — Deutsche Gesellschaft fuer Tecnische Zusammenarbeit)

Karmakar, K.G. (1999): *Rural Credit and Self-Help Groups: Micro-finance Needs and Concepts in India*, Sage Publications, India.

Khandker, S.R., Khalila, B. and Khan, Z. (1996): *Credit Programmes for the Poor: Household and intra-household Impacts and*

Programme Sustainability, Volume 1, Bangladesh Institute of Development Studies, Dhaka, Bangladesh,

LACRO (2008): *Savings-Led Micro-finance: An Introduction for LACRO*, Latin America and Caribbean Regional Office Christian Relief Services.

Mayoux, L. (1999): "The Magic Ingredient? Micro-finance and Women's Empowerment", www. gdrc.org/icm/magic.html.

Nair, A. (2005): *Sustainability of Micro-finance Self-Help Groups in India: Would Federating* Help?, World Bank Policy Research Working Paper No. 3516. February.

Rao, V.M (2002): "Women SHGs profiles from Andhra Pradesh and Karnataka". *National Bank News Review*. April- June 2002, 62-68.

Rutherford, Stuart (2000), "Self-Help Groups as Micro-finance Providers: How Good Can They Get?" Paper presented at the Workshop on Best Practices in Group Dynamics and Micro Credit, 15-17 February, Manesar, Gurgaon.

Sen, M. (2003): "*A Study of SHGs and Micro-finance in West Bengal*," State Institute of Panchayat and Rural Development, Kalyani, Nadia and CARE India.

Sinha, F (2005): "Access, use and contribution of MF in India Findings From a national study". *Economic and Political Weekly*, April 23, 1714-1719.

Tankha, A. (2002):"*Self-help Groups as Financial Intermediaries in India: Cost of Promotion, Sustainability and Impact*", A study prepared for ICCO and Cordaid, The Netherlands August.

Vajpayee, A.V., (2003), "*Promoting Poverty Eradication Potential of Women*", Text of Prime Minister of India's Speech while inaugurating the Gender Poverty Summit at New Delhi on November 2003, published by Ministry of Information and Broadcasting, Govt. of India.

12

Tribal Agriculture Development and Globalization : An Empirical Study

T. Krishna Kumar

The role of agriculture in the development of any country needs no emphasis. It has more strategic role in the process of development of developing countries like India. Agriculture continues to be the main stay of the Indian economy even after six decades of independence. As it is playing a vital role in the progress of the nation, it is considered as the backbone of economy. But the importance of the agriculture sector in the country is gradually declining. The share of agriculture in GDP has declined from 59.2 per cent in 1950-1951 to 34.9 per cent in 1990-91. It has now reached to 18.3 per cent by 2007-08. Similarly, the percentage of population who depend on agriculture for their livelihood has also declined from 70 per cent to 57 per cent.

Indian agriculture had reached the stage of development and maturity much before the advanced countries of the world embarked on the path of progress. At the time, there was a proper balance between agriculture and industry and both flourished hand in hand. The Indian agriculture in the pre-independence period can be correctly described as a 'subsistence' occupation. It was only after the advent of planning that some farmers started adopting agriculture on a commercial basis. At the time of the First World War, the agriculture contributed two-thirds of national income. After the initiation of planning in India, the share of agriculture has persistently declined on account of the development of the secondary and tertiary sectors of the economy. The share of agriculture in national income is often take as an indicator of economic development.

The Government of India has given top priority to the agriculture sector during first five-year plan, which is popularly known, as primary sector in India. Agriculture sector is the mainstay of the tribal and rural Indian economy around which socio-economic privileges and deprivations revolve. No strategy of economic reform can succeed without sustained and broad based agriculture development. At present most of the tribal families are still depending on agriculture but they are not getting the reasonable price for their agriculture yields, therefore they are not able to develop economically and financially.

Agriculture is a backbone of Indian economy. Agriculture is rural and cradled civilization worldwide. Its development has contributed to the food security, industrial growth and rural prosperity. More than 75 per cent of the population is depending on the agriculture sector. Indian agriculture plays a dominant role in India's role.

The globalization is an ancient issue started at least 2000 years ago when global exchange relations among three major centres of the world China, India and West Asia, America, Europe and Japan were not part of global exchange. It promotes the universalism through exchange of religious philosophies and knowledge. It had brought the world economy on to one platform.

Objectives

The starting point for any area of study is to set forth its boundaries and determine its objectives. The following are the objectives of this study:

1. To know the agriculture status of the residents of the Three Thandas.
2. To study the interest of the tribal towards agricultural operations.
3. To extract the types of crops that they cultivate.
4. To educate farmers the use of manure which is cost-free fertilizer?
5. To know the types of crops are being cultivated.

Data and Methodology

For the purpose of the empirical study the data has been collected from primary sources by using a structured questionnaire designed for this particular purpose. The respondents are the farmers of these 3-Thandas.

Sample Size

The total families who are living in these thandas were 225, out of which 100 farmers have been selected at random for the purpose of the study.

Scope of the Study

The study has been confined to the Thandas adjacent to Mulkanoor town in Bheemadevarapally Mandal of Karimnagar District, Andhra Pradesh where the World famous Co-operative Bank "Mulkanur Co-operative Rural Bank(MCRB)" has been established. These 3-thandas consists of 225 families and their main occupation is agriculture.

Analysis of the Study

On the basis of the collected data through a structured

questionnaire has been tabulated for the purpose of presentation to understand the tribals life in interior places and to interested people. This field survey gives us the pertinent and trustsworthy information, which is quite useful for selecting the beneficiaries for certain Government financial schemes. The tabulated results are presented below:

Table 12.1 : Age of the respondents

Age	*Actual Number*	*Percentage*
20-30	40	40
31-40	40	40
41-50	20	20
Total	**100**	**100**

Source : Field survey.

The above table reveals that the age composition of the respondents. It is evident from the given data that majority of the respondents from the age group of 20-40-, this indicates that the youth is inclining towards agriculture. It shows that this profession is coming from their ancestors.

Table 12. 2 : Educational status

Education	*Actual Number*	*Percentage*
1-6	60	60
7-9	30	30
SSC, and above	10	10
Total	**100**	**100**

Source: Field survey.

The above Table 12.2 shows that the education background of the respondents, the majority 60 percentage of the respondents are falling under the elementary education standard, with this it can be easily inferred that the farmers not have education and making use of the developments which are taking place in the agriculture sector on account of globalization.

Table 12.3 : Use of Latest Techniques

Age	*Actual Number*	*Percentage*
Using	50	50
Not using	40	40
Planning to use	10	10
Total	**100**	**100**

Source: Field survey.

The study reveals that majority (50 percentage) of the respondents are implementing the latest techniques of farming. It is clear that the tribal people are in the globalization and getting fruits of globalization.

Table 12.4 : Opinion on latest farming methods.

Farming methods	*Actual Number*	*Percentage*
Very good	10	10
Good	20	20
Satisfactory	70	70
Total	**100**	**100**

Source: Field survey.

The above Table 12.4 presents the lucid idea of the farmers with regard to latest farming methods. The opinion poll focuses that the majority of the respondents are just satisfying by using these latest methods of farming which have emerged due to globalization. The latest methods of cultivation are good but sometimes the farmers are not in a position to get the required mechanical tools so easily.

Table 12.5 : Types of crops. (Food crops)

Type of crops	*Actual Number*	*Percentage*
Paddy	60	60
Maize	20	20
Groundnut	20	20
Total	**100**	**100**

Source: Field survey.

The above Table 12.5 throws light on the types of food crops, which they cultivate in a particular season. The elicited data indicates that the majority of the farmers cultivate paddy which is the main food of the south Indians. The remaining i.e. minority of the respondents are inclining towards the cultivation of both groundnuts and maize. It can be concluded that cultivating paddy is beneficial and advisable to demographic conditions which are prevailing in this particular area.

Table 12.6 : Types of crops (cash crops).

Type of crops	*Actual Number*	*Percentage*
Cotton	80	80
Chillies	20	20
Turmeric	–	–
Total	**100**	**100**

Source: Field survey.

The above Table 12.6 exhibits the cultivation of cash crops by the tribal farmers. Majority of the farmers are evincing interest in cotton crop because it gives not only good yield but also good cash benefit. Therefore, majority of the farmers are cultivating cotton. But it has been observed that the Government is not supplying the quality seeds for cultivation to extract good yield.

Table 12.7 : Mode of water facility for farming

Water facility	*Actual Number*	*Percentage*
Canals	20	20
Wells	70	70
Rain water	10	10
TOTAL	100	100

Source : Field survey.

The above Table 12.7 shows that the source of water, which is used for agricultural operations. The study reveals that majority of the farmers are depending upon the well source of water for cultivation but at the same time the farmers are not in a position to get sufficient electricity supply from the Government source. It has become a chronic problem in almost all the areas in this area as well as whole Telangana districts. Therefore, the farmers are pleading the Government to supply the uninterrupted power during a certain period of time so that they can properly use for the right purpose.

Table 12. 8 : Logistics Status

Mode of transport	*Actual Number*	*Percentage*
Tractor	60	60
Auto Trolley	30	30
Bullock cart	10	10
TOTAL	**100**	**100**

Source : Field survey.

The above Table 12.8 shows the mode of transportation used for transporting the agricultural output to the grain market by the farmers. The study shows that majority of the respondents have expressed that they use the tractor mode of transportation for reaching their output to the market on right time to get the right price for the products. Some of the farmers who are getting the limited yield are using the second mode of transportation for moving the output to the market.

Conclusion

From the respondents opinion that the Agriculture is the backbone of any individual farmer and the country but the Globalization has broken the backbones of the agriculturists of Andhra Pradesh. in the particular and the country in general by making the seeds and fertilizers scanty and dear. The farmers are not able to get the required quantity of fertilizers and seeds of the good quality. Due to this the farmers are not in a position to get the quality output for getting the reasonable or good price for their yield. At the end of the study it has been concluded that the globalization is both boom and bane to the tribal agriculturists. And the agencies, government has to take an oath to develop the tribal agriculturist.

References

B. Suresh Lal and others "Rural Development in the era of Globalization", Serials Publications, 2008, ISBN: 978-81-8387-213-3.

Field Survey.

Magazines on Tribal Development issues.

S.K. Misra and V.K. Puri : *Indian Economy* 24th Revised Edition-Himalaya Publishers.

Sanjiva Kshva Panday, *Globalization Policy and A.P. Agriculture,* Navarthiks, 2004.

S.P. Gupta, *Statistical Methods*, 31st revised edition, Sulthan Chand & Sons, 2002.

13

Empowerment of Rural Women through Self-Help Groups and Microcredit

Anita Modi

Gender discrimination is a challenge for the whole world. Gender gaps are widespread in access to and control of resources, in economic opportunities, power and political voice. Although women are described as the better half of men, but the reality is totally different. The condition, status and position of women are deplorable in all terms whether social, economic and political. Specially, rural women of India are victims of gender discrimination and their sad plight is a challenge for us. Rural women are the major workforce in the agricultural sector of our economy, but their work could not get the recognition in the society. They have no property, no education and no skill to get employment in the formal and organized sector.The sad plight of women is evident from the fact that women constitutes almost half of the population, performs nearly two-third of work hours, receives one-tenth of the world's income and owns less than one hundredth of the world property. Gender discrimination involves the huge cost in the form of great poverty, slower economic growth, weaker governance and a lower living standard of the people.

To ensure the overall growth of the economy in real terms, it is essential to empower women in all spheres of life.

Empowering women should include changes in women's mobility in the social ladder, changes in women's labour patterns, changes in women's access to control over resources. This empowerment is a process by which women can take control and ownership of their choices. The government has implemented several developmental programmes for poverty reduction and empowerment of poor women in rural areas in the country. The Government of India had ushered in the new millennium by declaring the year 2001 as 'Women's Empowerment Year' to focus on a vision 'where women are equal partners like men'. The last decades have witnessed some basic changes in the status and role of women in our society. There has been shift in policy approaches from the concept of 'welfare' in the seventies to 'development' in the eighties and now to 'empowerment' in the nineties.

Nowadays, it is recognized that a diverse range of financial services is required to the rural poor women so that they can participate in the mainstream activities, their standard of living, quality of life, self-esteem and self-dignity can be improved. It is a known fact that rural poor women are deprived of rural institutional credit because of high cost of administering small loans and lending risk involved. To solve this critical problem, the concept of Self-Help Group (SHG) and micro-finance has been adopted in the country. Now-a-days, SHGs and micro-finance have received extensive recognition as a strategy for poverty reduction and women's economic empowerment. Micro-finance institutions started in India in 1980s through Self-Help Groups (SHGs). In 1996, NABARD launched national-wide pilot projects to link SHGs to the banks. According to NABARD, "A SHG consists of an' average size' of 15 people from a homogenous social or economics class, all of who come together for addressing their common problems. The SHGs meet regularly and save small sums of money. They rotate these savings as loans within the SHG. Aftersome time, they get loans from banks on the basis of their accumulated savings.

Objectives of SHGs

1. To inculcate self-help approach among woman folk so that their dependence on other groups can be minimized.
2. To promote the habit of savings among rural women so that they can take loans from the banks on the basis of their collected savings.
3. To motivate women entrepreneurship to make them capable of establishing small scale and cottage industries.
4. To enhance the women's participation in their development programmes to make them more effective in improving the status of women.
5. To create awareness among rural women about their health, education and sanitation.
6. To develop skills and capabilities of rural women folk in various agriculture related activities.
7. To facilitate the involvement of NGOs to improve the living standard of rural women.
8. To develop collective leadership among rural women.
9. To provide access to money, infrastructure and marketing facilities to rural women so that their productivity and efficiency can be increased.

   SHGs have facilitated the process of micro-credit for the rural woman folk. An access to micro-credit has been helpful in improving their bargaining power, participation and decision-making power. Micro-credit is helping rural women to start income generating projects, take part in credit services and planning and freedom in expenditure management.

In relation to micro-finance, the concept of empowerment is defined as the process by which women take control and ownership of their choices. The core elements of empowerment are the ability to define one's goals and act upon them, awareness of gendered power structures, self-esteem and self-confidence. Thus, empowerment consists of greater access to knowledge and resources, greater autonomy in decision-making to enable them to have ability to plan their lives. SHGs are playing an effective role in prompting the empowerment of poor women. The existing literature on SHG bank linkage programme reveals that an access to credit has brought economics benefits to poor women in terms of employment, better living conditions and enhanced consumption levels. The improvement in economics position of poor women has increased their bargaining power, participation rate and decision-making powers. A positive and significant change has taken place in the standard of living, education, health and housing facilities among the women members of SHGs. Now the women associated with SHGs have become more conscious and aware about their roles, rights and status in the family as well as in the society. This process of awareness will go a long way in making the country modern, developed and civilized. The hidden talent of entrepreneurship among women is also being utilized only because of SHGs. A sense of responsibility and responsive behaviour has become part and parcel of women members of SHGs. Thus, women's financial contributions helped them earn gender respect from their husbands, children, and from society.

SHG movement has now been in operation for well over a decade in India. The social intermediation for forming and nurturing SHGs is handled by large number of NGOs, community based organizations like farmers club, local bodies, and social service oriented individuals. This programme has involved the entire banking system. The NABARD report (2005-06) suggests that the cumulative number of SHGs financed by banks till March 2006 was approximately 2.3 million across the country with a membership of 32.98 million persons.

The continued participation in SHGs is also enhancing the skills, capabilities and other abilities of women members. It is found in many studies that SHG women members are utilizing SHG loans for regular economic activities like animal husbandry, agriculture and petty business. About 70 per cent members of SHGs in Tamil Nadu have invested their money in various assets like land, livestock and household durables. Some members of SHGs are taking loans for housing purpose also.

Many studies have found that SHGs is Andhra Pradesh have been instrumental in augmenting the skills and capacities of rural poor women. The women members of SHGs have been assisted to have linkages with banks, NGOs and other financial institutions for the successful implementation of SHG movement. A case study of SHG of Karnataka has also concluded that SHGs are a catalyst of women empowerment and poverty eradication. Many studies have appreciated the people participating approach of SHGs. SHG programme has laid special emphasis on skill formation and capability development for the empowerment of women. To meet this purpose, many national and regional vocational training centres are providing training to women in various areas like embroidery, health care, skin care, fruit and vegetables preservation, tailoring and bag stitching.

As a result the level of income and standard of living of women's family have improved significantly. It is heartening to note that the women member of SHGs is now no more in the clutches of moneylenders. A study conducted in Andhra Pradesh clearly indicates that the repayment rates were high and the bank-linkage made difference in the lives of the SHG members.

SHGs have proved their significance at social front also. SHGs have provided a platform where poor women discuss the important issues related to their families, society, education, health and sanitation. Due to SHGs, the women members are actively participating in meetings, workshops and seminars, thereby playing crucial role in decision-making process. This exposure and awareness have enhanced the self-worth, self-confidence and communication skills of woman folk. The members of SHGs are now resisting those existing traditional norms and values which are hindering their path of development.

It is amply clear that collective work, leadership with fixed tenure, mutual trust and cooperation are the driving forces for SHGs. Even then many hurdlers and constraints are present in the successful implementation of SHG movement. First of all, the coverage of SHGs is mainly concentrated in the southern region of the country. The poorest of the poor women are deprived of the benefits of SHGs because of lack of savings to contribute as a member of SHG. The existing caste system and family attitude are also stumbling blocks in the smooth path of SHGs. In the same way, illiteracy and lack of awareness among women also put a question mark on the success of SHGs. Inadequate training and lack of skills and capacity building in members of SHGs are also responsible for the poor performance of SHGs. The emergence of SHGs has overburdened the women folk, causing deterioration in the health of rural women. It is a matter of concern that a major portion of the benefits of SHGs are being cornered by the dominant leaders of the rural society and poor needy women are deprived away from the benefits of SHGs.

The repayment of loans becomes burdensome for women members if the loans are used for meeting consumption needs or for purchasing durable consumer items. This has created a lot of tension among women. Even some women members are committing suicide in case of non-payment of loans.

To make SHG movement effective and successful for women empowerment, it is essential that the main motto of SHG "for the women, by the women and of the women" should be followed in every manner. There is an urgent need of massive support from the state, NGOs, civil society groups and local people to make SHGs more viable, successful and effective. Awareness camps, literacy campaigns and capacity building training programmes should be organized periodically to bring a large of women under the umbrella of SHGs and thus empowering them.

14

Capacity Building of Rural Poor through Micro-Finance : Role of Institutions

Jitendra Ahirrao

Poverty is the main cause of concern in improving the economic status of developing countries. India's rural poor currently have very little access to finance from formal sources. Micro-finance approaches have tried to fill the gap. Micro-finance has evolved as a need-based programme to cater neglected target groups especially rural poor. Its evolution is based on the concern of all developing countries for empowerment of the poor and the alleviation of poverty. If poor people are provided access to financial services, including credit, they may very well be able to start or expand a micro-enterprise that will allow them to break out of poverty. Thus, micro-finance has become one of the most effective interventions for economic empowerment of the poor. The access to credit and the opportunity to begin or to expand a micro-enterprise may be empowering to the poor, especially in comparison to other development initiatives which often treat these specific target group members as recipients.

A micro-finance institution is an organization that offers financial services to low income populations. Micro-finance institutions have a key role to play in creating economic opportunities for the poorest sections of the society by broadening their outreach. A great scale of organizations is regarded as micro-finance institutes. They are those that offer credits and other financial services to the representatives of poor population. Micro-finance is increasingly being considered as one of the most effective tools of reducing poverty. Micro-finance has a significant role in bridging the gap between the formal financial institutions and the rural poor. The Micro-Finance Institutions accesses financial resources from the Banks and other mainstream Financial Institutions and provide financial and support services to the poor.

Micro-Finance

India inherited a problem of mass poverty in rural areas along with its independence. Poverty in rural India has declined substantially. In recent times, micro-finance has been proposed as a strategy for self-employment through the promotion of micro-enterprises. Micro-finance has gained considerable importance in the last two decades as a tool of poverty reduction. It is also emerged as a powerful tool for rural development. Micro-finance is generally seen as small loans to poor people in general and rural poor in particular for self-employments that generate income allowing them to care for themselves. Micro-finance is providing of small loans that are repaid within short periods of time and are essentially used by low income households. Sometimes, little assistance from outside will speed up the process. The micro-finance through SHGs has undoubtedly begun to make significant contribution in poverty alleviation and empowerment of the women. Micro-financing through SHGs has transferred the real economic power in the hands of women and has considerably reduced their dependence on men. It is not only a financial system but also a tool for social change. Micro-finance provides the economic element to development. Rural people can earn income and build assets, families eat better, they can afford health care and children are more likely to attend school.

Micro-finance, the development buzzword of the nineties was meant to cure the illness of rural poverty. Micro-finance was launched to bridge the gap between demand and supply of funds in the rural area. This initiative was taken to develop a credit delivery mechanism basically in the rural area. In the recent years, most of the countries are to promote micro-finance institutions not only as a rural development tool but also as a rural development panacea. The success of micro-credit institutions in developed countries, the developing economies have increasingly become enthusiastic in the promotion of micro-credit as a rural development intervention. Although the basic philosophy behind the micro-credit movement is to eradicate poverty as it stimulates the growth of micro enterprises by developing new markets and by promoting a culture of entrepreneurship among the rural people.

Self-Help Groups (SHGs)

India has developed its own model of micro-finance organization in the form of *'savings'* and *'credit'* groups known as the Self-Help Groups (SHGs). Self-Help Groups have emerged as a means of providing poor people with the credit that they need to emerge from poverty. The groups initially draw on their own saving at an interest fixed by them to lend within the group and later, get linked to the formal credit system. SHG are small, economically homogeneous and affinity groups of rural poor not exceeding 20 members voluntarily formed to save and mutually agree to contribute to a common fund to be lent to its members as per group decision. The SHG model was largely inspired by the successful experiment of the *'Grameen'* Bank set up in 1976 in Bangladesh by Prof. Mohammad Yunus to empower the rural poor by means of the formation of 'saving' and 'credit' groups. These groups are usually formed by Governmental or NGOs with emphasis on both thrift and credit activities. The novel concept of SHG propagated by NABARD since 1992 has gradually received necessary support from the banking structure. The importance of SHG shall be evident from the fact that after the 2006 Assembly Election, the Government of West Bengal created a new department of SHG and appointed a Minister for the same.

Micro-Finance is emerging as a powerful weapon for poverty alleviation and women's empowerment. In India, micro-finance scheme is dominated by Self-Help Groups (SHGs) - Banks-Linkage Programme, aimed at providing a cost effective mechanism for providing financial services to the poor. Based on the philosophy of peer pressure and group savings as collateral substitute, the SHG programme has been successful in not only designing financial products meeting peculiar needs of the rural poor, but also in strengthening collective self-help capacities of the poor at the local level, leading to their empowerment. The genesis of the SHG Bank-Linkage Programme has its origin in the felt need for a subsystem to provide hassle free banking services to the rural poor in a sustainable and cost effective manner. Over a period of 20 years since introduction of SHG Bank-Linkage Programme, it has emerged as the largest micro-finance outreach programme in the world. That the programme is the most cost effective and fastest growing micro-finance world over initiative can be witnessed from the phenomenal growth in terms of coverage of a massive number of rural poor families and the financial support to the hitherto un-reached poor.

SHG — Banks-linkage programme

The SHG — Banks-linkage programme was conceived with the objectives of developing supplementary credit delivery services for the unreached poor, building mutual trust and confidence between the bankers and the poor and encouraging banking activity both on thrift as well as credit and sustaining a simple and formal mechanism of banking with the poor. The linkage programme combines the flexibility, sensitivity and respon-siveness of the informal credit system with the technical, administrative capabilities and financial resources of the formal financial sector. It is a design relying heavily on collective strength of the poor, closeness of NGOs to people and large financial resources of banks. Further, the SHGs have also undertaken effective social mobilization functions contributing to an overall empowerment process. The banks have externalized what would otherwise have been high transaction costs for mobilizing savings of the poor, appraisal and sanction of loans and improved loan recovery through the financial intermediative role played by SHGs.

During the year 2005-06, 6.20 lakh new SHGs were financed by banks to the tune of Rs. 44.99 billion by way of loans. Cumulatively, banks have lent Rs. 113.97 billion to 22.39 lakh SHGs. NABARD has extended a refinance of Rs. 10.68 billion to banks during 2005-06 bring the cumulative refinance amount to Rs. 41.60 billion. 44,362 branches of 545 banks (Commercial Banks- 47; Regional Rural Banks- 158; and Cooperative Banks - 340) situated in 583 districts in 30 states of the country are participating in the programme. About 32.98 million poor households have gained access to formal banking system through SHG bank linkage programme. Nearly 90 per cent of the groups are women groups.

Micro-Finance Institutions

Micro-Finance Institutions are the pivotal organizations that make individual microcredit loans directly to villagers, micro entrepreneurs, impoverished women and poor families. MFI is like a small bank with the same challenges and capital needs confronting any expanding small venture but with the added responsibility of serving economically-marginalized populations. Many MFIs are creditworthy and well-run with proven records of success, many are operationally self-sufficient. The micro-finance sector consistently focuses on understanding the needs of the poor and on devising better ways of delivering services in line with their requirements, developing the most efficient and effective mechanisms to deliver finance to the poor. Continuous efforts towards automation of operations is steady improving in efficiency.

NABARD

Ever since the pilot project for micro-finance was launched by NABARD a decade ago, the micro-finance programme has experienced a massive leap forward. Even today NABARD is one of the foremost institutions promoting micro-finance activities and supporting them on a large scale through bank-linkage programme. As on 31st March, 2009. NABARD had a provision of financial access to 16.7 million poor families through formation and credit linkage of 10.79 lakh self-help groups. One of its mission statements incorporates a target of formation and credit linkage of 5.85 lakh new SHGs by the year 2007 with 60 per cent of them coming from 13 priority underdeveloped states of the country. NABARD has set for itself an ambitious task of providing access to micro-financial services to about 50 million rural families by linking four million Self-Help Groups with the banking system in another four years. Interventions of NABARD in this regard would continue in the form of investments in development of Human capital through large-scale training of SHGs, NGOs and other SHG promoting agencies. NABARD—

- Provided inputs in capacity building for banks and partner agencies.
- Promoted the idea of organizing thrift and credit groups among the NGOs as an add-on activity and encouraged linking them with banks.

Provided loanable funds to banks and financial support to eligible MFIs, to ease the fund flow position to the sector.

State Bank of India (SBI)

Micro-finance is not new to State Bank of India. SBI has taken up SHG movement as a mission. A noble mission to reach those families who were hitherto having no access to the credit by any formal financial institution and, therefore, were depending on informal sources and moneylenders. SBI has actively participated in SHG-Bank Credit Linkage Programme since its inception in 1992 as a pilot project of NABARD. SBI is the largest bank in India with over 10,000 branches and is also the largest player in the micro-finance sector in India with a market share of around 20 per cent. It finances about 3 lakhs SHGs and has cumulative disbursements of Rs. 1,000 crore with Rs. 750 crore outstanding. SBI has taken several initiatives to expand its micro-finance portfolio covering one million SHGs. With passage of time, SBI has come out with innovative and varied products to expand micro-finance programme. Since, then the Bank has made a steady progress in financing SHGs. As on March 2006, SBI's branches spread throughout the length and breadth of the country have opened 6.30 lakh Savings Bank account of SHGs out of which more than 5.41 lakhs SHGs have been provided with credit facilities thus benefiting more than 75 lakhs poor people. Majority of these SHGs are women SHGs. SBI is maintaining its position as a leader among Commercial Banks in credit linking of SHGs and is a prime driver for the movement. As at the end of March 2006, SBI with a share of approximately 47 per cent of total SHGs financed by Commercial Banks is far ahead of others. The year-wise cumulative position of SHGs-Bank Linkage Programme for the last 4 years is as under:

Table 14.1: Year-wise cumulative position of SHGs-Bank Linkage Programme

Year	*March '03*	*March '04*	*March '05*	*March '06*
SHGs linked (financed)	1,07,553	1,74,666	3,43,691	5,40,481
No. of beneficiaries	12,33,660	21,50,752	48,11,674	75,68,842
Amount disbursed	324.84 cr.	614.87 cr.	1311.45 cr.	2262.95 cr.
Amount outstanding	269.43 cr.	462.77 cr.	872.08 cr.	1459.89 cr.
No. of SHGs maintaining Savings a/c in the Bank	2,79,466	3,69,568	5,08,396	6,36,067
Amount in Savings a/c (Amt. in Rs.)	261.36 cr.	348.31 cr.	411.82 cr.	434.07 cr.

(*Source* : State Bank of India Websites)

MAVIM

Maharashtra Mahila Arthik Vikas Mahamandal (MAVIM) is the women's economic development corporation under the Government of Maharashtra. It functions as and apex body for promoting activities including self-help saving groups, training programmes for women and seeking market for women's products. As early as 1975, Maharashtra pioneered the concept of a development corporation Mahila Arthik Vikas Mahamandal for economic support to women seeking self-employment if they were below the poverty line, providing them with training, credit and marketing facilities. The policy for women in Maharashtra Government envisages a greater role for MAVIM. MAVIM, a government agency, has played an important role in promotion of SHGs in the rural areas. The '*Sahayoginis*', the Field workers of MAVIM, have played a significant role in mobilization of rural women and their empowerment. The NGOs contracted by MAVIM and banks have also made significant contribution in the SHG promotion in the villages. MAVIM has itself new insights towards development and towards capacity building of women.

Maharashtra Gramin Bank

'Grameen Bank' was started by Muhammad Yunus, in 1976 to make available a credit delivery system for the poor, especially women, in Bangladesh. Impressed by micro-finance system of Grameen Bank in Bangladesh, the Maharashtra Government is planned to implement a similar model in the state. The work of Grameen Bank is extremely great and if implemented in the state, would help to finance women and self-help groups. Despite the easy processing of loan, the recovery rate is 99 per cent through Grameen Bank and the women get money on time without any delay. The Maharashtra Gramin Bank continues to work as Self-Help promoting institute so as to further consolidate the initiative taken it in the matter.

Regional Rural Banks have been in existence for around three decades in the Indian financial system. With joint share-holding by Central Government, State Government and the sponsoring bank, an effort was made to integrate commercial banking within the broad policy thrust towards social banking keeping in view the local peculiarities. RRBs were established with a view to developing the rural economy by providing, for the purpose of development of agriculture, trade, commerce, industry and other productive activities in the rural areas, credit and other facilities, particularly to small and marginal farmers, agricultural labourers, artisans and small entrepreneurs, and for matters connected therewith and incidental thereto Maharashtra Gramin Bank came into existence on 20th July, 2009 after amalgamation of erstwhile 'Maharashtra Godavari Gramin Bank' and 'Marathwada Gramin Bank' as per the notification of the Government of India. The Bank is sponsored by Bank of Maharashtra.

District Rural Development Agency (DRDA)

District Rural Development Agency (DRDA) is the principal organ at the district level that is vested with the responsibility of overseeing the implementation of various anti-poverty programmes. The DRDAs are expected to effectively coordinate with the Panchayati Raj Institutions, the banks and other financial institutions, the NGOs and the technical institutions, etc. with a view to gathering the support and resources required for poverty reduction effort in the district. DRDA is engaged in promotion of SHGs of BPL families under SGSY programme for which the services of NGOs are primarily utilized for promotion and nurturing of these SHGs. There is no subsidy element in SHG Bank linkage programme whereas Government is giving good amount of subsidy to the SHGs promoted under SGSY. The scheme provides that 75 per cent funding should be in groups. The group may consist of 10-20 persons of BPL families. 20 per cent non-BPL members in case of need can be added in the group. However, for minor irrigation and disabled persons, this number may be 5 members. The scheme is implemented under the supervision of Rural Development at the State level. At the District level, the implementation of the scheme has been entrusted to the District Rural Development Agency (DRDA) of Zilla Parishad. SGSY is being implemented by the DRDA with the active participation of Panchayati Raj Institutions (PRI), the Banks and Non-Governmental Organizations.

Conclusions

Micro-Finance can be a powerful instrument initiating a cyclical process of growth and development. Micro-finance is expected to play a significant role in poverty alleviation and development. Micro-finance activity improved access of rural poor to financial services, both savings and credit. Micro-finance has gained considerable importance in the last two decades as a tool of poverty reduction. SHG has gradually received necessary support from the institutional structure. Central Government should be promoted SHGs in a very large way to extend credit to the poor rural people under SGSY. SGSY is being implemented by the DRDA with the active participation of Panchayati Raj Institutions (PRI), the Banks and Non-Governmental Organizations. In India, a variety of micro-finance schemes exist and various approaches have been practiced by both GOs and NGOs. NABARD is one of the foremost institutions promoting micro-finance activities and supporting them on a large scale through bank-linkage programme. SBI is maintaining its position as a leader among Commercial Banks in credit linking of SHGs and is a prime driver for the movement. RRBs were established with a view to developing the rural economy by providing, for the purpose of development of agriculture, trade, commerce, industry and other productive activities in the rural areas, credit and other facilities, particularly to small and marginal farmers, agricultural labourers, artisans and small entrepreneurs. The Government can help by creating a flexible architecture for micro-finance innovations, including through a more enabling policy, legal, and regulatory framework.

References

Debendra Kumar Das, *Rural Sector and Development,* Deep & Deep Publications, New Delhi.

Kamdar Sangita, *Micro-Finance Self-Employment and Poverty Alleviation*, Himalaya Publishing House, New Delhi.

Prasada Rao, *Rural Poor and Institutional Credit – Rural Resources and Development Initiatives*, The Associated Publishers, Ambala.

Sagar Mondal & G.L. Ray, *Rural Development*, Kalyani Publishers, New Delhi.

Anupam Hazra, Poverty in Rural India: Jeopardizing the Future Growth – Kurukshetra – A Journal on Rural Development, Ministry of Rural Development, Vol.58, No. 1, Nov. 2009.

Gautam Patikar and Komal Singh, Scenario of Micro-Finance in India – An Overview, *Southern Economist*, Vol. 48, No. 17, Jan.1,2010.

P. Rajasekhar Reddy, Employment Through Women's SHGs - Ashwattha, *The Journal from Yashwantrao Chavan Academy of Development Administration*, Vol. 2, Issue-2, April-June, 2008.

Santosh Kumar & R. Vasanthagopal, Micro Credit Dispensation Models and Employment Generation, *Southern Economist*, Vol. 48, No. 17, Jan.1, 2010.

Thanksy Francis Thekekara, Sustainability Issue in Micro-Finance, Ashwattha – Kashada, Pune, Vol.1, Issue No. 3, July-Sept. 2007.

Informal Credit Delivery System, Prepared by NABARD officials, Jalna.

Annual Report, 2008-09 – Ministry of Rural Development, Government of India.

http://www.statebankofindia.com.

15

Performance of SGSY and SHGs in Bihar

B.C.Das

The Ministry of Rural Development, Government of India, on 1st April, 1999, by merging the Integrated Rural Development Programme (IRDP), Training of Rural Youth for Self-Employment (TRYSEM), Supply of Improved Tools for Rural Artisans (SITRA), *Ganga Kalyan* Yojana, Million Wells Scheme (MWS) and Development of Women and Children in Rural Areas (DWCRA), implemented a self-employment programme known as Swarnajayanti Gram Swarojgar Yojana (SGSY) with emphasis on formation of organisation of poor. The basic objective of the SGSY is to bring the assisted poor families above the poverty line by providing them income generating assets through bank credit and government subsidy. The approach of SGSY is based on mobilization of rural poor to enable them to organise into Self-Help Group (SHG) which are expected to act as financial intermediary for economic empowerment of the members. This programme has been conceived as a holistic self-governing programme covering all aspects of Self-employment of the rural poor such as organisation of poor into SHGs, their capacity building, credit arrangement, technology and market support, etc. In India, SHGs represent a unique approach to financial intermediation. The approach combines access to low-cost financial services with a process of self-management and development of rural poor who are SHG members. SHGs are formed and supported usually by NGOs or (increasingly) by Government agencies, linked not only to banks but also to wider development programmes. SHGs are seen to confer many benefits, both economic and social to women. SHGs enable women to grow their savings and to access the credit which banks are increasingly willing to lend. SHGs can also be community platforms from which women become active in village affairs, stand for local election or take action to address social or community issues.

Growth of SHGs under SGSY

At present, the SGSY programme is the biggest anti-poverty programme in world in terms of linking the rural poor through SHG to Commercial Banks, Regional Rural Banks (RRBs) and Cooperatives Banks. From 1999 April till January 2010, 36.78 lakh SHGs have been formed, of which 65 per cent have passed Grade-I (24.09 lakh), and 30.56 per cent Grade-II (11.24 lakh) and 22.72 per cent (8.36 lakh) have taken up economic activities (Table 15.1). The programme since inception has assisted more than 1.32 crore *Swarojgaris*.

The total funds made available for the programme since implementation was 20137 crore (Table 15.2) but the utilisation of fund was around 74 per cent.

Credit has been considered a critical input under SGSY which is made available to the *Swarojgaris* from financial institutions for creation of productive assets. The target, mobilization and disbursement of credit since implementation of SGSY indicate the moderate improvement over the years (Table 15.3). The ratio of credit to subsidy was about two during the above period and did not vary much from year to year, and it remained much below the target ratio of 3:1.

Table 15.1: Physical Progress under SGSY since Inception ('000)

Year	*SHGs formed*	*No. of SHGs passed Grade-I*	*No. of SHGs passed Grade-II*	*SHGs taking up Economic Activities*	*SHG Swarozgaris Assisted*	*Individual Swarozgaris Assisted*
1999-2000	292	125	—	29	35	586
2000-2001	223	214	74	26	319	687
2001-2002	434	176	54	31	365	573
2002-2003	399	190	95	36	414	412
2003-2004	392	205	91	51	578	320
2004-2005	266	220	106	68	789	327
2005-2006	276	211	92	80	873	278
2006-2007	246	222	156	138	1472	220
2007-2008	306	251	117	181	1154	254
2008-2009	564	322	139	114	1467	290
2009-2010 (January 2010)	278	273	100	82	957	143
Total	**3678**	**2409**	**1124**	**836**	**8739**	**4090**

Source : Various Annual Reports of MoRD, Govt. of India.

Table 15.2: Funds allocated and utilized under SGSY since inception *(Rs. crore)*

Year	*Total Allocation*	*Total funds available*	*Utilization of funds available*	*Percentage utilization of fund*
1999-00	1472	1962	960	49
2000-01	1332	1608	1118	70
2001-02	775	1300	970	75
2002-03	756	1178	921	78
2003-04	1066	1214	1043	86
2004-05	1333	1510	1291	85
2005-06	1333	1559	1339	86
2006-07	1466	1724	1424	83
2007-08	2269	2394	1966	82
2008-09	2692	3003	2285	76
2009-10 (December 09)	2689	2683	1548	58
Total	**17183**	**20137**	**14866**	**74**

Source: Various Annual Reports of MoRD, Govt. of India.

Table 15.3 : Credit Mobilization and Disbursement since inception of SGSY

(Rs. crore)

Year	*Total Credit Target*	*Total Credit Mobilized*	*Total Subsidy disbursed*	*Ratio of Credit to Subsidy*
1999-2000	3205	1056	542	1.95
2000-2001	3205	1459	702	2.01
2001-2002	3201	1330	666	2.00
2002-2003	2525	1184	606	1.95
2003-2004	2129	1302	713	1.83
2004-2005	2508	1658	859	1.93
2005-2006	2516	1823	905	2.01
2006-2007	2869	2291	971	2.36
2007-2008	3744	2760	1289	2.14
2008-09	3930	3530	1742	2.03
Total	**29831**	**18395**	**8994**	**2.03**

Source: Various Annual Reports of MoRD, Govt. of India.

More than 15 lakh SGSY–SHGs were maintaining savings bank accounts with the banking sector with outstanding savings of Rs. 1563.38 crore (Table 15.4).

Table 15. 4 : Progress of SGSY–SHG during the last Three years

(Rs. in crore)

Particulars	*2006-07*		*2007-08*		*2008-09*	
	No. of SHG	*Amount*	*No. of SHG*	*Amount*	*No. of SHG*	*Amount*
Savings of SHG with Banks as on 31st March	956317	757.50	1203070	809.51	1505581	1563.38
Bank loan disbursed to SHG during the year	188962	1411.02	246649	1857.74	264653	2015.22
Bank loan outstanding with the SHGs as on 31st March	687212	3273.03	916978	4816.87	976887	5861.72

Source : Status of Micro-finance in India 2008-09, NABARD.

The Regional Rural Banks had the maximum share of savings from 4.33 lakh SGSY-SHGs with savings amount of Rs. 775 crore (49.50%) followed by Commercial Banks with savings bank accounts of 9.31 lakh SGSY-SHGs with savings amount of Rs. 681 crore (43.60%) and Cooperative Banks having savings bank accounts of 1.40 lakh SGSY- SHGs with savings amount of Rs.107.24 crore (6.90%) in the year 2008-09 (Table 15.5).

Table 15.5 : Savings of SGSY-SHG with Banks-Agency-wise as on 31st March, 2009 *(Rs. in Crore)*

Agency	*Position as on*	*No of SHG*	*Amount*	*% Share of amount*
Commercial Banks (Public and Private Sector)	31.03.2008	765775	527.02	65.10
	31.03.2009	931422	681.60	43.60
	% growth	21.6	29.3	
Regional Rural Banks (RRB)	31.03.2008	357004	210.83	26.05
	31.03.2009	433912	774.55	49.50
	% growth	21.5	267.4	
Cooperative Banks	31.03.2008	80291	71.66	8.85
	31.03.2009	140247	107.24	6.90
	% growth	74.7	49.7	
Total	**31.03.2008**	**1203070**	**809.51**	**100**
	31.03.2009	**1505581**	**1563.39**	**100**
	% growth	**25.1**	**93.1**	

Source: Status of Micro-finance in India 2008-09, NABARD.

The banks have financed 2.64 lakh SGSY-SHGs, including repeat loan to existing SHGs with bank loan of Rs.2015.22 crore during the year 2008-09. The RRBs and Cooperative Banks have disbursed more credit to the SHSY-SHGs in the year 2008-09 than 2007-08 (Table 15.6).

Table 15.6 : The Bank Loan disbursed and outstanding against SGSY-SHGs

(Rs in crore)

Agency	*During the Year*	*Loan Disbursed*			*Loan Outstanding*		
		No. of SHG	*Amount*	*% Share of amount*	*No. of SHG*	*Amount*	*% Share of amount*
Commercial Banks	2007-08	160674	1103.70	59.40	638283	3225.92	67.00
(Public and Private	2008-09	133117	1102.38	54.70	645145	3961.53	67.60
Sector)	% growth	-17.2	-0.1		1.1	22.8	
Regional Rural	2007-08	64678	597.71	32.18	223191	1332.33	27.70
Banks (RRB)	2008-09	81662	655.27	32.50	258890	1508.10	25.70
	% growth	26.3	9.6		16.0	13.2	
Cooperative Banks	2007-08	21297	156.33	8.42	55504	258.62	5.30
	2008-09	49874	257.57	12.80	72852	392.09	6.70
	% growth	134.2	64.8		31.3	51.6	
Total	2007-08	**246649**	**1857.74**	**100**	**916978**	**4816.87**	**100**
	2008-09	**264653**	**2015.22**	**100**	**976887**	**5861.72**	**100**
	% growth	**7.3**	**8.5**		**6.5**	**21.7**	

Source : Status of Micro-finance in India 2008-09, NABARD.

The branches of Regional Rural Banks and Cooperative Banks are mostly found in rural areas, and these banks play very important roles in implementation of SGSY. Regional Rural Banks play a leading role in rural areas than any other Banks.

The success of any anti-poverty programmes depend on how successfully these programmes are implemented in most poverty stricken states of the country. In terms of percentage of poor people in the States–Orissa, Bihar and Jharkhand are having more number of poor people than any other states of the country. Reduction of the poverty in the country depends upon the successful implementation of SGSY in these states. Besides other aspects of SHG development, SHG members under SGSY need systematic and guaranteed credit facility from the financial institutions to increase their level of income through various entrepreneurial activities. A major cause of the poverty among rural people is lack of access to financial resources to acquire productive assets to improve living standard. This is caused by the fact that the formal credit institutions that function smoothly in developed urban areas cannot cater to the credit need of rural poor due to lack of information about the borrowers and lack of proper collateral among the poor people. In the rural areas, the RRBs are one of the important sources for the poor people to get credit. The access to credit and continuance with bank by poor people in high poverty states are very important. In the present paper, the performance of SGSY-SHGs financed by RRBs in the state of Bihar is studied. As on 31st March, 2009, 43,361 SHGs have saved around Rs. 22.31 crore in five Regional Rural Banks in Bihar (Table 15.7).

During the last three years, RRBs in Bihar have disbursed more than Rs. 172.73 crore to the SGH members under SGSY (Table 15.8).

Table 15.7 : Savings of SGSY-SHGs with RRBs in Bihar as on 31.03.2009

(Rs. in Lakh)

Name of the RRBs	*No. of SHGs*	*No. of Members*	*Amount of Savings*
Bihar Khsetriya Gramin Bank	2964	34097	14.22
Kosi KGB	NA	NA	NA
Madhya Bihar Gramin Bank	15241	15295	914.00
Samastipur KGB	1575	17325	37.52
Uttar Bihar Gramin Bank	23581	238109	1266.00
Total	**43361**		**2231.74**

Source : Status of Micro-finance in India 2008-09, NABARD.

Table 15.8 : Loan Disbursed to SGSY-SHGs by RRBs in Bihar *(Rs. in Lakh)*

Name of the RRBs	*2006-07*		*2007-08*		*2008-09*	
	No. of SHGs	*Amount*	*No. of SHGs*	*Amount*	*No. of SHGs*	*Amount*
Bihar Khsetriya Gramin Bank	275	403.25	2001	1235.78	488	472.16
Kosi KGB	823	506.12	NA	NA	NA	NA
Madhya Bihar Gram in Bank	1294	902.00	1155	1042.00	1101	1126.00
Samastipur KGB	580	144.00	934	240.00	1030	295.14
Uttar Bihar Gramin Bank	2828	2167.21	1754	3116.00	3314	5625.00
Total	**5800**	**4122.58**	**5844**	**5633.78**	**5933**	**7518.30**

Source : Status of Micro-finance in India 2008-09, NABARD.

Against these background discussions, the present study attempts to find out the performance the SGSY-SHGs financed by the RRBs in the state of Bihar.

Methodology and Study Area

Bihar, one of the most backward states in India where

concentration of rural poor is much higher than most of the other states, was selected purposively for the study. From the state, two Regional Rural Banks (RRBs) having more than 25 branches were selected at the first phase. Again from each RRB, 25 branches were selected and from each branch, one SHG financed under SGSY for income generating activities prior to March 2007 were taken for the study. The reason for such selection of the SHG was that the groups those were financed at least two years before the data collection would have manifested some economic development.

Therefore, 50 SHGs financed under SGSY by the 50 branches of two RRBs, viz. Bihar Khestriya Gramin Bank and Uttar Bihar Gramin Bank constituted the sample of this study. Primary and secondary data for the study were collected during December 2009 to February 2010.

For the purpose of measuring and ranking the performance of the group, a maturity index was developed with 20 key performance indicators. For each indicator, values (marks) were assigned as per the actual performance of the group. The maximum values allotted to each of the indicator aggregates to 100. The performance of SHG is assessed on the basis of total marks obtained on 20 indicators.

Results and Discussions

(1) ***Meeting Frequency :*** The group members are expected to meet at a certain interval to conduct their transactions. A maximum five marks were allotted if the group conducts their meeting weekly, 3 marks if conducts fortnightly and 2 marks if conducts monthly. The performance of the group on this indicator presented in Table 15.9 indicates that 84 per cent group conducts meeting monthly once.

(2) ***Regularity of Meetings :*** The members are expected to participate in the meeting regularly so that they may own the group. The meeting of the group is required to transact various activities like savings, repayment of loan, maintenance of registers, community development activities, etc. Attendance, participation in decision-making and sharing responsibilities are important activities of the member in group. To measure the regularity of meeting, a maximum 15 marks were allotted if the group had held 75 per cent and above the schedule meeting, 10 marks if it had 75 to 25 per cent scheduled meetings and 0 marks if it had less than 24 per cent scheduled meetings. The analysis of data presented in Table 15.9 reveals that 30 groups out of 50 groups conducted 25 to 75 per cent of their scheduled meetings in last year.

(3) *Democratic Character of the Group:* Philosophy of SHG is based on collective decision-making. Every member is expected to shoulder certain responsibility as per the need of the group. The practice of rotational leadership provides opportunities and challenges to each member to handle group activities. This practice also helps to reduce the dependency of the group members on few members for operation of the group. It also reduces the conflict. For this indicator, if changes of the office bearer had been made at least once since inception then it was considered as democratic and maximum 6 marks was assigned otherwise it was considered as undemocratic and 0 mark was awarded. Eighty-four per cent of the group reported that there was no change of leadership in the group.

(4) *Sanction against Deviant Behaviour:* Discipline is prerequisite for effective functioning of the group. To ensure discipline, the group must formulate some rules and regulation to govern them. It is expected that all should obey the rules and regulations, and work accordingly. However, it is not true in all cases. There are some deviants in social system. To deal these deviants, there must be existence of some fine/sanction procedure. Under this indicator, if such rules are existing and they are being enforced than a maximum 2 marks were awarded to the group otherwise 0 mark was awarded. Data on this indicator revealed that in majority cases (66%) the groups were not having any such rules to discipline the errant members.

Table 15.9 : Performance of the Groups on indicators 1 to 5

Sl. No	*Indicator*	*Category*	*Bihar Kshetriya Gramin Bank*		*Uttar Bihar Gramin Bank*		*Total for two RRBs (50 SHGs)*	
			f	*%*	*f*	*%*	*f*	*%*
1.	Frequency of Meeting	Weekly	1	(4)	4	(16)	5	(10)
		Fortnightly	1	(4)	2	(8)	3	(6)
		Monthly	23	(92)	19	(76)	42	(84)
2.	Regularity of Meeting	< 24 per cent of the scheduled meeting	7	(28)	8	(32)	15	(30)
		25 per cent to 74 per cent scheduled meetings held	17	(68)	13	(52)	30	(60)
		>75 per cent scheduled meetings held	1	(4)	4	(16)	5	(10)
3.	Democratic Character of the Group	Democratic	9	(36)	2	(8)	11	(22)
		Undemocratic	16	(64)	23	(92)	39	(84)
4.	Sanction against deviant behaviour	Groups having rules and also enforced	4	(16)	13	(52)	17	(34)
		No such measures	21	(84)	12	(48)	33	(66)
5	Homogeneity of the Group	Homogeneous	13	(52)	12	(48)	25	(50)
		Partially homo-geneous	9	(36)	13	(52)	22	(44)
		Not homogeneous	3	(12)	0	(0)	3	(6)

Note : Figures in parentheses are percentages

Source : Field Survey.

(5) ***Homogeneity of the Group:*** One of the ideal characteristics of the group is that it should be homogenous. The members from similar occupation, sex, caste, ethnic and socio-economic status participate in a cohesive manner in decision-making process. Heterogeneous group most of the time encounter conflicting situations. A maximum of 2 marks were allotted if all the members are from BPL, 1 mark was allotted if more than 50 per cent members are from BPL and 0 mark was given if less than 50 per cent members are from BPL. Fifty per cent of the groups were found having only BPL members.

(6) ***Book-Keeping:*** It is not possible to run a group without registers. There are various activities like discussions, attendance of the members, savings, deposit, loans, etc. which needs to be recorded to know by the members, officials and developmental functionaries. As per the maturity of the group and level of transactions, the number of registers in the group increase. A maximum score of 4 was allotted if the group is having more than 6 registers, 3 marks was given if the group is having 5 to 3 registers and 2 marks was given if the group is having 2 to 1 registers for their record-keeping. Majority (62 %) of the groups were found having 3 to 5 registers.

(7) ***Maintenance of Registers:*** Regular update of registers is very important to ensure transparency and reduce conflict in the group. To evaluate this indicator, a maximum of 6 marks were allotted if more than 6 registers are update, 4 marks were allotted if 5 to 3 registers are update, 2 marks were allotted if 2 to 1 registers are update and no mark was allotted if no register is found up-date. Maintenance of the register was found very poor in the study region and in majority (64%) of the cases only 1 or 2 registers were found update on the date of investigation.

(8) *Members' Saving:* "Savings first-Credit later" should be the motto for every SHG member. Regularity in saving by the group members takes them towards self-dependence. Members learn financial discipline through savings and internal lending. It also helps in growth of corpus so that the group can meet the credit needs of their members. A maximum mark of 4 were allotted if all members save regularly, 2 marks allotted if some members report regular saving and no mark was allotted if members savings are found not regular. The analysis presented in Table 15.10 reveals that savings pattern is not uniform, and savings of the members was found irregular in majority (52%) of the groups.

(9) *Members' Access to SHG Records:* Records, registers and assets are common property of the group. In an ideal situation, each and every member should have access to the group's books and records. Access to records breeds transparency in the group. This indicator was allotted maximum of 2 marks if the group members have access to records otherwise no mark. The frequency analysis presented in Table 15.10 indicates that half of the SHG members did not have access to SHG record. It was also found that the majority (80%) of the group's members under Bihar Kshetriya Gramin Bank did not have access to SHG record. It was observed during the field investigation that in most of the SHGs, the registers were kept with the NGO facilitator.

(10) *Participation of Member in Decision-Making*: For effective functioning of the group, all members should understand each issue and participate in decision-making process. This participation goes a long way in empowering the member and increasing their ability to take right decision. A maximum of 4 marks was allotted to this indicator if most of the members participate in decision-making process, 2 marks were allotted if some of the members used to participate and no mark was awarded if it is found lack of participation of members in decision-making process. The RRB-wise as well as total of two RRBs analysis of members' participation in decision-making is presented in Table 15.10. The analysis reveals that in majority groups there was very low level of participation of members in meeting.

Table 15.10: Performance of the Groups on indicators 6 to 10

Sl. No	*Indicator*	*Category*	*Bihar Kshetriya Gramin Bank*		*Uttar Bihar Gramin Bank*		*Total for two RRBs (50 SHGs)*	
			f	%	*f*	%	*f*	%
6.	Book-Keeping	>6 Registers	2	(8)	3	(12)	5	(10)
		5-3 Registers	14	(56)	17	(68)	31	(62)
		2-1 Registers	9	(36)	5	(20)	14	(28)
7.	Maintenance of Register	More than 6 Registers are update	2	(8)	0	(0)	2	(4)
		3 to 5 registers are update	7	(28)	8	(32)	15	(30)
		1 to 2 registers are update	15	(60)	17	(68)	32	(64)
		No Register is update	1	(4)	0	(0)	1	(2)
8.	Members' Saving	Regular	8	(32)	8	(32)	16	(32)
		Some members regular	11	(44)	16	(64)	27	(52)
		All are not regular	6	(24)	1	(4)	7	(14)
9.	Members Access to the SHG records	Have access	5`	(20)	11	(44)	25	(50)
		No access	20	(80)	14	(56)	25	(50)
10	Participation of Member in meeting	Majority Participate	6	(24)	5	(20)	11	(22)
		Few Partici-pate	8	(32)	16	(64)	24	(48)
		No partici-pation	11	(44)	4	(16)	15	(30)

Note : (Figures in parentheses are percentages)

Source : Field Survey.

(11) *Internal Lending :* One of the basic objectives of group formation is to increase the socio-economic condition of the group members. As the members are resource poor, they need credit for consumption, emergency and production activities. Internal lending from the corpus to the group members help them to learn to priorities the credit needs, developing repayment schedule, fixing rate of interest, etc, and most importantly the importance of financial discipline. The internal lending process enables the group to develop skills in financial management, maintenance of accounts and establishing rapport with the banks. To this indicator, a maximum of 10 marks was allotted if the group has lent 3 times or more , 8 marks if group has lent 2 times, 4 marks if group has lent 1 time and 0 mark if group has not taken up any internal lending. The performance of groups presented in Table 15.11 reveals that majority (52%) of the groups under these two RRBs had availed two times of internal loan before IGA.

(12) *Loan Repayment:* Loan Repayment characteristic is an important manifestation of maturity of the group as well as member. Timely repayment of loan indicates that the loan was availed as per the repayment capacity and sound business plan. A maximum of 8 marks were allotted if the groups are repaying their loan regularly, 2 marks if the repayment is irregular and no mark if there is no repayment. The performance of the groups on this indicator reveals very unsatisfactory situation. It was observed that the repayment of loan after availing credit for IGA was irregular in majority (64%) of the groups.

(13) *Loan Size:* Loan size was taken as an indicator to measure the maturity level of the group. Disciplined

Table 15.11: Performance of the Groups on indicators 11 to 15

Sl. No.	*Indicator*	*Category*	*Bihar Kshetriya Gramin Bank*		*Uttar Bihar Gramin Bank*		*Total for two RRBs (50 SHGs)*	
			f	*%*	*f*	*%*	*f*	*%*
11.	Internal Lending	No internal lending	0	(0)	0	(0)	0	(0)
		One time	0	(0)	8	(32)	8	(16)
		Two times	13	(52)	13	(52)	26	(52)
		Three times and above	12	(48)	4	(16)	16	(32)
12	Loan Repayment	As per the instalment	0	(0)	0	(0)	0	(0)
		Irregular Repayment	5	(20)	11	(44)	16	(32)
		No Repay-	20	(80)	12	(48)	32	(64)
		ment	0	(0)	2	(8)	2	(4)
13.	Loan Size	Loan Size has increased	2	(8)	10	(40)	12	(24)
		Loan Size has not increased	23	(92)	15	(60)	38	(76)
14.	Supported by Professional Agencies	Supported	10	(40)	9	(36)	19	(38)
		Not Supported	15	(60)	16	(64)	31	(62)
15.	Credit Plus Activities	Involved in Credit Plus activities	5	(20)	3	(12)	8	(16)
		Not involved in credit plus activities	20	(80)	22	(88)	42	(84)

Note : (Figures in parentheses are percentages)
Source: Field Survey.

groups make timely repayment of loan, and gradually become eligible for higher dose of loan. Under this indicator, a maximum number of 4 were allotted if the size of the loan availed by the group has increased over the time otherwise 0 mark was allotted. It was found in the study sample that in majority of the cases the loan size has not increased in their long career exceeding five years.

(14) *Support by Professional Agencies:* SHG is an institution. Various problems may arise from time to time which require assistance of expert to solve or provide guidance. Support by NGOs and government agencies help increase the maturity level of the group. A maximum 4 marks were allotted if the group is supported by the professional agency otherwise no mark was allotted to this indicator. The findings presented in Table 15.10 reveals that the majority (62%) of the groups were not supported by any professional agencies.

(15) *Credit Plus Activities*: SHG is not an institution which is engaged only in saving and credit activities. It should look beyond credit related activities, and engage various community welfare activities like primary education, immunization, family planning, sanitation, anti-dowry, anti-child labour, etc. to make it a socially responsible institution. A maximum of 2 marks were allotted if the group has taken up any community welfare activities in last year otherwise no mark was allotted to the group under this indicator. The findings presented in Table 15.11 indicate that the most of the groups were confined to their saving and credit activities.

(16) *Social and Political Participation of members in other Organisation:* Panchayati Raj Institution (PRI) plays very important role in community development. The member of SHG becoming member of PRI may extend benefit to the group on various ways. Similarly, by becoming member or office bearer in other organisation may enhance the status of the group. A maximum of 4 marks were allotted to the group under this indicator if it is found that any of the member of SHG is holding office bearer position in PRI, 2 marks were allotted if any member is holding office bearer position in any organisations other than PRI, 1 mark for ordinary membership in any organisation and no mark if SHG members are neither office bearer nor ordinary member of any organisation. The analysis of the findings is presented in Table 15.12 indicates that very few members were holding in formal or office bearer position in other organisation. Only some members of 4 groups were holding official position in PRI. The SHGs in Bihar has to go a long way to establish itself as an important institution in the community.

(17) Member of Federation: Membership in federation provides a sense of security to the group. Federation also facilitates SHG to gain greater access to banks, establish links with government and non-governmental organisation. A maximum of 4 marks were allotted if the groups are federated. SHGs without membership in federation are not assigned any mark. It was found that no group from Bihar has been federated.

(18) SHG Audit: Auditing of the records by external agencies enhances the credibility of the records. It also reduces chances of wrong doings in accounting. If the records of the SHG are audited by an external agency, the SHG is allotted maximum 2 marks under this indicator and no mark was allotted if the records are not audited by an external agencies. It was found that not a single account or record of sampled SHG was audited by external agencies in Bihar.

(19) Members' Training: Members training is critical for sustainability of the group. Different types of training are required at different stages of group. Capacity building of the members through various training programmes helps the member to understand the importance of group for their development. A maximum 4 marks were allotted if

Table 15.12 : Performance of the Groups on indicators 16 to 20

Sl. No	*Indicator*	*Category*	*Bihar Kshetriya Gramin Bank*		*Uttar Bihar Gramin Bank*		*Total for two RRBs (50 SHGs)*	
			f	*%*	*f*	*%*	*f*	*%*
16	Social and Political Participation of Members	Without any membership/ official position	15	(60)	12	(48)	27	(54)
		Formal Membership	5	(20)	5	(20)	10	(20)
		Official position in any formal organisation other than PRI	2	(8)	7	(28)	9	(18)
		Official position in PRI	3	(12)	1	(4)	4	(8)
17	Member of Federation	Member of Federation	0	(0)	0	(0)	0	(0)
		Not a member of federation	25	(100)	25	(100)	50	(100)
18	SHG Audit	SHG audited	0	(0)	0	(0)	0	(0)
		SHG not audited	25	(100)	25	(100)	50	(100)
19	Members Training	More than 50 per cent members attended training	16	(64)	10	(40)	26	(52)
		Less than 50 per cent members attended training	9	(36)	15	(60)	24	(48)
20	Corpus Fund	<50 per cent of corpus fund in circulation	8	(32)	2	(8)	10	(20)
		50 to 75 per cent corpus fund in circulation	17	(68)	17	(68)	34	(68)
		>75 per cent corpus fund in circulation	0	(0)	6	(24)	6	(12)

Note : (Figures in parentheses are percentages)
Source: Field Survey.

more than 50 per cent of the members have attended skill development training otherwise 0 mark was allotted. The performance of the SHG on members' training presented in Table15.12 reveals that around half of the members have not attended any skill development training although these groups were financed under various projects.

(20) Corpus Fund : Circulation of corpus fund among members increases corpus. However, it is seen most of the time that the major chunk of the corpus fund remains idle in saving bank account. This is not an ideal situation for the group. The group should meet their small credit need from their own corpus fund rather than from other sources by paying interest. Therefore, the rotation of corpus fund for internal lending is considered as important indicators to measure the maturity of the group. A maximum of 8 marks were allotted if more than 75 per cent of the corpus fund is in circulation, 4 marks were allotted if 75 to 50 per cent of the corpus fund is in circulation and no mark was awarded if less than 50 per cent of the corpus fund is in circulation. The performance of corpus fund circulation of SHGs is presented in Table 15.12. In the study, 68 per cent of the groups reported 50 to 75 per cent utilisation of the corpus.

Aggregate Score of the Maturity Index of Group

Indicator-wise score and aggregate score of maturity index of sampled SHGs under different RRBs is presented in Table 15.13 which gives a comprehensive profile of the maturity level of the group. The SHGs under RRBs in Bihar were found to be very weak and immature. They scored less than 50 marks. It is important to mention that the groups for the study were taken from those groups who were financed for IGA prior to

Table 15.13: Maturity Score of SHGs (Indicators as well as Total Mean Score)

SHGs under RRB	No of SHGs	INDICATORS 1	2	3	4	5	6	7	8	9	10	11	12	13	14	15	16	17	18	19	20	*Total*
Bihar Kshetriya Gramin Bank	25	2.16	7.60	2.16	0.32	1.40	2.72	2.80	2.16	0.40	2.08	8.96	3.20	0.32	1.60	0.40	0.76	0.00	0.00	1.44	2.72	43.2
Uttar Bihar Gramin Bank	25	2.56	7.60	0.48	1.04	1.48	2.92	2.64	2.56	0.88	2.08	7.04	4.48	1.60	1.44	0.24	0.92	0.00	0.16	2.40	4.64	47.2
Maximum Marks		**5**	**15**	**6**	**2**	**2**	**4**	**6**	**4**	**2**	**4**	**10**	**8**	**4**	**4**	**2**	**4**	**4**	**2**	**4**	**8**	**100**

List of Indicators

1. Meeting Frequency
2. Regularity of Meetings
3. Democratic Character of the Group
4. Sanction against Deviant Behaviour
5. Homogeneity of the Group
6. Book Keeping
7. Maintenance of Registers
8. Members' Saving
9. Members' Access to SHG Records
10. Participation of Member in Decision-Making
11. Internal Lending
12. Loan Repayment
13. Loan Size
14. Support by Professional Agencies
15. Credit Plus Activities
16 Social and Political Participation
17. Member of Federation
18. SHG Audit
19. Members' Training:
20. Corpus Fund

2007. It is expected that the groups those who are financed for IGA must have passed through various evaluation processes, and have developed some capacity to govern themselves. However, from the maturity scoring, it is revealed that the groups of Bihar were linked to banks for IGA without properly assessing their capacity to utilize the loan for their benefit. Due to low maturity level of the sampled groups in Bihar, it was found that majority of the groups/ members have stopped transaction with bank after availing subsidy.

Relationship Between SHGs' Maturity Level and Bank Credit Availed

It is expected a high correlation between the level of maturity and the size of the bank credit availed by the group. To examine this, aggregate maturity score of SHGs along with the mean bank credit availed by the group since last five years were studied. The findings of relational analysis of maturity level of SHG with bank credit availed is presented in Table 15.14. The finding suggests a positive and significant relationship between the maturity of the SHGs and the size of the bank credit availed by the group. This finding confirms the finding of Purushotham (2009) reported in a study on "Institutional Credit for Rural Livelihood— A Study of SGSY in the Regions of High Poverty".

Table 15.14: Relational Analysis of Maturity level of the SHG with bank credit availed by the group

(n=50)

State	*Mean Maturity Score*	*Mean Bank Credit availed (Rs.)*	*Correlation Coefficient (Rs)*
Bihar	45.18	2,59,180	0.33*

*Significant at 5% level.

Conclusion

The SHGs of the study sample were formed in a very routine manner without giving much emphasis in the process part. They were recommended to bank for revolving fund and credit for IGA without following right grading process. It was found that the most of the SHGs did not take up sufficient number of times of internal lending to acquire the minimum level of skill to manage their own fund before opting for higher amount of credit from bank. Many of the SHG members were found ignorant about the quantum of subsidy, interest rate and terms of loan repayment. The maturity level of the sampled SHGs was very poor and they performed very badly in all 20 performance indicators. These immature SHGs were not reckoned by the banks as serious micro-credit clients and the SHG-bank linkage process was not pursued seriously. To establish an effective linkage between SGSY-SHG and bank, the performance of the SHGs on the above discussed 20 indicators has to be improved through capacity building of different stakeholders involved in the process.

References

Annual Reports of Ministry of Rural Development, Government of India, 2008-09

Purushotham, P. (2009), "Institutional Credit for Rural Livelihood: A study of SGSY in the Regions of High Poverty", National Institute of Rural Development, Hyderabad.

Status of Micro-Finance in India: 2006-07,2007-08 and 2008-09, NABARD.

16

Rural Credit Access through Micro-finance

A Road to Women Empowerment

B.Vanitha

Introduction

The concept of empowerment has its origin in the experiences of social movements in Latin America in their attempts to carry out social transformation. Since then it has entered many fields of theory and practice and well established throughout the development discourse. Empowerment is the process by which those who have been denied the ability to make strategic life choices acquire such ability. It is viewed from the expansion in people's ability to make strategic life choices in a context where this ability was previously denied to them. As it is a process and is not therefore, something that can be given to the people.

Women Empowerment

Women empowerment is a process whereby women become able to organise themselves to increase their own self-reliance, to assert their independent right to make choices and to control resources which will assist in challenging and eliminating their own subordination. The goal of women empowerment is to address issues relating to women's subordination, inequality and inequity. Hence, women empowerment is a process where women are able to change from a state of powerlessness *(I cannot)* to a state of collective self-confidence *(We can).*

Framework of Women Empowerment

The core of the women's empowerment framework formulated by UNICEF (1993) lies in the argument that women's development can be viewed in terms of five levels of equality.

1. *Welfare :* It is the first level which addresses only the basic needs of women without recognizing or attempting to solve the underlying structural causes, which necessitate provision of welfare services. At this point, women are merely passive beneficiaries of welfare benefits.
2. *Access :* It is the second level, which is essential for women to make meaningful progress. This involves equality of access to resources such as educational opportunities, land and credit.
3. *Conscientisation :* It is a crucial point in the empowerment framework for women to take appropriate action to close gender gaps and gender inequalities from inherent structural and institutional discrimination. They must also recognize the role they can often play in reinforcing the system that restricts their growth.
4. *Participation :* It is the point where women are taking decisions alongside men equally. To reach this level, however, mobilisation is necessary. By organising themselves and working collectively, women will be empowered to gain increased representation, which will lead to increased empowerment and ultimately greater control.

5. *Control* : It is the ultimate level of equality and empowerment. Here, the balance of power between men and women is equal and neither party has dominance over the other. At this stage in the empowerment framework, women are able to make decisions over their lives and the lives of their children, and play an active role in the development process. Further, the contribution of women are fully recognised and rewarded.

Using the empowerment framework, development planners can determine whether a project is at the welfare, access, conscientization, participation or control level, and determine the point of intervention, to move women to higher levels of equality and empowerment.

Women Empowerment and Micro-Finance

From the early 1970s, women's movements in a number of countries have identified lack of credit provision as a major constraint on women's ability to earn an income. Since 1970s, many women's organisations worldwide have included credit and savings, both as a way of increasing women's incomes and to bring women together to address gender issues. The 1980s saw the emergence of poverty-targeted micro-finance institutions and implementation of poverty alleviation programmes. In the 1990s, there was increasing emphasis on targeting women in micro-finance programmes towards their empowerment.

Women access to savings and credit gives them a greater economic role in decision-making through their decision about savings and credit. When women control decisions regarding credit and savings, they will optimise their own and the household's welfare. The investment in women's economic activities will improve employment opportunities for women and thus have a *trickle down effect* and leads to economic empowerment.

Micro-Finance

Micro-finance is nothing but the provision of financial services dealing with very small deposits and loans. Micro-finance Programmes (MFPs) based on this ideology operates from an integrated approach, where financial and social intermediations are endogenous to programme delivery. This approach goes beyond merely increasing income/consumption measures to increasing capacities and choices and thereby decreases the vulnerability of poor people by focusing on protection strategies.

Swarnjayanthi Gram Swarozgar Yojana (SGSY)

Swarnjayanthi Gram Swarozgar Yojana (SGSY) was launched by the Government of India on 1st April, 1999. It replaces all the earlier poverty alleviation programmes. The programme aims at establishing a large number of micro-enterprises in the rural areas, building upon the potential of the rural poor. The poor can fight poverty only collectively, not individually. Therefore, people who are homogeneous in terms of socio-economic background or traditional occupation come together and get organised into Self-Help Groups (SHGs) to attain a collective goal for a common cause for the benefit of group members.

The objective is to bring the assisted poor families (*Swarozgaris*) above the poverty line by providing them with income generating assets through a mix of bank credit and government subsidy by ensuring appreciable sustained level of income over a period of time. A variety of approaches have been adopted under SGSY.

SGSY focuses on group approach. This involves

organisation of the poor into Self-Help Groups (SHGs) through a process of social mobilisation and their capacity building. It aims at establishing a large number of *micro enterprises* in rural areas based on the potential and competencies of the rural poor. In establishing the micro enterprises, the emphasis is on the *cluster approach,* which helps in providing the backward and forward linkages in a cost-effective and sustainable manner. The success of micro-enterprises often depends on the choice of the activity, which should be based on local resources, aptitude and skills of the people. Accordingly, the bulk of the assistance under SGSY were channellised for a few select activities termed as *key activities* identified for each block, based on their potential, from which the swarozgaris can draw sustainable income. SGSY will adopt a *project approach* for each key economic activity which would outline various elements such as training, credit, technology, infrastructure and marketing and also indicate the number of people to be covered under the activity. Provision of adequate infrastructure is essential for sustainability of micro-enterprises. Therefore, importance is attached to plug the critical *infrastructural gaps* for identified clusters/key activities.

A special emphasis is placed on imparting the requisite technical and managerial skills of the rural poor under the *skill building approach* through well-designed training programmes to meet the minimum skill requirement for the identified activities. SGSY will ensure *upgradation of technology* in the identified activity clusters to add value to the local resources. SGSY will provide for *promotion of marketing* of the goods produced by the *swarozgaris*. By providing market intelligence, market development, consultancy services as well as institutional arrangement for marketing of goods including exports. SGSY is a *credit cum subsidy programme* for self-employment of poor families where credit is a critical component and subsidy is a minor and an enabling component. Subsidy is envisaged only as an incentive for prompt repayment by swarozgaris and thereby reduces their loan burden. Once, the *swarozgaris* establish their creditworthiness by way of prompt repayment under the first dose of credit, they look forward to repeated doses of credit for expansion of their economic activities. Therefore, SGSY lays stress on providing *multiple doses of credit* in deserving cases based on the credit history of *swarozgaris*.

Statement of the Problem

Experience has shown that many of the poverty alleviation programmes through organised credit channels have not achieved the required success. Compared to the earlier self-employment programmes, which resulted in a lack of proper social intermediation, SGSY is a holistic programme covering all aspects of self-employment centred in organising the women into Self-Help Groups. Apart from creation of micro enterprises and elimination of poverty, women empowerment is a major concern and prime priority of the SHGs formed under initiatives, of SGSY. Kabeer's work (1997) suggested that the assessment of the empowerment process is not only qualitative but subjective as well. Accordingly, the subjectivity of the process should also extend to measuring of empowerment in terms of women's own interpretation rather than relying on what is valued by the evaluators of the programmes. The process of empowerment should be judged as having occurred if it is self-assessed and validated by women themselves.

Hence, this study has been taken up to assess the level of empowerment interventions on the SHG members in Coimbatore District due to the implementation of SGSY.

Methodology

Though the scheme was implemented from first April 1999, the groups have become eligible to receive the economic assistance to take up the economic activity only from September 2001 onwards. Therefore, those groups, which have been involved in the economic activity for a period of more than five years after availing the economic assistance, were only considered for the study. Out of 19 blocks in Coimbatore District ten blocks were selected, where the SGSY interventions were considered to be very prominent. Out of nearly 40 activities 10 major activities were considered.

The details of the groups involved in the various economic activities in the selected blocks and the number of groups chosen for the study are shown in Table 16.1. As the average number of members in each group was found to be 12, three members (25 per cent) were interviewed from each group with the sample size of 108. Convenient sampling method was used for the purpose of data collection.

The Table 16.2 shows the statements of individual interventions listed on a five-point Likert's summated scale. On observing the summated score for each statement of individual intervention, it was found that the intervention level varied to each type of empowerment intervention. The statements arranged in the order of the ranks of individual indicators are listed below.

1. Freedom to choose economic activity.
2. Recognition/identification at the society level.
3. Freedom to spend the earnings.
4. Change in bargaining power.
5. Ability to move with the society.
6. Knowledge about investing the capital amount.
7. Importance within the household.
8. Improvement in capacity/skills.
9. Change in income due to economic activity.
10. Extent of male co-operation.
11. Knowledge in marketing a product.
12. Access to credit facilities.

Table 16.1 : Selected Block and Groups with activities

S. No. Economic Activity Block	Grossary Shop	Milch Animal	Thatches	Ready made	Calf & Rearing	Canteen	Handloom Weaving	Stone Quarry	Coir	Goat/ Sheep	No. of Groups Selected for Study	No. of Members Inter-viewed
1. Gudimangalam	2	11	19	3	7	_	3	_	17	_	(5)	15
2. Karamadai	8	10	2	3	7	_	4	_	_	19	(5)	15
3. Madathukulam	2	9	2	2	1	_	–	2	3	2	(2)	6
4. Pollachi (N)	_	2	2	_	3	_	4	_	28	_	(7)	21
5. Periyanaicken Palayam	8	4	2	1	3	3	_	_	_	_	(2)	6
6. Palladam	15	1	1	1	19	_	2	1	4	_	(5)	15
7. Sultanpet	3	_	_	_	_	_	6	_	7	_	(2)	6
8. Tiruppur	19	1	4	5	3	6	4	_	13	_	(2)	6
9. Thondamuthur	23	17	1	2	5	2	_	_	2	9	(4)	12
10.Udumalpet	5	_	13	3	9	6	_	_	2	10	(2)	6
Total											**36**	**108**

* Figures encircled represent number of group's involved corresponding to the activity chosen for study*Interventions on the Individual Members.*

Table 16. 2 : SGSY Interventions on the Individual

S.No.	*Empowerment Intervention*	*Welfare (1st level)*	*Access (2nd level)*	*Conscientisation (3rd level)*	*Participation (4th level)*	*Control (5th level)*	***Total***
1	Freedom to choose economic activity	–	12 (24.00)	3 (9.00)	48 (192.00)	45 (225.00)	**108 (450.00)**
2	Access to credit facilities	–	30 (60.00)	42 (126.00)	33 (132.00)	3 15.00)	**108 (333.00)**
3	Knowledge about investing the capital amount	–	3 (6.00)	42 (126.00)	48 (192.00)	15 (75.00)	**108 (399.00)**
4	Knowledge in marketing a product	–	14 (28.00)	49 (147.00)	38 (152.00)	7 (35.00)	**108 (362.00)**
5	Change in income due to economic activity	–	3 (6.00)	34 (102.00)	68 (272.00)	3 (15.00)	**108 (395.00)**
6	Freedom to spend the earnings	–	11 (22.00)	–	78 (312.00)	19 (95.00)	**108 (429.00)**
7	Extent of male co-operation	–	3 (6.00)	42 (126.00)	57 (228.00)	6 (30.00)	**108 (390.00)**
8	Importance within the household	–	6 (12.00)	32 (96.00)	60 (240.00)	10 (50.00)	**108 (398.00)**
9	Improvement in capacity/skills	–	3 (6.00)	39 (117.00)	57 (228.00)	9 (45.00)	**108 (396.00)**
10	Ability to move with the society	–	3 (6.00)	14 (42.00)	81 (324.00)	10 (50.00)	**108 (422.00)**
11	Change in bargaining power	–	4 (8.00)	15 (45.00)	75 (300.00)	14 (70.00)	**108 (423.00)**
12	Recognition/identification at the society level	–	3 (6.00)	2 (6.00)	79 (316.00)	24 (120.00)	**108 (448.00)**
	Total	–	**95 (190.00)**	**314 (942.00)**	**722 (2888.00)**	**165 (825.00)**	**1296 (4845.00)**

Apart from knowing the level of interventions corresponding to each attribute of intervention, the overall level of intervention is ascertained from the total summated score using the Likert scale. As the instrument consists of 12 statements, and interviewed 108 members, the following score values would be revealing.

12×108× 1 = 1296	–	The maximum possible score corresponding to **'welfare'** level.
12 x 108 x 2 = 2592	–	The maximum possible score corresponding to **'access'** level.
12 x 108 x 3 = 3888	–	The maximum possible score corresponding to **'conscientisation'** level.
12 x 108 x 4 = 5184	–	The maximum possible score corresponding to **'participation'** level.
12 x 108 x 5 = 6480	–	The maximum possible score corresponding to **'control'** level.

The total score would fall between 1296 (if all the 108 respondents happened to express that there is access to the measured dimensions) and 6480 (If all the 108 respondents happened to express that they have control over the measured dimensions.) As the total score is 4845 it may be ascertained that some of the members among the SHG members, have crossed the conscientisation level and reached the participation level. It showed that women were in a position to take decisions alongside men equally. It would become possible due to the collective strength achieved through mobilisation and organisation among the members.

However, the result cannot be interpreted to say that every member in the group has reached the fourth (participation) level of empowerment. In fact, there is difference in the level of empowerment among the members of the group. For example, those who are in a position to assume leadership and additional responsibilities would have reached the *participation* level while majority of the members who are active participants but not assuming any additional responsibilities, are in the *conscientisation* level. It is also observed that there are few members in the group who continue only with their contribution of savings and satisfied with the small amounts of internal borrowing still in the *access level*.

Conclusion

This study has revealed that there are indications of positive interventions in the women empowerment process due to the implementation of SGSY in Coimbatore District. From the stage of mere passive beneficiaries of welfare benefit, women are tending towards the stage of taking appropriate action to close gender gaps and inequalities. It has been found that there have been improvements in the financial position, income control and skill levels besides access to savings and credit.

Experiences over the years have shown that simply putting financial resources in the hands of poor women is not enough to bring about empowerment and improved welfare. Micro-finance programmes like SGSY when properly designed can make an important contribution to women empowerment by adopting a holistic approach that takes into account cultural, economic and political factors affecting empowerment. The schemes like SGSY can be ensured that women are more deeply and consistently empowered. Apart from the revolving fund and economic assistance extended to the SHGs, there should be more emphasis on other elements of empowerment such as leadership, self-management, and entrepreneurship in order to inch towards the overall empowerment of women.

References

Ela Bhatt (2005), Barrier to empowerment of poor women, excerpts of the 11th Justice Sunanda Bhandare memorial lecture on women, money and power, *The Hindu*, October 19.

Kabeer, N. (1998), Money can't buy me love? – Re-evaluating gender, credit and empowerment in rural Bangladesh, Discussion paper No.363, Institute of Development Studies, University of Sussex, Brighton, UK.

Manoharan Nair K. (2005), Micro-finance: The new development paradigm for poverty eradication and women's empowerment, *Kurukshetra,* April. Vol.53, No.6. pp. 18-20.

Priya Basu and Pradeep Srivastana (2005), Micro-finance and rural credit access for the poor in India, *Economic and Political Weekly Vol. XL. No.17, pp. 1747-1756.*

Satish, P. (2005), Mainstreaming of Indian micro-finance, *Economic and Political Weekly*, Vol. XL, No.17, pp. 1731-1739.

17

Self-Help Group—Micro Credit Linkage for Rural Development in India

G. Prasad Babu and *Rajkumar Josmee Singh*

Self-Help Group (SHG) is a registered or unregistered group of micro entrepreneurs having homogenous, social and economic background; voluntarily coming together to save small amounts regularly. They mutually agree to contribute to a common fund and to meet their emergency needs on mutual help basis. The group members use collective wisdom and peer pressure to ensure proper end-use of credit and timely repayment thereof. In fact, peer pressure has been recognized as an effective substitute for collaterals. Usually, the number of members in one SHG doesn't exceed twenty.

In India, NABARD initiated SHG's in 1986-87 for providing credit facilities to the poor, especially women, in both urban and rural areas. These SHG's stumbled upon a surprising finding; by targeting women, repayment rates came in well over 95 per cent, higher than most traditional banks. Impressed by those repayment rates, institutions like NABARD and SIDBI began increasing their lending to SHG's in India. The activities undertaken by SHG members include dairying, basket weaving, tailoring, pickles manufacturing, papad making, weaving, petty shops, sheep rearing, goat rearing, cotton coir rope making, coconut leaf thatching, group leaf plate making, spices production, honey and food processing, agarbatti making etc. have proved to be most viable economic activities in the country to earn sustainable income and livelihood.

Characteristics of SHG

- ❖ Homogeneous membership
- ❖ No discrimination
- ❖ Small membership
- ❖ Regular attendance
- ❖ Record-keeping
- ❖ Transparency in functioning
- ❖ Set of byelaws
- ❖ Thrift
- ❖ Utilizing savings for loaning.

Aims and objectives of SHG's

1. SHG is important for women and households headed by women, who often have difficulty in getting credit.
2. Micro-finance institutions locally mobilize voluntary savings the households as an enterprise gets the benefit.
3. SHG act as a forum for the members to provide space and support to each other and also enables the members to learn to cooperate and work in a group environment.
4. Micro-finance programmes, which build social capital, can indeed make significant contributions to women's empowerment.
5. SHG's have emerged as alternative development

strategy to promote the common interest of the weak and the vulnerable sections of the society.

6. As a risk management tool the key strength of micro-finance programme is the knowledge that loans will be available in time of need, making it possible for households to dispense with less effective and less desirable strategies like child labour money under the mattress.
7. Ability to turn individuals problems into collective one.
8. Develop human dimension of sharing.
9. It inculcate the principle of "each for all and all for each" among the members.

Micro-credit

Micro-credit is defined as provision of thrift, credit and other financial services and products of very small amount to the poor in rural, semi-urban and urban areas for enabling them to raise their income levels and improve living standards. Micro credit institutions are those, which provide these facilities. Muhammad Yunus, born 1940, is a Bangladeshi banker and the developer and founder of the concept of micro-credit. He is considered as father of micro-finance and he was also given Nobel Peace Prize in the year 2006. In 1976, Yunus founded the Grameen Banks to make loans to poor Bangladeshis. Since then the Grameen Bank has issued more than $3 billion in loans to some 2.4 million borrowers.

SHG-Bank Linkage Programme, since its pilot in 1992, has emerged as the leading micro-Finance (mF) programme in India. It is recognised as an effective tool for extending access to formal financial services to the unbanked rural poor. Encouraged by the success, the programme has been adopted by State Governments as a major poverty alleviation strategy. It has also led to the emergence of Micro-Finance Institutions (MFI) as a bridge between the banking sector and the rural poor. Experience of different anti-poverty and other welfare programmes implemented throughout the world have shown that the key to their success lies in the evolution and participation of community based organizations at the grass roots level. People's participation in credit delivery and recovery and inking of formal credit institutions to borrowers through intermediaries of SHG's have been recognizes as a supplementary mechanism for providing credit support to the poor.

Why we need micro-credit?

The importance of the micro-credit lies in the fact that the formal/institutional banking sector has not lived up to its social responsibility of meeting the financial needs of the poor due to –

- Lack of adequate branch network in the rural areas.
- The inability of the poor to offer satisfactory collaterals for the loans.
- Lack of education and awareness among the poor world.

The credit requirement of the poor has been estimated to be Rs.50,000 crore/annum. Against this requirement the credit outstanding of the poor with the formal banking sector is stated to be Rs.5,000 crore or 10 per cent of the total demand. According to sample survey conducted by bank and NCAER in 2003 in Andhra Pradesh and Uttar Pradesh, around 87 per cent of marginal or landless labourers do not access credit from the formal banking sector.

The principal objectives of the Micro-Credit programmes are —

1. To make the participating agencies well acquainted with the needs of different target groups e.g. Women,

tribal's, Scheduled Castes, Scheduled Tribes, micro-entrepreneurs and unemployed youth.

2. To initiate and implement micro-enterprises development programme and support the programme by way of an effective micro-finance delivery mechanism.
3. To strengthen capabilities of micro-finance organizations in the areas of planning, managing and coordinating micro-entrepreneurs to execute these projects and supporting them with managerial, financial and marketing assistance.

SHG - Bank linkage for micro-credit

A most notable milestone in the SHG movement was achieved when NABARD launched a pilot phase of the SHG Bank Linkage programme in February 1992. This was the first instance of mature SHG's that were directly financed by a commercial bank. The informal thrift and credit groups of poor were recognized as bankable clients. Soon after, the RBI advised commercial banks to consider lending to SHG's as part of their rural credit operations for creating SHG bank linkage. The linking of the SHG's with the financial sector was good for both sides. The banks were able to tap into a large market, namely the low-income households, transactions costs were low and repayment rates were high. The SHG's were able to scale up their operations with more financing and they had access to more credit products.

SHG-Bank linkage models

Under this model, groups are formed by different agencies known as Self-Help Group Promoting Institutes (SHGPI). These include NGO's, Voluntary associations, Govt. agencies, Panchayati Raj Institutions (PRIs), Vikas Volunteer Vahini (VVV) clubs, banks, Co-op. societies, etc.

(a) Without financial intermediation of NGO's/VA's

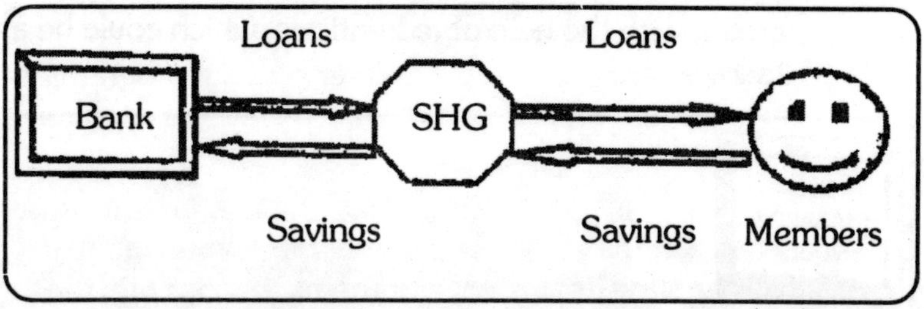

(b) With the financial intermediation of NGO's/VA's

In this model, a part of bank's work is externalized to NGO/VA

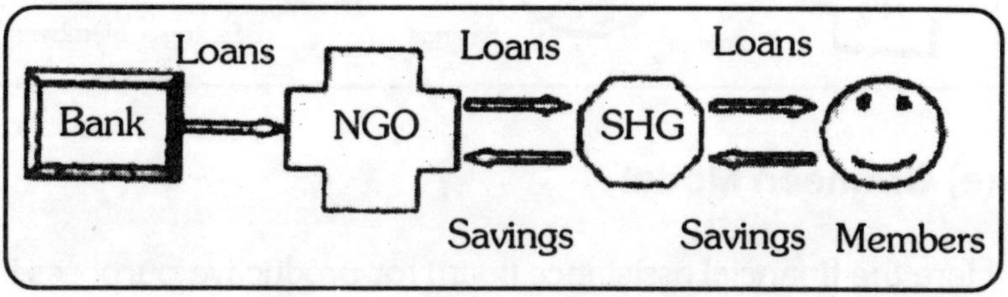

(c) Micro-Finance Institutions (MFI's)/NGO-SHG Models

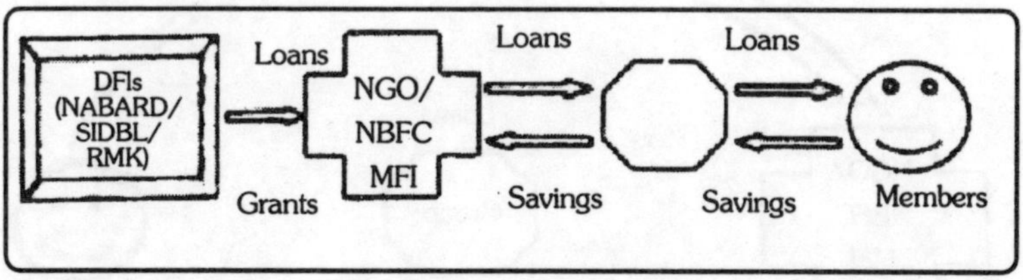

In this model, NGO, VA's, MFI's, NBFCs, etc. accessing funds either from banking system and or from Developmental Financial Institutions (DFIs) like NABARD and SIDBI for giving loans to SHGs either in group of individual mode.

(d) NGO/MFI Federation-SHG model

Here SHG get financial services, mostly savings and credit, with the help of federations, which could be as follows:

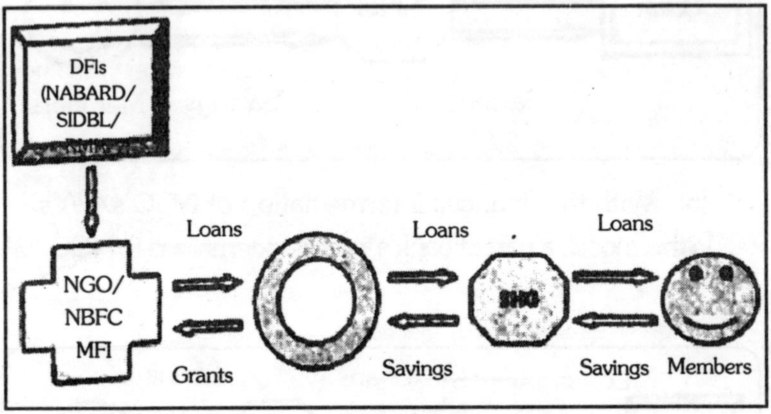

(e) Grameen Model

Here the financial assistance (loan) for productive purposes is provided by the MFI's/NGO's directly to the members of small groups directly on the strength of group assistance.

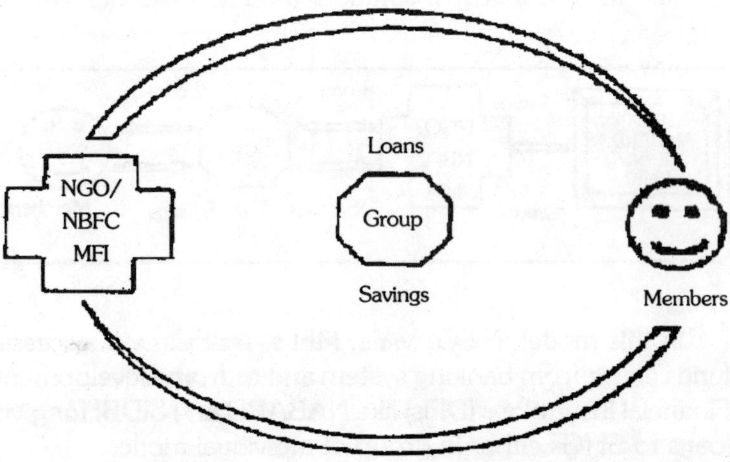

During the year 2008-09, 10,81,474 SHG were credit linked with banks and bank loan of Rs.11,131.74 crore (including repeat loans) disbursed taking the number of SHG credit linked to Rs.47,07,415 SHG as on 31st March, 2009. As on 31st March, 2008, 50.09 lakh SHG maintained savings bank accounts and had savings worth Rs.3,785.39 crore. The programme has covered more than 7 crore poor households, making it the largest Micro-Finance programme in the world. The overall progress of the Micro-Finance programme is given in the Table 17.3.

Recognizing the potential of micro-finance to positively influence the economic conditions of the poorer sections of the society, the Reserve Bank has been providing a facilitating environment for development of the micro-finance sector in the country. The SHG-Bank Linkage Programme, being implemented by commercial banks, RRBs and cooperative banks, is the major channel for providing micro-finance in the country, with more than 7.01 crore poor households covered. At end-March 2008, a total of 3.6 million SHGs with a total outstanding bank loan of Rs.17,000 crore were credit linked with the banks (Table 17.4). As on March 31, 2008, a total of 5.0 million SHGs were having savings bank accounts with the banking system of which the commercial banks had the maximum share (56.0 per cent) followed by the RRBs (28.0 per cent) and co-operative banks (16.0 per cent).

Advantages of SHG-bank linkage programme

- Significantly improved access to financial services of the rural poor,
- Positively impacted socio-economic conditions thus reducing poverty of members and their households,
- Empowered women members substantially
-

Table 17.3 : Progress of the Micro-Finance Programme (As on 31st march)

(Rs. crore)

Particulars	*Self-Help Group**				*Micro-Finance Institutions**			
	2007		*2008*		*2007*		*2008*	
	No.	*Amount*	*No.*	*Amount*	*No.*	*Amount*	*No.*	*Amount*
Loans disbursed	11,05,749 (1,88,962)	6,570.39 (1,411.02)	12,27,770 (2,46,649)	8,849.26 (1,857.74)	334	1,151.56	518	1,970.15
Loan outstanding	28,94,505 (6,87,312)	12,366.49 (3,273.14)	36,25,941 (9,16,978)	16,999.90 (4,8,16.87)	550	1,584.48	1,109	2,748.84
Savings accounts with banks	41,60,584 (9,56,317)	3,512.71 (757.50)	50,09,794 (12,03,070)	3,785.39 (809.51)				

* Figures in parentheses Indicate the share of SHG covered under SGSY. (@) : During the year

\# Actual number of MFI provided with bank loans would be lower as several MFI have availed loans from more than one bank.

* Due to change in data and MIS, the reporting is for the position as on 31st March, 2008.

Table 17.4 : Bank Loans Outstanding against SHGs as on March 31, 2008

Agency	*No. of SHGs*	*Share in per cent*	*Amount (Rs. Crore)*	*Share in per cent*	*Per SHG Out-standing Loan (Rupees)*
1	2	3	4	5	6
Commercial Banks (Public Sector)	22,98,200	63.4	10,930	64.3	47,560
Commercial Banks (Private sector)	80,647	2.2	545	3.2	67,596
Sub-Total (Commercial Banks)	23,78,847	66.6	11,475	67.5	48,240
Regional Rural Banks	8,76,716	24.2	4,421	26.0	50,485
Co-operative Banks	3,71,378	10.2	1,103	6.6	29,711
Total	**36,25,941**	**100.0**	**17,000**	**100.00**	**46,884**

Source : Status of Micro-finance in India 2007-08, NABARD.

Region-wise spread of SHG-Bank linkage (%)

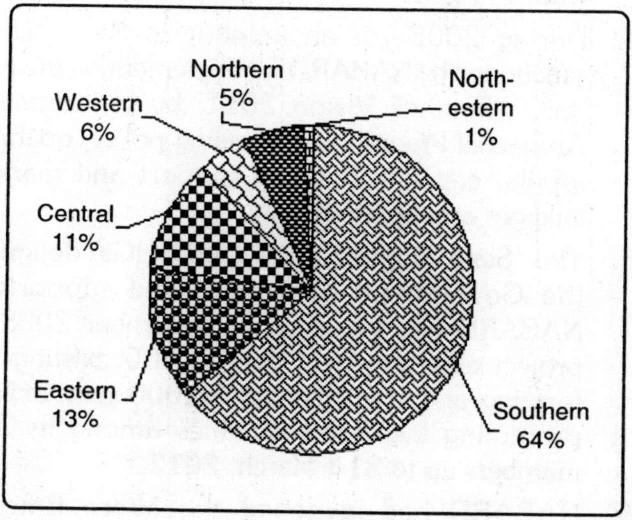

Recent initiatives of Central and State Government's vis-à-vis SHG-micro credit promotion

1. 2009-10 Budget set a target - Reach of SHGs to be widened to enroll at least 50 per cent of all rural women in India as members of SHGs over the next five years.
2. Andhra Pradesh Government started three programmes for the welfare of the SHG's viz. insurance on bank loan, Jana Shree Bima Yojana and insurance cover for milch animals. The first one is to protect the loan obtained by the SHG members under the loan/ credit insurance. Second one is to insuring the spouse of SHG member. The third one is to get the insurance coverage for the milch animals given to the groups.
3. The Rajiv Gandhi Mahila Vikas Pariyojana (RGMVP) is a special initiative of the Rajiv Gandhi Charitable Trust (RGCT) for promotion, credit linkage and formation of SHG federations in select districts of Uttar Pradesh.
4. During 2008-09, an amount of Rs.39.15 lakh sanctioned by NABARD for implementing the project 'micro-Finance Vision 2011' by Government of Arunachal Pradesh for providing policy, operational inputs, capacity building support and marketing linkages among the SHG's.
5. The 'State Support Project on SHGs' designed by the Government of Tripura and supported by NABARD was launched in December 2008. The project aims to credit link 11,500 existing SHG, forming and credit linking 35,000 new SHG and promoting livelihood activities among its 3 lakh members up to 31st March, 2012.
6. NABARD had launched the Micro Enterprise Development Programme (MEDP) during 2005-06

for skill upgradation, development of sustainable livelihoods and venturing into micro enterprises by matured SHG members.

Conclusion

SHG Micro-finance has significant role to play in Indian economy for boosting micro entrepreneurial activities for creating productive assets coupled with employment generation. So, in order to cover all the poor households, particularly BPL households, there is need for providing full support by the Government, financial institutions, NGO's, SHG Promoting Institutions (SHGPI) to SHG's programmes. Political interference in the functioning of self-help groups should be avoided. The bottlenecks like indifference attitude of bank officers, exploitation by promoting NGO's, lack of marketing facilities for product/services. These bottlenecks should be rooted out on priority basis. Women groups should be given responsibility of running Anganwadi, fair price shops, so that they become permanent entities and also transparency and accountability can be maintained. The concept of financial inclusion should be followed by giving the equal opportunity to all the BPL families in the country so that balanced growth is maintained and also ensure social, economic empowerment of the downtrodden.

References

1. NABARD Annual Report, 2008-09, URL – *www.nabard.org*
2. Reserve Bank of India, annual report 2008-09, : URL - *www.rbi.org.inthe*
3. J.C.Mishra, R.K.Thanvi., Indian Banking System and Micro-finance, *Kurukshetra*, February, 2004, Vol.52, No.4., pp.12-15.

18

Bharat Nirman
A New Deal for Rural Development

R.C. Mishra **and** ***K.C. Mishra***

India is predominantly a rural economy where more than 70 per cent of the total population lives in the rural area. So Rural Development is indispensable for India's economic development. As a result, rural development has been treated as one of the important objectives of planning in India. Rural development may be defined as a policy of bringing about a structural change in the socio-economic situation to achieve improved living standard of the poor residing in rural areas and making the process of their development self-sustaining. Rural development became a planning concern as the programmes and strategies adopted in India remained largely ineffective in removing unemployment, ensuring distributive justice and alleviating poverty. Besides the exodus from rural to urban India proves beyond doubt that the development process of the last half a century of independent India has left rural areas far behind the cities. Apart from an effort to increase agricultural and industrial production it is also necessary to address directly the problems of education, health service, safe drinking water, employment, poverty etc. in rural areas. In view of this, an ambitious time bound programme namely "Bharat Nirman" was launched in 2005 by UPA Government as a new deal for rural development in India.

Objectives

The present study is a modest attempt :

(i) To study the earlier major rural development programmes and throw light on the emerging challenges found in rural development.
(ii) To study the components and significance of Bharat Nirman which is a new deal for rural development.
(iii) To provide suggestions and conclusion.

Major Rural Development Programmes

The Community Development Programme (CDP) was the first major rural development programme launched after independence in October, 1952. This programme aims at transforming the social and economic life of the rural community as a whole. Due to paucity of funds and personnel, it was realized that the whole country could not be covered under CDP. Thus, the National Extension Service (NES) was launched in October, 1953 with a reduced number of personnel and modest financial provision so that development work could proceed on the basis of self-help efforts. Although the programme has certain achievements like establishment of an organized administrative set up, introduction of modern technologies in agriculture, etc., yet it had some limitations like social imbalance, inadequate attention paid to people's participation, inadequate fund, administrative weaknesses, etc.

Secondly, in view of the emerging food shortages and stagnant agricultural production during the Second Plan (1956-61), the approach of rural development took a new direction in the Third plan (1961-1966) with increasing emphasis on agricultural production. Accordingly Intensive Agricultural Area Programme (IAAP) were launched on a pilot basis for rural development. This has been described as the Green Revolution

Phase which is otherwise termed as technocratic phase of rural development. Although it resulted in revolutionary change in the production of agricultural output, yet it created regional imbalance and social imbalance leading to the aggravation of poverty.

Thirdly, in view of the inter-linkages of crop production, livestock economy and environment, development of Wasteland and degraded land has emerged as an important issue in rural development. Thus, special programmes like the Drought Prone Area Programme (DPAP) and the Desert Development Programme (DDP) were launched in 1973-74 and 1977-78 respectively for area development and poor farmers in combating drought and erasing desert.

Besides, the several other programmes like the Integrated Wasteland Development Programme (IWDP) in 1989-90, the Investment Promotion Scheme (IPS) in 1994-95 and the National Watershed Development Project for Rain-fed Areas (NWDPRA) in 1990-91 were launched to develop wasteland, to promote the participation of the corporate sector in the development of non-forest wastelands and to improve agricultural production in rain-fed areas through participatory approach. Due to a plethora of bottlenecks the area development programmes cut little ice for rural development.

Fourthly, along side the area development programmes, another stream of programmes were evolved to directly benefit the poorer sections of the rural population. Thus, the Small Farmer's Development Agency (SFDA) and the Marginal Farmers and Agricultural Labourers Agency (MFAL) were launched. Seeking to improve upon SFDA and MFAL and to overcome the Financial crunch, these two schemes were merged in the Integrated Rural Development Programme (IRDP) which was launched in 1978-79 and its allied programmes are the Training of Rural Youth for Self-employment (TRYSEM), the Development of Women and Children in Rural Areas (DWCRA), the supply of improving Toolkits to Rural Artisans (SITRA) and the Ganga Kalyan Yojana

(GKY), etc. with a view to overcoming rural poverty as the beneficiary approaches. In view of the little impact upon the rural poverty, IRDP and its allied programmes were merged into a single programme known as the Swarnajayanti Gram Swarozgar Yojana (SGSY) in 1999 with the objective of encouraging Micro Enterprise, organizing rural poor into Self-Help Groups (SHGs), Infrastructure support, technology, credit and marketing linkages among the rural poor.

Finally, wage employment programmes form an important component of the anti-poverty strategy with the twin objectives of creating rural infrastructure to support further economic activity and to create additional demand for labour in times when there is maximum unemployment. Accordingly, the various programmes like the National Rural Employment Programme (NREP), the food for work programme, the Rural Landless Employment Guarantee Programme (RLEGP) were launched. But both NREP and RLEGP were merged in the Jawahar Rozgar Yojana (JRY) in 1989 which included the Indira Awaas Yojana (IAY) and the Million Wells Scheme (MWS) which were two independent schemes in 1996. Besides the Employment Assurance Scheme (EAS) was launched in 1993 in drought prone areas and basically tribal and hill area blocks but it was later extended to all the blocks in 1997-98 and the Food-For-Work Programme was started in 2000-01 as a component of EAS. A major proportion of JRY was renamed as the Jawahar Gram Samridhi Yojana (JGSY) in 1999. Recognising complementarily of the JGSY, the EAS and the Food-For-Work Programme, they were merged under the Sampoorna Grameen Rozgar Yojana (SGRY) with effect from 2001 with the objective of generating wage employment, creating durable economic infrastructure in rural areas and providing food and nutrition security to the rural poor.

The Emerging Challenges

Towards the end of the Ninth Plan (1997–2002) and the

beginning of the Tenth Plan (2002 – 07) it was evident that the centrally sponsored schemes and central schemes for rural development had proliferated enormously. But the various programmes did not have any visible impact upon the rural development. Despite continuing efforts of the Government. of India to address the challenges of rural development, the incidence of unemployment and underemployment still persists along with poverty. Land and forest degradation in the rural areas and over exploitation of ground water is seriously threatening sustainability of food production. On account of Globalization and privatization, public investment in general and irrigation in particular have fallen resulting in the low productivity of agriculture. Development and dissemination of agricultural technologies, diversification of agriculture, development of processing and marketing arrangements, development of health services and rural connectivity demand greater attention while formulating new strategies for rural development. Besides, a large number of schemes and programmes, already launched having common objectives and meant for the same beneficiary groups invariably get diluted in terms of impact. The duplication of delivery structures and the procedural hurdles invariably curtail the flow of assistance to the targeted beneficiaries. Therefore, a large number of rural development programmes were rationalized and merged and there is need to introduce new scheme to ensure the convergence among the sub-programmes around a few clearly identifiable themes and objectives of rural development in India.

Bharat Nirman Programme: A New Deal

Keeping the emerging challenges in view, a new deal for rural development was made to foster rural development in India. Thanks to UPA (United Progressive Alliance) Government. which launched the Bharat Nirman Programme in 2005 with a thrust to improve physical and social infrastructure in rural areas. This is otherwise a programme of infrastructure development. It is a time bound programme from 2005 – 09 for development of infrastructure in the rural India for the rural development. The basic infrastructure in rural areas must change in four years to bring basic amenities to the doorstep of the rural folk was the motto of the programme. Rural infrastructure is not only a key component of rural development but also an important ingredient in ensuring success of any sustainable poverty reduction programme. The effective development of infrastructure in rural areas improves rural economy and quality of life. It promotes better productivity, increased agricultural income, adequate employment etc. leading to rural development.

Six core areas of infrastructure development were identified under Bharat Nirman Programme for implementation in a time bound manner. These six core areas are irrigation, rural roads, rural housing, rural water supply, rural electrification and rural telecommunication. The components of the 'Bharat Nirman Programme' are explained below :

- *Irrigation :* Bringing an additional 1 crore hectares of unirrigated agricultural land under assured irrigation by 2009.
- *Rural Roads :* Connecting all habitations having a population of one thousand (500 in hilly and tribal areas) with all weather roads through Pradhan Mantri Gram Sadak Yojana (PMGSY) by 2009.
- *Rural Water Supply :* Provision of safe drinking water to all villages and habitations in the country by 2009 through Accelerated Rural Water Supply Programme. (ARWSP).
- *Rural Housing :* Construction of 60 lakh houses for the rural poor by 2009 through Indira Awaas Yojana (IAY)
- *Rural Electrification :* Provision of electricity to all

villages by 2009 through the Rajiv Gandhi Grameen Vidyutikaran Yojana (RGGVY).

- *Rural Communication:* Provision of telephone connectivity to all villages by 2007.

Along with the Bharat Nirman Programme, the Government has launched various other initiatives for rural agricultural development. Eight Flagship programmes namely, the Sarva Shiksha Abhiyan, Mid-day Meal Scheme, Rajiv Gandhi Drinking Water Mission, Total Sanitation Campaign, National Rural Health Mission, Integrated Child Development Services and National Rural Employment Guarantee Scheme (NREGS) have been emphasized for rural development in India.

The Bharat Nirman Programme along with eight flagship programmes will develop social and economic infrastructure in rural India. The building and development of infrastructure in rural areas will ensure that every household will have a roof over head, a square meal, market access, higher productivity, road connectivity, electricity, communication facilities, better health facilities and better environment by 2009. As a result, it will not only help to develop agriculture, industry, trade and commerce in the rural areas but also help to banish poverty and unemployment from the rural areas. It is expected that through these programmes, provision of urban amenities in rural areas will check the exodus of rural people to the cities and minimize the rural–urban divide. Thereby it will bring about sustainable development.

Although the programme is implemented by the State Governments through PRIs. Yet it is not a programme of the state Government alone. It is an agenda for everybody and in fact every Indian is either a user or a partner in this gigantic task of nation building. The Union Government. has shown its commitment in the very first year of the 4-year programme. The National Committee on Rural Infrastructure chaired by the Prime Minister directly monitors the progress of implementation of all programmes taken up under Bharat Nirman.

Bharat Nirman: Progress so far

The ambitious Bharat Nirman Programme proposed to invest about Rs. 1.74 lakh crore. Till March 2009 about Rs. 1.14 lakh crore have been spent under Bharat Nirman.

Under the Bharat Nirman at the current pace, on each day of the year, 290 habitations are provided with drinking water and 17 habitations are connected through an all weather roads. On each day of the year, 52 villages are provided with telephones and 42 villages are electrified. On each day of the year, 4113 rural houses are completed. The Budget 2009-10 provides Rs. 31,280 crore and the Budget 2010-11 provides Rs. 48,000 crore for Bharat Nirman. The progress of Bharat Nirman till March, 2009 has been given below :

Bharat Nirman : Status Summary

Component	*Financial Status Expenditure (Rs. Crore)*	*Physical Status*			
			Target	*Achieved*	*% achieved*
Rural Roads	30,737	New Road Length (km.)	146185	72,185	49
		Upgraded Road Length (km.)	194132	106284	55
		Habitations (No.)	50948	25068	49
Electrification	11,275	Villages (no.)	470039	128072	27
Telephones	137	Villages (no.)	66822	56030	84
Irrigation	29,349	Area ('000 hact.)	10000	5583	56
Drinking Water	20,588	Villages (no.)	603639	479898	80
Rural Housing	22,172	Houses (lakh)	60	61	102
Total	**1,14,257**				

Source: Various nodal Ministries.

- One of the celebrated components of Bharat Nirman was the scheme for building all weather roads for unconnected habitations. Launched during the NDA rule, the Pradhan Mantri Grameen Sadak Yojana (PMGSY) was made part of the fast track Bharat Nirman process. In 2005, there were over 50,000 habitations with no road connections. Four years later, half of these have got the promised road. Also included under Bharat Nirman was upgradation and renewal of 3.4 lakh kilometers of existing roads. Around 1.8 lakh km. have actually been improved. Thus around 49 per cent of total habitations were provided road connectivity by March, 2009. it is found that more vulnerable sections like dalits living in smaller habitations and tribals living in forests, would have largely been neglected.
- The most crucial component of Bharat Nirman was irrigation. About 60 per cent of India's cultivated land is dependent on rain and it is estimated that crop yields will double if water is assured through surface irrigation. Bharat Nirman was to bring 10 million hectares under some form of surface irrigation. But, only about 5.6 million hectares could be covered. More and more funds have been allotted for this purpose in the subsequent years. Thereby the target can be achieved.
- Rural housing for Below Poverty Line (BPL) families is the only area where targets have been met, with over 61 lakh dwelling units getting built. This was done under the ongoing Indira Awaas Yojana, which is routed through the Panchayats. Selected families were given Rs. 27,500 for building a small pucca house in 2008-09. This has been increased to Rs. 45,000 in the Budget 2010-11.
- Under the Rajiv Gandhi Grameen Vidyutikarana

Yojana by March 2009, 128072 villages have been electrified. But the achievement is only 27 per cent of target. Thus more emphasis has been given in the subsequent years to achieve the target.

- By March, 2009, 56030 villages out of 66822 villages have been provided with telephone connectivity. The remaining villages are getting connected very soon. So rural telecom density is increasing by leaps and bounds.
- Under the Accelerated Rural Water Supply Project (ARWSP), over 4.8 lakh of the targeted 6 lakh villages were covered by March, 2009. Thus 80 per cent achievement can be found in case of Drinking Water. For ensuring sufficient and safe drinking water, *Swajaldhara* and National Water Quality Monitoring and Surveillance programme have also been started.

Progress of 8 flagship Programmes

Sarva Shiksha Abhiyan (SSA)

It was launched in 2001. In the last 3 years 140,000 schools have been opened. 13 crore children additionally enrolled and 5.76 lakh new teachers were appointed. For primary education the Government has emphasized on Sarva Siksha Abhiyan (SSA) and provided the scheme a budgetary support of Rs. 13,100 crore in 2009-10. With a view to shifting from access and infrastructure at the primary level to enhancing retention and improving quality of learning. However, the number of out of schools children too has dropped from 3.2 crore in 2001 to 76 lakh in 2008.

Mid-Day Meal Scheme (MDMS)

In a country where an estimated 41 per cent of children are

under weight due to poverty, the provision of hot, cooked meals at schools has been spectacularly popular programme. Initiated in typical half-hearted fashion in the 1990s, MDMS actually got traction after a landmark direction from the Supreme Court in 2001 making it mandatory for schools to provide cooked meals. Since then, over Rs. 33000 crore have been spent on implementing the programme. As of 2009, about 11.74 crore children studying in Classes I to VIII are getting mid-day meals, making it the largest school meals programme in the world. Of these, 8.24 crore kids are in primary sections (Class I to V). The scheme is also a key factor behind rocketing growth in enrolment in the primary sections. It was extended to classes VI to VIII in 2008.

National Rural Health Mission (NRHM)

The National Rural Health Mission which was implemented from April, 2005 envisaged accessible, affordable and accountable quality health services to the poorest households in the remote rural regions of the country. The goal of NRHM is to establish a fully functional community owned decentralized health delivery system. NRHM aims to build or upgrade infrastructure, appoint medical personnel and address key issues like infant/maternal mortality. A key element is the Accredited Social Health Activist (ASHA), roughly one for each village. In four years, nearly 6.47 lakh ASHAs have been appointed. But only about 40 per cent have been trained to level 2 while only 1 per cent have completed all 5 levels. Drug kits have been given to 64 per cent. Infrastructure has been built up and facilities are improving, but trained staff are still lacking in large parts.

Total Sanitation Campaign (TSC)

A long running programme for building toilets in rural areas was reoriented and renamed TSC in 1999. The aim was to discourage open defection and thus reduce the spread of various diseases. However, the goal of TSC is to keep the environment clean, healthy and promote the rural sanitation on the country. Over Rs. 51,000 crore has been spent on construction of nearly 5.2 crore household toilets and over 10 lakh institutional toilets (in schools and balwadis). Thus under Total Sanitation Campaign (TSC) remarkable progress has been achieved. Further, solid waste management has been highlighted in TSC. Because waste is a form of resource and its proper and efficient use would be promoted.

Integrated Child Development Services (ICDS)

This mammoth scheme provides nutritional supplements, health checkups and immunization coverage to children up to the age of 6 years to reduce mortality and disease. It also provides nutritional supplements to pregnant and lactating mothers. These services are delivered through a vast network of 12.43 lakh anganwadi centres of the estimated 20 crore children in the 0 – 6 years age group, over 7 crore are officially benefiting from ICDS. In the Budget 2008-09, the remuneration of Anganwadi workers has been increased from Rs. 1000 to Rs. 1500 per month. Likewise, the remuneration of Anganwadi helpers has been increased from Rs. 500 to Rs. 750 per month. Thus more and more allocation for ICDS in the subsequent Budget has been made for successful working of ICDS.

Jawaharlal Nehru National Urban Renewal Mission (JNNURM):

Nearly one-third of India now lives in urban areas. Cities and towns are in dire need of expansion of basic services like roads, sewerage, electricity, housing, etc.. JNNURM was launched in 2005 as the main vehicle for improving urban infrastructure.

Its objective is to build basic infrastructure improve governance and provide basic facilities to the urban poor. JNNURM has two main components – Basic Services to the Urban Poor (BSUP) Programme and Integrated Housing and Slum Development Programme (IHSDP). BSUP was launched to assist cities and towns in taking up housing and infrastructure facilities for the Urban Poor in 63 selected cities in the country. IHSDP, which was launched simultaneously with BSUP in December, 2005 is taking up housing and slum upgradation programmes in non-BSUP cities. Thereby it will have trickle down effect on rural development.

Rajiv Gandhi Drinking Water Mission (RGDWM)

The goal of the mission is to supply safe drinking water to uncovered habitations and slipped back habitations as well as to address issues of quality. Thus more and more funds have been allocated to improve the quality.

National Rural Employment Guarantee Scheme (NREGS)

The most publicized of the flagship schemes, NREGS was launched in 2006 and rolled out over the country in phases. Now, the scheme has been implemented in all 596 rural districts in India. The enactment of such an act has undoubtedly marked a paradigm shift from the existing wage employment programmes and necessitated formulation of State Specific Rural Employment Guarantee Schemes with a view to ensuring legal right to at least 100 days wage employment to the unemployed rural household. This is primarily to be achieved by taking up project oriented activities covering works on water conservation/harvesting, drought/flood control, plantation, land development, rural connectivity etc. NREGS has generated over 391 crore person days of employment by March, 2009 (a person day is one person working for one day). Over Rs. 44,480 crore have been spent.

Implementation has been highly uneven across states. The share of registered households given work varies from as high as 73 per cent in Rajasthan, 68 per cent in Chattisgarh and 63 per cent in Assam to a dismal 13 per cent in Maharastra, 30 per cent in Gujurat and 31 per cent in Orissa. In NREGS, the budgetary support has been provided to the extent of Rs. 39100 crore for 2009-10; which is an increase of 144 per cent over the previous budget. Further, Rs.40,100 crore has been provided for NREGS in the Budget 2010-11.

Suggestions

The following suggestions may be made for the effectiveness of the new deal programmes with a view to fostering rural development in India.

First, people's participation is one of the important requirements for the effectiveness of the programme. People must feel the ownership of such programmes and must contribute towards them. They should forget to expect the government to do everything for them. This could be done by involving the people through PRIs, local groups, self-help groups, user groups, associations, etc.

Secondly, in order to make the programme effective, it is necessary to make information available as a matter of right, to the citizens. As a result, people can know about the programmes and schemes available for them.

Thirdly, rural development must be approached holistically. It is necessary to adopt a holistic approach to rural development with suitable inter-sectoral linkages for maximizing impact. Besides special attention ought to be given for closure partnership with the State Government, District Administration, PRIs & NGOs to bring about synergy in collaborative effort and long-term sustainability of the programmes.

Fourthly, corrupt practices among the officials relating to the programmes ought to be checked. Stringent and exemplary actions ought to be taken against the officials resorting to fraudulent practices. Besides accountability and responsibility ought to be fixed upon the officials who fail in executing the programmes duly.

Finally, efforts have to be made to improve and strengthen the monitoring mechanisms with a view to monitoring and evaluating the programmes from time to time for their effective implementation.

Conclusion

In fine, the Bharat Nirman programme along with eight flagship programmes if implemented with strong determination and true spirit will no doubt change the face of rural India. As a result it will not only alleviate poverty and unemployment in rural India but also provide urban amenities in rural areas leading to rural development in India. It is however concluded that just as Roosevelt's New Deal Policy could overcome the Great Depression of the Thirties, the Government of India's new deal for rural development will not only banish poverty and unemployment in the rural areas but also bring about sustainable development in the rural areas within a short span of time.

References

Annual Report 2008 and 2009, Ministry of Rural Development, GoI.

Datt Ruddar & Sundharam, K.P.M.; (2009); *Indian Economy*, S. Chand and Company, New Delhi.

Government of India, Economic Survey, 2008 – 09 and 2009 – 10.

Gulati Ashok, Will Bharat Nirman Make Bharat Mahan?, March,03, 2005, *Financial Express*.

IGNOU, MRD-102, *Rural Development Programmes*, Vols. I, II & III.

Mahipal (2006); Panchayati Raj and Bharat Nirman: Role in Effective Implementation, *Kurukshetra*, Vol. 54, No. 12, PP. 65 – 67.

Mishra, K.C. & Mishra, R.C., (2008), "Rural Development in India: Challenges & Task – Ahead", *Sourthern Economist*, Vol. 47, No. 8, PP. 5 – 8.

Sankaran, P.N. (Oct. 2006), BHARAT NIRMAN Towards unlocking Growth Potential of Rural India, *Kurukshetra*; Vol. 54, No. 12, PP. 3 – 8.

Subodh Verma, "Bharat Waits for Real Nirman", June 4, 2009, *The Times of India*, Pune, P. 13.

www.rural.nic.in.

19

Krishi Rath
An innovative Approach
Towards Rural Development

Niti Mehta and *Anita Arya*

This chapter provides an overview of the "Krishi Mahotsava" or "Rath" being conducted annually by the Government of Gujarat since 2005. The "Rath" is held in the months of May-June just preceding the kharif season. The purpose of this note is to speculate upon the future course of action that the government could pursue and the manner in which this rather unique exercise can be institutionalized for addressing the needs of holistic, sustained and systemic agricultural and overall rural development. The envisaged functions would require the Rath to be modified in its present state as also certain organizational tenets would have to be imbibed into the extension exercise. To convert the Krishi Rath into a permanent entity there is a need to identify and internalize the key features of the "best practices" that aim at poverty alleviation and holistic rural development. This would enable the Rath to serve as a replicable model for extension and dissemination of scientific agricultural practices. In addition the Rath would facilitate village level planning, provide expertise on allocation of crucial resources as well as provide guidance to the farmers on application of scientific know-how. Clearly such a system would have to be made an integral part of the decentralized planning machinery at the sub-state level, preferably the block or taluka.

The next section discusses the compulsions being faced by the agriculture sector, arising from the increasingly globalised scenario that necessitates technology adoption for enhanced productivity and incomes. This calls for more effective extension services and technology dissemination. Subsequent section entails a description of the Krishi Rath and a resume of the activities undertaken. Section four would highlight the need for transforming the Rath into a single window access system of information and agriculture related technology for the farming community and other stakeholders. Similar experiments, to make available technical know-how at the farmers' doorsteps (e.g. cooperatives, corporates, credit and input agencies, etc.) undertaken on pilot basis would be discussed. The fifth section discusses how the "Rath" could imbibe for instance the organizational strengths of successful rural development and micro-finance initiatives. Krishi Rath though entails a much larger portfolio of activities; it could incorporate organizational aspects of Grameen Bank, specially its decentralized nature and outreach for enhancing productivity and incomes. The concluding section summarizes all the major arguments put forth in favour of transforming the Rath into a decentralized "Information Bank" facilitating agricultural growth and transformation.

Agricultural Extension for Holistic Development

Agricultural growth is largely determined by the rate of technological change, which in turn depends on the adequacy and efficiency of agricultural research and extension systems. The transformation of agricultural production system and its impact has been quite dramatic in the recent years. Rapidly changing traditional system of agriculture means that the agricultural research and extension systems are facing unprecedented challenges as well as new opportunities. It is evident that agricultural knowledge and information are critical inputs, however to be useful, these must be effectively communicated to farmers (Sharma *et al*., 2004). Challenges before the extension system/machinery are manifold.

At the forefront are the new learning needs of farming communities. Globalization is bound to bring both risks and market opportunities to the farmers in the less developing economies. The farming community thus needs to be educated and prepared to modify their agricultural operations and practices. Agricultural extension services by the governments have to play a new role and serious attention has to be given by policy-makers for its reform and modernization. In order to improve quality of life extension now has to provide need and demand based knowledge and skills in a non-formal participative manner to rural men, women and youth. Apart from advice and information on production technology, farmers need a wide range of services, with improved access to markets, research, credit infrastructure and business development services. For this to take place the government has to facilitate information flows across different organizations and bring all the stakeholders together for effective dissemination and problem solving.

Secondly, adequate extension and information percolation has assumed worldwide importance to fight the menaces of hunger and rural poverty. Non-price factors and technology would be crucial in productivity and income growth. While India has one of the world's most extensive systems of agricultural research in place, breakthroughs achieved by the Agricultural Universities and Research Institutions are often mere academic achievements and rarely do the technologies developed reach down to the field level in an effective manner. There also remains tremendous chasm between the yields achieved by the demonstration farrns and that in the farmers' fields. The lacunae lies in improper dissemination of scientific knowledge and technology transfer from the lab to the farms. Resource poor small and marginal farmers, and those residing in the remote reaches of the country are particularly slow to adopt new technologies and scientific practices. A concerted effort is required to address the needs of these categories of farmers. The yield gaps can be bridged through an integrated package of technology, services and public policies.

Thirdly, as revealed through research, increasing monetization of inputs does not seem to be paying off significantly. Agriculture is increasingly marked by rising cost of cultivation with declining output. The major factors impeding productivity growth are depleting water table, deterioration of soil and water, erratic monsoons and frequent droughts. The share of agriculture in the domestic product of Gujarat has been declining, but the people employed in the sector have declined much more slowly than the income generated. Agriculture continues to be a major source of employment in the rural areas. Overall declining returns imply that agriculture requires technological and scientific inputs in order to come out of the prevalent stagnancy and achieve a sustainable growth. Higher investments in irrigation, research and extension are recommended for a beneficial impact on agricultural output.

Keeping the volatile and fluctuating nature of the agriculture sector in view, and compulsions of globalised era to make agriculture withstand competitive pressure, the Government of Gujarat adopted a new extension approach to information dissemination to the rural sector. The Krishi Rath, being organized since 2005, is a step towards integrated eradication of poverty in rural areas.

The Programme

The Krishi Rath— a month long agricultural festival is a unique programme and first of its kind in the country. It is an intensive programme to facilitate agricultural planning and overall rural development with the objective that the state's per capita agricultural income doubles in a sustainable manner within five years of the programme's inception. The event aims at development of not only agriculture, including crop and livestock sectors, but touches the entire gamut of agricultural research and education, land resources, water management, cooperatives, marketing and processing, livestock, fisheries and inputs (see charts 1 and 2). The programme spans the whole of rural Gujarat, covering all the 18600 villages. The major activities encompass individual beneficiary schemes (drip irrigation, soil health cards, krishi credit cards, distribution of kits, credit schemes, etc.) and community oriented schemes (establishment of cooperative societies, kisan shibirs, water harvesting, e-gram, etc.). Scientific inputs are imparted by the agricultural scientists together with market guidance, formation of self-help groups, awareness generation and demonstration exercises. Gram Sabhas are organized in each village prior to the main event to decide on the beneficiaries of input kits, the location for construction of water harvesting structures, canal cleaning programmes, applications for kisan credit cards, bankable yojnas and other government schemes.

The programme is implemented through massive preparatory activities and monitoring from the village, taluka and district levels to the highest levels of decision-making. Large number of personnel and agencies are involved in the conduct of the event. All this is achieved incurring high administrative and monetary costs. The Junagadh Agricultural University carried out an evaluation of the Krishi Rath held during 2005 in order to ascertain the extent to which the farming community benefited from the various activities undertaken (JAU, 2006). The exercise was carried out by interviewing farmers in the different Saurashtra districts, belonging to different age groups, educational status and size group of landholding. The study revealed that nearly 60 per cent of the farmers adopted scientific crop sequences as suggested by the scientists,

Chart 1 New Approach—Krishi Mahotsav
Individual Beneficiary Scheme

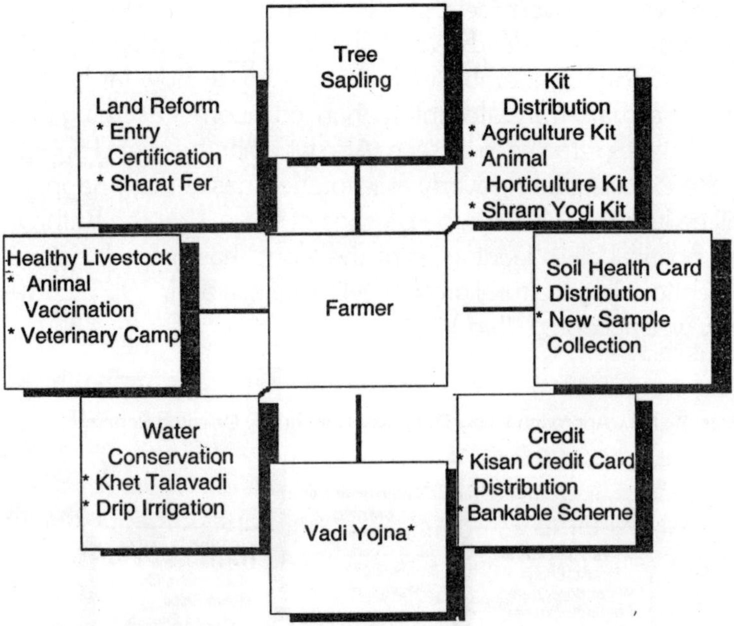

* Under the Vadi Yojna, farmer are persuaded to grow horticulture crops in small portions of Their farms along with main crops.

Source: http//agri.gujarat.gov.in/hods/dir.agriculture.him. Accessed on 4/2/2010.

81 per cent of the farmers interviewed initiated judicious usage of the sparse irrigation facilities as suggested, 74 per cent started undertaking the recommended crop protection measures and 33 per cent of the respondent farmers agreed that the Krishi Rath had succeeded in disseminating knowledge related to better and scientific farming practices. It is heartening to note that 17 per cent of the farmers had already started implementing up to 75 per cent of the knowledge disseminated. Several other beneficial effects of the 'reinvented extension model' have been reported. For instance, "Gujarat farmers have moved wholesale from a 13:7.5:1 nitrogen-phosphorus-

potassium composition to a 6.5:3.5:1, thereby reducing cost, optimizing production and improving net income. The farm credit system too has been revitalized. Agricultural loan disbursements in Gujarat have clocked 22-25 per cent annual growth rate, thanks to supportive government policies." (Shah *et al.*, 2009, pp.47). While these are indeed remarkable achievements, and possess potential for considerable increases in output, how far have the actions actually translated into enhanced incomes accruing to the beneficiaries remains to be seen. Also whether the overall objective of the exercise, i.e., poverty amelioration has actually happened will be known only with the passage of time. That the Rath with the political class leading from the front, has helped Gujarat's exceptional agricultural growth performance after 1999-2000 is now well accepted (*Ibid.*).

Chart 2 : New Approach-Krishi Mahotsav Community Oriented Scheme

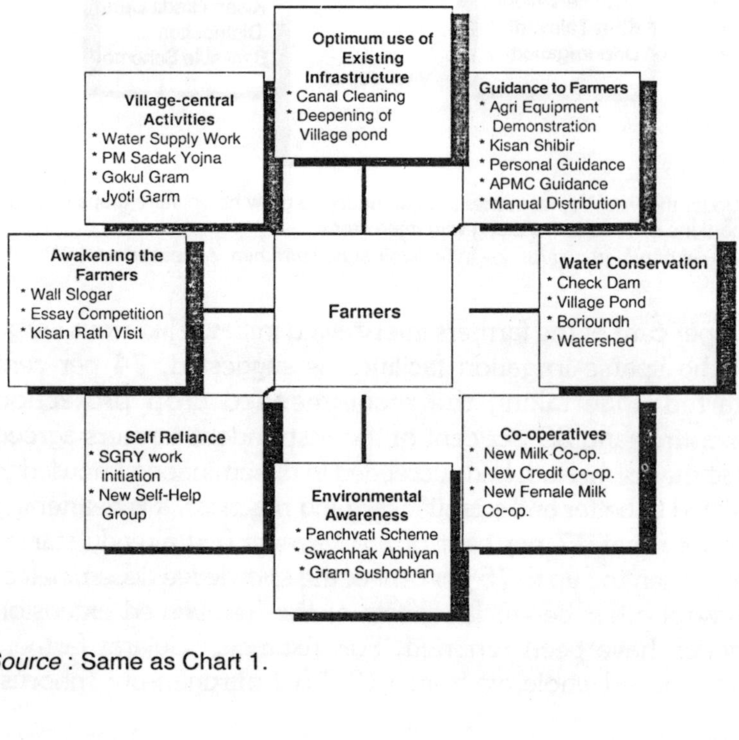

Source : Same as Chart 1.

The Krishi Rath is undoubtedly a holistic approach, addressing the entire gamut of problems confronting agriculturalists in a systemic manner. To that extent it differs from the target oriented approaches and schemes already in place. The effort is a step towards direct involvement and participation of communities in their development wherein the success depends to a great deal on the level of personal commitment by all the stakeholders. It is in consonance with the basic tenets of the "Karmayogi Approach", and hence underscores the desired impetus and push required for administrative and bureaucratic reforms for good governance. Earlier efforts of similar nature, such as loan melas was too narrow an approach and distorted the normal functioning of the banking structure. While it is early days yet to comment of the fruitfulness of the Krishi Rath for rural poverty amelioration, it has so far played a catalytic role in accelerating agricultural output in Gujarat. Nonetheless, for the Rath to emerge as a successful and replicable model it needs to be modified into a stable structure catering to needs of local rural based activities.

Transient "Rath" or Single Window Information Bank

There are several issues that have a bearing on rural livelihoods such as productivity enhancement, sustainability, resource management, poverty alleviation, food and nutritional security, globalization, liberalization of world trade, etc. In addition agricultural producers and small farmers require location specific information on technologies, best practices, market and price information on agricultural inputs and outputs. Specific information on soils, pests, crops, weather forecasts and expert systems for sustainable management of production systems is also required. At present all the elements, i.e. information regarding new agricultural technology and beneficiary schemes of the government, etc. are dispersed, present either with the agricultural universities, or the line departments, input agencies, research organizations and so on. For the Rath to usher in holistic development of rural areas it should be institutionalized into an area based stable structure having permanence and continuity. Institutionalization of the Rath into a "single window bank" for dissemination and monitoring purpose is thus required. By being a part of the decentralized planning process, it would also remain free from political compulsions and bureaucratic dependence.

A framework for such a bank was conceived and tried on a pilot basis under the aegis of the Agro-Climatic Regional Planning Project (ACRP). The bank became dysfunctional as the Project concluded. However, we would like to stress upon its importance and revival in the changed form of a more permanent Rath. The ACRP approach at the district level had marked significant departures over the "scheme-oriented" departmental approach to planning. Details of the project and the approach are documented elsewhere (Basu, Guha and Kashyap, 1996). A significant section of the strategies suggested therein required action under the public domain (i.e. integrated watershed development, provision of overall infrastructure, etc.). But a large part of the strategy was such in which effective action could be taken by individual farmers or groups of farmers, notably, crop sequencing, crop combination, diversification of agricultural activities, etc. The final decision on these issues rests with the cultivators. The farmer's decisions no doubt hinge upon factors such as availability of water, inputs, overall infrastructure and markets. Yet within these broad contours he has a variety of options. He needs to be guided keeping in view the external factors. For taking informed decisions, farmers not only need a plan detailing out the possibilities, but also technical and market information. The Agro-climatic Planning and Information Bank (APIB) was conceived to help farmers / groups use the integrated vision of the regional plan in their decision-making (Basu and Hashim, 1996). It was to be an effective interface with the farmers in the field. The main premises on which the concept was mooted were:

- For effective decision-making access to knowledge base, including technical and economic data, tools, studies are essential.
- To provide wider access to user groups it would be necessary to create single window to reach out to all the actors on the ground.
- Substantial information has been generated under the Indian Council of Agricultural Research (ICAR) system, Indian Space Research Organization (ISRO), Agricultural Universities, State Line departments etc. pertaining to agriculture and allied activities. It would be useful to consolidate the efforts and refine them to suit local needs.

The bank was tested on a pilot basis in two blocks of Karnataka to be a model for countrywide application of the concept. Its areas of operation were envisaged to be homogenous resource regions and two regions, representing primarily dryland area and other diversified region were selected. The information required for the purpose of crop planning, land and water assessment and utilization was stored and processed at the lowest level of disaggregation, which varied depending upon the source of information. Thus crop data was at village level; resources at cluster of villages; information on prices, credit availability was at level of sub-region or block. Given the concept of the bank, the following were considered to be the major tasks of the pilot bank:

1. Compilation of information, area specific development strategies
2. Computerized storage and retrieval of information and tools
3. Dissemination of information in appropriate formats
4. Providing specific planning services and integration with macro level planning exercises.

The Krishi Rath can be crystallized into a permanent entity on the lines of the APIB.

Technologies and tools that have developed in the recent information technology revolution can play a vital role in overcoming most of the present problems related to agriculture and rural development. New approaches to productivity improvement and employment generation are largely knowledge intensive. The new Information and Communication Technologies (ICTs) provide a potentially powerful tool for improving communication between research, extension and farmers and promote sustainable agriculture and rural development. What is required is rendering of generic information into locality specific knowledge that can be utilized by the farm families. Restructuring extension services to take advantage of the information age would help small and marginal farmers by bridging the knowledge gap (Swaminathan, 2000). However, what is needed are approaches which can take ICT to the farmers. A second example of taking knowledge to the farmers door step is the "Village Knowledge Centres" propagated by the MS Swaminathan Research Foundation. The centres set up on a pilot basis in Pondicherry serve to bridge the disconnect between what the farm families need by way of generic information and what the conventional extension agencies are able to provide. The centres focus on skill building and information empowerment with the help of ICT tools, mainly data cum voice communication tools. The hub provides connectivity to the internet and the staff creates locally useful content in the local language. In addition to the provision of data and information, the centres are operational contact point between the government agencies and local families. These are used by various line departments to disseminate information. Significantly assetless and extremely poor families are among the major users. (Vasanth and Kumaran, n.d.).

The Agricultural Extension Division of the ICAR has also taken initiative of technology dissemination through Agricultural

Technology Information Centres (ATIC) which are in the process of development under the National Agricultural Technology Project (NATP). ATIC is a 'single window' support system linking various units of research institutions with intermediary users and end users (farmers) in decision-making and problem solving exercise. The centre provides diagnostic services for soil and water testing, plant and livestock health; supply research products such as seeds, planting material, poultry strains, livestock breeds, fish seed, processed products etc. for testing and adaptation; provide information through published literature and communication material as well as audio-visual aids (Sharma *et al.*, 2004).

The above examples serve to highlight the tried and tested initiatives which have served as specialized windows providing access to information in a comprehensive fashion to the farming communities in addition to other interested parties, such as cooperatives, corporations, financial institutions, etc. The Krishi Rath has tremendous potential of developing as single window access system providing back-up information and expert advice. No doubt such a permanent structure would gain much by supplementing with periodic campaigns (at least once a year) where top officials and politicians of the state interact with the farming communities. Such a campaign would provide a platform of airing grievances and also guard against spurious products, inputs and other negativities. The permanent window can also develop into a valuable tool for decentralized and scientific planning at the village and taluka levels. The organizational structure for such a system however needs to be thought out carefully for imparting it continuity and relevance.

"Rath" and Decentralization

The organisational structure of the Grameen Bank of Bangladesh, a pioneer in rural micro-credit deserves highlighting. While the Grameen Bank is focused on delivering microcredit to marginal and landless cultivators, it would be interesting to examine whether its organization pattern and democratic nature can be adapted to the "Rath" initiative. The dominant activity that the bank engages is group based credit disbursement. It is done in the hope that if some funding could be made available to the landless and poor on reasonable terms, they could engage in productive self-employment thereby overcoming poverty. The innovation of Grameen Bank micro-finance is to collateralize the asset of future access to loans. This is combined with another design element- default by one member leads to loss of access for all members. The main cause of success of Grameen Bank is cited to be the way it is organized and managed in response to the specific needs of the target groups. The delivery system has a decentralized structure. Basic decision making authority is devolved to the operational levels of which the staff and clients are an integral part. Such a decentralized architecture facilitates openness and transparency. Micro credit availability has enabled wider adoption of HYV crop production and enhanced productivity, along with higher employment. Bank lending has also been successful in expanding the opportunities for self-employment (mainly in service sector) for its members; this generates higher returns than wages. Grameen Bank's success in reducing poverty and vulnerability is questioned. But the bank has itself given birth to highly profitable business enterprises. "The long history of micro-finance movement....and the incidence of high aggregate poverty situation seems to remind policy-makers about the limitations of micro-finance in alleviating poverty." (Rahman and Khandker, 2000, cited in Muhammad, 2009, p. 40). Also, "...its success lies in creating profits by integrating the poor into the market." (Ibid, p.41).

Here the example of Basix India, another NGO, needs emulating. Basix follows the approach of shifting from micro credit to livelihood finance, since few beneficiaries under micro credit reported change in their poverty status. The reasons found by the programme operators were "..unmanaged risk, low productivity in crop cultivation and livestock rearing and inability to get good prices from the input and output markets." (Bera, 2008, p.81). Livelihood finance encompasses in addition to lending, efforts in savings mobilization, insurance and assisting in distributing and marketing clients' output. The growing realization that low income households can benefit more through a broader set of financial and non-financial services than just credit, led Basix to revise its strategy. Thus the organization offers to its customers in addition to credit, agricultural and business development services, facilitates market linkages and encourages formation of producers' cooperatives (Bera, 2008; Mahajan, 2005).

Rath's relevance could be sustained and it could be replicated if it is developed as a model that gives continuity in the state. For this, its institutionalization into a decentralized area based stable structure is needed, staffed by dedicated personnel who are knowledgeable about the local issues. The educated rural youth, oriented as they are to the needs of the local farmers, could be provided employment. As an institution it could function as a store house for knowledge, create locally usable value added content, and disseminate technical information, enabling transfer of knowledge to the farming community and other stakeholders. Propagation of relevant government schemes and incentives could also be routed through this structure; as often in the remote areas there are serious information gaps with regard to government initiatives.

The "Rath" could have an important role in the emerging decentralization in rural India. The 73rd Constitutional Amendment gives constitutional status to the panchayats at the district and sub-district levels. The panchayats are entrusted with the task of preparation of plans for economic development and social justice and implementation of schemes for the same. For decentralized planning to be truly reflective of the felt needs of the people, it is essential that plan formulation is initiated at the local levels. Such an exercise would require database, technical expertise, studies etc. As a part of the decentralized planning process, the Rath could additionally function as an information support system and aid the village panchayats in formulating the integrated development plans to ensure judicious use of land and water resources. The need for area specific development strategies is more acute in the agricultural sector than perhaps any other sector. The Rath's role as a technical arm of the local level decentralized planning set up would lend it legitimacy and help in infusing technological inputs tc the primary economic sectors in a sustained manner. The "Rath" could thus emerge as an important change agent - promoting scientific agricultural practices, transferring knowledge and aiding decentralized planning.

The desirability of decentralized planning cannot be doubted. District level planning provides a scenario that is "consistent with the specific needs of the people, the growth potential of the area and budgetary allocations available" (Ghosh and Kashyap, 1996). Dantwala (1983, as cited in *ibid.*) has also argued that decentralized planning can play an important role in curbing exploitative instruments that generate and maintain poverty by strengthening "non-exploitative arrangements such as institutional credit, cooperative marketing and public distribution". Revitalization of the farm sector requires location specific technological and institutional input and a holistic approach to agricultural system where land and water resources development and conservation play an important role. Only bottom-up and resource based planning can effect prioritization of development initiatives and investment decisions. Otherwise continuation of hierarchical planning approach would only aggravate inter-regional imbalances and inequalities.

The local plans and development priorities arrived at with the help of technical inputs from a permanent Rath could be dovetailed with the district planning boards and state level plans. So far this has not been fully achieved and the Rath can play an important role here. The Regional Rural Banks (RRBs) are involved in catering mainly to the weaker sections of the rural community- the target groups comprise small and marginal farmers, agricultural labourers etc. The investment priorities arrived by way of village level planning could be dovetailed with that of RRB's for successful project implementation. Further mechanisms of cooperative action between the Rath with the RRBs and other credit delivery institutions could also be worked out. Krishi Rath thus needs to be modified and given a permanent structure for aiding rural development process in Gujarat. Gujarat can be a pioneer in this; other states would follow, learning from the state's experiences.

Summing Up

Agricultural research and extension play an important role in the growth of the agriculture sector. Efficiency and efficacy of the extension system are important determinants of technological change. The extension machinery faces tremendous challenges as of today. The farming community, if they are to reap the benefits of the globalized era, requires knowledge and scientific practices to modify their agricultural operations. In addition, sustainability of agriculture is being threatened; declining productivity, increased cost of cultivation, degradation of land and water resources are all playing havoc with the farm incomes and overall threatening the livelihood patterns of the rural population. In the process rural poverty and growing rural - urban disparities are becoming all the more glaring.

Gujarat Government's effort towards information dissemination for scientific agriculture by way of the month long Krishi Mahotsava is a commendable exercise in the direction of doubling rural incomes. The noteworthy feature of the programme is that it enables unprecedented convergence of activities from different departments and stakeholders. The programme enables micro level planning for every village with the help of experts on a scientific basis. The programme has reported initial successes, though it is yet early to comment upon its role in enhancing farm incomes and reducing poverty in rural Gujarat. The Rath followed a holistic approach to address the needs of the agricultural sector, but for it to develop as a successful and replicable model it needs to be institutionalized into a permanent and stable structure. It is recommended that the Rath be transformed into a block or district level "single window information bank" for dissemination of locally relevant information and aid decentralized village level economic planning activities. Such efforts at reaching out to the farming communities have already been made in the past. Agro-climatic Planning and Information Bank under the ACRP approach and the Village Knowledge Centres of M.S. Swaminathan Research Foundation have enabled knowledge dissemination through ICT, among other means, to reach out to the different stakeholders. The Rath can develop along the lines of these tried and tested examples and emerge as specialized windows for information access. Additionally it could also provide valuable technical inputs for economic and social planning at the village and block levels.

The organizational structure of such a permanent entity has to be well thought out for it to perform its role to the optimum. To that extent lessons can be learnt and imbibed from the successes of the Grameen Bank. The Krishi Rath can also be developed as a decentralized information bank besides being the technical arm to provide support for village level planning. In this image the Rath would have a continuous and sustained role to perform. It has the potential to act as a catalyst in transforming agriculture of the state, thereby ushering in rural prosperity.

References

Agriculture and Cooperation Deptt, Govt. of Gujarat (2005), *Krushi Kranti, Krishi Mahotsava* 2005, Gandhinagar.

Agriculture and Cooperation Deptt, Govt. of Gujarat (2005), *A New Approach to Agricultural Extension and Integrated*

Agricultural Development for Eradication of Poverty in Rural Areas, Gandhinagar.

Basu, D.N., G.S. Guha and S.P. Kashyap (1996) (Ed.) *Agro-Climatic Regional Planning in India*, Volumes 1 & 2, Concept Publishing Company Pvt. Ltd., New Delhi.

Basu, D.N. & S.R. Hashim (1996), "The Concept of Agro-Planning Bank: Carrying Plans to Farmers", in D.N. Basu, G.S. Guha & S.P. Kashyap (Ed.)

Bera, Sayantan (2008), "Programme Design and Impact Assessments: 'Success' of Micro-finance in Perspective", *Economic and Political Weekly*, August 9.

Dantwala, M.L. (1983), "Two Way Planning Process: Scope & Limitations", *Indian Journal of Agricultural Economics*, Vol 38, No. 2, April-June.

Ghosh, T.K. & S.P. Kashyap (1996), "District Level Planning in India: An Overview of ACRP Approach" in Basu, Guha and Kashyap (Ed.).

Junagadh Agricultural University (2006), *Kharif Krishi Mahotsava, 2005, Siddhio ane Arsro- Saurashtra Vistaar*, Junagadh. Mimeo.

M.S. Swaminathan Research Foundation (2005), "*Toolkit for Setting up Rural Knowledge Centres*", Chennai.

Mahajan, Vijay (2005), "From Micro credit to Livelihood Finance", *Economic and Political Weekly*, October 8.

Muhammad, Anu (2009), "Grameen and Micro credit: A Tale of Corporate Success", *Economic and Political Weekly*, August 29, XLIV:35.

Rajan, K (1996), "*Decentralized and Multi-Level Planning*" in Basu, Guha & Kashyap (Ed.).

Rahman, A and M.H. Khandker (2000), (Ed.) "Micro-finance and Development", Special Issue, *The Bangladesh Development Studies*, Vol. XXVI, Dhaka.

Roy Chowdhury, Indrani (2010), "Understanding the Grameen Miracle: Information and Organisational Innovation", *Economic and Political Weekly*, February 6-12.

Shah, Tushaar, Ashok Gulati, Hemant P, Ganga Shreedhar and RC Jain (2009), "Secret of Gujarat's Agrarian Miracle after 2000", *Economic and Political Weekly*, December 26.

Sharma, S.D., A.K. Shrivastava and U.C. Sud (2004), *Information*

Support, Volume 20, State of the Indian Farmer- A Millenum Study, Academic Foundation, New Delhi.

Swaminathan, M.S. (2000), "*Community led Approaches to Ending Food Security and Poverty*", UNESCO Chair in Eco Technology, Rome. Mimeo.

Vasanth, Anita and Senthil Kumaran (n.d.), *Reaching the Unreached*: The Use of Information Communication Technologies- Experiences of the MS Swaminathan Research Foundation, (Mimeo) MSSRF, Chennai.

20

Gene Revolution
A Sustainable Growth Approach for Food Crisis

B.K. Mohanty

The first signs of slowdown in agriculture were visible in the mid-1990s, mainly due to a decline, in public investment in agriculture. By the end of 1990s, the signs became ominous. The CAGR (Compound Annual Growth Rate) of food production has fallen from 2.9 per cent during 1980s to 1.7 per cent in the 1990s. The growth rate in rice production in 1990's has fallen to less than half of that in the 1980s while wheat fared only slightly better. When we analyse the trend a little closely, the foodgrain sector production was found much sharper after 1996-97. Almost all the crops have shown a stagnant or decelerating growth rates during the period 1996-97 to 2004-05. Therefore, it is clear that the country started facing severe supply side problems since the mid-1990s, which became acute by the turn of the century. In 1950, the world's population was about 2.5 billion. In 1999, it crossed the 6 billion mark. According to the United Nations population Division, the world population would be somewhere between 8 and 11 billion by 2050. These figures appear to suggest that it may indeed be difficult to feed everybody in the future.

In 1950, world foodgrain production was 631 million tonnes. It increased about 3 times to 1843 MT by 2000 and further 2075 MT in 2007. Thus between 1950 and 2007, the population increased by about 2.6 times but grain production jumped by 3.3 times. In 1950, each person had 248 kilograms of grain. In 2007, this increased to 314 kg. Similar increases have occurred in the whole range of food needed by humans — meat, dairy products, fruits, vegetables, sugar, etc. According to UN estimates there will be at least 800 million hungry people looking for the food. If the above food production figures remains true than why there will be hunger? The simple answer is that food is not available equally to all.

Table 20.1: World Population and Foodgrain Production

Year	*Population (Billion)*	*Production (Million Tonnes)*	*Availability kg Per Capita*
1950	2.54	631	248
1960	3.03	824	272
1970	3.77	1079	286
1980	4.45	1429	321
1990	5.29	1768	334
2000	6.12	1843	301
2007	6.60	2075	314

Source : UN Population Division and FAO.

Limits of Population Growth

There is a limit to how much the earth can yield. There is a limit to cultivable land, which is currently 11 per cent of the 13.2 billion hectares of the total land area of the planet, the rest being taken up by forests, settlements and grasslands, etc. There is also a limit to water. If everybody was to start consuming as much as, say, the American consume, than obviously the earth will not be able to sustain it. At the current population of about 6.7 billion people, a US level per capita consumption of 1046 kg would require world population of nearly 7 billion tonnes of foodgrain- three and half times the present production. The earth would become a wasteland by

2050. Now the question arises whether the earth feed an additional 3 billion people in the next 50 years? The answer is yes. The reason is that the full potential of agriculture is yet to be realised in most parts of the world.

An Outlook

For example, in Africa, the total harvested area under cereals is 98.7 million hectares, from which about 146 MT of cereals are produced. In North America (US and Canada) the harvested area for cereals is 71 million hectares but the production is 398 MT. They are producing 252 MT more despite cultivating 20 million hectares less land. So, it has been evident that Africa has a vast potential to improve its agricultural production. This discrepancy can be measured by checking out the yields per hectares of land as shown below in the Table 20.2.

Table 20.2 : Land Utilisation under Cereals

Name of the Country	*Area- Million Hectares*	*Production (Million Tonnes)*
Africa	99	146
North America	71	398
South East Asia	53	199
Europe	118	404
World	674	2221

Source : FAO.

Table 20.3 : Yield Rate of Foodgrains in Different Countries (kg per hectare)

Name of the country	*Rice*	*Wheat*
US	7694	2825
China	6265	4455
India	3124	2619
Nigeria	1440	1127

Source : FAO.

China produces 6,265 kg of rice, while Nigeria has to make do with just 1440kg and India with 3124kg. This is nothing but a division between rich and poor countries. Cereal yield per hectare is about 4 tonnes in the developing world, while it is over 6 tonnes in the advanced countries. There is also a vast difference in vegetable production. Vegetable production is just 10 tonnes in Africa and 9.6 tonnes in South East Asia. But in North America, it is 26 tonnes and in Europe it is nearly 21.21 tonnes. The reason of this difference is that more and better resources have been available to the farmers. If same amount of resources are made available to the farmers in India or Bangladesh no doubt they can also produce more food products and the yield rate will increase tremendously. It requires a shift of the method of cultivation both domestically and internationally. In this connection Greg Wagner, Director of a grain trade consultancy in Chicago told "Global economy continuing to expand, the demand base has been increasing the supply has been decreasing. As a consequence price must go high enough to cut back on demand otherwise there will not be any wheat left."

From the following Table 20.4 it has been revealed that there has been no remarkable increase in the yield rate of wheat, rice, corn, soyabean or sugarcane in any part of the world over last 10 years. Agricultural productivity has stagnated internationally, while the consumption of agricultural products has steadily increased with the increase of the income levels and population growth.

India's average rice yield today is 2.9 tonnes per hectare. By comparison, China's average rice yield, remained at 6.3 tonnes per hectare, is more than double that of India. South Korea has achieved an even higher rice yield i.e. 6.8 tonnes per hectare. Agricultural productivity has stagnated after the green revolution. What comes concern is that India's agricultural productivity is even lower than that of many other countries. India has 170 million hectares under foodgrain

Table 20. 4 : Yields of Various Crops (Tonnes/Hect.)

Year	*2002*	*2003*	*2004*	*2005*	*2006*	*2007*
Sugarcane						
Australia	73.80	82.60	82.60	87.10	94.10	88.80
Thailand	71.00	71.00	70.00	61.00	66.90	71.10
China	50.25	49.50	43.50	47.25	50.18	53.33
India	67.00	66.00	58.00	63.00	66.90	71.10
Brazil	70.00	71.00	73.00	75.00	66.90	71.10
Soyabean						
USA	2.66	2.56	2.28	2.84	2.89	2.87
China	1.63	1.73	1.65	1.81	1.70	1.72
Argentina	2.63	2.82	2.36	2.71	2.66	2.99
India	0.90	0.71	1.05	0.73	0.90	0.95
Brazil	2.66	2.82	2.37	2.31	2.56	2.85
Rice						
Thailand	2.62	2.57	2.65	2.63	2.70	2.69
Indonesia	4.41	4.50	4.56	4.64	4.59	4.60
China	6.16	6.19	6.06	6.31	6.26	6.23
India	3.14	2.67	3.13	2.95	3.17	3.18
Brazil	3.30	3.25	3.43	3.37	3.86	3.81
Corn						
South Africa	2.84	2.65	2.94	3.64	3.41	2.52
Argentina	6.00	6.33	6.52	7.37	6.48	8.04
USA	8.67	8.12	8.93	10.06	9.29	9.36
China	4.70	4.92	4.81	5.12	5.29	5.39
Wheat						
Canada	1.94	1.83	2.26	2.64	2.74	2.61
Turkey	1.82	1.96	1.95	2.15	2.15	2.03
USA	2.70	2.36	2.97	2.90	2.82	2.60
China	3.81	3.78	3.93	4.25	4.28	4.55
India	2.71	2.77	2.62	2.71	2.59	2.63

Source : The Economic Times of India, Dated- 21st July, 2008.

cultivation, producing 220 million tonnes of foodgrains in a year. China has only 60 per cent of this arable land area but it is able to harvest twice the quantity of foodgrains that India produces.

Sixty years after independence India produces on an average, only 14 kg of rice and wheat per person per annum, just a little over one kilogram per person over a month. Over 60 per cent of India's net shown area still remains at the mercy of the monsoon. About 60 per cent of our farmers own only 0.4 hectares of land each. Another 20 per cent of farmers hold an average of 1.4 hectares each. Therefore, 80 per cent of our farmers are small and marginal farmers. Nearly 87,000 farmers in India committed suicide between 2001 and 2005, within a span of four years. The per capita availability of foodgrains in India has declined from about 500 grams per day per person to less than 400 grams per day over the last two decades.

Since the mid-1960's, the traditional agricultural practices are gradually being replaced by modern technology and farm practices in India and a veritable revolution took place in our Country. The new technology was tried in 1960-61 as pilot project in seven Districts and was called Intensive Agricultural District Programme (IADP) and later High Yield Verity Programme (HYVP) was added and was extended to cover the entire country. This strategy was popularly known as "Green Revolution". Now it is the time to lunch a " Gene Revolution" instead of " Green Revolution" to feed the world and make Indian farmers rich.

A slowdown will have a serious effect on India's economy. Hence, we have no choice but to keep the growth story going, and to keep a check on inflation. The common man spends 50 per cent of his income on food. Therefore, food prices would have to top our long term approach to combating inflation. These prices have risen as a result of rising population and falling productivity.

Food security remains a global challenge today and famine still threatens several parts of the Globe. There is an urgent need to develop new agricultural technologies that will increase yields and eliminate crop failures and famines. Many scientists believe that new plants developed using modern Bio-technology will play an important role in increasing our ability to produce enough food. Advancement of Bio-technology is having dramatic impacts on Global agricultural production.

Bio-tech crops were planted on over 100 million hectares in 2006 by 10 million farmers in 22 countries and the results have been found well. In all countries where farmers have access to bio-tech crops, yields are higher and production costs are lower, making farmers more efficient than ever before. Since 2007, when bio-tech cotton was introduced India's cotton output has almost doubled to 27 million bales weighing 170 kilograms each, and average yields are up around two-thirds, largely because of lower rates of pest infestation. Unlike the original "Green Revolution" which saw large increase in use of pesticides and fuel, the new bio-tech crops of the "Gene Revolution" help reduce the use of inputs like pesticides, fuel and water. EU economists reported that biotech crops have been responsible for a decrease in pesticide use of over 200 million kg which has reduced the environmental impact by more than 15 per cent. Fewer pesticide applications mean less use of fuel and water on the farm. In India, pesticide use in Bt. Cotton has been reduced by half and this has reduced the use of fuel and water as well as reducing farmer exposure.

Agriculture is a contributor of green house gas and studies have shown that biotech crops help decrease these emissions. Scientists estimate that biotech crop planted in 2005 decreased global emission of carbon dioxide by 20 billion pounds. This is the equivalent of removing 4 million cars from the road for a whole year. These new crops are grown in a more sustainable manner, with less use of pesticides, fuel and water and less impact on the environment.

Improvements in agricultural technology are a critical component of meeting this challenge and bio-tech crops are already making a combination. Insect protected crops and herbicide tolerant crops allow farmers to achieve high yields even while using fewer pesticides. New drought tolerant crops, which will grow and survive even when rainfall is not optimal, are being developed through bio-technology.

Many Countries have tackled food scarcity in the past with the introduction of conventially bread, although gene-altered high yielding crops. Scaling up the genetic production potential of a crop through traditional plant breeding technologies is a long drawn out process. The problems plaguing Indian agriculture call for quick solutions that only molecular breeding can bring about.

Measures to Eradicate Food Crisis

Development of a Strong Agricultural Infrastructure Base

Now there is an urgent need to develop agricultural infrastructure to meet the rising demand in India for foodgrains and other Agri-products. Setting up storage facilities to processing facilities for our farm products is one big issue that needs to be tackled by the policy-makers in the country. Public goods, infrastructure, welfare imperatives other regulatory needs and areas of market failure will continue to need government intervention. Now it is a matter of concern that Globally the investment in the agricultural sector is shrinking. Building of rural roads, rural telecom and rural electrification need to be accelerated and coordinated. Farm subsidy amounts to about Rs. 1 lakh crore. The sector can be better off if this were to be spent as investment on the development of infrastructure towards agricultural sector.

Restructuring the Agricultural Sector

Now it is the time for re-establishing a trained and dedicated cadre of agricultural extension workers. It is also necessary for strengthening of agricultural research and technology development and institutional support system. There is an urgent need for augmenting the physical and economic connectivity of farm to market, post harvest operations including the role of food processing industries and ultimately enhancing farmers income, rural employment security and inclusiveness. Reform should be taken up to encourage private sector investment in agriculture.

Approach Towards Yield Gaps

Low yield areas are to be demarcated and an analytical measurement should be taken up to find out the reasons of yield gap and low factor productivity. Local farmers and private money lenders should come forward and extend their cooperation with the government officials in conducting various surveys relating to the growth of production in the agricultural sector.

Creation of Advanced Laboratories at National Level

A national network of advanced soil testing laboratories should be established to promote balanced nutrient application and advise the micro nutrient deficiencies. Farmers should be necessary to ensure timely availability of quality seeds and agro-chemicals to the farmers at the time of their need. Each farmer should be issued soil and water health cards. Just like carbon credits, the farmers should be given credit on the basis of the water used by him for the production purpose. Special emphasis and training should be given to the small and marginal farmers for the adoption of dry land farming in the country. Bio-diversity conservation and creation of livestock heritage on farm Gene banks should become an integral part of development programmes.

Organise Farmers into Bodies

Individual farmer has no bargaining power to sell the farm produce at the reasonable price. Companies or Co-operatives are capable of leveraging the opportunities afforded by the market. It is essential to encourage initiatives taken by ITC's E-Choupal and DCM Shriram's *Haryali stores* that offer farmers a host of inputs ranging from seed, fertiliser, tractor parts and disel for pump sets to agronomic advice and soil testing post harvest infrastructure should be modernised.

Institutional Support

The flow of credit, particularly to small and marginal farmers should be made speedier and hassle free. Whether based insurance products should be promoted to increase the coverage which is now at a nascent stage. SHGs (Self-Help Groups) should play more proactive role in the process. In Public Distribution System (PDS).Through SHGs micro credit should be opened to have an easy product delivery system.

Implementation of MSP in a Massive Scale

In India, the farmer sells his produce for about one-third the price the consumer pays. To increase the benefit of rising food prices to the farmer and to minimise the cost to the consumer, this huge margin between the farm and the consumer prices must shrink. For the removal of the gap the first step is to abolish the Mandi tax. Next step is to allow direct sourcing of farm produce by agribusinesses and organised retail and reduce several rounds of transportation and loading and unloading costs, etc. Appropriate policy interventions are needed to transfer the benefits of the rise to the farmers and at the same time to strengthen social safety programmes to assure access to food on part of the poor. The MSP must be fixed for all major commodities and implemented judiciously throughout the country.

Conclusion

Today's paramount need is to improve agricultural productivity across the Globe. Crop yields can be increased through the introduction of technologies such as drip irrigation or through education and training of farmers. If countries like India and China, which have large agricultural land, can boost their productivity to the levels attained by the developed world, it will no doubt mitigate food scarcity. From the first "*Green Revolution*" to the current "*Gene Revolution*", innovative new technologies have significantly improved our ability to feed our people. Farmers in India and around the world, who have pioneered the use of modern bio-technology have seen their innovation rewarded in terms of high production and lower environmental impacts. Further innovations like bio-fuels and drought tolerant crops will further contribute to sustainable production efficiencies.

21

Participatory Watershed Management for Sustainable Agriculture in North Eastern States

Rajkumar Josmee Singh, G. Prasad Babu, Vairagar Vishal Gulab and *Ram Kumar*

The richly vibrant north east region of our country is in a state of gradual, but steady transformation. North Eastern Region comprises of the states of Arunachal Pradesh, Assam, Manipur, Meghalaya, Mizoram, Nagaland, Sikkim and Tripura. It occupies about 8 per cent of the country's land area and accounts for about 4 per cent of the country's population. The development of these hilly and mountainous states and the protection of their ecology have become matters of national concern, as these are the recognized climate makers and repository of rich bio-diversity. Hills and mountains are the lungs of the country. Crop production, livestock, horticulture and farm forestry or agro-forestry are the recognized four major components of hill agro-ecosystem.

Due to increasing population pressure, the land on the hills, is not being cultivated on the scientific principles. Marginal and sub-marginal lands have been brought under shifting or *jhum* or swidden cultivation without taking adequate conservation measures. Shifting (Jhum or Swidden) cultivation is a primitive practice of cultivation in States of North Eastern Hill Region of India. Shifting cultivation in the present context has become not only unproductive because of the exposure of rocks due to soil erosion, heavy silt load in streams and drying of perennial water sources, loss of plant nutrients, loss of forestry resources and loss of flora of human and animal importance, but has also become hazardous to the environment, and act as a severe constraint to raise above the bare minimum level of subsistence for people who practice it. With reference to a report, as on March 2009, on Special Central Assistance to State Plan Scheme on Watershed Development Project in Shifting Cultivation Area (WDPSCA), it has been reported by Indian Council of Agricultural Research (ICAR) Complex for North Eastern Hill Region, Shillong, Meghalaya, about 14.66 lakh ha. area is affected by Shifting Cultivation mainly in States of Arunachal Pradesh, Assam, Manipur, Meghalaya, Mizoram, Nagaland and Tripura.

Today, it is universally accepted that conservation should be essentially an area approach and the unit of its adoption should be a watershed. Therefore a combination of few approaches is required to be adopted in a given watershed. Watershed management of the resources with people's participation should be a concept for the management of natural resources in an integrated approach, considering holistic development for all the users of the watershed.

Watershed and Watershed Management

A watershed is a topographically delineated natural unit that collects, stores and releases water. Collected water comes in the form of rain, snow and in coastal fog. It is stored in lakes, ponds and subsurface soils and geologic formations. Rivers and streams, as well as groundwater flow, then release this water. Watersheds also are referred to as drainage basins or catchments because they "drain" and "catch" rain and snowmelt water that falls onto the land.

Based on the size, shape and land use pattern of locations, watersheds are categorized into different groups. The categorization could also base on the size of the stream or river, the point of interception of the stream or the river and the drainage density and its distribution. The All India Soil and Land Use Surveys (AIS&LUS) of Ministry of Agriculture, Government of India, have developed a system for watershed delineation like water resource region, basin, catchments, sub-catchments, and watershed. The usually accepted five levels of watershed delineation based on geographical area of the watershed are:

(1) Macro watershed (> 50,000 ha)
(2) Sub-watershed (10,000 to 50,000 ha)
(3) Milli-watershed (1,000 to 10,000 ha)
(4) Micro-watershed (100 to 1,000 ha)
(5) Mini-watershed (1 to 100 ha)

Watersheds may also be categorized as hill or flat watersheds, humid or arid watersheds, red soil watershed or black soil watershed based on criteria like soil, slope, climate, etc. Depending on the land use pattern, watershed could again be classified as highland watersheds, tribal settlements and watersheds in areas of settled cultivation. From management point of view, watershed can also be described as a bio-physical, socio-economic and sometimes a political unit for planning and management of resources.

Watershed Management is a process of integrated decision-making regarding uses and modifications of lands and water within a watershed. It is a typical form of ecosystem management, which includes the entire watershed system, from uplands to headwaters, to wetlands and river channels. It focuses on the processing go energy and materials (water, sediments, nutrients and toxics) down slope through this system. A good watershed management therefore must consider the social, economic, environmental sustainability and institutional factors operating within and outside the watershed area.

Participatory Watershed Management (PWM)

What is PWM?

People's participation is recognized by government agencies as an essential component of all developmental efforts including watershed management. The implementation of participatory watershed management practices has enabled communities to overcome problems and gain more control over their natural resources and livelihoods. Increased expectation due to involvement of the local people may not always be accomplished. But the advantages of people's participation are not only many but sound also. Participation can ensure effective utilization of available resources. In real terms, community participation means voluntary sharing by the users group their time, energy and money on the programme and adopt the recommended measures and practices on a sustained basis.

Watershed initiates a participatory process for the optimum utilization of water resources in a given area. It promotes skill management, regulation, control and conservation of water to facilitate maximum agriculture and allied operations in watershed areas. The unique feature of watershed is that it involves all the stakeholders into the process of planning, decision-making and management of watershed. It enables willing and active participation of the farming community along with the implementing agency.

Why PWM?

In practice, people in North Eastern Region have varying goals and values relative to uses of local land and water resources.

Human modifications of lands and waters directly alter delivery of water, sediments and nutrients alter aquatic systems. The need for and significance of participatory watershed management is imperative with the following multiple advantages:

(1) Assess the nature and prevailing status of the watershed ecosystem;
(2) Define short-term and long-term goals for the system;
(3) Set objectives and determine actions needed to achieve the objectives;
(4) Assess both costs and benefits of each action;
(5) Protect hill slopes of Jhum areas through soil and water conservation measures on watershed basis and to reduce further land degradation;
(6) Encourage and assist Jhumia families to develop Jhum land for productive uses with improved cultivation and suitable package of practices leading to settled cultivation;
(7) Improve socio-economic status of Jhumia families through household/land based activities;
(8) Mitigate ill effects of shifting cultivation by introducing appropriate land use as per land capability and improved technologies;
(9) Evaluate the effects of actions and progress toward goals; and
(10) Re-evaluate goals and objectives as part of an iterative process.

Extension approaches for Promoting Participatory Watershed Management for sustainable agricultural development.

(1) Participatory approach for empowerment of community;
(2) Implementation of the watershed project through watershed community;
(3) Dynamic and vibrant role of extension personnel;
(4) Project proposals to be demand driven and reflect felt-needs of the community;
(5) Replication of successful watershed development projects;
(6) Adoption of watershed approach for treatment of degraded Jhum areas as cluster and contiguous manner;
(7) Integration of sectoral measures for comprehensive watershed development and maintenance;
(8) Consolidation of treatment efforts through projectised approach with proper choice of treatment measures;
(9) Emphasis on sustainability of treatment measures and providing means for settled cultivation;
(10) Multi-disciplinary approach at district and project level while evolving programme measures and conducting farmers training, involving various line departments like Agriculture, Forests, Horticulture, Animal Husbandry, Minor Irrigation, etc.;
(11) To mitigate ill effects of shifting cultivation by introducing appropriate land use as per land capability and adoption of improved technologies; and
(12) Promoting equity for resource poor and women.

Conclusion

Extension agencies should take dynamic and vibrant approaches to make Participatory Watershed Management for ensuring sustainable and productive agriculture. This long term strategy of Participatory Watershed Management is directed towards increasing or maintaining the adaptive capacity of natural resources to produce material goods such as food, fibre, fuel wood, timber, non-timber forest products, meat, dairy products, fish, etc. including their value addition wherever required including the conservation of bio-diversity and services such as clean air and fresh water not only for the present but for future generations also.

References

Agricoop (2003). Watershed Development. *http://www.agricoop.nic.in*

Food and Agriculture Organization (1999). *Preparation report for integrated watershed development (Hills II) Project* March 1999, Investment Centre Division, FAO/World Bank Cooperation Programme, Rome.

MANAGE (2000). Common principles for watershed development. *http://www.manage.gov.in.*

Seth, S. L. (2000). Watershed management in India. *Kurukshetra* 48: 2-7

22

Housing—A Multi-Dimensional Issue in Rural Kerala
Problems and Prospects

K.V. Ramachandran

For everyone on this Universe there should be a shelter to live in. Construction dating back to the very existence of man forms the basis of all developments. It is a vehicle for the growth of culture and civilization. Every rational beings longs to have a shelter to protect their families. Therefore, shelter occupies the most important position among the construction activities. People want not only mere physical shelter but also a home as part of the total way of life. It is a place where people in general fulfil the basic domestic and personnel functions of family life, physical and mental health, working efficiency, emotional security and social status. Therefore, shelter must be seen in the context of basic needs as critical to living, as food and clothing, hence bound up with individual's right to live and demanding an appropriate social context for its fulfilment. Thus, housing is one of the pressing needs of any country's population.

In India, the building need is very high. The need for housing consists of not only the demand for upgradation and renovation of existing housing stock but also the need for construction of new dwelling units. Therefore, to find a shelter for each one at a low cost is the greatest challenge of all times, though it is the moral obligation of every government to provide an adequate shelter to all.

However, the demand for a roof over one's head had been increasing continuously and there has been a severe shortage of housing due to the wide gap between the demand for and supply of housing stocks in India. This causes an acute shortage of dwelling units in the country. The problem is becoming grave mainly because the house construction has not kept pace with the growing demand. The major factor leading to the housing shortage is the slow increase in housing construction in relation to the population growth.

The pace of housing construction has been extremely slow because of the speculative increase in land price and rising wage rate and cost of construction. Hence, the achievement of housing is decreasing whereas the need for housing go on increasing year after year thus bringing about an imbalance between both the demand for supply of housing. Resultantly, for millions of people in India, the desire of owning a house remain only a long cherished dream unfulfilled so far. In our country, 80 per cent of the total population constitutes rural people and about 30 per cent out of this 80 per cent of the rural people are living under abject poverty. To provide an affordable shelter to these people would be a major task of the government. The housing shortage in urban India also presents a grim picture. The picture is abysmally dismal at the lower end of the economic ladder. The metropolitan cities like Mumbai, Kolkata and Chennai are the number one examples to this where the number of per dwelling unit was 5.6 in 1951, 6.01 in 1981, 7 in 1995 and 7.5 since 2005, thus creating congestion over time (survey by NBO — National Building Oganization, 1995 & 2005).

Housing-Still a Mirage to many in Rural Kerala

In Kerala, there is a persistent gap between both the aggregate demand for and supply of housing stocks which causes a high level of housing inadequacy in the state. Due to the escalating rise in price of building materials and labour the housing has become totally inaccessible to many. Now, the price of building materials alone contribute to 60-70 per cent of the over all cost of construction. Besides, the recent boosting up of the wage rate (i.e. in the year 2007–08, the maximum wage rate per day for the male worker in the construction field was Rs. 250 while that of the female worker was Rs. 180. But, by the beginning of the year 2009-10, the wage rate among the both workers suddenly increased to Rs. 450 and Rs. 300 respectively) has also added much to the intensity of the housing problem.

The predominant use of conventional construction materials like steel, cement, burnt clay bricks and timber clearly shows an increasing trend in the construction costs over the years. The cost of construction is increasing by 13-15 per cent each year even when the inflation is less than double digit. Therefore, the most important subject with immediate interest is the reduction in building costs. The cascading effect in the price of building materials stands as a major hurdle in the field of house-building. Therefore, a significant reduction in the construction cost is highly inevitable if any solution to the housing problem is to be sought for.

In the state, at present, it is seen that the high cost of housing is caused not only by the escalating rise in the price of building materials but also due to the "insane craze" for the so-called "new fashions" in house-building. The housing need is generally considered as a socio-cultural concept and determines the quantity and quality of the accommodation which the households are willing to pay for. But, the demand normally varies with the price of building, with household's income, their accumulated savings and/ or financial loans and constraints and as such.

The building construction today has grown in size, accelerated in pace and became so highly mechanized that it is nothing but an outdoor assembly plant. It is highly traditional, regionally and locally conditioned activity; bound up by a variety of cultural, social, climatic as well as technical parameters. In this era of rapidly rising prices of building materials, escalating wages, forced up by inflation and increasing energy costs the initial costs of construction has been rising at an ever increasing rate. Moreover, the follow on costs such as maintenance and operations have also escalated rapidly.

In such a situation, the technology transfer is highly inevitable. There should be a shift from conventional building technology to cost-effective technology in housing construction. Technology transfer has been given prominence in introducing innovation and technologies whilst transfer of technology is important in manufacturing, construction and processing industries. That is how, Japan which initially got technology from the west, improved upon them and took the lead in manufacturing and construction. Anyway, the houses built by the low-cost, cost–effective, and environment friendly technology is eminently suited to Kerala atmosphere and such houses ensure longer life, lesser maintenance, better aesthetic, and greater comfort. Thus, low- cost housing is still a hot topic among the researchers and planners as the construction costs have gone up over the period of last two decades.

Magnitude of the Problem in the State

The acute shortage of housing settlements is one of the basic problems confronted by the State at present. The soaring price of building materials is the main factor which causes this problem. It has a cascading effect on the overall costs of construction. If this trend is followed, the housing scenario in the coming years presents a grim picture. Housing has been a "neglected area" especially among the rural masses. It is still a "mirage to many". To the poor persons concerned, the "sky itself is their shelter". The non-availability of accessible land at reasonable price keeps the poor man away from building apartments. But, just converse to this, the need for more and more dwelling units arose on account of the formation of nuclear families caused by the rapid urbanization and development. It necessitates the construction of a large number of new houses in the State.

In 1991, out of the total housing shortage of 31 million units in India, 20.6 million in rural areas and 10.4 million in urban areas. But by the 21st century the total housing shortage is likely to reach a dismal condition. When we look into Kerala it can be seen that 20 per cent of the total houses are the huts of semi–permanent nature. About 50 per cent of this 20 per cent are substandard huts which are unfit for safe human living. Again, the 50 per cent of these substandard huts are required to be demolished (Government of Kerala, *Economic Review* 1994, State Planning Board, Thiruvananthapuram). It should also be noted that the average size of households (i.e. the average number of persons living in a house) in Kerala was 5.3 persons as against 5.6 for all India (Census by Government of Kerala, 2001).

Assuming the average household size of 5.3, the number of houses required for accommodating the increase in population would be around 7 lakhs (i.e.an increase in population about 37 lakhs by 2000 AD divided by the average household size of 5.3 persons). Moreover, the requirement of new houses by the formation of nuclear families by 2000 AD would be 4 lakhs and by 2010 it would be above 9 lakhs. Summing up all the requirements of new houses in the State by the year 2010, come to nearly 16 lakhs, creating severe problem of housing shortage and at the same time a colossal task to the government for bringing out any solution to this.

All these indicate the magnitude of the problem and the importance of bringing down the cost per house. So that, with the available resources more number of families can be provided with house if the resources are discerningly used. For this, the cost of construction must be reduced. The lowering the cost of construction emphasizes the need for adoption of new building materials and construction techniques which are capable of cost reduction.

However, the shortage of dwelling units around 16 lakhs for rural people in the State by 2010 indicates only the quantitative aspect of the housing problem. The poor condition of a large part of the existing housing stock and the overcrowding in houses and tenements show the qualitative aspect of the housing problem which is specially seen everywhere in the State.

The hardest hit by the spiraling cost of construction has always been on the lower, middle class and weaker sections of the population. Therefore, the rapid increase in the cost of materials became the main source of concern for the prospective house-owners. Thus, efforts have to be directed at improving the income status of the poor and at the same time working for solution towards reducing the cost of housing.

Reviews

Several studies have been made in this direction. Anyhow, a brief review of the available literature in this field is attempted as follows:

1. Robert M Buckley and Eugene N. Gurenko studied the *'Housing and income distribution in Russia"* in which they stressed that the housing allocation had progressive effects on the distribution of income in Russia. The increase in income inequality that occurred in recent years is significantly reduced. The study brings out the point that the progressive housing allocation enables the equitable income distribution.
2. Dinesh Mohan in his study "*Three Decades of Building Research in India*", pointed out that the

problems of modern India are, however, of an entirely different genre. We face the staggering shortage of shelters for teeming millions who live either under the sky without any roof or under appalling conditions of abject poverty. To find a shelter for each of them at a low-cost is the greatest challenge of all times. The study highlights the problem of severe housing inadequacy confronted by the country at present.

3. In the words of T. K. Majumdar, the inaccessibility of low-cost housing and the initial structuring of inequalities whether in land, housing, space standards or in allocation of resources for improving living environment of low- income population are the factors that oblige the rural migrants to build their own shelter on illegally occupied lands. According to him, the inaccessibility of housing especially to the rural migrants is the resultant effects of inequalities in land and allocation of resources.
4. Gopikuttan, G. in his study "*Housing Boom in Kerala-Causes and Consequences*"– examines the recent trends in the field of house-building and its causes and consequences on Kerala Economy. He says a construction boom that occurred everywhere in the State during the period in between 1990-1996. This is due to the massive inflow of foreign remittances through the NRIs. But, unfortunately, since 1996-97 there was a massive gulf return to Kerala (more than 46,000 Keralites) which adversely affected much to the rural housing in the State. Resultantly the housing construction activities in Kerala became a standstill.
5. Charles Correa in his study "*Housing Problems in Rural India*", says the materials and skills used for housing should be local and the settlement pattern as per the local needs. He further added that, the houses for the poor will have to be so cheap that masses can

afford it. These houses should also have minimum maintenance costs and they must fulfil the basic function of a house.

6. Indira Hirway in a study "*Housing for the Rural Poor*" – focused on the major problems of the rural houses that such houses have high recurring maintenance costs which the poor cannot afford and they are incapable of giving protection against natural calamities like floods, cyclones, earthquakes, and the surroundings of the houses lack the most fundamental requirements for hygiene. Therefore, Hirway stresses that the housing programmes should socially and culturally valid and should be suitable to the climatic as well as to the economic conditions of the poor. That is, the architecture of the house, the shape, the size, the layout, the materials used, etc. should be suitable to the local conditions and local needs.
7. The Census Report on Housing Problem in Kerala 1990 has recorded that in Kerala there were 42.89 lakhs of households and 41.33 lakhs of occupied dwelling units. Any scheme to wipe out the backlog and to cope up with the increasing demand every year should include programmes for conservation by repairs and improvement of the existing stock and for putting new houses in place of those which are fit for demolition and replacement minimum standard of stability and convenience to meet the new demand is also necessary. "A house saved is a house made".
8. Amrita Abraham in a study "*Housing for the Poor*" identified that the housing problem is the problem of housing for the poor. When population increases the shelter problem becomes more acute.
9. According to the Draft Eighth Five Year Plan (1992 – 1997) of Kerala, shelter is an instrument between man and his environment promoting his safety,

protection, privacy and prestige. Kerala's Eighth Plan has a slightly different emphasis mainly because the State has already achieved relatively a high level of development in social infrastructure as compared to other states. The Draft Eighth Plan of the State while recognized the need for giving top priority for poverty alleviation through increase in employment hold that the industrial and agricultural sectors and activities like housing, tourism, etc. should get the highest priority during the Eighth Plan period.

10. Prof. R. N. Iyengar in his study "*Rural Housing – a Discussion*" suggests certain policy issues to overcome the shelter problem. The policy issues he suggests are (1) To remove legal constraints with a view to increase supply of serviced land, (2) To provide stimulus and support for housing through credit finance mobilization, (3) To promote the use of Cost-Effective and appropriate technologies, and (4) To promote employment generation schemes which directly and/ or indirectly help housing activity.
11. K.R. Nayar in a study "*Housing Amenities and Health Improvement – Some Findings*" holds the view that housing is a health promoting factor. Cities like New York and Boston faced a complexity of problem like housing, water supply, etc. In this study he suggests that the improved housing has an influence on health improvement. The influence of housing and amenities on health is inconsistent.

When we go through these studies and findings it is apparent that though different studies had been made in this direction none of these studies bring out any pragmatic solution to the gigantic issue of housing inadequacies in the country as a whole. Several theoretical solutions are there but in practice all lacks a clear–cut practical dogma as how to approach to this problem. Therefore, here in this section, several pragmatic solutions to overcome such a multi–faceted problem of housing shortage especially in the State are hereby highlighted.

How to Solve the Problem of Rural Housing Shortage : Some Approaches

The main thrust of building research has been to improve upon the conventional practices and develop new prefabricated and cast-in-situ conventional practices and develop construction methods, mechanical aids, modern management techniques to achieve an appreciable reduction in cost and time of construction and to effect maximum possible saving in the consumption of costly and scarce materials like cement and steel as well as improving quality in construction. Techniques for construction of walls and roofs were developed with a view to make an optimum use of local materials such as soil, bricks, lime and timber.

Various cost reduction techniques and cost saving materials have been developed by the Central and State Housing Construction Departments, State Housing Boards, Central Building Research Institute (CBRI), Rookie, Structural Engineering Research Centre (SERC), Chennai, National for Cement and Building Materials (NCB), Ballagarh, Regional Research Laboratories, etc.

The various departments like National Building Organization (NBO), New Delhi, Building Materials and Technology Promotion Council (BMTPC), New Delhi, Housing and Urban Development Corporation (HUDCO) New Delhi, Housing Development Finance Corporation (HDFC), National Networks of Nirmithi Kendras under the aegis of HUDCO and COSTFORD (Centre of Science and Technology for Rural Development) centres, etc. throughout the State have been playing decisive role in the promotion of innovative and environment friendly low-cost construction techniques for the purpose of solving the problem of severe housing shortage in the country-wide scale.

Certain cost-saving building materials promoted by these departments are being: (1) Fly ash, Phosphogypsum, Blast Furnace Slag, etc. developed from industrial wastes, (2) Clay Fly Ash Burnt Bricks, Fly–Ash-Sand–Lime Bricks, Cellular Concrete Components, Alumina Red Mud Bricks and Phosphogypsum based Building Components, Sundried Bricks, Aluminium and Asbestos Sheets for Roofing, Glassed Shutters and Partitions , etc. The Table 22.1 shows some low-cost building materials employed by Nirmithi Kendras and COSTFORD centres in their pursuit of constructing low- cost residential projects in Kerala.

Table 22.1 : Low- Cost Building Materials Employed by Nirmithi Kendras and COSTFORD centres in the State.

Various Stages of Housing Construction	*Low-Cost Building Materials Employed.*
1. Foundation & Basement	Rubbles/Laterite Boulders (i.e. black coloured hard stone pieces) /Building Stones.
2.. Walling	Hollow Concrete Blocks/ Terra Cotta/ Burnt Clay Bricks/ Hollow Bricks/ Laterite Stones(locally available) / Wire- Cut-Bricks(a smooth and uniform sized Sundried Bricks)/ Concrete Wall Frames/ Hard Boards, etc.
3.. Roofing	Mangalore Pattern Roofing Tiles/ Terra Cotta Roofing Tiles/ Concrete Roofing/ Asbestos/ Galvanized Iron (GI) Sheets, etc.
4. Flooring	Flooring Tiles/ Red Oxide/ Cement/ Terra Cotta Tiles/ Mosaic/ Black Cement, etc.
5. Doors & Windows	Timber/ Concrete Doors & Window Frames/ Glassed Shutters/ Bamboo Ply Doors and Framed Windows/ Aluminium Sheets, etc.
6. Bonding & Finishing	Cement/ Mud/ Combination Mortar (i.e. cement, lime, and sand at 1: 2: 12 ratio)/ Cement Mortar/ Lime Mortar.

Source: Details collected from Nirmithi Kendra & COSTFORD centres in Kerala.

The popular cost-effective construction techniques employed in the large scale low-cost construction activities are: Rat Trap Bond, Filler Slab, Brick Arches and Waffle Shell System for Roofing, Thinner Walls or Single Brick Thick Walls, Bridge–on– Edge Cavity Walls, Pre- Cast Stone Masonry Blocks, Modular Brick Masonry Walls, Hollow Clay Blocks for Shell Type Houses, Sundried Brick Walls with Waterproof Treatment, Pre–Cast Hyperbolic Shell for Roofing, etc.

The most popular low-cost construction devices widely employing in Kerala are: Modular Constructions, Wood Frame Modular Constructions, Masonry Modular Constructions, Plant and Beam Constructions, etc. More than 1 lakh low-cost houses have been constructed by Kerala State Housing Boards, Nirmithi Kendras and COSTFORD centres as their attempt for solving the rural housing shelter less in the State. However, the innovations and their applications keep the society growing, dynamic and competitive and Help in improving people's welfare over time. We need to train our manpower resources in such a way that we can reach international levels of technology and quality in some fields and gain a reputation and self-reliance at international level.

Solutions to the Problem of Rural Housing Shortage : Different Views

At present, the most important subject with immediate interest is the reduction in building costs. The Cost-Effective Environment Friendly (CEEF) Technology is making sustained efforts to implement advance programming and architectural planning, rational and structural designs, organization, execution and management of works and using new materials and construction devices. So, the formidable problem of housing shortage is yet to be tackled on a country-wide scale. Different personalities, academicians, architects, researchers, economists, engineers and construction departments in their surveys, analysis and studies conducted; unanimously declare that the application of cost reduction techniques in building construction is eminently suited as some pragmatic solutions for tackling the severe problem of rural housing shortage elsewhere.

Mrs. Gillane Allam– Ambassador of Egypt to India underscored the need for the use of cost-effective and environment friendly technology if the commitment of the global community to provide affordable shelter to all is to become a reality.

Dr. Shankar Dayal Sharma–an erudite Scholar and former President of India said "human life would become richer and meaningful if human settlements are in tune with nature".

Narayana and M. Ramanjaneyulu in their study "*Rural Housing Shortage in India*", view that the rural housing under the employment programme has to satisfy the schematic norm of achieving the minimum of 50 per cent of the total cost as wage cost. Therefore, specification should be labour intensive and cost-effective. This can be enabled only through such low-cost technologies that can respond to the requirements of housing. Low–cost technology does not mean sacrifice of quality and durability. It only means avoidance of extravagance and minimizing the use of costly materials like cement, steel and wood.

The Draft Status Report on Housing and Construction Technology, July, 1975, focus on the fact that the gap between both the demand for and supply of housing is so wide which can be reduced by the choice of technology and effective management of resources.

Charles Correa in his study "*Housing Problem in Rural India*" says the materials and skills used for housing should be local and the settlement pattern as per the local needs. He further added that the houses for the poor will have to be so cheap that masses can afford it. These houses should also have minimum maintenance cost and they must fulfil the basic function of a house.

Vinay Lal in a study "*Budget and Housing Sector*" gives a picture about budget and housing and Murthy focuses on Indira Awaas Yojana, the construction of low–cost housing.

Jeethoo and Dipti Bhardwaj in a study "*Development of Mud Technology for Rural Shelterless*" highlighted the advantages of mud as a building material and mud technology should be developed for rural shelterless.

Gopalakrishnan in a "*Notes on Our Development Experience in Independence 1950-1985*" gives a vivid picture on housing and stresses the need for alternative techniques which will reduce the cost of construction.

C. V. Ananda Bose – the former Director of Kerala State Nirmithi Kendra (KESNIK) while analyzing the vexed question of housing in the country, keeping the essence of Nirmithi Movement in Kerala, underlines the need for propagating cost-effective environment friendly building technology to tackle the problem of rural housing. He emphasizes the need for bringing about a new design and construction culture avoiding unnecessary costs and eliminating wrong notions about low-cost housing. Remember, "We need a shelter and not a house to live in". On this context the rural housing is not a problem to be tackled for.

Dr. S. C. Lahiry in a study "*Rural Housing–An Overview*" says that the rising cost has a dampening effect on the housing sector and the need of the hour is to promote low-cost and environmentally appropriate technology and use of indigenous resources.

Dr. Neela Mukherjee in a study "*Rural Poor and Housing Issues and Approaches*" says that the present scenario calls for the formulation of a comprehensive housing policy. Among the measures suggested are, a detailed survey to identify the needy, popularization of cost–effective technologies, appropriate housing design and involvement of beneficiaries.

Prof: N.N. Chhabra in his study "*Low-Cost Rural Housing Design – A National Exposition*" views that "GRAMAWAS1995" was an effort at finding out a feasible solution to the rural housing shortage as well as applying innovations involved in the use of locally available building materials.

Dr. K. N. Raj in a study "*Rural Housing in India*" says that low-cost housing is the answer to the spiraling construction cost. People ought to be convinced and guided not only in adopting new technologies but also helped in designing and planning their own dwelling units. This calls for a change in the mindset and a new construction culture reducing costs and avoiding over designing and eliminating wrong notions. We should guard against the efforts of the powerful building lobby and the conventionally trained engineers to sabotage the low-cost technology and also put an end to our " West is Best Attitude" . Let us enrich further our rich building culture by assimilating only the best practices from the west.

Laurie Baker, the architect of low-cost housing technology in Kerala, said the construction techniques and materials need to be good, energy saving, strong, waterproof and so on. We cannot sincerely and effectively plan rural housing from a city office desk. We have to go to the villages and plan for their real needs.

Suggestions to overcome the Problem of Housing Shortage

It must be better to follow some useful steps to overcome the severity of the problem of rural shelterless. Some of them being are: - (1) Don't imitate others in house- building. Construct a shelter according to the income affordability of each. By doing so, the family's aggregate welfare need not be sacrificed. (2) Try to use locally available building materials and avoid high-priced scarce materials. So, we can avoid unnecessary costs and delay in construction. If the rural people at large are opt locally available low- cost building materials for their shelter, then about 30- 40 per cent of the overall construction costs can definitely be reduced. (3) Try to avoid the difference between actual costs and estimated costs of construction. Otherwise, they will be trapped into a huge financial debt. (4) The aspirants of a shelter should have a mind to accept the low-cost technology and locally available building materials for housing. So, try to eliminate the wrong notion about low- cost housing. (5) "Housing is a problem". But, it will not be a problem or a dream not to be fulfilled so far if cost- effective environment friendly building technology is opted.

References

I. Books.

Dinesh Mohan (1980)..... 'Three Decades of Building Research in India', Council of Science and Industrial Research in India.

Dreyer O (1976)... '*Cultural Changes in Developing Countries*', Progress Publishers, New Delhi.

Krishnaswamy, K. T, Gharpure. S. V. & Dr. Kulkarni. A. B. (1964)... *'Limit Design of Reinforced Concrete Structures* ', Khanna Publishers, Delhi.

Laurie Baker (1983).' Houses—How to Reduce Building Costs', published by COSTFORD, Kerala.

Majumdar, T. K. (1993)...' *Urbanizing Poor*', Lancers Publishers, New Delhi.

Mohammed Mohsin (1983), 'LIC and Urban Housing', published by Aligarh Muslim University, Aligarh. Ist. Edn.

Solomon, S. K. (1987)' *Design of Reinforced Concrete Structures*', published by International Book Traders, Derawal Nagar, Delhi.

II. Reports, Articles & Journals:

Anyanwa, J. C. (1990), 'Housing Finance in Nigeria', Prajnam, *Journal of Social and Management Science, vol.*XIX, No. 4.

Ananda Bose, C.V. (1996)......'.Rural Housing – Nirmithi Perspective' – *Kurukshetra*.

Chhabra, N.N. (1996)., 'Low- cost Rural Housing Design- Natural Exposition' – *Kurukshetra*.

Desarda, M. (1994)...' Rehabilitation of Earthquake Victims- Problems of Housing' *EPW*, Vol.XXIX, NO.6

Business to Business, product Update— an *Economic Times* Presentation, 1995.

Draft Status Report on Housing and Construction Technology, Research, Design, Development and Extension Requirements (July 1975), National Committee on Science and Technology, Government of India, Technology Bhavan, New Delhi.

Draft Eight Five Year Plan (1992- 97) Report of Government of Kerala, Kerala Development Review, January- March 1992, vol.1, No.1, published by Institute of Planning and Applied Economic Research, Dr. John Matthai Foundation, Dr. John Matthai Centre, Department of Economics, University of Calicut, Thrissur.

Economic Review— State Planning Board, Thiruvananthapuram.

Gopalakrishnan, P. K. (1985), Notes on Our Development Experience Since Independence, 1950- 1985. State Planning Board, Thiruvananthapuram, Government of Kerala.

Gopikuttan, G, (1998)., 'Housing Boom in Kerala, Causes and Consequences', Kerala University Ph.D. Thesis, Centre for Development Studies (CDS) Thiruvananthapuram.

Mrs. Gillane Allam (1997)' Report on Better Habitat for Harmonious Living.' a conference held in connection with Global Nirmithi Net (GNN) Indian Chapter, New Delhi, GNN News.

Jeethoo, A.S. and Dipti Bhardwaj (1992)...' Development of Mud Technology for Rural Shelterless', *Journal of Rural Development*.

Kiran Wadhwa (1994).' Housing Programmes for Urban Poor- Shifting Priorities', *Economic and Political Weekly*, Vol. XXIII, No.34.

Raj, K. N. (1996) ... 'Rural Housing in India-*Kurukshetra*.

Karim N. A. (1996)...' Shelter for All- Need for a Comprehensive Housing Policy', *Yojana*.

Mathew, M.S. (1995)...'Cost- effective Technologies for Housing'- a paper presented on the seminar organized by Kerala State Nirmithi Kendra, Thiruvananthapuram.

Reports of Government of Kerala 8th Five Year Plan (1990 – 95).

Reports from the Survey conducted by Awasvikas Sansthan, Jaipur (1998).

Shankar Dayal Sharma (1997)...'Report on Better Habitat for Harmonious Living'- a conference held in connection with Global Nirmithi Net (GNN), Indian Chapter, New Delhi, GNN News.

Virmani, B. R. and Kala Rao (1997), 'Economic Restructuring Technology Transfer and Human Resource Development' — *Journal of Social and Management Sciences*, Vol. XXVI. No. I.

23

NREGA and Sustainable Development
A Critical Analysis

Anupam Hazra

India is having a long history and experience in implementing wage employment programmes. However, beginning with Jawahar Rojgar Yojana in 1989, the outreach of these programmes increased significantly as in the period 1989 to 2006, ultimately culminating in NREGA. These wage employment programmes implemented by State Governments with Central assistance were self-targeting, and the objective was to provide enhanced livelihood security, especially of those dependent on casual manual labour.

Based on the experience of these programmes the NREGA was enacted to reinforce the commitment towards livelihood security in rural areas. It is one of the largest single rights-based social protection initiatives in the world. NREGA is the first ever law internationally, that guarantees wage employment at an unprecedented scale. The Act was notified on 7th September, 2005. The significance of NREGA lies in the fact that it creates a right-based framework for wage employment programnes and makes the government legally bound to provide employment to those who seek it. It is currently the biggest self-targeting programme in India, open to all rural people who are willing and able to undertake manual labour in their village. Government of India through National Rural Employment Guarantee Act, 2005 aims to provide for enhancement of livelihood security of the households in rural areas of the country by providing at least one hundred days of guaranteed wage employment in every financial year to every household whose adult member volunteer to do unskilled manual work. Through this Act the ultimate aim of the Government is to create durable assets in one hand and at the same time strengthen the livelihood of the rural poor needs a special mention. The choice of works suggested in the Act address causes of chronic poverty like drought, deforestation, soil erosion, etc., so that the process of employment generation can be carried out on a sustainable basis. Launched in February 2006, NREGA covers all the 614 districts across the country. In this way, the legislation goes beyond providing a social safety net, and towards guaranteeing the right to employment. The experience with NREGA so far suggests that it is one of the main planks of rapid poverty reduction in the Eleventh Five Year Plan.

NREGA ranks among the most powerful initiatives ever undertaken for transformation of livelihoods in rural India. The unprecedented commitment of financial resources by the largest employment programme in human history is matched only by its imaginative architecture. The emphasis on planning of works and mechanisms of social audit means that quality of works is centrally important. This is not a welfare programme dishing out doles. It is a development initiative, chipping in with crucial public investments for creation of durable assets, which can provide much-needed momentum to growth in the most backward regions of India. Perhaps the most remarkable feature of NREGA, making a decisive break with the past, is the complete ban on contractors. Ever since independence, most government programmes in rural areas have been implemented through the agency of local contractors, who have emerged as major agents of exploitation of the rural poor, especially women. They have run roughshod over basic human rights, paid workers a pittance and used labour-displacing machinery. NREGA bans the use of such machines, mandates payment of statutory minimum wages and provides various legal entitlements to workers. It visualizes the involvement of local people at every stage — planning, implementation and social audit. All of this is obviously incompatible with programmes where the main goal becomes maximization of profits of the contractor. The other Unique features of the Act include, time bound employment guarantee and wage payment within 15 days, incentive-disincentive structure to the State Governments for providing employment as 90 per cent of the cost for employment provided is borne by the Federal Government or payment of unemployment allowance at their own cost.

Great emphasis has been placed on transparency and accountability at every stage of the programme. There is also an unprecedented emphasis on the use of Information Technology (IT).This is meant to facilitate the right to information, more intensive monitoring of the programme, as also greater speed of execution.

The Act is also designed to promote the participation of women in the workforce as it mandates 33 per cent participation for women. In India, the majority of people living below the poverty line are women and globalization has tended to contribute to what can be termed the 'feminisation of poverty'. This is associated with a concentration of women in the informal sector and in agriculture, putting them beyond the reach of traditional social security measures. Rural employment schemes have even, on occasion, displaced women. NREGA, however, is intended to be gender-sensitive. It allows for worksite crèche facilities, pays equal wages and insists that one-third of all workers are women and that they participate in management and monitoring the programme.

A report Two years of the National Rural Employment Guarantee Act (2006- 08) brought out by the Ministry of Rural Development lists the achievements as seen by the government. It says that in the nine months of 2007- 08 till December 2007, 855 million person days of work were generated, compared to 905 million person days in the 12 months of 2006-07, 1.23 million works were undertaken compared to 0.84 million in the earlier period, and Rs. 9,106 crore was spent in nine months (or 60 per cent of available funds) compared to Rs. 8,823 crore in the previous period (73 per cent of available funds).

Employment demanded was the highest in states like Andhra Pradesh, Bihar, Chhattisgarh, Jharkhand, MP, Orissa, UP and West Bengal, all of which are poor states except AP. The lowest demand for employment came from Maharashtra, Gujarat, Punjab and Haryana, all rich states. Of the assets created, 57 per cent were in water conservation, 13 per cent in irrigation, 17 per cent in roads, and 14 per cent for land development. Of the water conservation works, 347,000 or 43 per cent of the total value were for water harvesting, 13 per cent or 98,000 for water bodies such as ponds and 20 per cent to irrigate land owned by SC/ ST's. There were 113,000 tree plantation works and 206,000 for roads. What it cannot say is how many of these assets were lasting ones.

NREGA and Sustainable Development: The Possibilities & Potential Impacts

Strengthening Democracy : NREGA visualizes the involvement of local people in every decision — whether it be the selection of works and work-sites, the implementation of projects or their social audit. It strengthens the democratic decentralization processes at the grass root-level by incorporating *Gram Sabha* in the entire planning and decision-making process. It also infuses transparency and accountability in grass root democratic processes through social audits.

Encouraging Natural Resource Management : Focusing on strengthening natural resource management such as afforestation, drought proofing, flood proofing, water conservation - the Act has become a significant vehicle for regeneration of India's depleting natural resource base. And it seems that in the long term, NREGA might have a huge impact on our countries environment and gross agricultural output as it emphasizes on works that target water conservation, afforestation and drought proofing.

Preventing Migration : By securing livelihood and creating employment opportunities at the village level itself - NREGA mitigates seasonal/distress migration which has been a significant source of employment and income for a large proportion of rural population.

Controlling Spread of HIV/AIDS : NREGA also has the potential to address other major sociological issues like the spread of AIDS, stop farmers suicides etc. since migration of rural population is one of the leading causes for the spread of AIDS.

Transforming rural economic and social relations : It is also increasingly recognized that the NREGA has the potential to transform rural economic and social relations at many levels. The legislation is having a positive impact on the socio-economic empowerment of women (as the Act mandates at least 33 per cent participation for women).Where the NREGA has led to a significant increase in women's paid work, there are likely to be substantial social changes as well. These would be in addition to other changes such as the decline in distress migration and the improvement in food consumption among certain families. Not only does the NREGA provide money incomes directly to those women participating in it, in many states the wage delivery mechanism is linked to the opening of post office or bank accounts. This involves the access of a much greater number of women in institutional finance from which they have been largely excluded. Intra-household gender relations are also likely to be affected, but these changes will occur over a longer time and would require more extensive sociological study to identify. Nonetheless, this greater participation of women in the NREGA, particularly in some states, is clearly a positive indicator that shows the inclusive potential of the programme in unanticipated ways.

Potentiality to improve Health Status : The village health status of the village is likely to improve through proper implementation of NREGA due to (1) regular availability of clean potable drinking water, (2) construction of drainage that will improve the cleanliness in the village, and thereby reduce the chances of occurrence of diseases, (3) construction of toilets will also improve the level of cleanliness in the village and public health status, (4) reduction in unpaid drudgery of women will reduce their time stress and provide them more time to relax or to work and (5) construction of child care centre will improve general health of children, who will receive nutritious food and clean environment. This will reduce their expenditure on health (which is usually private expenditure) and improve their productivity at work. Considering the fact that ill health is one of the major risks that throws people in poverty, the improved status of health will go a long way in reducing vulnerability and poverty of people.

Improvement of Rural Educational Status : Many children in school-going-age in the village are engaged in collection of fodder, fuel wood, water etc. or in animal grazing. Assuring water supply at the door step, regeneration of common lands for fuel and fodder as well as child care centres will reduce unpaid work of children. This will enable them to attend the school regularly. This will particularly be beneficial to girl children, who stay back at home either to take care of younger siblings or to help in collection of water, fodder etc. and other household work. Moreover, improved economic condition will encourage parents to send their children to school.

Source: *Hazra, Anupam (2009)*

Kannan has stressed that the potential of NREGA could be more fully realised if human development had been more fully prioritised, including, for instance, improved childcare facilities, which would help mothers to work under the scheme. Furthermore, NREGA limits employment to manual labour and does not include work or training (for example, in setting up local businesses) that could have a long-term impact on improving livelihoods.

The Growing Criticism and the Emerging Issues

Experiences across the country suggest that greater awareness among the people and greater systematic oversight by elected local bodies can help minimize misuse of the scheme and maximize benefits to the eligible population. It has also been reported from across the country that in sites where the NREGS has been effectively implemented, there has been a significant reduction in labour migration and an improvement in the livelihood of the poor. The programme has largely been self-selecting, with landless and land poor households, SCs and STs participating to a greater extent than other categories.* While the Act mandates that at least one-third of NREGS beneficiaries should be women, the percentage of women workers to total has exceeded this by a large margin in states like Tamil Nadu. In some parts of the country, women working in NREGS have been able to obtain the same wages as men possibly for the first time in rural India. Some basic data on NREGS provided by the Report on NREGA for 2006-08 of the Ministry of Rural Development of the Government of India is pasted below:

---

* A survey of NREGA implementation carried out in May-June 2008 in10 districts spread over six North Indian States found that 81 per cent of sample workers lived in kutcha houses, 73 per cent belonged to either SC or ST families, 72 per cent had no electricity at home and 61 per cent were illiterate. See *Frontline*, January 16, 2009, cover story.

	2006-07 (Up to March)	*2007-08 (Up to December)*
Employment Demanded	2.12 crores Households	2.61 crores Households
Employment Provided	2.10 crore Households	2.57 crores Households
Persondays Generated	90.5 crores	85.51 crores
SC	22.95 [25.35%]	23.29 [27.23%]
ST	32.98 [36.44%]	26.56 [31.06%]
Women	36.79 [40.65%]	37.72 [44.11%]
Others	34.56 [38.18%]	35.67 [41.71%]
Works Taken Up	8.35 lakhs	12.31 lakhs
Use of Financial Resources	Rs. 8823.35 crores [73% of available funds	Rs. 9105.74 crores] [60% of Available funds.

Source: www.nrega.nic.in

Despite certain strengths, several weaknesses are still there. The most important have to do with the quality of assets created. The government has not paid adequate attention to strengthening the process of people's planning and implementation of works. The immense potential of NREGA for transforming rural livelihoods thus remains completely unrealized. Social audit is, after all, mainly a post-facto exercise. More important is what is done prior to works being started. It must also be said that even social audit so far remains a process mainly driven top-down by the government.

There are also programmatic concerns such as the absence of worksite facilities for women with children and the need for a fair revision of the schedule of rates. These issues need to be addressed swiftly. None of them must be allowed to deter the wholehearted implementation of an Act that has become a lifeline for millions of Indians who have been left out in the cold by high economic growth.

The World Bank has criticized NREG as an obstacle to development and poverty alleviation because it discourages the migration of people, an important engine of growth and prosperity. The Bank's argument is straightforward: if people are paid a decent wage to work in their own village, they would have little incentive to seek work elsewhere. And traditional economic theory on development has always suggested that the rural workforce must move to towns and cities to find gainful employment to help ease the burden on agriculture and aid the move to higher value-added sectors.

Complaints about payment delays and even inadequate payment, lack of facilities at the worksite such as shade and safe drinking water are piling up. The financing of the scheme continues to be an issue of debate. The affordability of NREGA has been an issue of wide debate in India, and opponents have warned that the programme will contribute to a fiscal crisis. Estimates of how costly the programme will end up being vary between 1 per cent and 5 per cent of GDP. It has been argued that the programme is too open-ended — i.e. it entitles anyone to obtain employment, which could also lead to escalating costs (Patnaik, 2006).

From a poverty-reduction point of view, one of the most fundamental criticisms of NREGA is that the types of activities for which work can be funded — e.g. water conservation, land development, afforestation, provision of irrigation systems, construction of roads, or flood control — are prone to being taken over by wealthier sections of society. . In their monitoring study of NREGA in Madhya Pradesh, Samarthan and colleagues found that the types of activities undertaken were more or less standardised across villages. This raises the questions about whether effective local participation had taken place, and whether the activities would be relevant to improving livelihoods.

In most other locations, social status, social networks, nepotism, religion and politics have influenced access to the scheme, and wealthier sections of local society are, in some cases, manipulating the implementation of NREGA in much the same way as they do with other government initiatives.

Social audits have revealed discrepancies between the numbers of job cards issued at the panchayat level and the number of people working, suggesting that numbers have been inflated to generate more funds than needed, which are then embezzled by local officials. A delay in the distribution of cards is also common, which suggests that people are unable to work even though employment may be available.

There is conflicting evidence over how far the assets created by public works benefit the poor: some support the notion of substantial contributions to agricultural productivity from which the poor also benefit; others argue that the location of the assets has tended to benefit those in wealthier households with irrigation facilities, since their wells have been recharged through the various structures created or rehabilitated.

For the civil society, NREGA's implementation is marred by crucial faults. Studies and surveys indicate that Panchayati Raj Institutions (PRI's), the nodal bodies under the act, have not yet been empowered to implement the act yet. Going by the assessments, political intervention at local level is taking a toll on the authority of PRI's. Besides, the objective of creating productive assets under the act is not being adhered to, thus limiting its impact on local development. Assessments show that steps have not been taken to enable them to handle such work. Central guidelines mandate an employment guarantee assistant for each village panchayat to be recruited to assist in the scheme's implementation. But this has not been done in most of the states. As a result, panchayats have not completed selection and registration of employment seekers, thus leaving large gaps between registrations and providing jobs. "Without the functionaries, the panchayats cannot implement the functions under NREGA effectively," says Manoj Kumar of PRIA, a Delhi-based NGO.

"Too much paper work for NREGS" was cited as a problem by many GP members including the Sachibs. Schemes like NREGS involve huge amount of paper work which require dedicated technical (computer literate) staff, computer and photocopying machines. NREGA stipulates that GPs are required to prepare annual report containing the facts and figures on achievements regarding implementation of the scheme within its jurisdiction and a copy of the same is to be made available to the public on demand. All accounts and records related to the scheme are to be made available for public scrutiny.

Much greater use of information technology would be critical for transparency, accountability and speed at all stages, from sanction of works, release of funds and wage payments to social audit. Outmoded Schedules of Rates need to be revised, to bring them in line with a new programme that bans machines and contractors. Government should also mandate a role for Civil Society Organizations (CSOs) to work as support agencies for PRIs in NREGA planning, implementation and social audit. This would help institutionalize the CSO-PRI partnership, putting pressure on both CSOs and PRIs to learn to work together. Strictly speaking, these reforms should have been in place well before NREGA was launched. But it is obviously better late than never.

Conclusion

Under the social protection umbrella, public works have probably had the largest outreach. But these have been criticized because they often fail to generate employment through the creation of productive assets and, without this, they cannot contribute to the generation of sustainable and productive employment. NREGA in India is an example of a public works programme with diverse social protection objectives that include providing a minimum income alongside stimulating local development, and operating in a gender-sensitive manner. It can serve as a model and provide lessons for the development of similar social protection initiatives in developing countries. To conclude it can be said that NREGA is an unusual and instructive example of a social protection measure that is demand-driven and gender-sensitive, has nationwide coverage, and provides a minimum income alongside stimulating local development.

Without a doubt, NREGA has the potential to change the socio-economic landscape in rural India in the long term. But as with any other legislation, it is practically impossible to make it foolproof. Middlemen coming into Illegal nexuses with corrupt govt. officials to swig away the NREGA funds are to be expected. The only way corruption can be stemmed is by proactive people's involvement in the implementation process. People should start questioning the officials for transparency in the process and get proper information about creation of muster rolls and disbursement of funds. And as such, it feels like RTI (Right to Information Act) should and will become the primary weapon for people.

NREGA is already making a difference to the lives of the people. Yet there is a long way to go. There are some issues in terms of the benefits to be drawn from the assets created by the scheme. Also, the menial nature and the lack of encouragement for both skilled labour and further training is something that is of concern in the long run. Implementation issues like issuance of job-cards on time is also a concern. Facilities for workers would also have to be improved over time. From the labour market point of view, it would be important to create a safety net through NREGA for poor people without damaging the labour market and employment prospects.

References

Ambasta, P., Shankar P.S.V., Shah, M. 2008. 'Two Years of NREGA: The Road Ahead', *Economic and Political Weekly*, February, 23.

Bhatia, B and Dreze, J. (2006) 'Employment Guarantee in Jharkhand: Ground realities', *Economic and Political Weekly*, July 22.

Frontline, January 16, 2009, cover story.

Gaiha, R. (2005) 'Does the Employment Guarantee Scheme benefit the rural poor in India? Some recent evidence', *Asian Survey*,

November/December 2005, Vol. 45, No. 6.

Hazra, Anupam.(2009).'NREGA: Transforming Rural India', *Kurukhetra*, December 2009.

Jha, R., Gaiha, R., Shankar, S. (2008). 'Reviewing the National Rural Employment Guarantee Programme,' *Economic and Political Weekly*, 43(10), 44–48.

Kannan, K. P. (2005) 'Linking employment guarantee to human development', *Economic and Political Weekly*, October 15.

Malhotra, S. (2008). 'NREG Two Years On: Where Do We Go From Here?', *Economic and Political Weekly*, 43(31), 27–35.

Ministry of Law and Justice. (2005). 'National Rural Employment Guarantee Act, 2005,' *The Gazette of India* (September 7, 2005), New Delhi: Government of India Press.

Ministry of Rural Development. (2009). *Two years of the National Rural Employment Guarantee Act (2006- 08)*, New Delhi: Government of India Press.

Patnaik, I.(2006) 'Bad Economics Zone?', *The Indian Express*. June 21.

Powis, B. 2007. 'Systems of Capture: Reassessing the Threat of Local Elites,' Social Development Papers, South Asia Series Paper No. 109, December.

Ravallion, M. (2000). 'Monitoring Targeting Performance When Decentralized Allocations to the Poor Are Unobserved,' *World Bank Economic Review*, 14, 331–45.

Samarthan Centre for Development Support (2006) *Status of NREGA Implementation: Grass roots Learning and Ways Forward*. 1st Monitoring Report.

Website of National Rural Employment Guarantee Act i.e. *www.nrega.nic.in*

Index